Eugene Smolensky

PUBLIC PRICES FOR
PUBLIC PRODUCTS

PUBLIC
PRICES
FOR PUBLIC
PRODUCTS

Edited by *Selma J. Mushkin*

THE URBAN INSTITUTE
Washington · 1972

COPYRIGHT © 1972 THE URBAN INSTITUTE
ISBN 87766–010–7
Library of Congress Catalog Card No. 76–161578
UI 39–137–2   1972

Available from:

Publications Office
The Urban Institute
2100 M Street, N.W.
Washington, D.C. 20037

List price: $10.95

Printed in the United States of America

Contents

CONTENTS

vi

Tables

Figures

FIGURES

Foreword

In the industrial nations the city has drawn a major share of the national population to itself and its suburbs and in the process has reinforced or created problems which are increasingly in need of rational treatment. The problems range from poverty to waste disposal, from housing, congestion, and racial tension to welfare, crime, and education—and underlying them or intimately related to them is the strain on urban finance.

The origins of the financing crisis go back a number of decades. In the 1920s, the real city and the jurisdictional city were still identical for all practical purposes. But since then, city annexation did not keep pace as people and development overflowed corporate boundaries into new jurisdictions that press against the gates of what has now been retermed the central city. Richer citizens have moved outward, taking a large share of the city's revenue base with them—while still relying as commuters on city services for which they may not pay. Nonetheless, the poor remain, forming an increasingly higher percentage of the population and further burdening a city less and less able to meet its fiscal demands.

To reduce the widening gap between expenditures and revenues, the central city is often driven to short-term solutions, while it hunts for additional revenues on a stop-gap basis. Meanwhile the pressures for long-term solutions grow rather than decline. There is pressure for a thorough investigation of city expenditures, weighed in each case against value received. There is pressure for a full analysis of city revenue sources—whether from within or outside its jurisdiction—and of methods by which the city might efficiently and equitably apportion its demands for resources among its citizens. At a more far-reaching level, there is need for close analysis of the network of interdependencies, including those of demand and benefit, between the central city and other jurisdictional units included in the metropolitan area— as well as a need for analysis of organizational alternatives that are area-wide on a geographic or functional basis.

Several contributory investigations related to these issues are currently underway at The Urban Institute. One broad study of the municipal budget process includes the development of a model which simultaneously examines the demands for various categories of public services and the revenue sources used to finance them. When completed, the model can be used to estimate the responses of local expenditures and revenues not only to a variety of external influences such as population, income, and price changes but also to variations in the amount of aid received from higher-level governments. This research will also consider the effects of substituting revenue sources such as fees, charges, or income and sales taxes for the traditional property tax, and the extent to which tax—or expenditure—competition among jurisdictions within the metropolitan area can limit the flexibility of central city policy-making.

Another study in progress focuses on "fiscal flows" between jurisdictions within the metropolitan area—the "flow" being determined by the amount which nonresidents pay to another jurisdiction in taxes and user charges in comparison with the value of the public benefits they receive from it. By quantitatively measuring such flows, the study reveals the magnitude and direction of interjurisdictional transfers. It thus permits one to determine whether the central city is being exploited by tourists and suburbanites and whether additional taxes and charges might equitably be levied against them. For central city residents in different income classes, the study also measures the distribution of burdens and benefits in a selected number of tax and expenditure categories.

Both of these studies have an immediate bearing on the subject of the present volume in which eighteen essays—some written by internationally known scholars, others by undergraduate students serving internships at The Urban Institute—examine the theory and practice of using fees and charges to help finance urban public services. Recognizing that such pricing has already been long established for many urban services, ranging from water rates to marriage licenses and road tolls, the authors explore the advantages of using a pricing system in other areas where the units of service can be measured, where the individual user can be identified, and where charging the user does not run contrary to other overriding public objectives. If and where pricing is feasible, these essays point to certain gains in efficiency and equity: (1) the non-user is not penalized by having to support the service through taxation, (2) the added funds at least help to narrow the revenue-expenditure gap, (3) the costs of services will be partially defrayed by those who, like commuters, cross jurisdictional boundaries, (4) where comparisons exist, public pricing helps to correct distorted prices in the private market, and (5) taking the buyer's response as a signal of demand, the allocation of resources becomes more efficient in the public sector itself.

As the following pages make clear, this is not to suggest public pricing as a panacea. In one area of study after another, the authors indicate the inadequacy of the data on which they must base their analyses. The data are generally incomplete or nonexistent with respect to demand and use, to prices for similar services in different urban centers, to the economic and social characteristics of the users, and to the elasticities of demand with respect to prices. What may be most critically needed at this stage is the assembling of comparable data, on a city by city basis, for all of the services for which prices are presently set or for which pricing is considered possible.

In spite of—and possibly because of—the inadequacy of available data, this volume performs a valuable service in revealing the present state of inquiry, in defining investigative needs, and in pointing to options, including the suggestion that the central city and its suburbs may be moving to a new system of relationships in which jurisdictional and fiscal boundaries will not be coterminous.

William Gorham
President
The Urban Institute

Washington, D.C.

Preface

New understandings of the usefulness and limitations of user charges in the public sector have emerged in the past several years. However, the work done thus far is clearly just a beginning.

It is hoped this volume will contribute importantly to further clarification of the role of user charges in the allocation of resources and in providing correctives for the private marketplace. A number of the essays raise new questions about public services and the feasibility of directly pricing them.

Part I addresses the conceptual problems of public pricing. It presents data that shed light on these problems, and it deals with public prices in relation to revenue raising, equity, and efficiency in government. Part II describes the issues involved in improving price signals for both the private and public sectors in connection with specific services. This part asks whether these services lend themselves to public pricing, and if so, on what basis and with what effects. Finally, some crucial questions are identified as an agenda for new research.

No attempt was made to gain uniformity in opinion or approach from the separate authors. By posing sharply rather than trying to camouflage the divergencies, this volume highlights the need for and seeks to encourage further study.

The deep interest of scholars and practitioners in advancing knowledge about user charges is evidenced by the many authors who gave so willingly of their time and professional skills to prepare this volume. My thanks go out to all of them for their invaluable contributions, with special tribute to Jerome W. Milliman, William S. Vickrey, Eugene Smolensky, T. Nicolaus Tideman, Edward H. Clarke,

Allen V. Kneese, Paul H. Gerhardt, and John G. Duba for their excellent and voluntary labors.

Secretary George Romney's interest in policy research and application supported this volume through its months of gestation. The Department of Housing and Urban Development provided much of the funding. Special thanks are due Harold B. Finger, Assistant Secretary of HUD for Research and Technology, and Alan Siegel, his able assistant, for their interest and cooperation.

When the original compilation of chapters grew too long, Worth Bateman, Urban Institute Vice President, and Harold M. Hochman, Director of Studies in Urban Public Finance, arranged for Professor Richard M. Bird of Toronto to help bring the material back to manageable size. We are greatly indebted to Professor Bird for this work.

Thank-you's would not be complete without mentioning those who assisted in putting the volume together. Kathleen Sproul, in editing the manuscript, gave generously of her long experience as critic-writer. Virginia Herman assisted importantly in manuscript preparation and gathering of data. Charles Cole provided valuable assistance as copy editor. Harriet Cobern efficiently performed many coordinating tasks. Joseph L. Caulfield, Marcia Hampton and Elaine Worsley assisted with design of tabular material, handling of proofs and typing. Students assisting the project, in addition to those who contributed signed chapters, worked diligently on substantive issues; among them, special mention goes to Karen Nelson and Howard Chernick, the latter for his preparation of materials on the pricing of fire protection. Walter Rybeck of the Institute was editorial coordinator throughout final stages of the project.

Selma J. Mushkin

Washington, D.C.

PART ONE
The Theory of Public Prices

Chapter 1

SELMA J. MUSHKIN
RICHARD M. BIRD

Public Prices: An Overview

*P*RICING urban public services is an increasingly current topic.[1] Continued revenue pressure on urban finances has led many cities to consider carefully the prospect of augmenting their financial resources by introducing or increasing fees and charges for various local government activities. At the same time, the development of two previously disparate strands of economic analysis—marginal-cost pricing and "public goods" and externalities—has provided a more adequate conceptual basis for the use of the price system by governments, both to correct distorted private market prices and to improve the allocation of resources within the public sector itself.

The essays assembled in this book amply demonstrate both how far we have come in improving our theoretical and practical knowledge of the appropriate scope and nature of pricing for many services commonly provided by urban governments, and how very far we still have to go before our knowledge in either respect can be considered satisfactory. Rather than summarizing further this lengthy volume—most chapters of which are themselves already in part summaries of more specialized literature—this introductory chapter first presents the scanty data on the importance of prices in current city finance, then outlines briefly when pricing can and should be used by city governments. The final chapter reviews the findings and focuses on some of the major issues emerging from the extensive theoretical and substantive dis-

Selma J. Mushkin was Director of State-Local Finance Studies at The Urban Institute at the time she undertook this volume. She is now a Senior Fellow at the Institute and Director of the Public Services Laboratory of Georgetown University.

Richard M. Bird is Professor of Economics, Institute for the Quantitative Analysis of Social and Economic Policy, University of Toronto.

cussion in the book. This forms an agenda for further research and possible experimental design.

A Note on Definitions and Data

We use the term public prices to identify a method of payment for public services. In using this term we adopt in modified form a classification of revenues made by Seligman 75 years ago.[2] He classified revenue items (1) in terms of degree of volunteerism or compulsion under authority of police power, tax powers, or powers of eminent domain; and (2) in accord with the economic relation of the individual to his government or more particularly the degree of individual benefit and the degree of public purpose. Degree of public purpose in more modern economic terminology would be translated into degree of external or neighborhood effects. In this work we consider as public prices what Seligman classified as quasi-private prices, public prices, and fees. See Table 1.7 for Seligman's scheme. (p. 24).

For the purposes of giving new emphasis to a possible substitution of public prices for taxes, when the product produced by government has private good characteristics, distinction necessarily must be drawn between the two revenue sources. The distinction helps to sharpen the public policy issue. Yet if one seeks to assess a levy that measures benefits accruing from public activities, in some instances the most appropriate single measure of that benefit is property value. Property values, for example, are enhanced by neighborhood improvements such as cleaner streets, trash removal, adequate street lighting—also by the location of good schools.[3]

Milliman, in a recent essay, gave a more inclusive definition when he wrote: "There is no hard and fast definition and . . . the term 'beneficiary charge' can mean many things to many people. As a result, a beneficiary charge can refer to a whole host of charges ranging from the sale of postal services, rent charged for public housing units, inspection fees, sale of public utility services, local property taxes on properties served by sewers, property taxes to finance given school districts, charges levied upon irrigation districts in Bureau of Reclamation projects, gasoline taxes upon motorists, and perhaps even to federal income taxes levied to finance such collective goods as national defense."[4]

The U.S. Bureau of the Census provides the only comparative data on local government finances but does not use the public price terminology. The data collected by the Bureau as part of the statistical series on governments are termed "fees and charges," narrowly defined as amounts received from the public for the performance of specific services benefiting the person charged and from the sale of commodities. The amounts of general revenues reported as charges exclude all revenues from public utilities and sales of monopoly liquor stores. These items are shown separately. Also excluded are other contractual payments.[5] Intergovernmental purchases of products that are part of general expenditures are not reported as sales or charges even though such revenue is counted as a charge in public utility finance data. For example, the transaction of one government in paying another for the hospital care provided a specific beneficiary would show up in Bureau of Census data not as a charge item but as an intergovernmental payment. In contrast, an intergovernmental payment for water would become revenue to the public utility.

The Census data necessarily employed in the accompanying tables are thus not adequate for the analyses required to answer such relevant policy issues as how cities have exercised their option to finance either through general revenues or through specific service charges. The definition of the expenditure items that may be priced is either too inclusive or too narrow to compute specific price-expenditure ratios; the expenditure data for certain services are not uniformly reported by all cities, nor are the fee data uniform. For example, the amount of student tuition and fees is reported, but total higher education expenditures of the public colleges and universities include many major items, such as university research outlays, for which no student tuition is levied. Local school charges are principally school meal prices, and it would be misleading to conclude anything from the fee-intensity ratios for local schools with different school meal programs as well as different educational programs. Parking fees are reported; in some instances there is a corresponding expenditure amount, but in others, the parking expenditures are merged into another category, for example, police. Expenditures and user charges that are grouped within a single Census category may also vary from place to place, thus further reducing the significance of comparisons of share of outlays financed by user charges on a city-by-city basis.

An important research task is therefore to reassess carefully the

Census data on user charges and expenditures to determine what might be feasible by way of routine collection of the comparable detailed and specific data needed to provide a more adequate base for research and policy prescription.[6]

The product-price concept most useful in terms of public policy necessitates not only a definition of public prices but also a definition of product designed to measure what it is that the government, or the consumer-voter, is intending to buy with the resources spent. The difficulty in fulfilling this requirement even for such simple services as waste collection and disposal is amply demonstrated in the chapters of Part Two.

Prices in Current City Finance

Total revenues from fees and charges in American cities substantially more than doubled from 1957 to 1969–70, rising from $3.4 billion to 9.4 billion; revenues from the operation of city-owned utilities alone just about doubled during the period, from $2.4 billion to $5.0 billion (see Table 1.1). The utility operations of a municipal government are commercial operations, no different from similar activities carried on under private auspices. But city governments also assess charges for such diverse services as hospitals, parking, and recreation facilities. Charges are also derived from the city's policing or regulatory powers; such charges are not included in the Census definition of charges and

TABLE 1.1

User Charges in City Finance
(In millions of dollars)

	1969–70	1967–68	1966–67	1962	1957
Charges	$ 8,281	$ 6,900	$ 6,366	$4,724	$3,392
Utility revenue	5,047	4,361	4,043	3,136	2,378
Monopoly liquor store revenue	121	121	97	77	60
Other current charges	3,113	2,418	2,226	1,511	954
Taxes	13,647	11,291	10,507	7,940	5,908
Ratio of charges to $1 of taxes	.61	.61	.61	.59	.57

SOURCE: U.S. Bureau of the Census, *City Government Finances* (annual issues for the given year).

are not in the amounts shown in Table 1.1. Controls on many activities are maintained by the government for health, safety, or other protective purposes: examples include the rights to fish, to keep a dog, to run a taxi, and to operate certain types of businesses. When the governmental activity sanctions a particular individual or business action, the label of "license" or "license fee" is often attached, and the Census then reports this fiscal information. Table 1.2 illustrates something of the wide variety of fees, licenses, and charges currently existing in various cities.

TABLE 1.2

Types of Fees, Charges, and Licenses

Police protection
   special patrol service fees
   parking fees and charges
   fees for fingerprints, copies
   payments for extra police service
     at stadiums, theaters, circuses
Transportation
   subway and bus fares
   bridge tolls
   landing and departure fees
   hangar rentals
   concession rentals
   parking meter receipts
Health and hospitals
   inoculation charges
   x-ray charges
   hospital charges, including per
     diem rates and service charges
   ambulance charges
   concession rentals
Education
   charges for books
   charges for gymnasium uniforms
     or special equipment
   concession rentals
Recreation
   greens fees
   parking charges
   concession rentals
   admission fees or charges

   permit charges for tennis courts,
     etc.
   charges for specific recreation
     services
   picnic stove fees
   stadium gate tickets
   stadium club fees
   park development charges
Sanitation
   domestic and commercial trash
     collection fees
   industrial waste charges
Sewerage
   sewerage system fees
Other public utility operations
   water meter permits
   water services charges
   electricity rates
   telephone booth rentals
Housing, neighborhood, and
commercial development
   street tree fees
   tract map filing fees
   street-lighting installations
   convention center revenues
     event charges
     scoreboard fees
     hall and meeting room leases
     concessions

TABLE 1.2   (Continued)

Commodity sales	pawnbrokers
salvage materials	plumbers—first class
sales of maps	plumbers—second class
sales of codes	pest eradicator
Licenses and fees	poultry dealer
advertising vehicle	produce dealer—itinerant
amusements (ferris wheels,	pushcart
etc.)	rooming house and hotel
billiard and pool	secondhand dealer
bowling alley	secondhand auto dealer
circus and carnival	sign inspection
coal dealers	solicitation
commercial combustion	shooting gallery
dances	taxi
dog tags	taxi transfer license
duplicate dog tags	taxi driver
electrician—first class	theaters
electrician—second class	trees—Christmas
film storage	vending—coin
foot peddler	vault cleaners
hucksters and itinerant peddlers	sound truck
heating equipment contractors	refuse hauler
junk dealer	land fill
loading zone permit	sightseeing bus
lumber dealer	wrecking license

Public prices, customary for some types of services, are difficult to impose for others. Utility operations, for example, are generally "self-financed" by fees. Other functions that have high fee potential (i.e., a high ratio of charges to total expenditures) are health and hospitals; sewerage; recreation; transportation facilities and services, including harbors and airports; school meals; and public housing. On the average, revenues from utility charges are almost twice the size of those from all other charges. Of the remaining charges, over a third are derived from providing sewerage and hospital care.

City services can be grouped into several categories. First, there are household-supporting services such as water, sanitation, and sewerage. In a congested urban community these services depend upon collective action, but they clearly lend themselves to "prices" charged to the benefiting households. A second category of urban outlay is support of industrial development, e.g., airports, water transport, parking facilities, and manpower training; again, the services lend themselves to pricing or user charges. There are also expenditures for support of "amenities"—services that help improve the cultural and recreational environment, e.g., museums, art galleries, playgrounds, ballfields, swimming pools, bathing beaches, auditoriums, and libraries. These services also frequently lend themselves to pricing.

These three groups of services may be classed as "urban functions," i.e., those that require higher per capita outlays in urban than in rural communities. About 70 cents of each dollar of municipal outlay in the large cities (those, excluding New York City, with populations of 100,000 and over) goes for these urban services (Table 1.3). The remaining city expenditures, of which education and highways account for about two-thirds, are more universal in nature. In recent years, expenditures on these universal functions have grown more rapidly than those on urban functions.

TABLE 1.3

Expenditures in Cities with Populations over 100,000
(excluding New York City)

	1962	1967	Annual growth 1962 to 1967 (percentage)
	(in billions)		
Total expenditures	$7.1	$9.5	5.9
Urban functions	5.1	6.7	5.7
Universal functions	2.1	2.8	6.6

SOURCE: Compiled by Marjorie Lissy from U.S. Bureau of the Census, *Census of Governments, 1962,* and *1967,* and from *Compendium of Government Finances,* also *Finances of Municipalities and Township Governments,* (GPO), from 1964 and 1969.

Despite the common policy prescription to make greater use of public pricing, charge revenues in the large cities grew more slowly than city expenditures (see Table 1.4). The highest yearly growth rate in the period 1962–67 resulted from charges connected with education, airport activities, and hospitals. Charges connected with education (mostly school lunch charges and higher education fees) rose an average of 11.6 percent. Revenues from public hospital fees rose 9.3 percent per annum, probably reflecting the extended use of charges made possible

10

TABLE 1.4

Average Percent Increase per Year in Expenditures and Charges
(Cities with population of 100,000 and over,
excluding New York City, 1962–67)

	City expenditures[a]	City charges[a]
Charge-financed, urban services		
Water supply	2.5	3.4
Electric power	7.3	5.0
Gas supply	4.4	3.5
Airports	(decline)	9.5
Transit utilities	6.1	3.1
Water transport and terminals	(decline)	5.3
Partially charge-financed, urban services		
Housing and urban renewal	5.5	3.8
Sewerage	4.1	6.5
Parks and recreation	7.0	8.6
Sanitation	3.8	6.3
Noncharge-financed, urban services		
Police	6.2	—
Fire	5.1	—
Universal functions, charge- and noncharge-financed		
Education	9.5	11.6
Public welfare	7.4	—
Highways	2.8	1.9
Hospitals	4.9	9.3
Total	5.9	5.2

SOURCE: U.S. Bureau of Census, *Census of Governments, 1962* (and also) *1967; Compendium of Government Finances;* also, *Finances of Municipalities and Township Government.*
[a] Data for expenditures are not exactly comparable with charge data.

by new medical care programs. Charges for urban self-financed functions in the large cities rose more slowly than expenditures on those functions in some instances (electricity, gas, and transit systems) but more quickly in others (water supplies, airports, and water transport). Charges for sewerage, for outdoor and indoor recreational services, and for trash collection and other sanitation activities are among those with high rates of increase relative to the expenditures for the related functions.

Variations among cities in the services offered result in wide differences in "fee intensity," i.e., the ratio of fees and charges to taxes.

Large cities provide a wider range of services than do smaller places, but not all these services lend themselves to pricing. At the same time, smaller towns may provide only utility services and accordingly report a large share of revenues from fees and charges. The fees and charges collected by cities in 1969–70 are shown in Table 1.5 by size of city.

Table 1.6 presents 1966–67 data for 112 cities with 1960 population in excess of 100,000.[7] The table groups the cities into three categories: those with current charges only (Group 1); those with current charges plus water-supply revenue (Group 2); and those with current charges plus water and "other" utility revenue (electric power, gas supply, and transit system (Group 3). For purposes of comparison, the most relevant columns are 5 (the fee intensity ratio), 6 (the effective property tax rate), and 7 (per capita expenditures). The fee intensity rate for the first group is smaller than that for the second, which is, in turn, smaller than that for the third group.

The Efficiency Case for Pricing Urban Services

The economic case for the expansion and rationalization of pricing in the urban public sector rests essentially on the contribution it can make to allocative efficiency. Prices will provide correct signals to indicate the quantity and quality of things citizens desire and help bring about the proper balance between private and public production of these things. A properly designed price system can potentially serve this end whenever the public provision of a service, or the private use of a common property resource such as air or water, is accompanied by significant divisible or appropriable benefits accruing to identifiable individuals, provided the cost of its implementation and operation does not exceed the gains in terms of more efficient resource allocation. Many of the services provided by urban local governments appear to qualify by this criterion.

In practice, of course, it may not be desirable to exclude people by imposing user charges even when it is technically possible to do so; for example, because an objective of policy is to redistribute income in the form of a particular service, or because it is believed that individuals will, if faced with a money price, choose to consume less of certain services than is considered socially desirable.

Redistribution may take the form of a particular "free" service.

TABLE 1.5

Amounts of Municipalities' Own Revenue (By Source, and Ratios of Charges to Taxes, 1969–70)

City Size:	All munici-palities	1,000,000 or more	500,000 to 999,999	300,000 to 499,999	200,000 to 299,999	100,000 to 199,999	50,000 to 99,999	less than 50,000
	....dollars in millions................................							
General revenue from own sources	18,715	5,387	2,745	1,305	633	1,720	2,011	4,915
Taxes	13,647	4,394	2,039	826	455	1,271	1,469	3,193
Current charges	3,113	649	445	293	112	275	330	1,010
Other revenue	1,955	345	261	186	66	173	212	712
Water and Utility revenue	5,047	1,051	666	215	129	449	472	2,063
Water supply revenue	2,201	309	275	146	75	187	259	949
Other utility revenue	2,846	742	391	69	54	262	213	1,114
	....ratios in percentages................................							
Current charges to taxes	22.8	14.7	21.8	35.4	24.6	21.6	22.4	31.6
Current charges plus water and utility revenue to taxes	59.7	38.6	54.4	61.5	52.9	56.9	54.5	96.2
Current charges to own revenue	16.6	12.8	16.2	22.4	17.6	15.9	16.4	20.5
Current charges plus water and utility revenue to own revenue	43.6	31.5	40.4	38.9	38.0	42.0	39.8	62.5

SOURCE: U.S. Bureau of Census, City Government Finances in 1969–70, p. 7.

TABLE 1.6

Fees, Charges, and Selected Fiscal Characteristics of Cities [a]

(Aggregate dollar amounts in millions)

City	(1) 1960 Population (thousands)	(2) General expenditures	(3) General revenue from taxes	(4) Fees and charges	(5) Fee intensity (4) ÷ (3)	(6) Effective property tax rate	(7) Per capita expenditures (2) ÷ (1)
Group 1							
1. Paterson, N.J.	143.7	$ 28.8	$ 21.6	$ .4	.02	$3.19	$200
2. Gary, Ind.	178.3	15.9	12.0	.4	.03	1.53	89
3. New Haven, Conn.	152.0	49.3	25.9	1.4	.05	2.30	324
4. Peoria, Ill.	103.2	10.1	6.8	.5	.07	2.05	98
5. Baton Rouge, La.	230.1	25.9	16.9	1.2	.07	.36	113
6. Hartford, Conn.	162.2	51.5	38.2	3.2	.08	2.82	318
7. Bridgeport, Conn.	156.7	40.2	24.7	2.5	.10	1.45	257
8. Indianapolis, Ind.	476.3	54.1	32.2	3.9	.12	2.55	114
9. Omaha, Nebr.	301.6	27.6	18.7	3.1	.17	2.89	92
10. Kansas City, Kans.	121.9	15.1	7.0	1.3	.19	2.17	124
11. Oakland, Calif.	367.5	55.4	34.7	10.5	.30	1.71	151
12. Berkeley, Calif.	111.3	14.1	8.3	2.6	.31	1.74	127
Group 2							
13. Newark, N.J.	405.2	143.1	81.9	8.6	.11	4.06	353
14. Washington, D.C.	764.0	454.5	274.9	31.8	.12	1.19	595
15. Waterbury, Conn.	107.1	24.4	16.5	2.1	.13	2.58	228
16. New Bedford, Mass.	102.5	30.0	13.0	1.9	.15	2.54	293
17. Springfield, Mass.	174.5	52.5	29.9	4.5	.15	3.68	301

[a] Cities in each group are listed in order of lowest to highest fee intensity.

TABLE 1.6 (Continued)

City	(1) 1960 Population (thousands)	(2) General expenditures	(3) General revenue from taxes	(4) Fees and charges	(5) Fee intensity (4) ÷ (3)	(6) Effective property tax rate	(7) Per capita expenditures (2) ÷ (1)
18. Jersey City, N.J.	276.1	$ 69.9	$ 43.5	$ 6.8	.16	$2.85	$253
19. Boston, Mass.	697.2	345.3	155.6	27.0	.17	3.01	495
20. Yonkers, N.Y.	190.6	52.8	31.0	5.5	.18	2.53	277
21. Honolulu, Hawaii	500.4	97.6	67.9	12.9	.19	1.05	195
22. San Jose, Calif.	204.2	37.7	23.3	4.8	.21	2.14	185
23. Baltimore, Md.	939.0	347.8	177.9	37.2	.21	3.47	370
24. Trenton, N.J.	114.2	30.8	18.1	3.8	.21	4.31	270
25. Pittsburgh, Pa.	604.3	79.6	52.7	11.1	.21	1.68	132
26. Philadelphia, Pa.	2,002.5	362.7	255.0	53.0	.21	2.61	181
27. Providence, R.I.	207.5	47.2	30.6	6.4	.21	2.62	227
28. Dearborn, Mich.	112.0	17.3	14.3	3.2	.22	1.25	154
29. Buffalo, N.Y.	532.8	131.0	60.8	13.6	.22	3.07	246
30. Syracuse, N.Y.	216.0	55.5	29.1	7.2	.25	2.80	257
31. Worcester, Mass.	186.6	63.0	34.2	9.1	.27	3.86	338
32. St. Louis, Mo.	750.0	113.0	84.3	23.7	.28	1.70	151
33. Hammond, Ind.	111.7	12.8	6.6	1.9	.29	1.54	115
34. Chicago, Ill.	3,550.4	458.0	312.1	96.6	.31	1.94	129
35. Dayton, Ohio	262.3	37.5	24.6	7.7	.31	1.78	143
36. Rockford, Ill.	126.7	9.4	8.2	2.6	.32	1.87	74
37. Rochester, N.Y.	318.6	104.9	41.4	13.1	.32	2.30	329
38. St. Paul, Minn.	313.4	47.3	28.1	9.8	.35	1.98	151
39. Camden, N.J.	117.2	11.6	8.9	3.3	.37	3.25	99
40. South Bend, Ind.	132.4	10.6	7.6	2.9	.38	2.46	80
41. Milwaukee, Wis.	741.3	127.8	54.5	21.2	.39	3.31	172
42. Erie, Pa.	138.4	11.7	8.0	3.2	.40	1.36	85

TABLE 1.6 *(Continued)*

City	(1) 1960 Population (thousands)	(2) General expenditures	(3) General revenue from taxes	(4) Fees and charges	(5) Fee intensity (4) ÷ (3)	(6) Effective property tax rate	(7) Per capita expenditures (2) ÷ (1)
43. Miami, Fla.	291.7	$ 35.3	$ 27.9	$11.2	.40	$1.96	$121
44. Minneapolis, Minn.	482.9	59.4	34.2	14.3	.42	2.12	123
45. Kansas City, Mo.	475.5	74.1	43.9	18.6	.42	1.77	156
46. Youngstown, Ohio	166.7	15.0	9.0	3.8	.42	1.60	90
47. Allentown, Pa.	108.3	8.9	5.9	2.5	.42	1.73	82
48. Jackson, Miss.	144.4	17.5	12.1	5.4	.45	1.56	121
49. Charlotte, N.C.	201.6	25.9	15.2	6.8	.45	1.49	128
50. Shreveport, La.	164.4	11.5	9.1	4.3	.47	.48	70
51. Salt Lake City, Utah	189.5	15.4	11.8	5.5	.47	1.58	81
52. Norfolk, Va.	304.9	80.4	36.3	17.1	.47	1.18	264
53. Des Moines, Iowa	209.0	30.5	12.7	6.3	.50	3.06	146
54. New Orleans, La.	627.5	92.5	43.1	22.2	.52	.45	147
55. Canton, Ohio	113.6	8.5	5.8	3.0	.52	1.42	75
56. Denver, Colo.	493.9	102.8	52.8	28.9	.55	2.03	208
57. Greensboro, N.C.	119.6	19.3	9.1	5.0	.55	.80	161
58. Savannah, Ga.	149.2	11.3	6.9	3.9	.57	2.00	76
59. Tampa, Fla.	275.0	35.1	20.1	11.6	.58	.48	128
60. Portland, Oreg.	372.7	56.5	29.0	17.5	.60	2.37	152
61. Evansville, Ind.	261.7	31.8	9.7	15.8	1.63	1.57	122
62. Mobile, Ala.	141.5	11.6	6.0	3.7	.62	1.60	82
63. Birmingham, Ala.	202.8	17.3	11.5	7.4	.64	.76	85
64. Utica, N.Y.	340.9	28.7	18.4	11.9	.65	.92	84
65. Atlanta, Ga.	100.4	15.4	4.0	2.6	.65	3.40	153
66. Montgomery, Ala.	487.5	67.7	30.4	20.1	.66	2.41	139

TABLE 1.6 *(Continued)*

City	(1) 1960 Population (thousands)	(2) General expenditures	(3) General revenue from taxes	(4) Fees and charges	(5) Fee intensity (4) ÷ (3)	(6) Effective property tax rate	(7) Per capita expenditures (2) ÷ (1)
67. San Diego, Calif.	134.4	$ 8.8	$ 7.2	$ 4.9	.68	$ .54	$ 65
68. Phoenix, Ariz.	573.2	79.5	35.2	24.0	.68	2.02	139
69. Winston-Salem, N.C.	439.2	58.7	28.8	20.0	.69	2.44	134
70. Tucson, Ariz.	111.1	20.8	7.4	5.2	.70	1.34	187
71. Fort Worth, Tex.	212.9	27.2	11.4	8.2	.72	2.36	128
72. Akron, Ohio	356.3	35.4	19.9	14.8	.74	2.32	99
73. El Paso, Tex.	290.4	53.7	19.5	14.8	.76	1.73	185
74. Topeka, Kans.	276.7	22.9	13.0	9.9	.76	1.83	83
75. Wichita, Kans.	119.5	20.4	6.4	5.2	.81	2.44	171
76. Amarillo, Tex.	254.7	36.0	11.6	9.6	.83	2.58	141
77. Toledo, Ohio	138.0	13.5	7.1	6.0	.85	1.92	98
78. Spokane, Wash.	318.0	50.9	20.5	18.7	.91	1.54	160
79. Louisville, Ky.	181.6	16.0	6.6	6.0	.91	1.65	88
80. Cincinnati, Ohio	390.6	75.2	29.2	26.9	.92	1.39	193
81. Flint, Mich.	502.6	133.6	47.0	44.8	.95	1.86	266
82. Columbus, Ga.	196.9	38.7	16.2	20.4	1.26	1.68	197
83. Little Rock, Ark.	116.8	11.9	6.3	8.1	1.29	1.26	102
84. Tulsa, Okla.	107.8	9.4	4.2	5.9	1.40	1.18	87
Group 3							
85. New York, N.Y.	7,782.0	4,162.2	2,443.9	837.5	.34	2.00	535
86. Houston, Tex.	938.2	117.8	69.0	24.3	.35	1.79	126
87. Niagara Falls, N.Y.	102.4	11.8	9.7	3.8	.39	3.06	115
88. San Francisco, Calif.	740.3	274.9	167.4	87.1	.52	.88	371
89. Richmond, Va.	220.0	75.0	38.9	20.5	.53	1.51	341

TABLE 1.6 *(Continued)*

City	(1) 1960 Population (thousands)	(2) General expenditures	(3) General revenue from taxes	(4) Fees and charges	(5) Fee intensity (4) ÷ (3)	(6) Effective property tax rate	(7) Per capita expenditures (2) ÷ (1)
90. Detroit, Mich.	1,670.1	$292.3	$154.3	$93.9	.61	$1.91	$175
91. Albuquerque, N. Mex.	201.2	24.2	15.8	9.9	.63	1.30	120
92. Fresno, Calif.	133.9	27.9	12.4	8.0	.65	2.12	208
93. Sacramento, Calif.	191.7	34.8	17.3	11.2	.65	2.15	182
94. Dallas, Tex.	679.7	81.4	57.5	38.0	.66	1.48	120
95. Columbus, Ohio	471.3	77.0	24.2	20.2	.83	1.44	163
96. Oklahoma City, Okla.	324.3	39.4	20.1	18.3	.91	1.49	121
97. Nashville-Davidson, Tenn.	399.7	127.5	53.7	50.9	.95	1.33	319
98. St. Petersburg, Fla.	181.3	32.1	16.0	17.5	1.09	1.79	177
99. Los Angeles, Calif.	2,479.0	333.9	237.5	267.9	1.13	1.82	135
100. Cleveland, Ohio	876.1	104.5	60.0	74.1	1.24	1.75	119
101. Fort Wayne, Ind.	161.8	16.1	9.0	11.4	1.27	2.18	100
102. Corpus Christi, Tex.	167.7	20.1	8.9	12.9	1.45	2.17	120
103. Lubbock, Tex.	128.7	10.1	6.3	9.2	1.46	2.02	78
104. Lincoln, Nebr.	128.5	18.8	8.4	12.5	1.49	2.94	146
105. Pasadena, Calif.	116.4	21.9	9.9	15.1	1.53	2.07	188
106. Seattle, Wash.	557.1	74.1	34.3	80.2	2.34	1.05	133
107. Knoxville, Tenn.	111.8	49.0	13.1	31.1	2.37	2.10	438
108. Tacoma, Wash.	148.0	17.3	8.9	27.2	3.06	1.35	117
109. Memphis, Tenn.	497.5	146.4	35.0	110.2	3.15	2.00	294
110. Austin, Tex.	186.5	24.0	8.3	28.8	3.47	1.84	129
111. Lansing, Mich.	107.8	22.4	7.6	26.7	3.51	2.34	208
112. Jacksonville, Fla.	201.0	32.3	14.7	55.1	3.75	1.81	161

SOURCE: *City Government Finances in 1966-67*, U.S. Bureau of the Census, Vol. 2, 1967; *Census of Governments, Taxable Property Values*, U.S. Bureau of the Census.

However, redistribution objectives in some instances may suggest negative charges or "prizes" for use. Under the present welfare financing, higher and more charges may involve a larger federal share in local expenditures. This shift may improve the redistributive effect under a public pricing system. Not all the services provided by the public sector that can be categorized as containing significant private goods elements are necessarily suitable for pricing. Nevertheless, as cities begin to inquire more closely into the basis of their current charging practices and into the appropriate economic incentives for use of their air, water, and land resources, an extended and expanded use of public prices can be expected in the future. The margin for feasible use of market signals to guide public production, while not limitless, is clearly considerably larger than has been realized to date in most cities.

Correcting private market signals

Externalities are effects of production or consumption activities that are not accounted for by private market evaluations because the relevant benefits or costs are not appropriable, i.e., they cannot be attached to individual parties.[8] External economies and diseconomies of this sort affect not only the quality of life in urban areas but also the range of functions of the local government, which may, for example, provide services that "internalize" the externalities. Alternatively, the government may invoke ordinances and levy taxes that attempt to modify the social behavior of firms and households in order to achieve a more efficient allocation of resources.

Air, water, and landscape pollution, for example, with their attendant health hazards and aesthetic distortions, constitute important external technological diseconomies. The mounting pressure for local government to counteract external effects originating in the private sector has had an increasing impact on the size and composition of the municipal budget. Once it is determined that the private market cannot be relied upon for adequate provision of services such as waste collection and disposal, the decision to use public services is not sufficient; proper public pricing of these services also may well be needed for efficient rationing of scarce resources.

Police powers as well as services are used to affect private externalities by restraining private actions—for example, zoning laws that restrict the use of sites or pollution control laws that may prohibit private individuals from undertaking certain socially undesirable activities. Antilitter laws are an example of regulatory powers employed to rid the community of an externality by placing the burden upon those who do the littering.

A city can also approach the problems of private external effects through its taxing power. Within the limits of that power, a system of taxes and subsidies can conceptually be devised to modify the behavior of individuals or industries so that private levels of activity may be brought into conformity with the socially desired levels. By such tax and subsidy schemes, the city may seek to internalize social costs. These costs are brought into the decision calculus and affect behavior of the individuals or firms. An "optimal toll" on auto use, for example, will cause automobile users to include in their private accounts the social cost of their action. Such procedures may also reduce the amount of expenditures required for services (e.g., roads) that are now being provided by the city to meet externalities. Thus, this approach essentially requires a local government to develop the appropriate set of incentives, the government's "visible hand," to bring the behavior of individuals and firms into a better alignment with appropriate social actions.

Taxes may also be used to deal with waste residuals. Some cities now vary solid and liquid waste charges to take account of the extra damage done to the environment by the particular waste discharged. For the most part, however, private industry has no incentive to economize on its waste discharges. As indicated by Kneese in Chapter 6 and Gerhardt in Chapter 7, producers have an incentive, rather, to use the resource "discharge" in place of more costly methods of production, more costly materials of production, energy sources, or processes that would reduce noise, clean the air or water after use, or build in a scheduled reuse of solid wastes.

Economically efficient management of the quality of water, air, and land has not been achieved by traditional legal and regulatory steps. Effluent charges imposed by the national government on industrial water and air polluters have therefore been gaining support, as either a supplement or substitute for state or local regulatory activity.

A proper effluent charge is set in relation to the amount of the damage. It thus serves as an explicit price for the use of the waste assimilative capacity of water or air. Industry will thereby be encouraged to adjust waste discharge in relation to the added cost and the specific circumstances after taking account of its market. One problem with this approach is that differential damage costs in specific cities would lead to variations in effluent charges and would bring advantages to some firms and disadvantages to others. These disadvantages will therefore often conflict with local industrial development plans and sometimes also with federal regional development concerns.

Effluent or emission charges can also be imposed on certain products offered directly to consumers by industries and firms that impair the quality of the environment. In many cases the consumer has no idea of the hazards the products represent to himself or the world around him. These products include such familiar items as the internal combustion engine of the family car; the phosphates in household detergents; the "disposable" soft drink bottle; the new nonbiodegradable plastics; and the kerosene exhausts from jet airlines. The costs are now appearing in many ways: in ever-larger poundage of solid wastes to be collected and disposed of, in lakes choked with algae, in individual discomfort and ill health, and in property damage.

Imposition of a public charge that would take account of the damage to the air, water, or landscape would improve market tests of a product's comparative advantage. Economic efficiency suggests that such charges be tailored precisely to the amount of the damage so they would operate to redirect the choices of consumers toward the less damaging and therefore lower cost commodity. The resultant shifts in consumption should be toward those commodities, those brands, that could respond to the charge by altering content and reducing potential damaging qualities.

National charges that seek to alter the incentives for consumer choices may have the merit of uniformity; this would help avoid the problem of treating competing firms differently. But there also may be disadvantages of uniformity; one illustration of the disadvantages of uniformity can be seen in the case of throwaway bottles sold in rural or farm areas, where they become a by-product commodity useful as land fill. The distance between farm and retail store and perhaps between store and bottling plant makes the returnable bottle costly. If the environmental-use charges were imposed nationally on throwaway bottles, the farm community and the nonfarm community alike would be deemed to have the same damage costs. But that is hardly the case.

The returnable bottle serves to illustrate the common circumstance in which the damage to the environment is particular to a community and its characteristics. Though the costs of such circumstances can be determined with precision only for a particular location with its special characteristics of airshed, wind- and streamflow patterns, or land use, the community has scant access to some of the devices that could importantly influence consumer decisions. How does a municipality impose a charge on the phosphate content of detergents? How can it even require that all new car sales include antipollution control devices? Ease of movement into and out of the city makes such restrictive or charge measures difficult to enforce. The markets in many cities are too small to provide, by charge or restrictive regulation, incentives to producers to alter the content of their product. However, cities do have noise ordinances. And even small places such as Bowie, Maryland, are regulating against throwaway bottle containers. Also, some cities vary solid and liquid waste collection charges in accordance with the content of industrial wastes, and enforce air and water effluent standards.

Improving the public allocation of resources

Under present resource allocation practices within the public sector itself the wrong product is sometimes produced, in the wrong quantity, and with no (or inappropriate) quality differentiation. If it is feasible to determine benefit values and to identify the beneficiaries of a public program, pricing becomes a viable means of ensuring that the allocation of public resources becomes more efficient.

Clearly prices can be charged only when persons in the community will voluntarily purchase the priced service. The value of the product to the voter-consumer would determine the volume of demand. What is altered by introducing prices, assuming that prices are set efficiently, is the basis for managing the decisions on quantity and quality of production.

Resistance to new program offerings stemming from financial barriers in a city might be removed if the new offerings were originally planned to be self-financed out of fees and charges. Examples of such possible new service offerings are many; they include emergency first aid and ambulance services, foreign language instruction in the primary grade schools, children's music concerts, home health services that offer paramedical team services to patients at home or in nonhospital institutions, offstreet tree maintenance services, sidewalk snow clearance, outdoor street festivals, plays, concerts, and other performing arts services, mobile meals units, library collections, special transportation services for the aged, the disabled, and children that would increase use of community facilities, and trained child–nurse visiting services.

Asking consumers to pay for public services through the price mechanism gives them a chance to record their desire to have the priced service in at least that quantity for which the priced demand is registered. Externalities may well suggest larger resource commitments, but for many services at present there is no mechanism at all for recording demand. Pricing can also help signal to the city administration a shift of demand away from an existing service or facility and thus perhaps lead to a more rapid alteration of production than would current financial practices.

A direct charge on consumers would enable the community to meet the demands, for example, of those who would prefer more or different trash collection services, more policing services, more street-cleaning services, and more neighborhood improvement and maintenance services. A discriminatory pricing policy would permit consumers to buy the *extra* public services. It would then be possible to consider more frequent trash collection, with the additional days of collection offered at a price. Similarly, extra police patrol service could be purchased from public sources, just as those extra services in some instances are now purchased from private sources. Similarly, too, there might be a market for more frequent street cleaning, more street lighting, more public snow removal, more public offstreet parking, more public health surveillance of restaurants, and so forth. If public prices for those added public services were set to cover the incremental costs of the additional volume of service, and if the demand registered by payment of the price suggested expansions of city services, city administrators would have both a guide to decisions on added services and at least some of the funds for their production.

Price signals also offer a method for trying out and responding to the public's desire for quality changes in public services. The consumer who desires a quality differential could pay for that option—a choice now frequently denied him when quality changes must be financed from general revenue.

Elementary and secondary education has received much attention in the current discussions about new machinery or new methods for registering consumer preferences regarding quality differences. One proposal, as indicated in Katzman's Chapter 16, calls for the creation of a competitive market in the production of schooling services; parents would make a choice among the producers of education. In some variants, price might be held constant by a uniform educational allowance or "voucher" amount for schooling that would be the exclusive, authorized funding source. Optionally, minimum quality and quantity standards would be set by law, and some variation by school producers in methods and quality would be permitted. In still other variants, parents would select and pay for school services directly, within standards established by law. Since competition would be permitted or encouraged, consumers could more nearly purchase the education they seek for their children. (There are also problems, of course, with such schemes in the education area, some of which are discussed by Katzman.)

Pricing public goods

For those goods that can in fact be established as having significant public good characteristics (examples are "the image of the city" and mosquito control), a pricing system is not usually viable. A "public good" is one that cannot be divided into purchasable units. Consequently, no individuals or group in the relevant service area can be excluded from the benefits. The benefit of the service is available to the recipient whether or not he buys it and, because it is available, he has no incentive to reveal what his true preferences are. The production of public goods thus cannot be guided by demand. In the absence of market-type responses of demand to price, there is no conceptual procedure other than the cumbersome political process for signaling the decision-maker about the value of increments of output in relation to costs of those increments.

Even in the case of local public goods, however, ways can be found, at least potentially, to determine consumer demand more easily than the "package pricing" of tax levels and public service bundles now customarily employed. For example, in their articles in this volume (Supplements to Part One), Clarke and Tideman suggests ways to signal consumer-benefit price responses through use of systems relying on either a neighboring household or median response to provide information on quantities and second-tier incremental prices. Even if such ingenious devices become operative, however, the external or spillover benefits from individual consumption of certain public services may be so large that they will tend to impair the efficiency of the market as a resource allocator unless corrected by explicit governmental action as directed through the political (voting) system.

That substantial portion of nonpriced public outputs which is of the public good variety makes up, by definition, nonpriceable outputs. Within such larger service categories as fire or police, however, which are regarded by some as public goods, there are numerous subservices that provide essentially private benefits. For example, the police who handle crowds at ball games and direct traffic around large shopping

TABLE 1.7

Classification of Revenues

Type of revenue	Extent of individual benefit	Extent of public purpose
Quasi-private price	Special benefit the exclusive consideration	Public purpose incidental
Public price	Less special benefit although still preponderant	Public purpose of some importance
Fee	Special benefit measurable	Public purpose of still greater importance
Special assessment	Special benefit still assumed	Public purpose controlling
Tax	Special benefit only an incidental result	Public purpose the exclusive consideration

SOURCE: E. R. A. Seligman, *Essays in Taxation*, Macmillan, 1895, p. 302.

centers are providing services to identifiable beneficiaries on whom charges could be levied, even though the larger service of preventing crime may perhaps best be considered a public good. The subsequent chapters provide many other illustrations of the possible range and subtlety of a new look at the public pricing of public products.

NOTES

1. J. A. Stockfisch, "The Outlook for Fees and Service Charges as a Source of Revenue for State and Local Governments," in *Proceedings of the Sixtieth National Tax Conference* (National Tax Association, October, 1967); also, Dick Netzer, "Federal, State, and Local Finance in a Metropolitan Context," in Harvey S. Perloff and Lowden Wingo, Jr., eds., *Issues in Urban Economics* (Johns Hopkins Press, 1968).

2. Edwin R. A. Seligman, *Essays in Taxation* (Macmillan, 1895).

3. Although not further explored in this volume, property taxation, and especially the taxation of incremental property values as a reasonable proxy measure of the value of benefits from certain public services, has a long and venerable history as a benefit levy. See Dick Netzer, *Economics of the Property Tax* (Brookings Institution, 1966); Edwin H. Spengler, "The Property Tax as a Benefit Tax," in *Property Taxes* (Tax Policy League, 1940), p. 1970.

4. See Jerome W. Milliman, "Beneficiary Charges and Efficient Public Expenditure Decisions," in *The Analysis and Evaluation of Public Expenditures: The PPB System*, Joint Economic Committee (91st Cong., 1st sess.. 1969), p. 298.

5. Roland Teeples, *Some Problems Concerning the Magnitude of State and Local Government Revenues from User Charges* (Institute of Government and Public Affairs, UCLA, 1968), MR108.

6. Juan de Torres, *Financing Local Government* (National Industrial Conference Board, 1967), Chapter 5; and Gerald J. Boyle, *Use of Service Charges in Local Government* (National Industrial Conference Board, 1960).

7. Chattanooga, even though having a 1960 population in excess of 100,000, is omitted from the table because, alone among cities, it receives revenue from current charges and "other" utilities but not from water supply.

8. For alternative definitions, see J. M. Buchanan and W. C. Stubblebine, "Externality," *Economica*, 29 (November, 1962), 371–384; J. E. Meade, "External Economies and Diseconomies in a Competitive Situation," *Economic Journal*, 62 (1952), 54–67.

Beneficiary Charges—
Toward a Unified Theory

*U*NTIL more work is done on the theory of beneficiary charges in relation to the theory of demand generation for public services, empirical work on, and policy prescriptions for, user fees will lag and remain uncertain. This conclusion was drawn from an extensive review of the literature. The more I examined the literature, the more I realized that the issue of beneficiary charges and efficiency had not been worked out well in the theory.

The literature gaps have to be set alongside the many current opportunities for application of direct user charges. Possibilities for the application of beneficiary charges as an efficiency measure are literally everywhere—to ration airsheds, parks, water quality, highway use, city streets, urban public services, public housing and renewal, college facilities, hospitals, doctors, and so forth.

However, greater application of beneficiary charges to increase efficiency in the allocation of resources is still only a contingent possibility. It must wait on greater revenue sharing, and a clearer federal role in income maintenance. Until these large forward steps are taken by the federal government, the relation of beneficiary charges to efficiency will be subsidiary to questions of user charges and equity, or

Jerome W. Milliman is Director of the Center for Urban Affairs, University of Southern California, Los Angeles.

Note: This chapter is adapted from Milliman's article, "Beneficiary Charges and Efficient Public Expenditure Decisions," in *The Analysis and Evaluation of Public Expenditures: The PPB System*, Papers submitted to the Subcommittee on Economy in Government, Joint Economic Committee (91st Cong., 1st sess., 1969), Vol. I, pp. 291–318.

user charges and revenue growth. The literature is also deficient in its coverage of this linking of revenue sharing and income maintenance to both the equity and revenue potential of charges.

Three major strands of economic literature deal with the question of beneficiary charges: that on public finance, on public utility, and on welfare economics relevant to marginal-cost pricing. To my knowledge, no one has pulled these three strands together to present a unified theory of beneficiary charges. The arguments advanced for such charges are quite varied, often fragmented, and sometimes inconsistent. Three major arguments have been used by advocates of beneficiary charges: (1) *equity*, that is, fairness in charging beneficiaries; (2) *revenue production;* and (3) *efficiency* in the use and production of public services.

The Public Finance Literature

The economic analysis of public expenditure decisions has advanced a great deal in the last two decades. Public finance, which earlier was largely concerned with problems of economic stabilization and with the "finance" problems of how to levy taxes and sell bonds, has gradually turned to these long-neglected topics: what public goods and services should be produced and how; how much should be invested; and how public goods and services, once produced, should be distributed. A large body of literature now exists on the evaluation of "systems" approaches to public investment decisions. The techniques of benefit-cost analysis, program budgeting, systems analysis, cost-effectiveness analysis, and operations research are becoming accepted as standard tools to aid public expenditure decisions.

With these developments, it would seem that analysis of production and distribution of public goods and services would have come of age. As one studies the theory and practice of the production and distribution of public goods and services, however, large gaps are apparent in the knowledge of demand and supply relationships. On the supply side, there has been trouble in measuring outputs, and therefore we have very few empirical production functions expressing the technical relationships between factor inputs and product outputs. We have even fewer cost functions with which to determine the optimal combination of factors to produce given outputs. As a result, we have often relied on expenditure functions per capita to describe relations between costs and outputs. Changes in expenditures are clearly ambiguous numbers in the absence of independent measures of outputs. Moreover, we often tend to count expenditures on inputs as measures of output.[1] It is also evident that the demand for public services is often an ambiguous concept, and that scanty information exists on how well political processes reflect preferences of consumers and voters.

These knowledge gaps on both the demand and supply aspects of the production and distribution of public goods and services are clearly related to the question of beneficiary charges. On the one hand, if we do not have solid knowledge of outputs, costs, and demands, then attempts to determine optimal prices, charges, and taxes for these goods and services are clearly in a precarious state. On the other hand, such prices and charges might be helpful as a form of consumer voting that may supply (in many cases) valuable information about consumer demands. For example, if a public good is supplied at a zero price, we can expect that excess demand will develop, with "cries of alarm" suggesting that more production is needed. Yet we may have little information about the value of this service and the legitimacy of its claim on resources versus alternative claims on the same resources.

With a few exceptions, the public finance literature on beneficiary charges deals primarily with the question of the benefit approach to taxation. The question of how to levy fees or user charges is largely ignored; some of the best-known public finance texts do not even treat the subject. In general, the stress is on the equity and efficiency gains of having taxpayers pay for benefits received. However, these gains are still considered within the context of how to finance expenditures, and benefit taxes are a "fair" way to do it. Problems of optimal resource allocation and efficiency are introduced only indirectly and are usually more concerned with the longrun questions of investment in public facilities, rather than with the efficient use of facilities.

The equity aspects of benefit taxes are viewed generally as a matter of simple justice; i.e., users of a public service should pay for its costs when the benefits do not spill over to other people. For example, the benefits of irrigation water service provided by the Bureau of Reclamation accrue to the irrigators, and it would be "unfair" to require the public at large to pay for this service. By contrast, free hospital service to the poor might justify subsidies because of indirect benefits to the community at large. The usual textbook discussions do not elaborate on *which government community should subsidize the service*—federal, state, or local.[2] The answer would probably be: the community that receives the indirect benefits.

The principle that subsidies should be given on the basis of indirect benefits received is probably most clearly exemplified in relationships between local and federal levels of government. When benefits are provided to one group or region and the costs are borne by other areas or groups (who do not receive either direct or indirect benefits), income transfers are involved. Such redistribution must be justified on grounds *other than* the benefit principle of taxation. Yet it is very seldom argued in theory that local publics, for example, ought to share more fully in federal programs (such as flood control or urban renewal) because most of the indirect, as well as direct, benefits reside locally. The feeling seems to be that benefits which are widespread are automatically national in character.[3] The same point is made below in reference to collective consumption goods: the public character of such goods is often attributed to the nation as a whole when, in fact, collective consumption may be highly restricted to a given locality or user class. For example, how widespread is the collective consumption of the services of a lighthouse or those of a local police force?

In the traditional public finance literature, the efficiency aspects of benefit taxes (charges) are largely limited to the longrun questions of the "proper" investment in capacity or the optimal scale of service. Thus questions of how best to ration service from existing capacity are seldom discussed. The investment in public facilities is considered justified if consumer preferences (in the case of direct tolls) or taxpayers' preferences (in the case of benefit taxes) return funds to pay for the cost of the facility. The literature on cost recovery and cost reimbursement for public investment takes its rationale from the questions of equity and longrun efficiency discussed here. If the cost is not to be recovered from the beneficiaries, either an error has been made in the original investment, or (if the beneficiaries are not required to pay) there would be a transfer of income from other taxpayers to the beneficiaries of the service. If "profits" are earned, then the investment should be expanded.

Moreover, so the argument goes, if we do not require cost recovery from the beneficiaries, we will not *really* know whether the benefits from the service exceed the costs. This argument is often made both in an ex ante sense and in an ex post sense. The requirement of cost recovery from the beneficiaries as a precondition makes "sure" that the beneficiaries will carefully consider the worth of the benefits in relation to the costs during the plan-formulation period. Ex post calculations can point out past errors and serve as a basis for future improvements in decisions for new investments. All this seems reasonable, except that emphasis on cost recovery may be inconsistent with the best shortrun use of existing facilities. In addition, excessive emphasis is often placed on the recovery of historical or "sunk" costs, which may not be efficient for new investment decisions.

The economic costs relevant at any one time are the opportunity costs of resources and the alternatives sacrificed now and in the future. Although cost recovery from beneficiaries has many obvious virtues, recovery of historical (or sunk) costs will be inefficient because they are not likely to coincide with opportunity costs. We are always faced with the possibility of change in the future and the possibility of not making correct projections, when constructing long-lived facilities. To insist on cost recovery of historical costs in the light of greatly changed conditions may clearly result in charging too little or too much. Moreover, cost recovery tends to foster the idea that once facilities are "paid for," they should be free. More on this later.

The Public Utility Literature

The writings on public utility economics are the second major strand of the literature on beneficiary charges. The principles of public utility rate regulation are an uneasy blend of legal and economic principles tied together within a framework of cost accounting. The legal principles tend to be concerned with the financial requirements of the utility and with the notions of equity and fairness to stockholders and consumers. In general, economic theory in this area has been forced to adjust to legal and financial constraints.

This is not the place to launch into a full-scale examination of the principles of public utility rate regulation (usually these principles have been applied to both publicly and privately owned utilities). However, to sketch out the basic features of the principles will be helpful, because any study of the possible inefficiency generated from the failure to employ beneficiary charges must also come to grips with the possible inefficiencies from the use of improperly applied or incorrect user charges. I suspect that a thorough study of the matter would show that major efficiency gains could be achieved by a drastic overhaul of the system of rate regulation of public utilities (federal, state, and local).[4]

In large part, the level of public utility rates is determined by the following relationship:[5] $R = E + (V-D)r$, where R is the total revenue required to cover total costs; E is the full operation and maintenance expense; V represents the fair value when the facilities were new;[6] D is the depreciation allowed in the value of the facilities; and r is the fair rate of return to be allowed on the current fair value $(V-D)$.

This method of rate determination has the following schematic properties:

$$\text{Total Revenue (TR)} = \text{Total Costs (TC)}$$
$$\text{Average Revenue (AR)} = \text{Average Costs (AC)}$$

In short, public utility rates are based in large part upon two principles that are questionable from the standpoint of efficiency in the use of resources: (1) rates tend to be based upon recovery of historical or original costs, and (2) rates tend to be determined by the average cost of service as opposed to the marginal cost of supply. This sort of price policy probably represents a nice balance between such multiple objectives as equity in the distribution of wealth between consumers and stockholders, fairness among classes of service, and the provision of the financial needs of the utility companies. Yet it is questionable whether such a policy deals adequately either with efficiency in the use of existing services or with the development of optimal criteria for new investment. On the one hand, the scope of public utility operations is quite likely to be expanded and applied to an increasing range of public or quasi-public services. On the other hand, the opportunities to change or overhaul present practices and accepted principles of regulation are not bright because of the long weight of legal precedents supporting the present structure and because marginal-cost pricing has some practical and theoretical difficulties of its own.

The Marginal-Cost Pricing Literature

The third major body of economic literature bearing upon the theory and use of beneficiary charges is the writing of "welfare" economists who have developed the theory of marginal-cost pricing. Although some of the principles of marginal-cost pricing are now being absorbed or adopted in writings in public finance and in public utility economics, as yet a full-scale synthesis has not been achieved. For example, a public utility textbook will generally have a chapter on marginal-cost pricing, but then little is done to relate the implications for the theory and practice of rate regulation. Neither public finance nor the public utility literature has succeeded in rationalizing the needs for reimbursement of financial costs with the efficiency rationale of marginal-cost pricing that may generate surpluses or deficits. The theory of marginal-cost pricing stresses that investment and operating decisions on social investments should be made *independently* of reimbursement policies for individual lumps or units of productive capacity.

It seems clear that marginal-cost pricing is still a controversial topic, one on which economists have not reached a complete consensus. At one extreme are those who have accepted it as a major pillar of public policy;[7] at the other extreme are those who have rejected it as invalid or wholly impracticable.[8] Between these poles are many economists who have advocated changes or modifications in the principle itself or qualified the claims that its strict application will produce an optimal allocation of all resources.[9]

In its most simple form, the cardinal rule of marginal-cost pricing says that the demand price should be made equal to marginal cost, with marginal cost defined as the incremental costs of production (more technically, as the derivative of the total cost-function with respect to output). Since resources are drawn away from alternative uses, marginal costs should reflect accurately the social opportunities foregone. The equality of price and marginal cost ensures that consumers equate marginal benefits from this use of resources with the real alternatives foregone elsewhere. In a world of pure competition the market mechanism would operate to ensure this equality.

For some types of public goods, production is characterized by longrun decreasing costs or increasing returns to scale. Marginal cost will lie below average cost in increasing return cases.[10] If demand price is made equal to average cost (full-cost recovery), the price will exceed marginal cost. This result is inefficient because the value that consumers place upon extra output exceeds the cost of alternative production that could be sacrificed elsewhere to produce this extra output. It is therefore desirable to expand production to the point where price equals marginal cost. However, this solution will generate a deficit, and the goals of cost recovery come into conflict with efficiency. It is thus fair to ask why these costs should be borne by the general taxpayers, when the benefits are seen by the users of the facility. By contrast, equating price and marginal cost when the average cost of production is rising will require restricting output to the point where price equals marginal cost, even though total costs could be recovered at larger outputs and lower prices. In this case, marginal-cost pricing would generate surpluses.

These simple-sounding arguments may hide a whole set of complicating circumstances and situations. As C. J. Oort suggests (as expanded below), answers can be made to most of the theoretical and practical objections raised against the marginal-cost pricing principle. In particular, a whole set of devices has been proposed to deal with the troublesome problems of surpluses and deficits.[11] Also, economists always point out that the case for marginal-cost pricing is based upon three important conditions:[12] (1) that there are no important spillover effects in production and consumption that are not reflected by $P = MC$; (2) that the current distribution of income be acceptable or certainly not biased toward the particular measurement of prices and costs; and (3) that deviations from $P = MC$ elsewhere in the economy do not require compensating adjustments in this sector (the theory of the second-best).[13]

The efficiency arguments for beneficiary charges, although subtle and often complex, are the most persuasive and valid. To illustrate this point, I quote from a summary of a searching critique by Oort of the marginal-cost pricing principle.

We have shown that many of the objections to the principle are either invalid, or irrelevant for policy, or require certain more or less important modifications rather than a rejection of the principle. Invalid are all those objections to the rule which are based on alleged or actual indeterminacies of the marginal cost function; in most cases, the correct interpretation of the principle, which requires in the first place the equilibrium of demand and supply, will lead to a perfectly determinate solution in terms of optimum prices and outputs even where marginal cost is indeterminate. In particular, this holds for the cost of joint production in which separate marginal-cost functions generally speaking do not even exist, but in which the marginal-cost pricing principle nonetheless applies without any modifications. Irrelevant are those objections which apply to any and all rules of policy; this holds for the entire class of problems raised by the factor "uncertainty." Of the many modifications to which the marginal cost pricing principle must be subjected before it can be applied in practice, none appears to be so drastic as to actually imply the rejection of the rule as such. Most are in the nature of a compromise between the principle itself and some other economic objective such as the minimization of the administrative costs incurred by putting the proposed price and output policy into effect.[14]

Cost-Recovery, Marginal-Cost Pricing, and Efficiency

Krutilla is one of the few writers who has worried about the difficulties of determining the proper scale of facilities when no charge is to be levied on the beneficiaries:

We have on the one hand dicta that the scale of a facility should be extended to the point at which incremental benefit equals incremental cost. However, unless user charges are levied to cover the cost of providing the marginal unit of output, there will develop excess demand represented by those users who would not find incentive to use the services of the facility if charges appropriate to the design criteria were imposed, but who will make use of the facility at zero price. If such use by any beneficiary at capacity output adversely affects the utility of any other, the design criteria result in a project inappropriately sized relative to realizing the benefits estimated for purposes of design. At any rate, *it is clear that design criteria as presently advanced relate to the correct design for an irrelevent situation where reimbursement policies are at variance with design criteria.*[15]

Krutilla argues that the marginal-cost pricing doctrine makes the investment decision "independent of the reimbursement policy for individual chunks of productive capacity." He says that initially there may be excess capacity in facilities, justifying a marginal-cost pricing policy of not recovering full costs. However, as use of capacity increases, prices should be raised "to ration scarce capacity until a point is reached at which the revenue demonstrates a beneficiary willingness to pay for service sufficient to justify an expansion of facilities." If user-fees are raised to reflect congestion costs they will sooner or later equal the average cost of capacity: "In short, marginal-cost pricing under these conditions will result in exactly recovering costs of facilities of optimal scale and schedule of expansion."[16] All this seems to suggest that marginal-cost pricing, correctly applied, will provide for full cost-recovery and that cost-recovery is a desirable efficiency objective.

To make these relationships appear even stronger, Krutilla next points out the difficulties that may arise when criteria for project design and policies for cost reimbursement are not consistent. The design criteria require that the scale of the investment be extended to the point where marginal benefits equal marginal costs. Unless user charges are imposed to cover the costs of the marginal unit, he argues, excess demand will develop and use of the facility will be inconsistent with the design criteria. Therefore, reimbursement policies should be made consistent with design criteria.

I am not at all sure that the policies of cost recovery and marginal-cost pricing are nearly so compatible (as Krutilla suggests) when we apply the opportunity-cost concepts in a world of uncertainty and changing supply and demand relationships, especially when applying these concepts to long-lived facilities. Some difficult questions are raised when we ask about the relevant social costs, in terms of alternatives sacrificed the day before a project is built and the day after.

Even in a world of perfect foresight and with no unexpected changes in future supplies and demands, the day after a project is built most of the resources involved may be "sunk." The alternatives sacrificed from then on are usually only current operation and maintenance costs, which may be low. In such cases, prices should be set to ration supply and demand, and this may mean that deficits are the rule of the day. The common answer in the literature is that eventually prices will rise to ration demand as demand increases in the future, and that the later surpluses generated will balance the early deficits so that full costs will be recovered.

I do not find this line of reasoning convincing when the argument is placed in a context of uncertainty and unanticipated change.

The original investment costs the day after the project is constructed are historical costs—no more and no less—and they will not necessarily reflect changing supply and demand conditions and alternative social costs in the use of resources from that day on. Prices that correctly ration the use of capacity and deal with congestion may or may not return historical costs. Moreover, deciding whether the revenues generated justify an expansion of facilities should not be determined by covering the historical costs (even though such may be required for legal purposes), *but whether the revenues are sufficient to cover the costs of expansion or replacement costs at the time in the future when they are contemplated.* Clearly, future replacement or expansion costs may bear little relation to investment costs at an earlier period.

The Krutilla argument pointing toward consistency and compatibility of marginal-cost pricing and cost recovery would seem to hold only when the investment calculations are correctly made and when the future conditions are correctly forecasted. Not only can actual demands exceed or fall short of those originally forecast, but also the costs of future replacement or expansion may be greatly different from those that governed the cost of the original. investment. What I am saying is that the costs that should be recovered are the opportunity costs sacrificed at any time.[17] And it is highly unlikely that opportunity costs in the use, replacement, or expansion of long-lived facilities will be identical to those incurred the day a project is constructed. Why, then, is recovery of original costs efficient?

If my argument has validity it would mean that the recovery of historical costs should be viewed with suspicion when questions of efficiency in a world of change and uncertainty are relevant. The argument would also imply that repayment contracts and price policy should be made flexible in light of changing conditions. In other words, what would promote efficient resource use in a future world is only vaguely perceived at the time of project construction. The same logic would also apply to project operation. Sharp changes in operating rules and product mix of a multipurpose project may well be efficient and productive for the same reasons.[18] Although fixed repayment contracts, fixed beneficiary charges, and fixed operating rules may be necessary for legal and finance reasons, they may not be at all conducive to efficient resource use. These points may seem relatively straightforward from the standpoint of the efficiency of resource use, but they have not, to my knowledge, been carefully analyzed in the literature on public expenditure decisions.[19]

Notice, however, that the argument has now been shifted from emphasis on cost recovery and repayment to the "rule" that public projects should be operated to maximize their net social product. The *"cost recovery" that takes place is the meeting of opportunity costs.* The covering of opportunity costs will recover "historical" costs only in a world where future opportunity costs coincide with historical opportunity costs. I think we can agree with Krutilla that evaluation policies and design criteria should be made consistent, as far as possible, with assumptions about future price policies. But no amount of ex ante rationalizing can deal adequately with problems of uncertainty and change regarding future opportunity costs.

In spite of all this, it might be important to note that the idea of cost sharing (as opposed to cost recovery) appears to have a great deal of merit and could perhaps promote efficiency in terms of the *behavior* of the parties at issue. Fox has suggested that (1) cost sharing provides valuable information on the demand for the public service to policy-makers, and (2) cost sharing tends to keep the claims of perspective beneficiaries in check.[20] Note that Fox is apparently talking about cost sharing and not cost recovery. The arguments that I posed earlier for user charges based upon marginal costs would imply some degree of cost sharing, even though "original" costs may or may not be recovered. The fact that user charges would equate supply and demand would (or could) provide information to decision-makers, as well as provide discipline against excessive claims of beneficiaries. It also seems to me that the correct argument is *not* that zero prices are opposed to cost recovery (or cost reimbursement), but that prices will be used to ration service and to equate marginal social costs and marginal social benefits. Costs thus will be "shared" and perhaps "recovered," but they will probably not be original costs.

Most of this discussion is couched in terms that may be convincing to economists. But how does it stack up in the real world of affairs? If the original (financial) costs of construction are not recovered from the beneficiaries they still must be paid for by someone. If not by the beneficiaries, who will return the costs of funds with interest? In the business world, when the future is incorrectly anticipated, losses of a private firm are borne by the suppliers of equity capital and occasionally by the suppliers of debt capital. In the public world, the state governments and local governments have the power to tax, and the federal government has the power to print money as well as the power of taxation. The facts of the matter are that taxes will probably be employed to recover the costs in this case. The efficiency questions should be concerned with the possible *adverse effects of these taxes upon resource allocation versus the adverse effects of the levy of beneficiary charges* that might return historical costs but still be inefficient.[21]

It is difficult to see a clear-cut answer to the issues posed here. As far as I know, they have not been given careful treatment in the economic literature. The legal question of how to make repayment contracts and project operating rules more flexible in light of changing economic conditions over the life of a project are also a source of major difficulty. Clearly, these problems of cost sharing and efficiency are most likely to arise in the construction of large chunks of investment capacity with long lives. When public investments are relatively divisible and small in relation to the size of the market, the problems of future uncertainty and the large divergencies between average and marginal costs will not exist. However, one point made here still stands: the future opportunity costs to be covered may be more or less than historical costs. It is likely that recovery of historical or original investment costs is inconsistent with economic efficiency both in the short run and the long run.

Public, Private, and Merit Goods

A great deal of confusion exists about the conditions under which beneficiary charges are desirable and feasible. At this point it might be helpful to introduce the concepts of *public* goods, *merit* goods, and *private* goods. It is technically possible in the case of private goods to exclude persons who are not willing to pay for the goods or service. In private goods, the benefit is received largely by the individual person or household. As a result, private production is technically possible and usually desirable. However, a number of private goods and services are supplied by governments, particularly public utility types of services.

By contrast, a public good, in its pure form, is equally available to all, because (1) there are no feasible ways of excluding any consumer from enjoying the good, and (2) the consumption of one consumer does not interfere with the amount available to all others. Classic illustrations of a public good are national defense or a radio transmission that covers the whole area.

Merit goods have been defined in several ways, and admittedly this is not a clear-cut category. Perhaps it is easiest to say that a merit good is a private good that has been endowed with the public interest. From a merit good the individual receives more of a public service than he would have purchased on his own. Margolis states that:

The initial attitude toward merit goods was to see them as imposed on the population by a group of moralists, or the intellectual elite, or a pressure group with power, but with a recognition that the imposition might be a legitimate activity in a democratic society.[22]

However, it now seems less restrictive to consider a merit good a private good that has some public good characteristics.[23] That is, part of the benefit is "seen" by the individual consumer and part by persons external to the individual or by the public in general. Although it is possible to levy user charges, total production could be subsidized to the extent that collective benefits were perceived.

If the subsidy were supplied by a tax on the general public, it could perhaps be thought of as the most general form of benefit tax. This would not necessarily mean that the good must be supplied free of charge to the individual consumer. A proper user charge to the consumer would equate marginal private benefits to marginal private cost, with the extra consumption and production justified by collective benefits being subsidized by general taxes.

In some cases the external or collective benefits are satisfied by the first amounts consumed. Thus, *at the margin*, the benefits received may be largely individual in nature. As a result, we must be careful to distinguish between all-or-none decisions and those involving a little more or a little less consumption. For example, we can plausibly argue that an urban water supply confers a collective benefit on the community in the form of public health, in addition to the benefit received by individual households. On this basis, one could also argue that some form of public subsidy might be justified in support of urban

water investment and consumption. Yet all of the public health requirements might be satisfied by a per capita consumption of 60 gallons per person per day so that a consumption rate of 120 gallons per
person per day should reflect only the equation of individual marginal
benefits and marginal costs. However, the generation of collective
benefits at the margin for merit goods could justify prices at less than
marginal costs for individual consumers.

Shortrun efficiency

The efficiency problem in public production is twofold: (1) the
optimal level of investment in capacity (longrun efficiency) and (2)
the best use of existing facilities (shortrun efficiency). Clearly, the
longrun efficiency question is applicable to all forms of public production—public, merit, or private goods. But the shortrun efficiency question is not relevant to pure public goods nor to the collective (marginal)
aspects of merit goods. The shortrun question refers to the need to
ration private goods. For instance, my consumption may interfere with
your consumption. The shortrun question also refers to relevant marginal costs that are positive. For public goods, then, not only is it technically impossible (or difficult) to exclude or to ration service, *it is also
unnecessary and undesirable to do so.* The marginal cost of an extra
consumer is zero (or nearly so), and there is no excess demand; there
is therefore no need to ration. Even if it were possible to ration use,
the correct price would be zero.[24] Sometimes this point is not well
understood by students of public policy who want more cost sharing
employed to achieve efficiency in public expenditure. As we shall see
below, there are indeed many problems in trying to get the proper level
of investment for public goods, but this problem should not be confused with the role or need for user charges in the short run.

For example, the Federal Water Project Recreation Act of 1965
was hailed by many as a laudable advance in providing for cost sharing
by beneficiaries of recreation and fish and wildlife investments in
federal water projects.[25] The provisions of the act with respect to cost
sharing specify that non-federal agencies must bear 50 percent of the
separable costs allocated to recreation, fish and wildlife, and all of the
operation, maintenance, and replacement costs thereafter. The non-
federal share of the separable costs can be borne in two ways: (1) pay-

ment, or provision of land, or facilities for the project; (2) *repayment with interest within 50 years, provided that the source of payment be limited to entrance fees and user charges.*

Notice that repayments were restricted to entrance fees and user charges. We have just seen that employment of such charges is feasible only for goods of substantial private character where the benefit is largely individual and where it is possible to apply exclusion. Moreover, I have pointed out that rationing is needed only when *my* consumption interferes with *your* consumption, and when the marginal costs of extra consumption are positive. Apart from the legitimate question of whether the state and local agencies for recreation and fish and wildlife do have the necessary legal powers to incur debt and to collect fees, it is clear that many types of recreation services and fish and wildlife services are public in character. It would, in many cases, not be feasible to collect entrance fees and user charges nor would it be desirable to do so as long as congestion did not develop and cause my consumption to interfere with yours.[26] I am not suggesting that cost sharing per se is undesirable in this case.

It is clear that the discipline of cost sharing by local agencies would keep in bounds all sorts of exaggerated claims of benefits for recreation and fish and wildlife. Moreover, having to bear only 50 percent of the separable costs would not seem to be excessive when many of the collective benefits probably reside or accrue to people within the state or region. All these points are certainly desirable in trying to achieve *longrun* efficiency in the proper scale of facilities.

However, the restriction of repayment revenues to revenues from entrance fees and user charges could well cause shortrun efficiency problems to arise. Although such fees might be justified on efficiency grounds to ration service in some instances, they clearly would not be applicable across the board. Imagine trying to collect user charges on a long river when there are numerous recreation benefits downstream. On the basis of the argument here, it would seem desirable to modify the Federal Water Project Recreation Act to remove the restriction that repayments for cost sharing be *limited* to entrance fees and user charges. We must not confuse the rationale for cost sharing to promote longrun efficiency with the proper role of user charges in promoting shortrun efficiency.

However, we should stress that an argument could and should be made for user charges on recreation and fish and wildlife facilities *without any reference to cost sharing of original costs*. Instead, as we argued above, user charges should be based on rationing space and making the users see the congestion or pollution costs they impose upon others. A colorful statement of this point of view is provided by Gaffney:

As I recall the summer roar of Seahorse motors on peaceful lakes, the oil slicks, the loud speaker radios, the boat toilet problem, and the beer can outrage, I lose enchantment with the notion that the marginal boater is an innocuous fellow who sheds no external costs. The marginal swimmer, maybe, but how much space is he allowed? The age of genteel canoeing is dead. Man has so magnified his powers to invade his neighbor's privacy, and placed such terrible engines of nuisance in the hands of so many barbarians and adolescents who are enjoined from releasing their aggressions in useful labor that the marginal curve of psychic pollution rises vertiginously. So long as we refuse either to civilize or employ our young, the only salvation is to tax their more destructive pursuits, and certainly not to pretend they aren't bothering anyone.[27]

Before I turn to a discussion of the efficacy of beneficiary charges for promoting longrun efficiency in investment in public facilities, it will be helpful to emphasize three points on the role of user charges as a means of rationing use of existing capacity.

1. It is clear that as congestion develops and as the marginal user imposes congestion or pollution costs on others, a public good or service may become "private" in the sense that there is a need for rationing to make efficient use of a limited facility, watershed, or airshed.

2. Here the question becomes how best to ration. It could well be that some administrative rationing devices could function effectively and at less cost. This is the place to indicate that the administrative costs of collection of beneficiary charges, especially user charges, may or may not be low. Clearly, this may be an important factor governing their use.[28]

3. Zero prices for some public services may not always result in excess demand and congestion if there is some complementary factor of production employed in the process which may itself be rationed. Perhaps some examples will clarify this point. The provision of flood control protection to lands in a flood plain is a public good. The service is equally available to all persons occupying the plain, and my con-

sumption does not interfere with your consumption. However, the service of flood control protection is rationed to the extent that, to enjoy the service, one must buy or rent land (a location). The price of land will reflect the value of the service and serve to ration demand for the limited supply of lands protected.

In fact, most of the benefit over the life of the facility will tend to be capitalized in land values the day the project is built. If the flood control protection is provided free of charge to the flood plain, the gainers will be the initial landowners. Subsequent land users will be required to pay land prices or rents that reflect changing opportunity costs and that equate supply and demand. In most cases, it would be difficult to claim that such landowners should be classified as a disadvantaged group, so that the case for benefit taxation based upon land values to recover marginal costs would seem to be especially strong.

However, the fact that such windfall gains have a long history of political acceptance is indicative of the general observation that attempts to implement beneficiary charges for efficiency reasons may not be very successful. For the politician and for the man of affairs, the efficiency arguments for beneficiary charges are likely to carry less clout than would arguments based on possible rising demands for equity or for the needs for revenue production.

We might observe that rents for lands or houses may serve to ration the use of a public service but may need attention for another reason. In the case of merit goods we are presumably trying to subsidize a public service, e.g., public schools. If, however, excess demand develops, land values and housing rentals may rise so that the disadvantaged groups may be forced to pay the equilibrium price for the service in higher rent or else live elsewhere. Zero prices of services may thus generate shadow prices in complementary factors that are inelastic in supply. Although the rationing effect may be commendable from an efficiency point of view, we may not achieve the redistribution of income we sought in provision of the merit good. This perversity would be accentuated if the landowners and landlords received untaxed windfall gains in increases of housing and land values.[29]

Zero prices to users do not necessarily imply that there is no rationing involved in the consumption of the service. This fact leads to several interesting observations. One is that the real or shadow price to the user may be positive. It is therefore not always clear, as the literature often asserts, that the marginal benefits will be zero, leading to waste because the service is "free" when marginal costs are positive. In fact, the effect of nonprice rationing or the rationing of auxiliary factors may serve to stop consumption far short of the point where marginal values in use are zero, even though user charges are zero.

A second observation concerns the conclusion we can draw from attempts to construct demand curves and to estimate benefits on the basis of revealed behavior (consumption data) at zero prices. Suppose, for example, that actual consumption of a service is Q_1 in a zero-price situation. Without additional information on the degree of rationing (administrative, congestive, or the indirect, as in the price of complementary resources) we do not know whether to place Q_1 at point A on the implicit consumer demand curve or whether it should lie somewhere to the left of point A, say at B in Figure 2.1. The nature of the judgments we can make about marginal benefits in zero-price cases, and hence what we can infer about waste, is thus not intuitively obvious. Greater consideration needs to be given to the possibilities of hidden or implicit rationing in the analysis of revealed behavior in zero-price situations.

Fig. 2.1 *Estimate of Demand at Zero Prices*

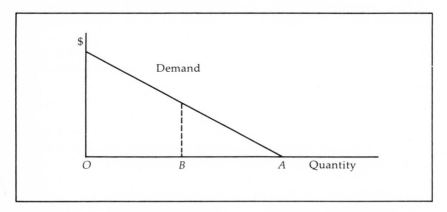

Clearly, this discussion does not refute the point made by Krutilla that subsidized facilities for one set of producer goods may distort the demands for auxiliary factors of production, so that the inefficiency effects may be found in the use of other inputs and investments, not just in particular service provided.[30] But it does mean that the question of possible inefficiencies generated in zero-price situations is apparently much more complicated than the existing literature suggests.

Longrun efficiency

Beneficiary charges can stimulate efficiency through the promotion of proper scales and levels of investment in two ways: (1) by imposing discipline on investment decisions and (2) by providing information to improve those decisions. The fact that beneficiaries will be charged will provide some discipline on the claims of benefits and will tend to force beneficiaries to consider these benefits and costs (the charges) in relation to alternative uses of their resources. If the burden of costs cannot be shifted, there will be less inducement to puff claims of benefits, and the relative allocation of factors will be improved.

The arguments made earlier that historical costs are not relevant to price policy based upon opportunity costs clearly raise many troublesome questions when we leave the static world and view investment in public facilities as a continuing process. Costs that may not be marginal in respect to output do become marginal in respect to the total question of whether to produce at all. Are the longrun marginal costs that we should be concerned with merely the derivative of the longrun, total cost-function with respect to output when the question is one of whether to produce at all? Also, are there not serious behavioral implications stemming from the dictum of ignoring historical costs the day after a project is constructed? Can you tell beneficiaries and public agencies that costs are important before a project is built and then not require cost-recovery the day after?

Unless substantial payment for benefits is required from beneficiaries or from the jurisdictions in which they reside, the forces to discipline public investment decisions will be very weak. Clearly when the discipline of the market is absent, there are serious problems of how to obtain responsible public investment decisions. We lack measures to reward good decisions and to penalize poor ones.

The discipline argument appears to be a powerful one, but there is not much I can add here. Further study of this line of thinking would accord with the suggestions to explore further political and behavioral models of the demand for public services.

Closely related to the discipline effect is the information effect cited above by Fox. That is, the application of beneficiary charges would provide decision-makers with valuable information about the benefit functions for public services. Provision of services at zero prices and failure to impose cost sharing makes it extremely difficult to estimate benefits received by users and to evaluate projects carefully.[31]

Just how difficult it is to estimate benefit functions in zero price cases is not usually appreciated. Some literature does exist on the problem of getting the public to reveal preferences, but the empirical problems of benefit estimation in zero-price situations are quite formidable. For example, suppose we have some revealed behavior on library circulation at zero price in an attempt to quantify some of the benefits of a public library. If the circulation is Q_1, we have to decide first whether to place it at point A or point B in Figure 2.1. But then how do we generate some sort of demand curve as a basis for benefit estimation? Unless we have another point, it is clear that we have little notion of the area to be measured and that points A and B could be consistent with an infinite number of demand functions. Benefit-cost analysis of public services supplied at zero prices is an incredibly difficult task, even when we have acceptable measures of the output unit. Revealed behavior at zero prices is extremely difficult to translate into meaningful benefit functions.

In general, I find the discipline and information arguments persuasive, yet I think that a great deal more study of the matter is required before we recommend the adoption of beneficiary charges for a greatly expanded range of public services. For goods that have substantial public content, the practical questions are: how do we get the public to reveal their preferences, and how do we collect beneficiary charges that may promote longrun efficiency and yet not cause shortrun inefficiencies?

For private goods, the problem is somewhat less. The people or consumers have to reveal their preferences because no other beneficiaries will do so, and "if I do not pay, I will not get the good." The efficiency problem with private good production in the public sector is how to reconcile desire to recover costs with the need to meet opportunity costs. As I suggested above, the theoretical conditions necessary for the reconciliation of these two kinds of cost recovery are not likely to be found in actual practice. However, we would hope that revenues generated by "correct" pricing policies would still recover some or all of the original costs so that the users would be more likely to bear the costs (as well as enjoy the benefits) rather than shifting the burden to other groups.

As Brazer, Gaffney, and others have pointed out, many kinds of public goods are, in fact, not equally available to all, but available only to particular regions, areas, or user groups. Although it may be difficult to estimate the amount of a policeman's service used by a particular family on the beat, it is clear that the policeman on a given beat provides protection primarily to that beat and only secondarily to other parts of the city and to other cities in the same region. For that commonly used example of a public good, the lighthouse, the service is certainly not provided to all, but only to boats in the vicinity of a given lighthouse. Flood control protection provides benefits mainly to users of the flood plain, fire protection to one area is not fire protection for the whole city, television signals may benefit only a limited service area, and so on.[32]

All this suggests that it may be easier than many writers believe to identify beneficiaries of a particular public good. If this is the case, the classic ingenuity of the American political system could be called on to provide decision-making institutions through which people's preferences can be revealed as a prerequisite for determining what types of beneficiary charges are appropriate and desirable.

NOTES

1. Werner Z. Hirsch, "The Supply of Urban Public Services," and Richard A. Musgrave, "Discussion of Part III," in *Issues in Urban Economics*, Harvey S. Perloff and Lowdon Wingo, Jr., eds. (Johns Hopkins Press for Resources for the Future, 1968). Hirsch and Musgrave cite examples of this tendency; on the demand for services, see Julius Margolis, "The Demand for Urban Public Services," in the same book.

2. James Buchanan, *The Demand and Supply of Public Goods* (Rand McNally, 1968) offers an exception.

3. As Edgar Olsen (one of the helpful critics who read my paper in an earlier draft) has suggested, the benefits of flood control and urban renewal are viewed as widespread because many communities have projects. The relevant question from the viewpoint of beneficiary charges is the extent of benefits from any one project.

4. William J. Baumol, et al., "The Role of Cost in the Minimum Pricing of Railroad Services," *Journal of Business* 35 (October 1961): 357–366; Jack Hirshleifer, et al., *Water Supply: Economics, Technology, and Policy* (University of Chicago Press, 1960), Chapter 5 (hereafter referred to as *Water Supply*); and William S. Vickrey, "Some Implications of Marginal Cost Pricing for Public Utilities," *American Economic Review* 45 (May 1955): 605–620.

5. Eli W. Clemens, *Economics and Public Utilities* (Appleton-Century-Crofts, Inc., 1950), p. 127, uses this formulation.

6. "Fair value" can mean values other than original cost. A better alternative from an economic standpoint would be replacement cost. In actual practice, as James C. Bonbright says, "all commissions administer, with more or less efficiency or laxity, versions of, or minor deviations from, an actual cost or sunk cost standard of reasonable utility rates" (Bonbright, *Principles of Public Utility Rates* [Columbia University Press, 1961], p. 283).

7. Abba P. Lerner, *The Economics of Control* (Macmillan, 1944).

8. I. M. D. Little concludes, "The general case against marginal-cost pricing is clearly overwhelming" (Little, *A Critique of Welfare Economics* [Oxford University Press, 1950], p. 194).

9. Nancy Ruggles, "The Welfare Basis of the Marginal-Cost Pricing Principle," *Review of Economic Studies*, 17 (1949–50): 24–46; and "Recent Developments in the Theory of Marginal-Cost Pricing," *ibid.*, 107–126. These articles give an excellent review of early marginal-cost pricing literature.

10. Several of my critics have objected to this statement, asserting that cases where longrun marginal costs diverge from longrun average costs are not frequent or important. Because our knowledge of cost functions for a wide range of public goods and services is so skimpy, it is apparent that neither position is presently supported by much empirical study.

11. See Hirshleifer, et al., *Water Supply* (see note 4 above).

12. Most of these qualifications apply equally well to any system of beneficiary charges, particularly to policies based upon average-cost pricing.

13. William Baumol and David Bradford, "Marginal-Cost Pricing and the General Welfare Revisited" (unpublished manuscript). The paper contains a valuable survey of earlier work. It reaches the disturbing conclusion that systematic deviations through the economy from marginal-cost pricing will be required for an optimal allocation of resources because all taxes (except Pigouvian poll taxes) to cover deficits will unavoidably make some prices depart from marginal costs.

14. C. J. Oort, *Decreasing Costs as a Problem in Welfare Economics* (Drak-

kerij, Holland, N. V. Amsterdam, 1958), Appendix on "The Marginal Cost Pricing Principle."

15. John V. Krutilla, "Is Public Intervention in Water Resources Development Conducive to Efficiency?" *Natural Resources Journal*, 6 (January 1966): 72.

16. *Ibid.*, pp. 66, 67, 68. Some of my critics think I have been unfair to Krutilla here; others agree with me. As I suggest below, Krutilla is correct only if he means recovery of new facility costs in an ex ante sense—not recovery of sunk costs.

17. Note the difficulties this argument implies for privately owned public utilities: investors must be paid, or the market for securities will be affected. Notice also that the argument has implications for all private firms—not just those with public utility status.

18. Maynard M. Hufschmidt (chairman), et al., *Report of Panel of Consultants to the U.S. Bureau of the Budget on Standards and Criteria for Formulating and Evaluating Federal Water Resources Developments* (U.S. Bureau of the Budget, June 30, 1961), p. 59. This report advances a similar argument.

19. One of my critics argued that more firms should be nationalized in the interest of efficiency to avoid the legal difficulties of deficits arising from the dictum not to recover historical costs. The deficits could presumably be paid for out of the general treasury. However, as Baumol has suggested, taxes *themselves* may introduce significant deviations from marginal costs.

20. Irving K. Fox, *Essays on United States Water Resources Policy* (University of Wisconsin, 1968).

21. My critics are of many voices on the questions raised here. Some say that recovery of historical costs involves no economic questions, and that my worries here are incorrect. Others see that failure to make beneficiaries share original costs will have dire consequences. Still others see beneficiary charges as second-best choices over tax levies. Finally, some worry about the meaning of the arguments for utility firms in the private sector.

22. Margolis, "The Demand for Urban Public Services," p. 541 (see note 1 above).

23. Several readers have argued that I ought to abandon the concept of merit goods. Considering both consumption and production externalities, almost all goods are part public and part private. Public and private goods are polar cases along a continuum.

24. Note that we must distinguish between the marginal cost of adding an additional TV set *once* the station is on the air and the marginal cost of changing the amount of production that is equally available to all. In the latter sense, each consumer is rationed to the quantity of the service that is actually produced. Here neither marginal utilities nor marginal costs are zero. Once the production decision has been made, the marginal costs of additional consumers are zero even though the amount and kind of service for each individual is fixed.

25. Public Law 89–72, passed July 9, 1965.

26. Robert Haveman (another of my helpful critics) suggests that if a local agency recognizes that user charges are not conducive to shortrun efficiency, it could choose to make the non-federal share in the form of an outright payment.

27. Mason Gaffney, "The Valuation of Public Goods—Discussion" in Morris E. Garnsey and James R. Hibbs, eds., *Social Sciences and the Environment* (University of Colorado Press, 1967), pp. 154–160.

28. Although many economists are sympathetic to Vickrey's plea for user charges to ration the use of city streets, they are skeptical of the proposal because the administrative costs of collection are likely to be high in relation to the efficiency gains perceived. Similarly, the desirability for underdeveloped countries to use water meters for rationing water supply may be doubtful if the costs of the meters themselves, their servicing, and the billing system are quite high in relation to the value of water saved and water investment avoided.

29. J. W. Milliman, "Land Values as Measures of Primary Irrigation Benefits," *Journal of Farm Economics*, 41 (May 1959); also, "Land Values—A Further Comment," *ibid.*, 42 (February 1960); and see Margolis, "The Demand for Urban Public Services," p. 546, and Gaffney, "The Valuation of Public Goods—Discussion" (see, respectively, notes 1 and 27 above).

30. Krutilla, "Is Public Intervention in Water Resources Development Conducive to Efficiency?" p. 69 (see note 15 above).

31. Roland McKean argues that admission charges supply important information about the nature of public demands and might be justified on the grounds of being the cheapest way for decision-makers to gain information about marginal evaluations by consumers. See McKean, *Public Spending* (McGraw-Hill, 1968), p. 73.

32. James M. Buchanan, "A Public Choice Approach to Public Utility Pricing," *Public Choice*, 5 (Fall, 1968). Buchanan advocates that a person have two roles—one as a taxpayer-purchaser and one as a consumer-purchaser, with separate marginal tax prices and marginal user prices. These suggestions have many attractive properties, but it is difficult to see how they could be implemented.

Chapter **3** WILLIAM S. VICKREY

Economic Efficiency
and Pricing

THUS far, most of the practical regulatory and other pricing policies associated with public goods and services have been primarily concerned with questions of equity, often to the detriment of economic efficiency. They have also often seemed oblivious of major gains in economic efficiency that could be realized without significant sacrifice of equity. The legal atmosphere within which regulatory agencies operate has tended to emphasize their role as arbiters between conflicting interests, while the concern of the regulated companies for the state of their earnings and their stance vis-à-vis the regulatory agencies has tended to cause them to pay relatively little attention to any efficiency-promoting innovations that would not yield them a fairly immediate financial gain.

This is the more unfortunate because criteria of economic efficiency, despite the overelaborate mathematical formulations of second-best optima often presented by theoretical perfectionists, can in practice usually be stated in fairly universal and well-defined terms, whereas the principles of equity to be applied often turn out to be poorly defined and even inconsistent. In the confusion over how to divide the pie equitably, much of the pie's substance gets frittered away, and the clients suffer pangs of hunger waiting for the slicing process to culminate. In extreme cases, the regulator finds himself cast in the role of a Solomon so absorbed in the niceties of dividing the baby

William S. Vickrey is Professor of Economics at Columbia University.

Author's Note: I wish to express my appreciation for the support and encouragement given by Professor Robert Haveman of the University of Wisconsin in the preparation of earlier material on which much of this article is based.

exactly in half that he ignores the inherent inefficiency of this procedure. Meanwhile, other issues remain largely disregarded, including the substantial possibilities for better utilization of resources, reduced levels of charges on the average, and improved service, all of which inhere in pricing policies that are imaginatively conceived in terms of economic efficiency.

Relation of Prices to Costs

The importance for economic efficiency of having prices closely related to costs is seen in its simplest form in a free enterprise system characterized by vigorous competition in all economic activities. In such a competitive system, prices tend to reflect the relative costs of providing additional quantities of various goods and services. Individuals and business firms, in pursuit of their private objectives, ordinarily select ways of providing the desired goods or services that minimize the sacrifice required by the remainder of the community. Thus the given level of production tends to be accomplished with the least possible expenditure of effort and resources.

This kind of pricing, conforming closely to the cost of serving additional customers, tends to arise through competitive pressures when production takes place either at constant or increasing unit costs and, to a somewhat less precise degree, when the economies of scale are moderate. But where costs decrease substantially as the volume of output increases, competition tends to break down, and prices in such areas may be too high relative to other prices from the standpoint of maximum efficiency. Clearly, when costs vary in proportion to output, a producer whose prices reflect the cost of additional output will recoup his costs, including a normal profit on his capital investment.

When economies of scale are moderate, a price that covers total production cost plus normal profit must exceed somewhat the cost of additional ouptut, but the difference may be small enough to avoid any gross inefficiency in the allocation of resources, so that the outcome would be tolerable from the standpoint of efficiency. But when economies of scale are substantial, there is a marked divergence between the price level that covers the entire cost and the price that properly reflects the cost of additional output. To the extent that the price is set to cover the entire cost, it prevents prospective buyers from buying as much of the product or service as would be desirable in terms of the impact of their decisions on the economy as a whole.

If the usage of the product is significantly responsive to changes in price, substantial inefficiency can be avoided only by lowering the price to a point approximating the cost of additional output. This in turn would involve operating at a loss, and will hence involve some degree of departure from the free competitive system.

Marginal Cost and Intramarginal Residues

Efficiency thus requires that prices be related to the cost of additional output, usually referred to by economists as "marginal cost." It is necessary, however, to be fairly precise about what is meant by the term, to avoid misconceptions often associated with it. For example, it is often loosely identified with the "variable cost" of the accountant, or with "out-of-pocket" costs, exclusive of the elements variously referred to as "fixed overhead" or "start-up cost." This identification is likely to be misleading, because marginal cost often contains an element of fixed cost, as it does when additional production requires new fixed plant or other additions to capacity. However, marginal cost will often not include *all* of the fixed cost since the total capacity of the fixed plant may increase more than in proportion to its cost. For example, when a highway is doubled from two lanes to four, its cost may be roughly doubled, but its capacity to carry traffic without undue congestion and delay is much more than doubled. In such cases marginal cost will include only a portion of the fixed cost on the books. Even in the short run, marginal cost may include a "quasi-rent" element determined by the scarcity or abundance of the fixed facilities relative to demand, which may be either greater or less than the historical "fixed cost" of these facilities. Also, marginal cost may not include all variable costs, where these do not vary strictly in proportion to output.

In the discussion of pricing for efficiency, therefore, it is desirable to avoid as much as possible the use of the terms "fixed cost" and "variable cost." Confusion will be avoided if the terms "marginal cost" on the one hand and "intramarginal residue" on the other are used. The latter term designates all cost other than marginal cost; it is calculated by subtracting from total cost the aggregate revenues that would be generated by prices set equal to marginal cost for each class of output.

Marginal cost as an absolute pricing standard

When the principle of marginal-cost pricing was first developed, its advocates generally held that the proper solution to the problem of achieving economic efficiency would be to set prices exactly at marginal cost, or as close to this level as would be feasible given difficulties in estimating marginal cost and in keeping prices in line with these estimates. The resulting deficit—the intramarginal residue—would be covered from taxes or other charges that are unrelated to the consumption of particular goods or services, in order to avoid interfering with efficient pricing in other areas. It was considered that only in this way could users of these goods and services make proper choices.

For example, suppose a shipment can be handled at a marginal cost of $100 by rail and $120 by truck. Unless the shipper valued qualitative aspects of the trucking service at $20 more than the rail service, the rail shipment would be most economical from the standpoint of overall efficiency. Yet, to fully cover its intramarginal residue, the railroad might have to charge $150, whereas the trucker, whose economies of scale are considerably smaller, might have to charge $130 at most. The shipper would then be induced to ship by truck, causing more resources to be used in transportation and leaving fewer resources available for other purposes, without yielding any comparable advantage to the shipper.

According to this analysis, the intramarginal residue of the railroad and trucker should be financed out of general tax revenues so that the shipper would be faced with prices—$100 and $120 respectively—that reflect the cost incurred by his choice of one mode or the other. Presumably he would then decide to use rail or truck (or operate his own truck) in a way consistent with overall efficiency, by balancing the advantage to him against the respective costs to be borne by the rest of the community.

There are, however, two major difficulties in applying this solution of marginal-cost pricing in its pure and simple form. One is that it would require great expansion of the role of government and a corresponding contraction of the free competitive sector. The other is that it would entail massive subsidies financed by taxes, which themselves may adversely affect economic efficiency. The next two sections deal with these difficulties.

Modification of the marginal-cost principle

Mild degrees of decreasing costs, with their attendant tendencies to imperfect competition and monopoly and with prices significantly above marginal cost, characterize a large proportion of modern industrialized societies. To attempt to bring all prices everywhere down to marginal cost and to subsidize the intramarginal residues of each industry would involve a vast expansion of government in the production and distribution of goods and services and a severe reduction in the role of free competitive enterprise. To apply simple marginal-cost pricing only to a selected group of industries where the economies of scale are particularly striking and the inefficiencies resulting from unsubsidized or unregulated prices are serious would go too far in the opposite direction. Services priced at marginal cost would be competing with services priced significantly above marginal cost. This competition would result in a substantial market distortion of the same character as, but in the opposite direction to, that produced by full-cost pricing of the decreasing cost services.

For instance, in the previous rail-truck example, suppose that only the railroad's intramarginal residue was subsidized. Rail service would be priced at the margin—$100. The trucker would have to add something to his marginal cost of $120 to cover other cost elements, assumed here to be $10, to reach his price—$130. If the shipper valued the extra convenience of the trucking service as worth $25 more than the rail service, he would still be inclined to use the rail. Yet overall efficiency in this case, with the $25 convenience value outweighing the $20 difference in marginal costs, would be better served by using the truck.

A better solution is to adjust subsidies so that the price difference of the two modes of shipment would be the same—$20—as their marginal-cost difference. If only rail is being subsidized, the rail shipment would then be priced at $110 as compared with the $130 truck price, calling for a $40 rather than a $50 subsidy. For inducing correct choices by shippers, this would be better than leaving the rail rate at $150. Yet it would still leave some distortion. This is evident when a shipper has his own trucks and makes a choice on the basis of a comparison between his own essentially marginal costs and the common-carrier rates that include marginal costs plus considerable excess, both for rail and truck.

The situation illustrates what is sometimes referred to as the "principle of second-best adaptation," i.e., that whenever there is a general rule that cannot be applied uniformly throughout all parts of an interrelated system, the best adaptation that can be made is likely to be a general modification of, or departure from, the theoretical rule. It is usually best in such cases not to try to follow the rule exactly for any limited area, but rather to allow for some appropriate deviation throughout. The application of this second-best principle to marginal-cost pricing, as has been seen, calls roughly for prices in the controlled sectors to be set above marginal cost by an amount corresponding to the differentials prevailing on the average in the uncontrolled sectors. The differentials encountered in the goods and services most closely competitive with those of the controlled sector should be weighted more heavily in determining the average.

It is sometimes claimed that allowing such margins would result in a policy too complex to be carried out in practice. Actually, rough rules of thumb for carrying out such a policy can be developed to produce results reasonably close to the best that would be theoretically possible (given the constraints against tampering with the uncontrolled sector), and vastly superior to full-cost pricing.

General tax support of marginal-cost pricing deficit

The second and more serious obstacle to carrying out marginal-cost pricing, either with or without the addition of a representative margin, is that the funds necessary to provide the required subsidies are not freely available without cost, but must in practice come from taxes that themselves have adverse effects upon economic efficiency. These adverse impacts arise not only from the high administrative cost of collection and the costs of taxpayer compliance, but also from the tendency of the taxes themselves to interfere with the making of efficient economic decisions.

This tax impact can be summarized as a coefficient termed the "marginal cost of public funds." Conceptually, this is the ratio of (1) the dollar equivalent of an added tax burden to (2) the net revenue from the tax increase after all additional expenses of collection have been met.

There are marked differences in the marginal cost of public funds obtained from various sources. If increased rates charged for a given service are considered as a kind of tax, it will be found that such revenues often have a very high marginal cost indeed. Transit fares are a case in point. Suppose that a municipally owned transit system increases fares from 15 to 20 cents and that, as a consequence of this 33 percent increase, ridership falls off 10 percent. Then for every 100 riders who previously paid 15 cents, yielding $15 of gross revenue, there will be 90 riders paying 20 cents and yielding $18, a net increase of $3. The burden per ride to the 90 continuing riders will be 5 cents each, or a total of $4.50. The burden to the 10 former riders, who were driven to an alternative form of travel they considered inferior to the 15-cent transit ride but preferable to the 20-cent transit ride, would range between 0 and 5 cents, or an average of 2.5 cents—a total of 25 cents for all 10 persons. The burden on continuing and former riders combined totals $4.75, or $1.58 for each $1 of new gross revenue. If operating costs are unaffected, as they may well be, this is also the marginal cost of net revenues.

The municipality could respond to the drop in patronage by reducing service, but this cost saving would be offset to a large extent by the decreased value of the service to remaining riders. Reducing service, indeed, could induce a further reduction in patronage and loss of revenue. So under the described circumstances, the marginal cost of public funds obtained from increasing transit fares is clearly of the order of 1.5 or more. While most large city governments are fairly hard pressed financially, it seems almost certain that substantial funds could be obtained from other sources at a much lower marginal cost. This is especially pertinent in transit funding since an increase in fares, when considered as a tax, is one of the most regressive taxes of any significance, imposing approximately the same dollar burden on individuals drawn from a wide range of income levels.

To recapitulate, two prescriptions emerge from considerations about the pricing of services subject to sharply decreasing costs or substantial economies of scale. First, a price should exceed marginal cost to the degree that prices of competing services exceed their marginal cost. Second, the price should be increased further to the point where the marginal cost of raising revenue in this way is roughly equivalent to the marginal cost of obtaining revenues from such other public sources as are likely to be used to balance the budget.

Self-Financing Public Activities

In cases where the economies of scale are not too extreme, or where usage is relatively little affected by the price changes over the range under consideration, it may prove desirable to set prices high enough to finance the operation on a self-liquidating basis, or on a basis of subsidies limited to specific forms, such as exemption from certain taxes or reducing or eliminating the charges for certain inputs. There are, indeed, many arguments for a pricing system that covers cost and avoids the temptations to lax administration that subsidized operation often seems to entail.

One such argument is that subsidized public operation may encourage users to demand that a service be unduly expanded or extended or improved in quality, especially where the circumstances are such that the consumers standing to benefit would not and perhaps should not be called upon to bear the full burden of the added cost, in that to do so would unduly limit usage. An agency subject to an immediate budget constraint may be better able to resist such demands than would an agency able to draw on an open-ended subsidy. A somewhat similar argument is that an operating agency may be less keen to hold costs down when it is able to draw on a subsidy than when it is required to function within the revenues available from charges it levies on its own responsibility. A third argument is that a subsidized operating agency may spend an excessive proportion of its administrative effort in trying to justify increases in the subsidy and in the scope of its own operations.

In any particular case, a decision whether to eliminate or limit the extent of subsidy should be made on the basis of weighing the above considerations against the loss of economic efficiency entailed by a limitation of the subsidy. If a limitation is imposed, it will no longer be possible to bring the marginal cost of net revenues to the operating agency into equality with the marginal cost of public funds generally. Limitation of the subsidy thus involves avoidable inefficiency in terms of prices and outputs, however much this may contribute to greater efficiency at the administrative level. This loss of efficiency can be minimized to some extent by a partial subsidy, and if the delimitation of the partial subsidy is fairly firm, so as to be an effective constraint not subject to modification by pressure from the agency or its consumers, much of the baneful effect of the subsidy on the efficiency of the administration of the service may be avoided.

The process calls for considerable caution, however. That such a subsidy be quite independent of the manner in which the service is supplied is very important, and especially that it not take the form of subsidizing a particular category of cost. Otherwise, distortions in the economical use of resources can be extremely serious. In New York City, for example, transit system expenditures that could be classified as capital outlays were for a long time subsidized from general city revenues while operating expenses had to be met from fares, with fare increases being mandatory if operating expenses were not so covered. As a result, levels of service were drastically cut and maintenance expenditures skimped. At the same time new appurtenances were furnished with a relatively lavish hand, new construction proceeded, often without adequate thought as to how the new facilities would be used when ready, and new equipment was purchased to replace equipment prematurely retired because of the poor maintenance.

Price discrimination

Even within the constraints of self-liquidating financing, a closer approach to maximum allocational efficiency can often be achieved if certain types of discrimination in the rate structure are introduced. A good example of this is the judicious use by the electric power industry of the classification of customers into residential, commercial, industrial, etc., combined with the use of block rates, sometimes referred to in the economic literature as a "multipart tariff." Through such multipart tariffs the larger customers, at least, have available an opportunity of buying additional service at rates close to the marginal cost, while making a substantial contribution to payment of the intra-marginal residue out of the higher rates they pay on the initial blocks of their consumption.

As generally practiced, however, this is discrimination that falls short of the ideal, because most small customers are at points on the schedule where the price they would pay for additional use is still far above the cost of supplying them with electricity. Moreover, such price discrimination has an undesirable distributional impact: the small customers who pay the higher rates are on the average poorer than the customers who are benefiting from the lower rates.

Discrimination by size of premises

This difficulty and the one above could be substantially mitigated if the block sizes in the residential rate structure were made to vary according to the extent of the premises served. A user in a large residence would then have to pay at the higher block rates for a larger amount of electricity than would a user in a small residence, before the lower rates approximating marginal cost would begin to apply. With judicious determination of such a rate schedule, even relatively small-volume residents, if living in correspondingly small quarters, would have available to them a low marginal rate for additional consumption. From the standpoint of efficiency, a larger proportion of the users would be in a position to make decisions regarding their use in terms of a rate close to marginal cost, thus promoting more efficient allocation of resources. From a distributional standpoint, also, the low-income customers would, on the average, pay relatively less and the wealthier customers living in larger quarters would pay relatively more.

This does not, however, fully meet the problem. Some consumers with an unusually large taste for housing relative to their consumption of electricity will still not have available to them rates that will be low enough at the margin to encourage full utilization of the facility. Moreover, basing utility rates on the size of the premises would have the effect of increasing the cost at the margin of occupying larger premises and thus lead to undue stinting in this direction, though possibly not to any serious extent, given the relative amounts involved. In the case of electricity, at least some of the service is close enough to a necessity so that few (if any) customers would give it up entirely because of high overall rates for relatively small levels of consumption, and the same is probably also true for water supply. But for other utility services—such as gas, telephone, or cable TV—there is a much more limited extent to which conventional forms of discriminatory pricing by the supplying agency will solve the problem of promoting efficient allocation of resources within the constraint of meeting full costs from revenues.

Property levies

There is indeed, much to commend going one step further by covering the intramarginal residues of utility services of this latter type, at least in part, by charges related to the occupancy or ownership of property to which the service is made available, independently of the amount of the service used, or indeed of whether the service is used at all. In this case the user could not reduce his contribution to the intramarginal residue by abstaining from use, so that he would be motivated to govern his use in terms of rates set close to marginal cost and would thus act in a way conducive to optimum utilization of resources. Ideally, the charges should be related to occupancy of land, independent of the improvements or structures erected on it but determined by site value and area, or possibly as a function of street frontage. If this were done, the charges would not constitute a deterrent to full development of the property, as would tend to happen if the charges were based in part on the value or magnitude of improvements.

The justification for assessing the nonusers is that the availability of the utility service is an essential element contributing to the value of the land. An individual who wishes to preempt the use of a parcel of land for some purpose not requiring a given utility service should not be excused from contributing to the cost of providing the service any more than a housewife who wants her refrigerator in a color that happens to be available only on models that include a freezer compartment should expect not to pay a price covering the cost associated with the freezer, even though she does not expect to use it. Indeed, such a method of covering intramarginal residues would go far to discourage inappropriate land use. Potential land occupiers who do not need the available utility services would be encouraged to locate elsewhere, unless the importance to them of the particular location is sufficiently great that they are willing to pay the charge. At the same time situations of inappropriate occupancy of sites located farther out on the fringes of the service area by those who do need the utility services and require costly extensions of service into new territory would be avoided. A more rational pattern of development would be encouraged, and leap-frogging and sprawl would also be reduced.

This assessment approach to the financing of the intramarginal residues involved in the provision of utility services, radical as it may appear at first mention, is nevertheless quite in line with one traditional justification for taxing land. The locational value of a site, usually the major element in urban land value, has been explained as a value created by the community to the extent that occupancy of the land provides access to goods and services provided by the remainder of the community. In return for enjoying the benefits this value measures, the property owner should be called upon to make a special contribution to the overhead costs of the activities that make these goods and services available. The argument is usually advanced with respect to governmental and other public services, but there is no inherent reason to prevent its application to utility services. Indeed, in some areas water supply is financed by charges against the property served, either on a value or on a front-foot basis. There have been recurrent suggestions that rapid transit extensions should be financed at least in part by special assessments against the property benefited. Financing other utilities in this way is but a logical extension of the same principle.

Equalizing the marginal cost

In many cases, however, the political structure will preclude the financing of intramarginal residues out of land taxes, especially for types of service where the potential users are not sharply localized, while at the same time the possibilities for covering the intramarginal residue through intramarginal charges in a multipart tariff may be limited. For many utilities, even with the best possible price policy, substantial inefficiencies will result under any scheme that is in any significant sense self-liquidating. Passenger transportation by common carrier, both urban and intercity, is a striking example of this. Telecommunication in its various forms, especially over longer distances, is probably another. Even here, however, there is often room for minimizing this inefficiency within the constraints imposed by the self-liquidation requirement.

Of course, if the independent operation has only a single price to be determined, as is substantially the case with many transit operations having a single flat fare, the level of this single price is ultimately determined by the financial requirement, and there is no further room for discretion. But in most cases a number of interrelated rates are capable of being adjusted, and even where only a single price is currently being charged, the possibilities for suitably differentiated prices often offer large returns. A workable principle is needed for adjusting the various rates so that a reasonably close approach to the optimum will result.

One fairly straightforward approach is to use again the principle of equalizing the marginal cost of net revenues for each of the rates under the control of the agency, but without requiring that this uniform internal marginal cost of net revenues equal the marginal cost of public funds. Take the case where an operating agency requires additional net revenue of $100 and can obtain this from customers in Group A at a cost to them of only $120, while to obtain it from Group B would cost them $130. It will be possible to decrease the aggregate burden imposed on the customers by increasing rates to get additional net revenues from Group A and lowering the rates on group B so as to give up a corresponding amount of net revenue. If this procedure is carried out until the marginal cost of net revenues has been equalized, the aggregate of benefits to customers will be maximized.

Such a rule can be justified only when it appears in the decision-making process that a dollar of benefit to Group B will weigh as much as a dollar of burden to Group A. This judgment would obviously not be valid if group A were known to be significantly underprivileged relative to group B. In practice, however, there is often no significant difference between the average income levels of two groups. Indeed, two groups may frequently be found to consist in large measure of the same individuals in different capacities and, in extreme cases, may be almost indistinguishable. This fact may be obscured by the way groups are defined: e.g., they may be classified as business firms rather than as individuals who are the ultimate customers, employees, or stockholders of the firms.

To deal properly with equity considerations usually requires attention to individuals or families as units rather than separately in each economic capacity in which they function. For example, in considering a proposal to raise rush hour traffic fares while lowering offpeak fares, it should be recognized that many rush hour riders also ride at other times, or if not, members of their families do. Or consider a proposal to lower railroad freight rates on coal relative to the rates on steel sheets. Suppose this led to a $120,000 saving to shippers of coal and an added burden of $100,000 to steel shippers. It is extremely unlikely that any one ultimate consumer could expect to emerge with a net burden as these freight rate changes become reflected in the costs of electric power, canned goods, autos, or the like. For this to happen would require that his direct and indirect consumption of coal relative to steel in all forms exceed the average relationship by more than 20 percent.

Moreover, even though two groups of ultimate consumers in a particular situation might be distinguishable, and it would seem unjust to impose a burden on one group even for the sake of a substantially greater benefit to the other, the specific decision should not be considered in isolation. Rather, the net result of a large number of similar decisions—each made to maximize the net balance of gains minus losses—should be weighed, since an individual who came out on the short end of one of these decisions would gain on others and almost certainly gain relatively more. If one thinks of applying this policy to a whole class of decisions ranging into the future, practically every individual could expect to benefit, as compared with any other reasonably uniform rule applied consistently.

Thus here, more than in most situations, there is good reason to aim for economic efficiency rather than to be held back by rules of justice or concepts of equity applicable to the individual case.

Yet ideas of justice cannot be disregarded entirely. Cases of immediate, flagrant, and substantial injustice call for setting aside or moderating the rule of efficiency. If, for example, a new rapid transit line at first is very lightly loaded, the marginal cost of carrying additional passengers is low, and efficiency would indicate a correspondingly low fare. Meanwhile, marginal cost on crowded lines in other directions would call for a correspondingly higher fare on the same basis—but this would understandably strike many riders as piling insult on injury. It may be regarded as a sufficient, though perhaps necessary, discrimination (simply because one must do one thing at a time) to single out one particular area for the new line. To give the beneficiaries of the new line a lower fare than those on the older, crowded line may not only provoke hard feelings but also create a disruptive political climate preventing the construction of new lines in rational sequence. In short, the felt injustices involved and the political tensions generated in adjusting rates for maximum efficiency must be taken into account. From a purely economic standpoint, also, the negative redistributive effects in some cases may be so substantial and so concentrated on identifiable individuals as to make it unlikely that adequate compensation would come from the random occurrence of countervailing decisions resulting from applying the efficiency rule elsewhere.

One advantage of the property tax approach noted earlier is that it can help rebalance these inequities. Since land values tend to reflect social benefits, it is both possible and logical to recover some of the advantages conferred on particular segments of a community through levies on the affected properties, as when transit lines serve one area but not another. Even here, however, market imperfections may be such that those who pay the higher fares are unable to secure corresponding rent reductions for some time, and vice versa.

When the property levy cannot be used to redress the felt inequities, retention of somewhat uniform rates or fares may be in order to preserve a sense of equity. However, this retention tends to encourage overutilization of old facilities and underutilization of new ones. It should be stressed that deviations from the efficiency rule are justified chiefly when there is a big and direct impact on identifiable individuals —and generally not when the impact is on businesses or industries.

The Case of Urban Area Transportation

Subsidization of commuters

Both equity and efficiency issues are involved in considering subsidies out of general revenues for rail commuter service to the wealthier suburbs (as distinct from local transit service). In this case, it might well be held unconscionable to provide additional subsidies out of funds that at the margin would be derived largely from added taxation that impinges on lower incomes. The situation here is particularly acute because such subsidization would be added to other inequities that run in the same direction, e.g., tax advantages of homeowners relative to tenants, the avoidance by many suburbanites of a large part of their share in the burden of supporting metropolitan amenities and obligations, and the various income tax loopholes that favor upper income groups.

In practice, however, the question of such subsidy to suburban mass transportation must be considered in the light of the even heavier subsidy of the alternative mode of commutation—the private automobile, often carrying only its driver. Failure to subsidize mass commutation facilities may merely mean that more traffic is diverted to highways, generating added congestion that impinges not only on the commuters themselves but also on people who are trying to move about within the suburban area. This congestion is likely to lead in turn to a demand for additional facilities constructed in considerable measure with federal funds or with revenues derived from motorists using the facilities at noncongested times and places and deriving relatively little benefit from expansion and duplication of facilities for commuters. Thus the end result of a failure to provide an obvious mass transit subsidy to suburbanites may be a far greater, though less obvious, subsidy to these same commuters as motorists.

Moreover, the existing and prospective subsidies to the motorist commuter are so great that in many cases not even the offer of *free* mass transportation service would suffice to produce an efficient choice of mode of travel as between private automobile and mass transit. The subsidy to the motorist commuter, computed in marginal terms, often far exceeds the entire marginal cost of the mass transit service. Assume that the automobile trip involves a subsidy of $1 on a marginal basis and the marginal cost of the corresponding mass transit trip is 60 cents. Then a bonus of 40 cents would have to be paid to each mass transit rider at rush hour if the cost differential involved in his choice between the two modes is to be correctly reflected to him. Only then would he be induced to make a proper choice in terms of weighing his own preferences against the resources used in making the two alternatives available to him. However, even if such a bonus could be financed, it would be a mixed blessing. It would begin to bias the choice of people to live in the city or the suburbs and, in either case, to live close to their jobs or commute.

Pricing of facilities threatened with congestion

So far, there seems, indeed, no adequate solution to the problem of inducing efficient patterns of commuter travel and providing the facilities for satisfactory service at minimum cost unless, in one way or another, the motorist commuter can be made to feel the full social costs of his trip. These costs, in principle, should include many items, among them: the full cost of duplicating or enlarging facilities to take care of peak-hour traffic; a major share of the cost of routes and facilities that also provide substantially improved service for off-peak users; the still unreckoned costs of automobile traffic's contribution to air pollution; and the cost of automobile accidents, to the extent these are not fully covered by insurance or are covered in a way that does not suitably affect the decision to make a particular trip. (These costs must of course be brought home to all users of the congested facilities at congested times, and not just to the regular daily users.)

This suggestion does not imply that toll booths should sprout everywhere, with the queues at the booths and the salaries of toll collectors eating up most of whatever benefits might be derived from improved management of the traffic. There are in fact a number of alternative devices available for the collection of tolls without excessive expense for collection and without delay and inconvenience to motorists. They are flexible and adaptable enough to vary the charges so as to promote approximately the desired optimization. The simplest of them would be a license or pass to enter designated congested areas; the pass would be purchased in advance and then marked, torn, or chemically activated before use to indicate time and place of use, and provision may be made for returning the license for reimbursement of the unused portion of the purchase price. Another system involves a meter attached to the vehicle, actuated by pulses emitted from roadway cables. Still another uses scanning or locater systems to monitor automobile use and thus permit a bill for each vehicle to be computed and mailed monthly to the registered owner. Institution of such congestion tolls would not only facilitate a rational solution to the commuter problem but also vastly increase the efficiency and utilization of the central city's downtown street facilities.

What drastic improvement can be achieved with relatively slight reductions in the amount of travel is seldom realized. For example, a reduction of only 10 percent in the vehicle-miles traveled over a given street network can easily result in a 25 to 50 percent reduction in the number of cars attempting to move at any one time. This reduction corresponds to an increase in speed of 20 to 80 percent, depending on the severity of the initial congestion conditions. Add to this the provision of adequate incentives to move as much of the truck freight as possible at night and other uncongested periods, and deterrents to preemption of street space by excessively protracted parking, double parking, and the use of excessively large vehicles, and an almost revolutionary improvement in downtown traffic conditions is within reach in relatively short order. Thus the use of congestion charges would not only reduce the subsidy to the private automobile commuters from the wealthier suburbs and thereby reduce the need for subsidy to the competing mass transit, but also have a crucial revitalizing impact on the core cities and the central business district. The contribution of the resulting revenues to hard-pressed city treasuries is by no means a negligible element; it would be one source of revenue with a marginal cost of public revenue of much less than one to one. In many instances, motorists paying the added charges would find themselves better off than they were originally, so that the marginal cost of public revenues might be zero or even negative.

Factors in Evaluating Economies of Scale

In addition to the many situations where a decline in costs with increasing volume is explicit and easily recognized, there are a number of situations in which the same principles of maximizing efficiency apply but where the economies of scale take forms that are not so obvious, and thus tend to be underestimated. It is important that these less obvious instances not be overlooked, and that the full extent of the existence of economies of scale be properly appreciated.

For example, the decreasing costs involved in a rail transit service are usually readily recognized where the minimum right-of-way provides more capacity than is likely to be needed in any but the most exceptional cases. Even where the system is being operated at maximum capacity, as with many of the central trunk routes in the New York metropolitan area during rush hours, outlying routes are generally operated at less than capacity. The economies of scale involved in operating a bus line, on the other hand, while not so apparent, are also substantial. The operating costs may indeed tend to vary fairly directly in proportion to the number of bus miles traveled, at least as long as the relative daily pattern remains unchanged, and this direct relation may be thought of as indicating an absence of economies of scale. Nevertheless, there may be substantial economies of scale in terms of passenger miles in that the higher density of operation may permit higher average load factors to be achieved. And even where load factors remain the same, a strong element of increasing returns may result from the fact that, as the volume of traffic goes up and with it the number of bus miles operated, the increased frequency, and possibly also the increase in variety of routes and types of service offered, is an improvement in the quality of service. If credit is taken for this increase in the value of the service to the former passengers against the cost of providing the additional bus miles that accommodate the additional traffic, the net cost of providing the service to the new passenger is less than the average cost per passenger of the entire operation. Where density is light, indeed, marginal cost may be so low that free service would be the most desirable mode of operation, with further savings resulting from the abolition of fare collection.

In transportation or communications generally, increased traffic usually leads also to the establishment of more direct routes. Thus, in freight transportation, even though costs per ton-mile were to remain constant or decline only very slightly with increased density of traffic along a given route, as more direct routes are established it becomes possible, for example, to ship twice the volume of traffic between the various origins and destinations according to the same overall pattern, but with less than twice as many ton-miles. If we use the number of ton-miles over which the freight is actually carried as a measure of the volume of service, the economies of scale in accomplishing the carriage of freight from point to point may be significantly underestimated. For example, suppose that cities A, B, and C are located at the vertices of an equilateral triangle 100 miles on a side, and that each point ships ten tons of traffic per day to each of the other two. If at this level of traffic, a direct link between A and C in addition to the AB and BC links is not found worthwhile, so that traffic from A to C moves via B over the AB and BC links, total traffic will be 8,000 ton-miles per day. Suppose then that activity doubles and each city ships 20 tons per day to each of the other two, and that with this increased traffic the construction of the direct line AC becomes worthwhile. Then total ton-miles will increase to only 12,000 per day, an increase of only 50 percent resulting from a 100 percent increase in demand.

On another level, statistical studies that attempt to estimate marginal cost and economies of scale by comparing the cost of operations in different areas, involving different densities of traffic or intensities of operation, often fail to isolate the element in the situation that is of importance for efficient price-making purposes. For example, the cost per telephone connected is generally found to be greater for large cities and metropolitan areas than for smaller towns and cities, from which it is sometimes concluded that local telephone service operates under a condition of increasing rather than decreasing cost. This statistical conclusion is sometimes buttressed by arguments based on the increase in the complexity of the switching equipment and in the number of stages of switching that each call must go through because of the increase in the number of telephones out of which the desired one is to be selected.

Such an analysis, however, leaves out of account the longer distances involved in the typical call in the larger city, as well as the fact that the telephone plant must be to a larger extent placed underground, with an increasing degree of difficulty of threading through a maze of other utilities as the city grows larger. The relevant question is not whether costs would go up or down if the city expands, but what would happen if there were a significant increase in the number of telephones connected, possibly in response to a rate reduction, within a given area and with a given physical environment to contend with. Considered in this way, it seems clear that the substantial reduction in cost per circuit-mile as more circuits are placed on a given pole or in a given set of ductways in a trench along a given route will more than outweigh whatever diseconomies of scale there may be in having to provide a more complex switching apparatus in the central exchanges.

Somewhat similarly, studies have been made that purport to determine the economies of scale in the railroad industry by comparing the costs of large railroads with those of small ones, without considering that the relevant variable is not the size of the railroad as a whole, however measured, but the density of the traffic. Thus the Richmond, Fredericksburg & Potomac Railroad, with a relatively small total volume of operations in terms of ton-miles, can be expected to have a relatively low level of average costs because of the high density of traffic over its relatively short route, whereas the Southern Railway, though a much larger railroad, however measured, might not be able to achieve comparably low costs because its traffic is spread out over a much larger network of route miles. Comparisons which deal with entire railroads, accordingly, are unlikely to generate a relevant estimate of marginal cost or of the extent of economies of scale.

Economies of scale as related to pricing policies discussed here may thus be much more significant than appears from a cursory study of the statistics. It is important not to be misled into thinking that the problem is relatively insignificant, or that the efficiency problems are minor compared to the probem of securing equity.

Pricing Rules
and Efficiency

THE rule of marginal-cost pricing of a commodity can be stated simply. The price should be set at the point where demand intersects the marginal-cost curve. In Figure 4.1 the demand schedule for Product A depicts the amount consumers are willing to buy at different prices. The marginal-cost curve shows the incremental cost of producing an additional unit of output. At the point of intersection, the price is determined—shown in the figure as P_1—and the output, often called the "ideal output," would be Q_1 of Product A.

If the total cost (and derivatively marginal cost) is calculated correctly, it measures what society has foregone in alternative uses of resources in order to produce this commodity. The marginal-cost curve shows the additional cost to society involved in getting one more additional unit of output. If the community as a whole is sufficiently competitive and other conditions are satisfied, following this marginal-cost pricing rule in each industry would enable the community to produce the maximum amount of output in goods and services. In order to increase the output of any one good, the output of all other goods or services would have to be decreased. And the consumer, by looking at the price facing him, can decide whether it is in his interest to increase his consumption of the commodity or to forgo its use and spend his income on something else in order to maximize his satisfaction. When the marginal-cost pricing ruling is followed everywhere, the marginal worth per dollar spent by each consumer is just equal to the marginal

E. Stanley Paul is an economist and a member of the Senior Research Staff of The Urban Institute.

Fig. 4.1 *Price and Marginal Cost*

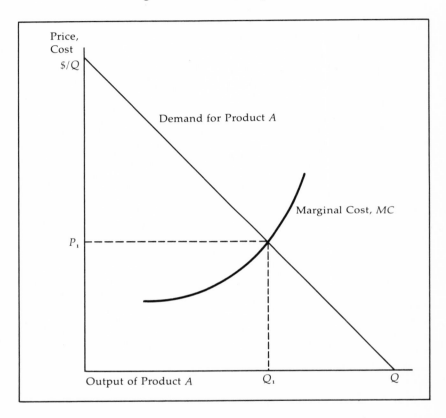

cost of producing goods and services, and there is no way in which reallocating resources can increase welfare or reduce total cost to the community.

Further Problems of Efficiency

This simple statement does not, however, resolve the efficiency issue. Three relevant questions may be asked.

1. How does marginal-cost pricing contribute to the most efficient use of an existing facility? (This is a shortrun pricing problem.)

2. Should the facility be expanded or contracted—or even built? (This question raises the problems of distinguishing shortrun marginal-cost pricing and longrun marginal-cost pricing.)

3. How are costs to be covered if marginal-cost pricing does not generate sufficient revenue?

Efficient use of a given facility

How a given facility should be used so that it achieves maximum efficiency is a common problem. Consider a swimming pool of a given size that permits a given maximum number of users per time period in the pool per day.

Following the rule, we must first determine the pool's total costs. This involves two components—variable cost and fixed cost. The variable cost consists of the operating cost and the maintenance cost, both of which vary with the number of users: e.g., as the number of users increases, the number of lifeguards must be increased and water quality maintenance must be upgraded. The fixed cost is the original expenditure on building the pool; this is a sunk cost, since resources have been committed, and they will not vary with the level of output.

The relevant costs for setting prices are the variable costs. As the output increases, the operating and maintenance costs will increase. The rate of variable cost change is the marginal-cost curve: that is, for each additional unit of output, the marginal-cost curve up to capacity shows the additional cost that is incurred when one more person uses the services of the pool. In Figure 4.2 marginal costs are increasing to capacity, Q_2; at that point they become infinite, or undetermined. The reason is that at capacity, although variable costs will increase, no further additional users can utilize the pool.[1] The interpretation of the vertical portion of the marginal-cost curve is that the marginal costs are undefined at that point. Figure 4.3 shows the total-cost function; its slope is the marginal cost shown in Figure 4.2, which also shows the demand for the swimming pool (represented by curve DD).

Suppose initially that, for whatever reason, the price for the use of the pool was set at P_0 or, to pick an arbitrary number, 25 cents. At the price of 25 cents, the frequency of the use of the pool, as reflected by the demand, would be Q_0. However, at this level of demand, Q_0, the frequency of use exceeds the capacity of the pool, which we have denoted by Q_2. There is an excess demand, the difference between Q_0 and

Fig. 4.2   *Price Rule: A Swimming Pool Case*

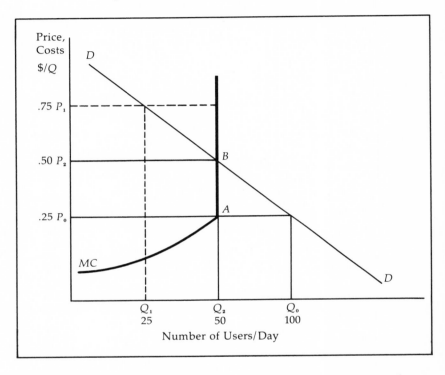

Q_2. Using arbitrary numbers, the frequency of use per time period (say a day) would be 100 at Q_0, 50 at Q_2, which is the capacity, and 25 at Q_1. Therefore, the excess demand with the price at 25 cents is 50 persons.

The excess demand can be rationed by price, by administrative fiat, or by waiting lines and queues. If queues are used to ration, the rule could be on a first-come, first-served basis: individuals would have to wait in a queue for their turn to use the pool. Those who did not want to wait would leave the queue.

To ration by administrative fiat requires that rules be developed and applied. For instance, it could be ruled that 8- and 9-year-olds could use the pool from 9 to 10 a.m.; 10- and 11-year-olds could use it from 10 to 11 a.m.; and so on.

To ration by price requires that when there is excess demand the

Fig. 4.3   *Cost Function: A Swimming Pool Case*

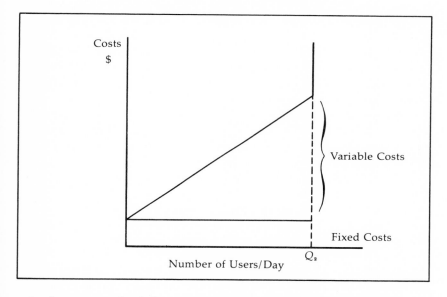

price be increased. If the pool operator were to increase the price to 75 cents (to P_1 in Figure 4.2), the quantity demanded would decrease from 100 to 25. Consumers will decide that at this higher price it is not worthwhile to use the swimming pool as frequently as before. In fact, an excess supply will exist at this price: the capacity of the pool allows use by 50 persons per day, but the consumers who will use the pool at a price of 75 cents will number only 25. The marginal cost of 25 additional users is now considerably less than the price. The marginal benefit the community would receive from having an additional unit of output is greater than the marginal cost to the community of providing that additional output. As the price is slowly lowered from P_1, consumers are willing to use the swimming pool more frequently. On the other hand, marginal costs would be increasing. Eventually the price falls to 50 cents (or P_2 in Figure 4.2). At this price, the demand is just equal to the capacity of the pool: i.e., there is neither excess demand nor excess supply.

Notice that we have here a seemingly anomalous position. At capacity the marginal cost becomes indeterminate, as indicated by point A in Figure 4.2. On the other hand, the price we are charging is greater than the 25-cent price at which marginal cost becomes indeterminant. This difference between point A and point B is the economic rent accruing to the swimming pool. The pool, whether publicly or privately owned, would be receiving income greater than the amount needed to pay for the operating and maintenance expense. Economic rent is often thought of as some kind of surplus. But notice that if we should decrease the price, say, from 50 cents to 45 cents, excess demand would result with the development of waiting lines. And devices other than prices would be required to ration the use of the pool. Consequently, the economic rent is a necessary complement to the efficient use of the pool.

Throughout, we have specified a fixed period of time, say, a week, for cost determination. The short run occurs when there is at least one fixed resource whose cost cannot be changed within a given period of time. Those costs that can be varied determine the shortrun marginal cost, which is the relevant cost for pricing. An extreme example of marginal-cost pricing is the situation in which all costs are sunk and marginal costs are zero. Under the marginal-cost pricing rule—that is, price equal to marginal cost—price would be set at zero.

Investment for expansion of facilities

Marginal-cost pricing does not always lead to a viable decision rule in terms of an optimal level of investment, because there is often indivisibility or lumpiness in investment. A basic condition required for application of the pricing rule on marginal costs is that capacity expansion can be undertaken in small divisible units. In the swimming pool case there need not be lumpiness, because small additions can be made to the pool's capacity. But for many investments this is not true. For example, between two points a highway and a bridge each have a minimum size. Moreover, the correct time period for establishing marginal cost is frequently difficult.

To illustrate the marginal-cost rule's application to investment decision, we assume in Figure 4.4 a constant return to scale activity. Constant return to scale means that, if we double all inputs, outputs will also double. The longrun total cost is shown in Figure 4.4. In the long run, there are no fixed costs. For this reason, our longrun costs start at the origin and increase by constant increments with increasing

Fig. 4.4 *Shortrun and Longrun Total Costs*

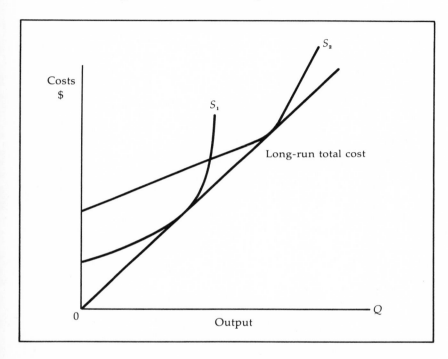

output. The longrun marginal cost is the horizontal line as shown in Figure 4.5, which means that the value of the resources foregone in alternative uses has a constant value to society.

The total shortrun cost, given the scale of plant shown in Figure 4.4, is denoted by S_1, the marginal-cost curve of which is MC_1 (Figure 4.5). Given the demand, DD, in Figure 4.5, the shortrun marginal-cost pricing rule is met when the price is set at P_1 and the rate of output is Q_1. At this level of output, the facility is being utilized at optimum level. However, notice that the price exceeds the longrun marginal cost (MC). The marginal benefit to the consumer as represented by price is greater than the longrun marginal cost.

An expansion from S_1 to S_2, the optimum plant size (see Figure 4.4), is now assumed. The price of the expanded output is equal to the longrun marginal cost, and the "ideal" rate of output or service would

Fig. 4.5 *Shortrun and Longrun Marginal Costs*

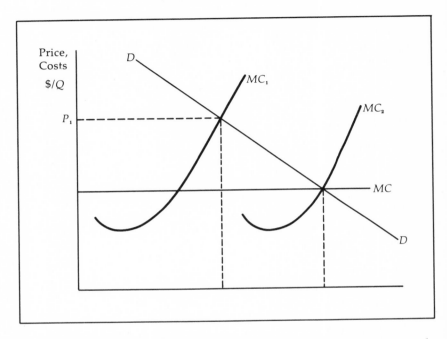

be Q_2. At level of output Q_2, price is also equal to the shortrun marginal-cost curve (MC_2).

Under the appropriate conditions, we can thus use the longrun marginal-cost rule on pricing as a guide to making the decision to invest.[2] After this decision is made, the question is again how to utilize the facilities efficiently, and, as before, marginal-cost pricing is the appropriate pricing rule.

If indivisibilities are present, however, and particularly if there is no market to reveal effective demand (as is true for many city services), other criteria must be used in making the investment decision. For instance, there is no market for highways, and thus the decision to extend, contract, or build highways must be based on other criteria. However, once the highway is built, the problem is to control frequency of use. If there is no congestion, the price should be set at zero. If there is congestion, a price can be found that will equal the marginal social cost. And at that price, we will have the optimum use of the highway in terms of frequency of use.

A city is continually faced with investment decisions. Some are on a large scale, such as expanding the water supply; others are on a relatively small scale, such as increasing the refuse collection fleet. Benefit-cost analysis has recently been applied to guide the city in making better decisions when it must undertake an investment project. The difficulties encountered in estimating benefits and costs are the same as those arising in the pricing of public services, and the cost estimates required for a benefit-cost analysis are the same as those needed in setting prices. When there is no market, estimation of benefits or demands is especially difficult. If there is a pricing system, however, analysts would have some information on benefits: this, of course, is one reason for the use of prices.

Another factor is also involved here. Suppose that for a project a good benefit-cost estimate is made (see Figure 4.6). The benefit-cost

Fig. 4.6 *Price and Marginal-Benefit–Marginal-Cost Ratios*

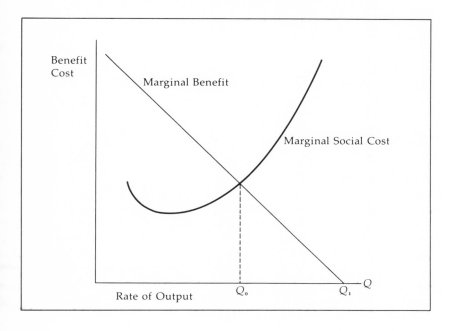

ratio is found to be greater than one, and the city invests in the project. The scale of the project is determined so that the marginal benefit equals the marginal social cost. In Figure 4.6, the ideal rate of output is shown to be Q_0. If there were no price charged for the output, however, the community would be willing to purchase the amount Q_1, which occurs where the marginal benefit (demand) intersects the output axis. Clearly, the marginal social cost exceeds the marginal benefit at this intersection. Such a zero-pricing rule would raise cries about the inadequacy of the project, and there would probably be pressure to increase the size of the facility. Any charge or pricing system below the marginal-benefit/marginal-social-cost point would lead to excess demand and, again, to pressures to increase the size of the facility. If a charge were levied at the point at which marginal benefit equaled the marginal social cost, that is, where price equaled marginal cost, we would then be using the project in the most efficient manner. Thus the use of prices can (1) give information to the decision maker in estimating benefits—in particular, helping to avoid an overestimation of benefits—and (2) assure that the project is efficiently used once it is established.

The costs of implementing and maintaining a pricing system are often called transaction costs. In any cost analysis, the costs of an optional pricing system should be included. For instance, what is the cost of implementing and maintaining a congestion toll on a highway? Transaction costs sometimes are so prohibitive that a market cannot come into existence; that is, the net benefits to be realized by pricing a product may be less than the transaction costs in setting the price and administering it.

Covering costs

The third problem raised above is how to cover a project's total cost through prices. Under the marginal-cost pricing rule, costs would not be covered if the service or project is characterized by decreasing costs per unit. Figure 4.7 illustrates the typical longrun average and marginal-cost curves for a decreasing-cost activity. Under our rule, output would be expanded to the point where the demand curve, DD, intersects the longrun marginal-cost curve (MC). The total revenue generated at the point where price equals marginal cost is not sufficient to cover the total cost. The loss would be equal to the cross-hatched area.

Fig. 4.7 *Price, Average Costs, and Marginal Costs*

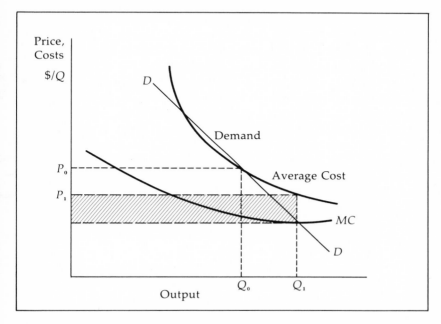

When cities use charges or fees, the emphasis is often on covering costs, and an interesting anomaly occurs. If the activity—for example, a water system operated by the city—is characterized by decreasing costs, the marginal-cost rule would cause the city to operate its water system at a loss. To many individuals this would suggest that the system is being operated inefficiently. However deplorable the loss may be, the system is producing at a rate that leads to the optimal output. Any rate of output other than Q_1 would not be, from society's viewpoint, the "ideal output." If the price were to be raised to cover costs, the community's benefit loss would outweigh the added revenue.

Second-Best Pricing Rules

Once the rule that price equals marginal cost is widely violated in the economy, alternative pricing structures are required if welfare is to be maximized. The general proposition suggested by the theory of the "second-best" is that if resources are to be efficiently allocated in these circumstances, prices will have to diverge from marginal cost in a systematic manner, even in the absence of externalities.[3]

Second-best theory shows that price should diverge from marginal cost in a systematic way that depends on the relative and relevant price elasticities. If there are no close substitutes, and we are considering an activity that produces only one output, the divergence of price from marginal cost will depend on the price elasticity of demand. The smaller the elasticity, the greater the divergence in price from marginal cost, and for a given price increase, the demand which is less elastic also will result in a smaller loss in welfare. This proposition is illustrated in Figure 4.8.

Fig. 4.8 *Second-Best Pricing and Elasticity of Demand*

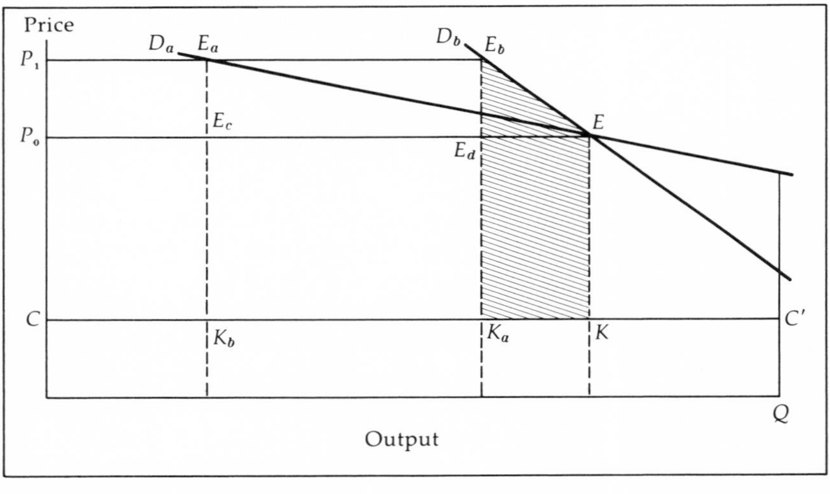

SOURCE: Adapted from testimony of William Vickrey, Federal Communications Commission hearings, July 22, 1969.

Two segments of two demand curves, D_a and D_b, are shown to intersect at E. CC' is the marginal cost curve. If we use Marshall's consumer's surplus—the amount the consumer is willing to pay for a commodity rather than do without—as the measure of welfare to the community, and if demand is given by the less elastic curve, D_bE, and price rises from P_0 to P_1, then the loss of consumers' surplus will be the area $P_0EE_bP_1$. On the other hand, the gain in producers' surplus because of the price change will be the area $P_0E_dE_bP_1$ minus K_aKEE_d. The net reduction in welfare is the shaded area E_bEKK_a. Also, if demand is given by the relatively more elastic demand curve, D_aE, the rise in price from P_0 to P_1 will result in a loss of welfare measured by E_aEKK_b. Thus, when marginal costs are constant, a given price rise will result in a larger welfare loss when demand is relatively elastic than it will when demand is relatively less elastic.

Second-best analysis can be extended to the pricing rules that could be applied to multiservice activities of the local government, where there are cost and demand interdependencies among those activities as well as between the public and private sector. Such an analysis requires knowledge about elasticities and cross-elasticities of demand that is not generally available. But such rules of pricing, with suitable modification, suggest the direction that would need to be taken if the pricing of public services is to be done in such a way as to reduce social loss.[4]

Peak Pricing

Many public services and nonstorable commodities offered by the cities experience periodic fluctuations in demand. The periods can be daily (e.g., the commuter flux), or weekly and seasonal (e.g., the weekend and seasonal use of parks and beaches). This fluctuation in demand poses two problems with respect to marginal-cost pricing: (1) efficient utilization of the existing facilities, and (2) the amount of needed capacity to meet the peak demands.[5]

Once a measure of welfare is specified—usually consumers' and producers' surplus—and assumptions are made with respect to the behavior of the shortrun marginal costs and the marginal-capacity costs, the peak-pricing rule can be determined. Given constant returns to scale, the price in each period is to be set equal to the relevant shortrun marginal costs, and the capacity of the activity is to be extended to the point where the weighted average of the shortrun marginal cost is just equal to the marginal-capacity costs, which are generally assumed to be constant. The weights are determined by the fraction of the different demands over the cycle to the total period. When this condition prevails, then consumers' and producers' surplus will be maximized.[6]

One thing to note about such a pricing rule is that capacity is not taken as a parameter; it is variable. If capacity is fixed, then to achieve maximum consumers' and producers' surplus requires setting the price equal to the relevant marginal cost in each period. This means that if in the relevant short run the marginal costs are zero—e.g., a bridge with zero maintenance cost and no congestion—the price is equal to zero. On the other hand, if capacity is variable, then even though the marginal costs in the relevant subperiod may be zero, a positive price would be charged.[7]

The theorems in the literature generally specify the behavior of costs carefully. The difficulty in actual pricing policy is that determining the relevant shortrun marginal-costs curves may be difficult—there may be lumpiness on indivisibilities that affect the marginal-capacity costs. Capacity costs are further confounded and difficult to assess because of the continual change in technology.

Demand fluctuations and the swimming pool

To illustrate a pricing strategy for a service experiencing periodic demand fluctuations, we again consider a hypothetical swimming pool. To get at the peak-pricing problem of determining how the use of an existing swimming pool is to be rationed and what the optimal size of the pool is, we shall put aside the problem of where various pools should be located within a city, what size each one is to be, and the possibility of different demands by different citizen groups.

Before specifying the demand and costs that are relevant to the problem, an objective function has to be specified. What goals do the city authorities have in mind with respect to the pool? In the spirit of "welfare economics," we shall assume that they want to maximize the net benefits. To specify the net benefits more carefully, we shall assume that the public authorities desire to follow those pricing rules and determine that size of the swimming pool maximizing the consumers' and producers' surplus. This means that if the city government wished to be a completely unscrupulous blackmailer, it would extract from each user of the pool the greatest amount he is willing to pay, rather than forego the use of the pool.

Two demand functions hold over the cycle, one for the peak, the other for the offpeak. For every positive price, the amount of swimming pool services demanded during the peak exceeds that of the offpeak. The demands are assumed to be independent. The cycle of demand will be, say, one week, and the offpeak demand will hold for three-fourths of the week, and peak demand for the other fourth. Figure 4.9 shows the two demand curves.

Fig. 4.9 *Swimming Pool Demand: Peak and Offpeak*

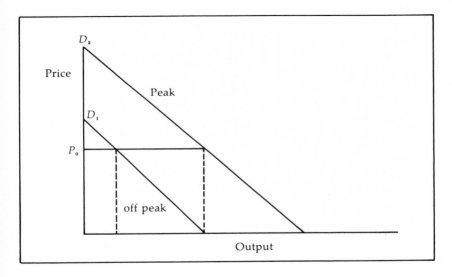

Several measures of output could be devised. The measure chosen here is an obvious one—the number of users per period—that will accord with costs. If the emphasis were on congestion and "psychic" use, some measure of density combined with the number of users would be appropriate, but this combination would add a new dimension. One way around this problem is to assume that density, a measure of quality, is a joint output with the number of users up to capacity of a pool of a given size. If the product of density-users is somewhat variable, and density is a surrogate for quality, a better specification of costs requires that output be measured by both user-frequency and density.

The relevant costs hold over the cycle. The operating, variable-maintenance, and repair costs (called here the running costs) are proportional to output up to capacity (Q_0 in Figure 4.10) and then can rise indefinitely. In Figure 4.10, the slope of the running costs is the marginal cost of the swimming pool. Because the running costs increase proportionally to output, the marginal costs are constant up to capacity. At capacity, the marginal cost is infinite. The marginal costs will be denoted by b.

Fig. 4.10 *Swimming Pool Costs and Output*

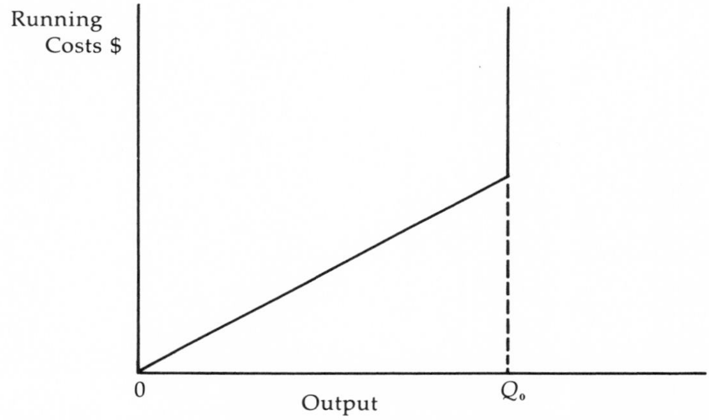

The assumption of constant shortrun marginal cost is not crucial to the argument. The argument could be reformulated to handle the situation in which marginal costs were not constant up to capacity. The problem requires that "capacity costs" be carefully defined. The appropriate formulation of capacity costs also permits the correct formulation of the objective function and allows us to determine the optimal capacity.

To make our swimming pool somewhat realistic, we shall assume that it can only be built in indivisible units, or multiple integers, of output of size E and at a cost R. Included in these costs are maintenance costs that do not change with outputs. The opportunity cost or the value of the foregone alternative will be measured by an equivalent-risk annuity paying S dollars per period. The average capacity cost per period for a fully utilized pool is equal to S/E, which shall be called B. Given this indivisibility, if "constant returns to scale" holds, then the longrun marginal cost is equal to $b + B$; that is, we are assuming that the longrun marginal cost equals the shortrun marginal running cost, b, plus the average-capacity cost.[8] The costs for two periods are shown in Figure 4.11.

Fig. 4.11 *Consumer Surplus and Peak and Offpeak Demand*

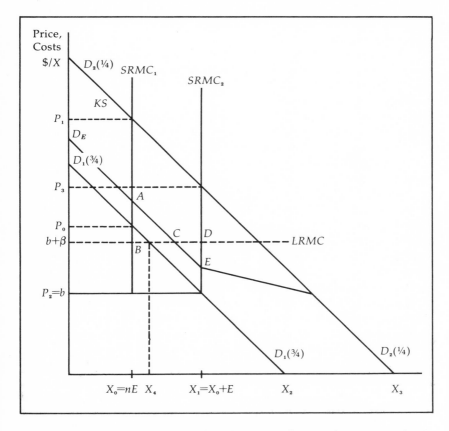

SOURCE: Oliver Williamson, "Peak-Load Pricing and Optional Capacity Under Indivisibility Constraint," *American Economic Review*, 56 (September 1966): 810–27.

The pricing problem is (1) to set prices such that the facility's use is limited, and (2) to determine the optimal size of the swimming pool. Williamson has suggested a simple geometric method to devise an appropriate price rule that will, under simplifying assumptions, maximize customers' surplus.[9] The technique is to combine the individual periodic-demand curves to obtain what he calls the "effective demand for capacity" relation. The use of this relation ensures that the optimal capacity that should be provided can be determined. Moreover, if there is no lumpiness in investment and if there are constant returns to scale, then the effective demand for capacity will determine the optimal size of plant such that the revenue will equal cost with prices set equal to shortrun marginal costs.

To construct the effective demand for capacity, the vertical distance between each individual demand curve and the shortrun marginal cost, b, in our example is multiplied by the weighting factor for each period's demand curve, w_1 and w_2. Adding vertically each of these desired curves, we obtain the effective demand for capacity curve. This is shown in Figure 4.11 as D_E.

Suppose that the size of the swimming pool is such that it can accommodate X_0 users per period. If the price for using the pool were zero, there would be X_2 offpeak users and X_3 peak users demanding use of the pool, but only X_0 users could be accommodated in each period. In both cases, excess demand exists and use of the pool must be rationed. In the absence of prices, the rationing would have to be by administrative fiat. If average-cost pricing were to be used, the price would be equal to $LRMC$ ($b + \beta$). But even at this price, excess demand exists for peak and offpeak use. The pool users would have to be rationed by some nonprice device: first-come, first-served, or some other administrative rule. If the price for the offpeak were set at P_0 and for the peak at P_1, then there would be no excess demand for the pool use in either period. By using a policy of price discrimination, the use of the facility is rationed among users and is used efficiently.

The revenue received from the facility's use would more than pay for the total costs. Is this a welfare maximum? Should the capacity be expanded? If the next-size plant generates output equal to X_1, should the plant then be expanded? The answer is yes if the effective demand for capacity curve (D_E) exceeds the longrun marginal costs. If the size of the swimming pool is increased, the effective demand for capacity now lies below the longrun marginal cost.

Under the welfare criterion of maximizing consumers' surplus, the pool should be expanded as long as the gain in consumers' surplus exceeds the loss in producers' surplus. In this example, so long as the area ABC is greater than the area CDE, welfare will be increased. In Figure 4.11, this is the case. The capacity should therefore be expanded. It follows from the construction of the effective demand for capacity that the prices will be set equal to the shortrun marginal costs. The offpeak price P_2 thus equals b, and the peak price equals P_3.

Notice that, in the offpeak period, revenue just covers the operating or running costs. The offpeak users do not contribute to capacity costs, which are borne by the onpeak users. In fact, the price the latter pay, P_3, is greater than $b + \beta$. In both cases, there is efficient use of the existing facility. In this example, there would be an equal number of users; the facility would be equally congested.

Contrast the situation with average-cost pricing. The price would be set equal to $b + \beta$. In the offpeak period at average-cost pricing, X_4 users would use the pool, and the pool would have excess capacity. By lowering the price we can accommodate more users, which leads to an optimal use of the pool.

Our illustration of the peak-pricing rule has been based upon hypothetical swimming pools. But the analysis applies to any activity experiencing periodic fluctuations in demand over time, such as highway traffic, and generation and distribution of electrical power. The problems of estimating relevant costs to be used and determining the demand in each period for such activities are difficult indeed. Our example, however, gives us a pricing rule that (1) utilizes facilities efficiently over the demand cycle and (2) simultaneously determines the optimal scale of plant. Thus, the rule can act as a guide in the choice of appropriate prices and in evaluating current pricing practices of activities that experience periodic fluctuations in demand.

NOTES

1. Algebraically, the marginal costs can be represented as the ratio of the change in total cost to changes in output. If $\triangle C$ is the increase in total cost resulting from an increase in output, $\triangle Q$, then an approximation to marginal cost for small changes in Q is

$$\frac{\triangle C}{\triangle Q} = \text{marginal cost.}$$

At capacity, $\triangle Q = 0$; thus, we are dividing zero into a given number $\triangle C$. And the resulting number is undefined.

2. Ralph Turvey, "Marginal Cost Pricing," *Economic Journal*, 79 (June 1969): 282–299, has recently said that if the longrun costs are properly calculated, the issue between shortrun and longrun marginal-cost pricing dissolves. What he does is calculate the present worth of capital costs. In this way, the capital costs of optional scales would be explicitly brought into the decision process and made consistent with the annual operating and maintenance costs.

3. W. Baumol and David F. Bradford, "Optimal Departures from Marginal Cost Pricing," *American Economic Review*, 60 (June 1970): 265–283, give four propositions relating to this second-best theory and discussion of their historical antecedents.

4. R. Rhees, "Second-Best Rules for Public Enterprise Pricing," *Economica* (new series), 35 (August 1968), provides a general theoretical analysis of second-best pricing rules. David F. Bradford and William J. Baumol, "Quasi-optimal Pricing with Regulated Profit and Interdependent Demands" (forthcoming), also examine pricing rules for public utilities.

5. Hendrik S. Houthakker, "Electricity Tariffs in Theory and Practice," *Economic Journal*, 61 (March 1951): 1–25; Peter O. Steiner, "Peak Loads and Efficient Pricing," *Quarterly Journal of Economics*, 71 (November 1957): 585–610; Jack Hirshleifer, "Peak Loads and Efficient Pricing: Comment," *Quarterly Journal of Economics*, 72 (August 1958): 451–468; Oliver Williamson, "Peak-Load Pricing and Optimal Capacity Under Indivisibility Constraint," *American Economic Review*, 56 (September 1966): 810–827. In these articles, the application of pricing rules to electricity shows the stimulus to the current theoretical work on the peak-price problem.

6. Williamson, "Peak-Load Pricing and Optimal Capacity Under Indivisibility Constraint" (see note 5 above), develops the argument in a context of indivisibilities in plant expansion.

7. See A. A. Walters, *Economics of Road User Charges* (International Bank for Reconstruction and Development, 1969), for a discussion on the differential between frequency of road use and the investment in the road. He would have a zero price charged any time the marginal social costs were zero, but the investment decision of the "road authority" is to be made by using the consumers' surplus maximization criterion.

8. The formulation of longrun marginal cost is not precisely accurate: this cost is exactly equal to the shortrun marginal cost except at the point of discontinuity occurring at capacity. But the argument is presented as if $b + \beta$ (which is also the longrun average cost at the point of discontinuity and is well defined) approximates the longrun marginal cost. Or alternatively, if the plant were divisible, then $b + \beta$ would be the relevant longrun marginal cost. An alternative geometric way of looking at this problem in the context of roads or highways is given in Walters, *Economics* (see note 7 above).

9. Mathematically, the consumers' and producers' surplus which is to be maximized is given by the following function,

$$W = w_1 \int_0^{X_1} D_1(X_1)dX_1 + w_2 \int_0^{X_2} D_2(X_2)\,dX_2 - b(w_1X_1) - \beta X^*$$

where W is the total consumers' and producers' surplus, or welfare; X_1 and X_2 are the outputs in periods one and two respectively; w_1 and w_2 are the weights; and X^* is the capacity output. Let P_1 and P_2 be the prices for offpeak and peak periods. Taking the partial derivatives of W with respect to X_1 and X_2, the first order conditions for a maximum specify the following pricing rules:

(i) If $X_1 = X_2 = X^*$ (capacity used in both periods), then
   $w_1P_1 + w_2P_2 = b + \beta$
(ii) If $X_1 \neq X_2 = X^*$ (capacity used only at peak period), then
   (a) $P_1 = b$
   (b) $P_2 = b + \beta/w_2$

EUGENE SMOLENSKY
T. NICOLAUS TIDEMAN
Chapter 5 DONALD NICHOLS

Waiting Time as
a Congestion Charge

QUEUES can be viewed as prices assessed in time, and time prices, like money prices, ration according to the tastes, income, and opportunity costs of buyers; hence they have an economic rationale. Time prices also have an intuitive appeal because time as such is more equally distributed than money.

A queue constitutes a peculiar kind of price in two ways: (1) The buyer pays the cost of the time spent, but no extra revenue thereby accrues to the seller of the product or service for which the queue forms. (2) It is a discriminatory price. The first peculiarity constitutes the major drawback to using queues as a policy instrument. Its second peculiarity constitutes its outstanding virtue for, if we assume that the opportunity cost of time is the buyer's money wage, time prices are analogous to a tax proportionate to wages. Whenever, in the interests of equity, the subsidy inherent in publicly provided goods needs to be varied by income class, queues can serve that function. They provide a test for rationing without requiring that resources be expended on an explicit means test. In particular instances, the costs of an equally effective means test may be far higher than queuing costs, making queues an efficient way to meet an equity objective.

Eugene Smolensky is Professor of Economics at the University of Wisconsin. T. Nicolaus Tideman is Assistant Professor of Economics at Harvard University. Donald Nichols is Associate Professor of Economics at the University of Wisconsin.
Note: A version of this chapter was presented before the Regional Science Association. See "The Economical Uses of Congestion," *Papers, Regional Scence Association*, Vol. 26, 1971.

The proper public policy issue is not so much whether to make a money charge at a particular congested public facility to make users aware of the negative externality for which they bear responsibility, but whether to allocate a scarce resource—the time of users—equitably but efficiently over a set of partially substitutable facilities. Paradoxically, queues may have an important role to play in achieving that optimal outcome. Their primary virtue is that they make it possible to provide consumers with a broadened range of choices. Some consumers will prefer faster service and higher money prices; others slower service and lower money prices; still others, moderate prices and moderate time costs. Those constituents who prefer paying in money to buy time can do so, but those who do not prefer to pay in money will be able to avoid doing so.

Queues in the Private Sector

The special cases discussed below illustrate some of the important attributes of queuing. We argue by analogy and hence discuss queuing in the private sector first. Since the costs to an entrepreneur of varying his equilibrium money price, over the day or week, depend very much on how often he would have to vary his price to maximize profits, we contrast the case in which consumers arrive in a steady flow with the case in which consumers arrive at irregular intervals. With each of these situations we also distinguish between the profit-maximizing shortrun (actually instantaneous) solution (quantity supplied per time interval fixed but money price and waiting time variable) and the longrun solution (optimal money price, queue length, quality supplied, and capacity are all variable). We also contrast the case where the buyer's direct participation in production or his willingness to spend time affects the seller's unit cost of production with the case where it does not.

Fixed frequency or regular demand

Queues will not arise when buyers arrive at regular intervals and each can be served in the same length of time; furthermore, a buyer's use of his own time cannot affect the seller's unit cost of production. Thus profit maximization will lead to zero queues both in the short run and the long run. The result is obvious, since prices need not vary from a single equilibrium price and hence there need be no costs due to varying them. A simple example will suffice to make the case.

Since it is now fashionable to study profit-maximizing in not-for-profit institutions, we consider a girl at a charity fair who is selling kisses at $1 per kiss. Each kiss takes ten seconds. The line before the booth has stabilized at 36 men because people are passing by in large numbers and because since that stability was reached a man has passed every ten seconds who is willing to pay the price in money and time. The price paid by each buyer now joining the queue is $1 plus six minutes. The girl, being a profit-maximizing charity, raises her price to $1.10. Fewer men now enter the queue at this higher money price and the line gradually shortens to 18 men. The price to new buyers is now $1.10 and three minutes, from which we deduce that the opportunity cost of time of these men is 10 cents per three minutes, since, the commodity itself being unchanged, there is no reason for the men to alter their total expenditure. If someone continues to pass by exactly every 10 seconds who is willing to pay the prevailing price, this canny lass would raise the money price to $1.20, thereby eliminating the queue, internalizing the externality, and maximizing profits—all in the name of charity.

We have shown that when demand is a steady flow through time, and when the buyer's time does not influence production costs, there will be no queues at any shortrun equilibrium.

Variable but deterministic demand

Suppose that demanders do not arrive in a steady stream during the day, that the opportunity cost of time is equal for all buyers, and that the buyers' time does not influence selling costs. With money prices constant, queues of varying length would then arise periodically throughout the day. If varying money prices were costless, the seller could continuously change the price to prevent a queue from ever forming. Assume, however, that changing the price at all during the day is so expensive that the seller realizes that a single supply price throughout the day is optimal. Assume further, that demand varies each day in a known way. What, in the long run, is the optimal money price, the optimal quantity supplied, and the optimal capacity?

As the Mathematical Appendix to this chapter indicates, the only novel point introduced by taking account of the cost of queuing to buyers is that the increased sales associated with greater capacity derive in part from reducing queue lengths and that permitting queues to lengthen is analytically equivalent to raising marginal-variable costs. Increasing capacity lowers profits by creating excess capacity at some periods during the day, but raises profits by increasing revenue in other periods. To maximize profits, capacity ought to be expanded until the increased sales revenue equals the marginal cost of expansion. The equilibrium price is as usual that price at which a use of a dollar would just be offset by the decline in profits on lost sales.

If we now relax the assumption that the opportunity costs of time are the same for all buyers, and if we permit the buyers' time to enter into the production process, we can state quite generally when there will be queues, on the average, at an establishment in longrun equilibrium.

Because the opportunity cost of time varies among buyers of a given commodity, the private sector differentiates among otherwise identical products by varying the time it takes to acquire them. A shop can save its buyers some time by carrying large inventories or by having many knowledgeable clerks always available. Another shop providing the same commodity can rely on self-service entirely. The money price of the goods will be cheaper in the self-service store, of course, because it costs—in salaries or inventory carrying costs, or more fixed capital—to conserve the customers' time.

In Figure 5.1 the opportunity cost of time is represented by the slopes of the lines and falls from customer A, to B, to C. If the production possibilities are such that there is some concave production frontier (i.e., if there is some fixed factor that makes saving the customers' time increasingly difficult), these individuals might end up at points a, b, and c respectively. Individual A would gladly pay a relatively high money price and low time price, while C pays a relatively low money price but a relatively high time price for otherwise identical commodities.

If there is competition, each kind of seller will in equilibrium earn zero profits. The proportion of stores of each kind will depend on the technical ability of stores to substitute time for money and on the distribution of buyers according to the value they place on their time. In the limiting case a continuum of money prices would be created; as-

Fig. 5.1   *Opportunity Costs of Time*

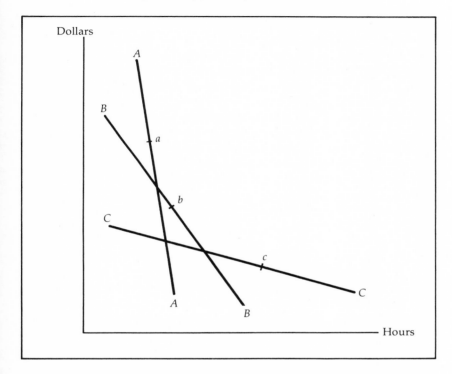

sociated with each money price would be a particular time cost, the largest time cost being associated with the lowest money price.

Because consumers differ in the value they place on their time, when there are variations in demand during the day, the same sort of time-price pairings could be offered to consumers without altering the production process directly. The only necessity is a constant money price that differs from firm to firm.[1]

A seller who has a higher money price at all times, but otherwise does business exactly as his lower-priced competitors do, will send some, but not all, buyers elsewhere. Given this competitive market, at peak periods the high money price will be associated with a low time price and thereby be attractive to those buyers with a high opportunity cost of time. Different individuals would offer a different money amount to reduce the waiting time by the same number of minutes during peak periods of demand.

But if zero profits are to exist at every money-time pairing, there must be some factor that raises costs when the number of buyers falls to the extent of producing a concave production frontier. The source of that extra cost is, of course, the capacity that goes unused at nonpeak hours. Buyers who want to face a smaller queue at peak hours must pay for capacity that goes unutilized during offpeak hours. Supermarkets, for example, product-differentiate by varying the number of cashiers. Stores with a larger number of cashiers have less frequent and generally shorter queues, but money prices are higher.

The illustrations we have presented draw on the private sector to indicate that queuing is part of the process of product differentiation. It is a way to respond efficiently to the variations in opportunity cost of time among consumers.

Queues in the Public Sector

As long as public services are offered on a "no-charge" basis, queues will exist in the public sector. Pricing of no-charge services in the short run will not necessarily eliminate queues. If queues are to be eliminated, the burden will fall totally on increased capacity, which must be expanded until demand is satiated. In that case, the optimizing public planner must set the scale of facilities on criteria analogous to those of the private sector. (This is, of course, not meant to imply that the elimination of queues is a legitimate social objective.) Efficiency considerations suggest that capacity be expanded only so long as the annual increase in consumer surplus from the expansion equals the annual cost of the increment in capacity. There can be no guarantee that the increment in the consumer surplus in going to zero congestion at zero money price will be justified on benefit-cost criteria. (Zero money prices need not result in nonprice rationing in the long run, but such a result seems likely.)

Excess demand at zero money prices depends in part upon the smoothness of longrun marginal cost in the timesaving activity. If the technology of the timesaving activity is lumpy, then the probability arises that the public good will have a positive shadow price at

Waiting Time as a Congestion Charge
Eugene Smolensky
T. Nicolaus Tideman
Donald Nichols

optimal scale, although conceivably the lumpiness could also yield excess capacity.

Indivisibilities in the costs of raising product prices are found more often in the public sector than in the private, simply because such indivisibilities are at times a source of private market failure and hence are an important reason for an activity being performed in the public sector. One such indivisibility occurs when going from a zero price to a positive money price. Thus, governments may want to charge congestion costs, and these charges might shorten or eliminate some queues, but the process of instituting the charge may itself not pass a benefit-cost test. Unable to charge a money price, queues become a substitute rationing device.

All this is of course a part of the existing literature. What we believe has not been fully appreciated is that a constant time charge will be the equivalent of a variable money charge, so that the good provided publicly at a congested facility is not a "public good," but one whose implicit price is a function of the opportunity cost of time. A queue rations out users with a high opportunity cost of time, shifting them to quicker substitutes with a higher money cost. Instituting a money charge equal to the congestion costs of the marginal user will also ration consumers out by the opportunity cost of time, but now it is those with a high opportunity cost who will remain. In the absence of a social welfare function, it is difficult to choose between these two rationing devices when considering the single congested facility, though the deadweight loss associated with queuing would tend to support rationing by money prices. (Efficiency requires that the effects of various pricing practices on substitute facilities also be considered, but we defer that class of problems for the moment.)

Variable transaction times and the peak-load problems are also an important source of fluctuations in demand and hence of queues in the public sector. The buyers' time can enter the production of some publicly provided goods; it can also be conserved through the expenditure of additional resources by the agency providing the product. In these two cases the problem of responding to different values of time for different consumers is, in essence, the same in both the private and public sectors.

Most of the discussion of policy responses to congestion in the public sector has been concerned either with using more resources to save the customers' time or with the appropriate congestion charge that is required to make users of a congested facility aware of the negative externalities for which they are responsible. The advantages of simply varying money prices at otherwise identical public facilities to produce different queue lengths that would be responsive to variations in the valuation of time by buyers has not been fully appreciated, even though Vickrey, the most ardent supporter of user charges, has given it effective justification, apparently without recognizing it.

Vickrey's example relates to equilibrium in a competitive highway industry, but it applies to any set of congested public facilities in which the buyers' time enters into production.[2] He assumes that (1) production functions are linear, (2) travel time is proportional to the number of vehicles passing a point, and (3) the sum of the tolls collected on any road must pay for its costs. He concludes (as have others before him) that in equilibrium there will exist fast roads with high tolls and few users and slow roads with low tolls and many travelers, each of the latter impeding one another's progress and inflicting time and resource costs upon one another.

In a very important paragraph, Vickrey goes on to show that, for the purely competitive case, when a continuum of money prices exists, the appropriate congestion charge is the money price already being paid for the commodity. He argues that an efficient toll would exist if a user, when entering a road, is required to pay the other users for the loss of utility he has caused them, in addition to paying the road owner for his increased costs. (Vickrey assumes the increased costs of production to be zero.) The presence of the new user causes the road to be a bit more crowded—in fact, as crowded as the adjacent road in the money-price continuum. Since the initial users were indifferent as to choice between the two adjacent roads at their respective prices, the loss in utility must be exactly equal to the difference in money price on the two roads. The appropriate congestion charge for the new user must, therefore, be equal to the difference in price between adjacent roads times the number of users on the road. But with total revenue (PQ) constant (total revenue equals total cost, which is a constant), the difference in price times the number of users ($-dPQ$) must be exactly the price that the entrant would have to pay anyway (PdQ) in this purely competitive market. Thus Vickrey's perfectly competitive set of money prices is the set of efficient money tolls in the sense that they force new entrants to pay an amount exactly equal to the value of the utility lost by others due to their entrance.

In particular circumstances, in short, assigning a set of money prices arbitrarily to a set of roads will lead drivers to distribute themselves according to the opportunity cost of their time in an optimally efficient way by forcing them to make appropriate use of their time. Efficiency comes about through varying the amount of the buyers' time that will be used in production on the different roads.

However, quite analogously to our previous discussion of queues in the private sector, simple waiting time (where the time spent is a pure deadweight loss) can also serve the cause of efficiency in the public sector. The relevant case has the following characteristics: (1) the commodity is a merit good for which the public benefit is inversely related to income; (2) the opportunity cost of time for the consumers is adequately measured by their money-wage rates, which vary, and (3) the buyers' time does not enter directly into production.

To make the discussion more concrete, consider the case of health services for which it seems reasonable to assume that the lower the permanent income of a potential patient the more willing is the public to provide him with care, *ceteris paribus*. Wishing to subsidize this service only for low-wage earners, the government can offer it at a low (even zero) money price, but then offer so little of it that a substantial queue results. Those with a high wage who are sick will then find the costs of the queue to be greater than the value of the money subsidy, and they will not choose to consume in the public sector. Low-wage people will find the subsidy to be smaller than the government reckons the money subsidy to be, by the value of their waiting time, but they will nevertheless consume in the public sector. The waiting time of those who choose to consume in the public sector is wasted, of course, but if it is cheaper to discriminate by income in this way than by using an equally effective means test, then this use of waiting time constitutes an efficient way to suboptimize.

A single money price and hence a single money-subsidy level for each consumer will add to the welfare loss of the resulting queue. Think of the government choosing the desired quantity of the service it wants consumed by some low-income individual whose demand function it knows. One option open to the government is to set a money price that induces the desired consumption—with the government paying the implicit subsidy (the difference between the price it charges and the marginal costs of producing the service). Alternatively it can charge a zero money price, but set capacity at that level which would produce a queue of the length which would make the cost, in the foregone uses of the waiting time, equal to the money price at which the desired consumption level would be chosen.

If the government took the latter approach, as it now nearly always does, it would then be confronted by the fact that different individuals value their time differently. At the subsidy implicit in the existing queues, some individuals would receive more of a subsidy than the government wished them to have and others less. In either case a welfare loss is generated that adds to the welfare loss of waiting in the queue. Obviously different subsidy levels are required for different individuals, and one way to achieve that is to vary money price and capacity at different facilities (of course, the different facilities, as the term is being used here, could be at the same site). There is some set of capacities and money prices and resultant time prices that, if chosen by the government, would minimize the sum of the welfare losses due to waiting plus the sum of the welfare losses that arise because in some cases the implicit subsidy would be too large, while in other instances the subsidy would be too small. Finding that set of money prices and capacities requires that there be a specified welfare function, a known production function, and a known probability distribution of arrival times. If the minimum welfare loss is less than the resource cost of setting a means test, than the outcome will be efficient.

It is also highly likely that equity will be improved. The current practice of offering public services on a first-come, first-served basis at a zero money price arbitrarily differentiates consumers from non-consumers, within the target population, by the opportunity costs of time, thereby violating vertical equity. The current system, for example, serves the working poor poorly. Further, each additional money-time price pairing made available improves vertical equity so long as those who consume at the zero money price facility face an unaltered time price. The a priori case for adding facilities with partial subsidies and some user charges to the set of zero-priced facilities is quite strong on equity as well as efficiency grounds.

Conclusion

Consideration should be given to introducing many money-price and time-price pairings into the public sector. Current practice consigns only the lowest-income classes to the public sector, while everyone else is put in the private sector. The effect is to narrow the political base of support for the public provision of merit goods. We suspect that there would be a much larger effective demand for the provision of merit goods if capacity and money prices were set in the optimal way. Finally, we need to consider the benefits and costs of offering a wider range of choice in the public sector apart from variations in waiting time.

We think that on a priori grounds we have justified a substantial investment in research time on studies of the costs and benefits of widening the spectrum of choices made available in the public sector in general, and the economical uses of queues in particular.

MATHEMATICAL APPENDIX

Variable price

We first set out to show that if buyers arrive with a known frequency and if there is no cost to changing price, then profit maximization will lead to zero queues.

We assume the following simple five-equation model to describe the firm on a particular business day, in the short run.

$$QD\tau = K\tau - \gamma PD\tau \tag{1}$$

The quantity demanded (QD) at a particular time of the day (τ) is a simple linear function of the price paid $(PD\tau)$, where the price may have a money component and a waiting-time component. Buyers appear in a steady stream, each buyer buys the same quantity, and the time it takes to complete each transaction is the same.

$$QS\tau = QS \tag{2}$$

The quantity supplied $(QS\tau)$ is fixed in the short run, and always the same.

$$L\tau = \alpha \int_0^\tau [QD(t) - QS(t)]\, dt \tag{3}$$

The length of the queue at any time $(L\tau)$ is proportional (α) to the cumulated excess demand (positive and negative) that has arisen during the day. The integral is over the time interval from the most recent instant when there was no queue.

$$W\tau = \lambda L\tau \tag{4}$$

Waiting time $(W\tau)$ is proportional (λ) to the length of the queue.

$$PD\tau = (PW)(W\tau) + PS\tau \tag{5}$$

The price paid is conceived of as consisting of two components: the price received in money by the sellers $(PS\tau)$ and the opportunity cost of time of the buyer. The latter consists of the time spent in line $(W\tau)$ weighted by the value of time to the buyer (perhaps the wage rate) expressed in dollars per hour. We assume that the opportunity cost of a unit of time is the same for every buyer at all times. The change in queue length during the day can be obtained by differentiating equation (3) with respect to τ and substituting successively (1), (2), (5) and (4) yielding equation (6):

$$\frac{dL}{d\tau} = (K\tau - QS - \gamma\lambda PWL\tau - \gamma PS\tau)\alpha \tag{6}$$

For every seller's price $(PS\tau)$, there is a queue length $(L\tau)$ that makes (6) equal to zero, thus stabilizing the length of the queue. Decreasing the money price increases the length at which the queue will stabilize.

At the equilibrium queue length during any time period, demanders are arriving at the counter at a rate that makes the quantity demanded equal the quantity the firm can supply during the period, and sales of $\bar{Q}S$ are made during each time period. The equilibrium queue length therefore varies inversely with the money price received by the supplier and is given by the linear function:[3]

$$L^* = \frac{K\tau - QS}{\lambda\gamma PW} - \frac{PS\tau}{\lambda PW} \tag{7}$$

By substituting (7) into (4) and the result into (5) we get an expression for the total price paid by the buyer that is independent of the price received by the seller.

$$PD\tau = \frac{K\tau - QS}{\gamma} \tag{8}$$

$$\text{when} \quad \frac{K\tau - QS}{\gamma} \geq PS\tau$$

In short, the total price paid has a minimum below which it cannot fall, no matter what the money price received. When the money price is below that money price which would just clear the market in any period, queue length adjusts to hold the price per unit to each buyer unchanged. Any price involving a queue cannot be efficient because the seller's price (and revenue) could be raised without affecting the buyers' price or the quantity sold.

Constant price

We now set out to derive the conditions for optimal price and capacity when demand varies but price cannot vary.

Total price, $PD\tau$, is the sum of money price and time price, so that one may write instead of (1),

$$QD\tau = f\tau(PS + PW \cdot W\tau) = f\tau(PS + PW\lambda L). \tag{9}$$

But L (queue length) is a negative function of capacity output (QS), so that:

$$QD\tau = g\tau(PS, QS). \tag{10}$$

If C_1 is the marginal cost per period of increments in capacity (and equal to average fixed costs) and C_2 is the marginal cost per period required for an increment of sales (and equal to average variable costs) equation (11) defines profits:

$$\pi = PS\tau \cdot QD\tau - C_1QS - C_2QD\tau \tag{11}$$

We differentiate (11) to find optimization conditions. Remembering equation (10),

$$\frac{\partial \pi}{\partial QS} = \frac{\partial QD\tau}{\partial QS} \cdot PS - C_1 - C_2 \frac{\partial QD\tau}{\partial QS} \tag{12}$$

setting 12 equal to zero and rearranging terms produces

$$PS = C_2 + \frac{C_1}{\dfrac{\partial QD\tau}{\partial QS}} \tag{13}$$

In this equation $\frac{\partial QD\tau}{\partial QS}$ is the marginal utilization of capacity at time τ. The equation may be understood as an optimization condition when the average value of the marginal utilization of capacity over all times τ is substituted. Then the equation says that capacity ought to be expanded until the average marginal utilization of capacity falls so low as to make further expansion inefficient. Increased sales at higher capacity derives from reducing queue length, which is akin to lowering price.

$$\frac{\partial \pi}{\partial PS} = QD\tau + PS\,\frac{\partial QD\tau}{\partial PS} - C_2\frac{\partial QD\tau}{\partial PS} \qquad (14)$$

Setting equation 14 equal to 0 and rearranging terms yields:

$$PS = C_2 - \frac{QD\tau}{\dfrac{\partial QD\tau}{\partial PS}} \qquad (15)$$

which is the usual result when, again, $\frac{\partial QD\tau}{\partial PS}$ is replaced by its average value through time: in equilibrium a price rise of a dollar would just be offset by the decline in profits on lost sales.

NOTES

1. D. Nichols, E. Smolensky, and T. N. Tideman, "Discrimination by Waiting Time in Merit Goods," *American Economic Review*, 63 (June 1971): 312–323.
2. William Vickrey, "Congestion Charges and Welfare," *Journal of Transport, Economics and Policy*, 2 (January 1968): 107–118.
3. For $\frac{QD\tau-QS\tau}{\gamma} \geq PS\tau$; $L^* = 0$ when $PS\tau > \frac{QD\tau-QS\tau}{\gamma}$.

SUPPLEMENT

TO PART ONE

Two Approaches
to Pricing
Public Goods

A   T. NICOLAUS TIDEMAN

The Efficient Provision
of Public Goods

*T*HE classic problem of public goods is to devise a set of rules such that persons, in following their own self-interest, would provide information that revealed the optimal expenditure on a public good. Samuelson has pointed out that simply prescribing rules through which individuals report their benefits is not a solution because, "by departing from his indoctrinated rules, any one person can hope to snatch some selfish benefit in a way not possible under the self-policing competitive pricing of private goods."[1]

This chapter describes a mechanism that, in theory, can solve the classic problem. Under the rules described, individuals have incentive to reveal the true value to them of marginal changes in expenditure on a public good. This information can be used to move to an optimal level of expenditure.

The Contribution of Majority Voting

The problem of public goods is dual: (1) sufficient information must be obtained to determine what level of provision is efficient, and

T. Nicolaus Tideman is Assistant Professor of Economics at Harvard University.

Author's Note: After writing this I learned that J. H. Dreze and D. de la Vallee Pousin had made a similar analysis, now published as "A Tâtonnement Process for Public Goods," *Review of Economic Studies*, 38 (April 1971): 133–50. Their work is more sophisticated mathematically, but their continuous adjustment process (in contrast with the discrete process offered here) gives participants no incentive to provide truthful responses outside of equilibrium. I also wish to acknowledge the Travelers Insurance Company for its support of my research for this chapter.

111

(2) revenue must be obtained to finance that level of provision. Linking the two aspects of the problem in a straightforward fashion produces an incentive for falsification. If you ask people how they would benefit from different levels of public goods, under the condition that they will be taxed in proportion to the value that they claim, then it is in their interest to claim almost no benefits.

There are ways to solve the problem through the use of simplifying assumptions. The simplest of these is that benefits are distributed equally to a given group of people. Then, under the rule of equal taxation among that group, everyone would agree on the appropriate level of expenditure. A slight variant that works just as well is to assume that benefits are distributed in known proportions, with an unknown constant of proportionality. If taxes were distributed in the same proportions as benefits, there would again be unanimous agreement on the appropriate level of expenditure.

To assume that relative benefits could be determined precisely is highly artificial, and there are weaker assumptions that produce efficient allocation. If taxes are distributed equally while the marginal benefits of expenditure on a public good vary among individuals, but the distribution of marginal benefits is such that the median and mean marginal benefits are equal, then an election process with majority rule will converge on the most efficient level of expenditure.[2] The theorem rests on the fact that efficiency occurs when the mean marginal benefit is equal to the marginal tax, while voting equilibrium occurs at the expenditure level such that the individual with median marginal benefits has marginal taxes equal to his marginal benefits. A more general version of the theorem is that with one distribution of marginal taxes and another distribution of marginal benefits, efficient allocation will result from majority rule voting if and only if the distribution of discrepancies between marginal benefit shares and marginal tax shares is such that the median discrepancy is zero. (The theorem is proved in a mathematical section starting on page 117.)

This is as far as ordinary voting theory goes. If the distribution of discrepancies between marginal tax shares and marginal benefit shares is likely to have a median other than zero, then the voting equilibrium is correspondingly likely to be inefficient, but it will not be clear whether expenditure is too high or too low. The system described below offers a voting procedure in which there are no obvious gains from lying and the equilibrium is efficient.

The Proposed System: An Example

The system may be illustrated with the example of a decision about expenditure on a public park. Assume that the appropriate level of expenditure on the park is uncertain. Assume also that the people involved have a procedure (possibly the majority voting) for arriving at a provisional level of expenditure that is not obviously biased. The provisional expenditure will be the actual expenditure if no better level is found. Included in the provisional decision is a rule about each person's share of cost of the park, if the provisional level is implemented. Each person involved is then questioned in the following manner:

The city is thinking about building a $50,000 park in your neighborhood. If the plan goes through, your share of the cost will be $28 per year. No final decision will be made until the value of the project is checked. In case a $45,000 park or a $55,000 park is built, how much should a $5,000 change in the expenditure on the park be valued in terms of your benefits? Whatever figure you give will be used in adjusting your taxes. For instance, if you say that $5,000 of park is worth $3 per year to you, your bill for the $55,000 park would be $31, and for the $45,000 park it would be $25.

Would a respondent reveal his true marginal benefits? That would depend on his expectations. If he expected the level of expenditure to be revised upward, then it would be in his interest to understate his benefits, to avoid higher taxes. On the other hand, if he expected a downward revision then it would be in his interest to overstate his benefits, so that his taxes would be reduced by more than his loss of benefits. If the possibility of lower expenditure just balances the possibility of higher expenditure (if the mean of his subjective estimate of the change in expenditure is zero) then neither an overstatement nor an understatement of his benefits will involve expected gain. As long as there is some positive probability attached to both an increase and a decrease, telling the truth about his marginal benefits will be the only action that an individual can take that will protect him from loss because of a change in expenditure. (A slight exception to this is discussed later.)

When the marginal benefit statements are returned, the provisional level of expenditure can be revised. If the stated aggregate marginal benefit of $5,000 of additional park expenditure is greater than

$5,000, the expenditure can be considered too low. If the stated aggregate marginal benefit is less than $5,000, the expenditure can be assumed to be too high.

To make an accurate revision of expenditure, some knowledge about the rate at which marginal benefits change as expenditure changes (the slope of the aggregate benefit function) is needed. One might think that the knowledge could be acquired simply by asking each person about the rate of change of his marginal benefits and then using the answer to determine his benefits at any other level of expenditure. That procedure, however, is unacceptable because it would give each person an incentive to overstate the rate at which his marginal benefits declined as expenditure increased. Any person with a very high rate of decline attributed to his own marginal benefits would be considered a recipient of almost no gain from an increase in expenditure, while a decline in expenditure would be treated as being very costly to him. If all persons concerned sought such treatment simultaneously, almost no revision of the level of expenditure would be possible. Using the same elasticity of marginal benefits with respect to expenditure for all persons solves this dilemma, though somewhat imperfectly.

The problem is what elasticity to use; the most convenient seems to be the median of reported elasticities. (The mean would be inappropriate because it would be subject to manipulation.) Thus participants in the public expenditure program must be asked a question somewhat as follows:

> To revise the level of expenditure on the park appropriately, we need to know how the average person's benefits from additional expenditure change as the level of expenditure changes. So please tell us the percentage by which your benefits of additional expenditure drop when expenditure is increased by 10 percent. An answer of 8 percent, for example, would mean that the benefits of increasing the expenditure from $50,000 to $55,000 would be assumed to be 8 percent more than the benefits of increasing it from $55,000 to $60,000. (You should be aware that the same percentage rate is necessarily being applied to all persons. The median answer—that is, the one with just as many answers above it as below it—will be used.)

With this information from participants, the taxation and expenditure decisions would proceed as follows. The stated marginal benefits would be used to estimate the aggregate marginal benefit of

$5,000 of expenditure when the level of expenditure is $50,000. Then the median reported elasticity would be used to estimate the level of expenditure where $5,000 of additional expenditure was worth precisely $5,000. That would be the revised level of expenditure.

Then the tax bills would be calculated. Each person's bill would have three components: (1) his share of the original $50,000 expenditure; (2) his calculated increase or decrease in benefits resulting from the revision in expenditure; and (3) a share (based on his contribution to the original $50,000) of the net gain from revising expenditure.

The third element of the calculation (net gain) appears whenever expenditure is revised either upward or downward, because any apparent need to revise expenditure implies an opportunity to achieve gains in efficiency. If each person's tax is adjusted in step two by the amount of his estimated change in benefits, then there are necessarily some funds in efficiency gains to be distributed in step three. The existence of this step, in which all persons gain, means that there is some room to compensate for losses caused by inappropriate adjustments in step two. Among persons who reveal their true marginal benefits, the ones who lose in step two will be those who have demands more inelastic than the median. The compensation offered in step three would more than make up for any loss in step two as long as a person's demand was more than about half as elastic as the median. (See the mathematical section at the end of this Supplement A.)

Under these circumstances, would individuals reveal their true benefits? The horizontal axis of Figure A.1 shows the change in expenditure resulting from the questioning process; the vertical axis shows the net benefit to an individual. Functions relating net benefits to the change in expenditure are shown as A, B, and C. All pass through the origin because if there is no change in expenditure there can be no change in benefits.

Curve A represents the outcome for a typical truth-teller. His gain is in proportion to the square of the change in expenditure. Curve B shows the outcome for a person with very inelastic demand, who reveals his true marginal benefits. He loses for any change in expenditure. Curve C shows the consequences for a person who understates his marginal benefits. An increase in expenditure benefits him, while a decrease causes him to lose. All curves are parabolas, passing through the origin. The slope of a curve at the origin is determined by how

Fig. A.1 *Expenditure Changes and True Net Benefits*

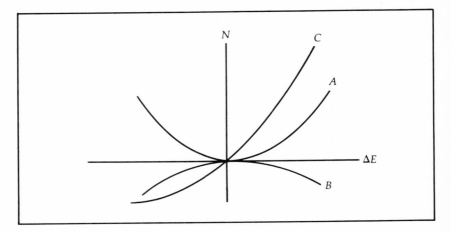

E, change in expenditure resulting from the questioning process; N, net benefit to an individual; A, B, C, functions relating net benefits to change in expenditure.

accurately a person reports his marginal benefits: understatements result in upward slopes, overstatements in downward slopes, and the truth in a zero slope. The rate of change of the slope is determined by the elasticity of demand. A more elastic demand results in a more rapidly rising slope. An elasticity of less than about half the average can cause a falling slope, as in curve B.

In these circumstances it would seem that revealing true marginal benefits would be an acceptable strategy to most persons. Except for persons with unusually inelastic demand, revealing true marginal benefits would guarantee that no loss would be suffered. No other strategy could do this. For persons who chose to misstate their benefits, an introduction of risk aversion into the analysis would be needed to limit the magnitude of their lies. Up to the point where a person's own misstatement dominated the determination of the change in expenditure, he could gain more the more he lied, *if* he could determine the direction of change in expenditure.

The presence of some persons who misstate their benefits need not make the procedure inefficient. If there is disagreement among these speculators as to the direction of the change in expenditure, their actions may cancel out. To allow for the possibility that such canceling may not occur, and for other imperfections in the process, there could be successive revisions of expenditure. If speculators were clever, they would allow expenditure to change only very slightly on each round and thus would capture nearly all the benefits. On the other hand, if speculators were not so clever, expenditure might oscillate to equilibrium, with speculators sometimes gaining and sometimes losing. Persons who revealed their true benefits would gain in proportion to the square of the change on each round.

The system described need not be hampered by respondent apathy. Standard or average values of the parameters can be used for nonrespondents. The problem of nonconvexities cannot be handled by the system. If there is a better maximum at a much different level of expenditure, this process will not find it.

The key feature of the process is the uncertainty in the direction of the change in expenditure combined with the fact that one's claimed share of marginal benefits is applied only to the change in expenditure. This might appear to be inequitable. A person can reveal benefits of double or triple those that went into his first-round tax without producing a revision in his tax for the initial expenditure. Is that fair?

It probably is. People will not report their true benefits if their total taxes vary with their shares of reported benefits. If we cannot otherwise determine efficient expenditure, we could at least improve on the equilibrium from majority voting through the process described above, which is Pareto-efficient for almost all persons who reveal their true benefits.

MATHEMATICAL APPENDIX

Efficiency and voting

THEOREM: *The equilibrium resulting from voting is efficient if and only if the median of the distribution of discrepancies between marginal benefit shares and marginal tax shares is zero.*

Proof: Let $\{b_i - t_i\}_E$ be the distribution of differences between marginal benefits and marginal taxes at the expenditure level, E, that results from majority-rule voting. The distribution of discrepancies between marginal benefit shares and marginal tax shares may be indicated by

$$\left\{ \frac{b_i}{\Sigma b_i} - \frac{t_i}{\Sigma t_i} \right\}_E.$$

If, by hypothesis, the median of this distribution is zero, then, multiplying by Σb_i, the median of

$$\left\{ b_i - t_i \left(\frac{\Sigma b_i}{\Sigma t_i} \right) \right\}_E$$

is also zero. This may be represented alternatively as the median of

$$\left\{ b_i - t_i - t_i \frac{\Sigma b_i - \Sigma t_i}{\Sigma t_i} \right\}_E.$$

Since E represents voting equilibrium, the median of $\{b_i - t_i\}_E$ is zero. Thus there are two distributions with the same median, differing by the quantity $t_i \left(\frac{\Sigma b_i - \Sigma t_i}{\Sigma t_i} \right)$. The first component of the quantity, t_i, is positive and the remainder is constant for the distribution. To add a constant multiple of a positive factor to a distribution without changing the median, it is necessary that the constant multiple be zero. That is, $\Sigma b_i - \Sigma t_i = 0$, or aggregate marginal benefits equal aggregate marginal costs, implying efficiency.

Similarly, if the median of

$$\left\{ \frac{b_i}{\Sigma b_i} - \frac{t_i}{\Sigma t_i} \right\}_E$$

is not zero, then the median of

$$\left\{ b_i - t_i - t_i \frac{\Sigma b_i - \Sigma t_i}{\Sigma t_i} \right\}_E$$

is not zero. But from voting equilibrium, the median of $\{b_i - t_i\}_E$ is zero. To change the median of a distribution by the addition of a constant multiple of a positive factor, it is necessary that the multiple not be zero, implying that $\Sigma b_i \neq \Sigma t_i$, which means that the level of expenditure is inefficient.

Mathematics of the proposed system

Let t_i be the tax shares of beneficiaries. Let $\hat{E}$ be the first approximation for expenditure. Provisional tax bills are given by

$$\hat{T}_i = t_i \hat{E}. \tag{1}$$

Two parameters are solicited from each beneficiary: his reported marginal benefit of a dollar of expenditure, $\hat{M}_i$, and the elasticity of his benefits with respect to expenditure, $\hat{e}_i$. (Note that $\hat{e}_i$ is the reciprocal of elasticity of demand.) Define the reported aggregate marginal benefit of a dollar of expenditure at $\hat{E}$ by $\hat{M} = \Sigma \hat{M}_i$. If the level of expenditure were precisely correct, $\hat{M}$ would be unity. It will be useful to have another symbol for the discrepancy between $\hat{M}$ and its equilibrium value. Thus the surplus in M is defined by $S = \hat{M} - 1$.

Next, assign a marginal benefit schedule to each person. Individuals must not have control over the elasticity of the schedules assigned to them. Therefore the same elasticity will be used for all individuals. The elasticity of the aggregate (vertical) sum of benefit schedules as reported, is

$$\frac{\Sigma(\hat{M}_i \hat{e}_i)}{\Sigma \hat{M}_i}.$$

However, if this figure were used it would be subject to manipulation by individuals by claiming extreme values of $\hat{e}_i$. Therefore, the weighted median of the $\hat{e}_i$'s is used, that is, the number $\hat{e}$ such that when the weights $\dfrac{\hat{M}_i}{\Sigma \hat{M}_i}$ are applied to the $\hat{e}_i$'s, half the weight lies below $\hat{e}$. If the distribution of the $\hat{e}_i$'s is believed for some prior reason to be such that $\hat{e}$ is a biased estimate of the aggregate elasticity, then the point not subject to such bias can be used as the standard elasticity.

In addition to the elasticity at $\hat{E}$, an assumption is needed about the shape of marginal benefit schedules at other levels of expenditure. For analytic convenience, the assumption here is that the schedules are linear, with point elasticity of $\hat{e}$ at $\hat{E}$. The level of marginal benefits assigned to each individual at $\hat{E}$ will be his reported level, M_i. These assumptions imply that at any level of expenditure, X, a person's marginal benefits at that level of expenditure, $\hat{F}_i(X)$, are given by

$$\hat{F}_i(X) = \hat{M}_i \left[1 + \frac{(\hat{E} - X)\hat{e}}{\hat{E}} \right]. \tag{2}$$

The efficient level of expenditure is then

$$E = \hat{E} \left(1 + \frac{S}{\hat{e}\hat{M}} \right), \tag{3}$$

since (2) implies that

$$\hat{F}i\left[\hat{E}\left(1+\frac{S}{\hat{e}\hat{M}}\right)\right]=\hat{M}_i\left(1-\frac{S}{\hat{M}}\right)=\frac{\hat{M}_i}{\hat{M}}, \tag{4}$$

which implies that the sum of the marginal benefits at this level of expenditure is unity.

Now consider the benefit that can be attributed to an individual from the change in the level of expenditure from $\hat{E}$ to $\hat{E}$. (While the word "benefit" implies an increase in expenditure, the same formula will apply if S is negative and a decrease results.) Since a linear marginal benefit schedule is assumed, the integral under the function can be found by applying the formula for the area of a trapezoid. The change in expenditure is $\dfrac{\hat{E}S}{\hat{e}\hat{M}}$ and the initial and subsequent levels of marginal benefit to the ith person are $\hat{M}_i$ and $\dfrac{\hat{M}_i}{\hat{M}}$ respectively, so that the benefit to the ith person of the change in expenditure, indicated by $\overline{B}_i$, is

$$\overline{B}_i=\tfrac{1}{2}\left[\frac{\hat{E}S}{\hat{e}\hat{M}}\left(\hat{M}_i+\frac{\hat{M}_i}{\hat{M}}\right)\right]=\frac{\hat{E}\hat{M}_i}{\hat{e}\hat{M}^2}\,(S+\tfrac{1}{2}S^2) \tag{5}$$

The aggregate of benefits over all individuals is

$$\overline{B}=\Sigma\overline{B}_i=\frac{\hat{E}}{\hat{e}\hat{M}}\,(S+\tfrac{1}{2}S^2). \tag{6}$$

The next step is to assign revised taxes to take account of the changes in expenditure and in benefits. The formula used for this is

$$\overline{T}_i=\overline{B}_i+t_i\,(\overline{E}-\overline{B}). \tag{7}$$

In other words, a person's revised taxes will be equal to the benefit attributable to him from the increase in expenditure, plus a share (equal to his original tax share) of the difference between revised expenditure and the aggregate benefit of the revision. The key feature of this formula is that an individual has almost no effect on his tax bill other than through the estimate of his benefits from the *change* in expenditure. Note that the sum of the revised taxes is the revised expenditure.

An individual's increase in taxes is given by

$$\overline{T}_i - \hat{T}_i = \overline{B}_i + t_i(\overline{E} - E - \overline{B}) = \frac{\hat{E}}{\hat{e}\hat{M}}\left[\frac{\hat{M}_i}{\hat{M}}(S + \frac{1}{2}S^2) - t_i(\frac{1}{2}S^2)\right]. \quad (8)$$

To describe the net effect of the change on an individual, the concept of true marginal benefit schedules, as distinct from those which people report, must be introduced. Thus, modifying equation (2), the true marginal benefit to a person, F_i, at any level of expenditure X is

$$F_i(X) = M_i\left[1 + \frac{(\hat{E} - X)e_i}{\hat{E}}\right], \quad (9)$$

where M_i is the true marginal benefit at $\hat{E}$, and e_i is the true elasticity of the person's demand schedule. Using (9) to revise (5),

$$B_i = \frac{1}{2}\frac{\hat{E}S}{\hat{e}\hat{M}}\left[M_i + M_i\left(1 + \frac{e_iS}{\hat{e}\hat{M}}\right)\right] = \frac{\hat{E}M_i}{\hat{e}\hat{M}^2}\left[S + \frac{1}{2}\left(2 - \frac{e_i}{\hat{e}}\right)S^2\right], \quad (10)$$

where B_i is the true benefit to the ith person of the change in expenditure from E to E. The net benefit to person i of the combined change in taxes and in expenditure, indicated by N_i, is

$$N_i = B_i - (\overline{T}_i - \hat{T}_i), \quad (11)$$

which, upon substitution, becomes

$$N_i = \frac{\hat{E}}{\hat{e}\hat{M}}\left\{\frac{M_i - \hat{M}_i}{\hat{M}}S + \frac{1}{2}\left[\frac{M_i\left(2 - \frac{e_i}{\hat{e}}\right) - \hat{M}_i}{\hat{M}} + t_i\right]S^2\right\}. \quad (12)$$

Equation (12) expresses N_i as a quadratic function of S, the difference between reported aggregate marginal benefits and its equilibrium value. The reason individuals are likely to report values of M_i and e_i is as follows. The sign of the linear term, $\dfrac{M_i - \hat{M}_i}{\hat{M}} S$, could be either positive or negative. To keep the contribution of this term to N_i positive, an individual would want to understate his benefits when S was positive and overstate them when S was negative. But he will not know the sign of S when he chooses $\hat{M}_i$. If he believes that zero is an unbiased estimate of S, that is, if 1 is the mean of his prior distribution on aggregate reported marginal benefits, then there is no gain in misstating M_i unless he has a preference for risk. Reporting the true value of M_i makes this term zero. By the same token, if an individual feels that M will be greater than 1 or if he feels that it will be less than 1, then there is an incentive to lie. However, such expectations cannot be held confidently because if aggregate marginal benefits are obviously greater or less than 1, then so many people may misstate their benefits that the change occurs in the wrong direction. Thus there are no obvious gains from lying. It might be easier to make money in wheat futures.

The quadratic term of equation (12) is almost always positive. The coefficient in brackets is positive as long as

$$e_i < \hat{e}\left(2 + \frac{\hat{t}_i\hat{M} - \hat{M}_i}{M_i}\right). \tag{13}$$

The two components of the numerator of the fractional term will be about equal since they have the same mean, so that the quadratic term will not be negative except for persons with elasticities of demand (the reciprocals of e_i) less than about half the median reported elasticity. The larger one's tax share is, compared to his marginal benefit share, the larger e_i can be without making the quadratic term negative. Thus for all except persons with unusually inelastic demand, the quadratic term provides nonnegative benefits. Therefore, telling the truth would probably be a satisfactory strategy for most persons: It would provide gains proportional to the square of the change in expenditure and would uniquely guarantee no loss for most persons.

Persons who chose to lie would be inclined to lie excessively, except for risk aversion, because until $\hat{M}_i$ approached S in absolute value a person who could predict the sign of S could do better the more he lied.

Now consider the question of whether it pays an individual to lie about e_i. Differentiating (12) with respect to $\hat{e}$, setting that equal to zero and solving for $\hat{e}$ yields

$$\hat{e} = e_i \frac{1}{1 + \dfrac{M_i - \hat{M}_i}{M_iS} + \dfrac{t_i\hat{M} - \hat{M}_i}{2M_i}} \tag{14}$$

as a person's preferred value of $\hat{e}$. For truthful responses about M_i, the second term in the denominator will be zero and the third term will be zero if t_i is the true marginal benefit share. The third term will be very close to zero on average since $\hat{M}_i$ and $\hat{t}_i\hat{M}$ have the same mean. For persons who believe they know the sign of S and adjust M_i accordingly, the second term will be positive, imparting a downward bias to $\hat{e}$.

NOTES

1. Paul Samuelson, "The Pure Theory of Public Expenditure," *Review of Economics and Statistics*, 36 (November 1954): 389.

2. Howard R. Bowen, "The Interpretation of Voting in the Allocation of Economic Resources," *Quarterly Journal of Economics*, 58 (November 1943): 32–42. This theorem was proven by Bowen for the slightly stronger assumption that marginal benefits are distributed normally.

B EDWARD H. CLARKE

Multipart Pricing of
Public Goods: An Example

*I*N the first part of this appendix, "The Efficient Provision of Public
Goods," Tideman proposed a voting procedure that would reduce
some of the incentive for individuals in a public goods interaction
to hide their true preferences and would also remove some of the inefficient equilibrium that usually results from majority voting. This appendix chapter discusses a multipart pricing system that also applies to
the classic "free-rider" or revealed-preference problem and might, in
other respects, be a socially preferred arrangement for public choice.[1]

The system proposed here would confront each user of a *pure*
public good, one from which potential users cannot be excluded without additional cost, with a two-part tariff. Each individual would pay
a *fixed charge*, over which he has no control, but which is determined,
in part, by the demand revelations of others. In addition, his contribution reflects a (positive, negative, or zero) *variable charge* that is
equal, at the marginal unit of provision, to his revealed demand price
and which, on certain inframarginal units of output, is determined by
the difference between the cost of producing the good and the revealed
demand prices of *all other* participants in the public goods interaction.

A genuinely simple illustration of the proposed system below
assumes two possible discrete levels of public good output: zero output,
q_0, or positive output, q_1. The potential users of the good, n in number,
include Mr. K and *all others*, each of whom is given an opportunity

Edward H. Clarke is Economic Advisor to the Director, Bureau of the Budget,
State of Illinois.

Author's Note: I wish to acknowledge the Ford Foundation for its support
of my research in this field.

to reveal a demand price for q_1. A positive output, q_1, will be produced when the sum of the revealed demand prices of Mr. K and all others, $RB_k + RB_0$, is greater than or equal to the cost of producing the good, $\emptyset$.

Consider the mechanics of the proposed system as illustrated by Mr. K's contribution, which will be precisely equal to his fixed charge if he does not choose to reveal a demand. To determine this fixed charge under the proposed system, Mr. K is *assigned* a price, $\bar{p}_k$, which is taken to be his revealed demand price, RB_k, in the absence of any other demand revelation from him. The output (q_0 or q_1) which would be produced based on summing Mr. K's assigned price, $\bar{p}_k$, and the revealed demand prices, RB_0, of all others is Mr. K's *assigned output*. Mr. K's *fixed charge* is simply his assigned price, $\bar{p}_k$, times his assigned output, $\bar{q}_k$, where $\bar{q}_k = q_0$ or q_1.

The assigned prices to Mr. K and all others may be arbitrary, subject only to the constraint that the sum of the assigned prices, $\bar{p}_k + \bar{p}_0$, be equal to the cost of producing the good, $\emptyset$. These prices may be assigned by government but must not change as a result of individual demand revelations. Under conditions where the revealed demand price of each individual, including Mr. K, is greater than or equal to his assigned price, a positive rate of output, q_1, will be produced and the contribution of each will be simply his fixed charge. The sum of the individual fixed charges will be equal to the cost of producing the good. In a like manner, where the revealed demand price of each individual is less than his assigned price, zero output will be produced. Individual fixed charges and contributions will also be zero.

Consider the more complicated case where the revealed demand and assigned price orderings vary among the n participants. Suppose that the sum of the revealed demand prices of all others, RB_0, is *less* than the sum of their assigned prices, $\bar{p}_0$, but that Mr. K's revealed demand price is greater than or equal to a *variable price, p_k'*, determined by subtracting the sum of the revealed demand prices of all others, RB_0, from the cost of producing the good, $\emptyset$.[2] Application of the output decision rule above will result in a positive output, q_1, when $RB_k \geq p_k'$ $= \emptyset - RB_0$, because the sum of all revealed demand prices is greater than or equal to the cost of production.

Given the demand revelations of all others, both Mr. K's assigned output and his fixed charge are zero. However, because actual output, q_1, is greater than his assigned output, q_0, which would be produced in the absence of a demand revelation from him, Mr. K pays a *variable charge* equal to his *variable price*, $p_k' = \emptyset - RB_0$. His contribution, $\bar{p}_k \bar{q}_k + p_k'$, thus consists of a zero fixed charge and a positive variable charge. Assuming all others behave alike, their assigned outputs will be equal to actual output and their total contributions will be equal to $\bar{p}_0$ times actual output. Total contributions from Mr. K and all others will be in excess of production cost.[3]

Alternatively, for all others, let the sum of revealed demand prices, RB_0, be greater than the sum of assigned prices $\bar{p}_0$, but let Mr. K's revealed demand price be less than his variable price, p_k', again determined by subtracting RB_0 from $\emptyset$. Application of the output decision his fixed charge must be positive. However, because actual output, q_0, rule will result in zero output, q_0, but both Mr. K's assigned output and is less than his assigned output, $\bar{q}_k = q_1$, Mr. K receives a *rebate* equal to his variable price, $p_k' = \emptyset - RB_0$. His contribution is thus $\bar{p}_k \bar{q}_k - \bar{p}_k'$, where $\bar{q}_k = q_1$. If all others behave alike, their contributions will be zero but Mr. K's contribution will represent an excess over the zero production cost.

In each case, the incentive is lacking for Mr. K to hide his true preferences. His fixed charge being genuinely fixed to him, he can maximize only when his true demand price, B_k, and his revealed demand price, RB_k, bear the same greater than (or equal to) or less than relationship to his variable price. That is, for Mr. K to maximize, $RB_k > p_k'$ must hold when $B_k > p_k'$. Alternatively, $RB_k < p_k'$ must hold when $B_k < p_k'$.

In effect, the proposed system motivates each individual to respond to his *variable price* in choosing the actual output. In so doing, each chooses an output that will be agreed upon by all others because the inequality relationships between revealed demand and variable prices must be the same for all individuals. For example, when Mr. K's revealed demand price is greater than his variable price and a positive output is produced, none of the remaining participants can have revealed demand prices less than their individual variable prices. The reason for this becomes clearer in the nondiscrete output case considered below.

The above example, which assumes that an individual is given information regarding the demand revelations of all others and, in turn, his variable price for a discrete rate of output, demonstrates that

the usual incentive to hide one's preferences is lacking. Let us now relax both (1) the assumption that he is given his variable price prior to
revealing his demand and (2) the discrete output assumption, to demonstrate why individuals are motivated to reveal *precisely* their true
demand prices for a range of possible outputs.

When Mr. K does not know his variable price prior to revealing
his demand, he must reveal it so that both his revealed and true demand
prices will bear the same relationship to his variable price—whether
greater than, less than, or equal to it. When any number of variable
prices are feasible, he can maximize only by revealing his true demand
price.

In the nondiscrete, continuous output case, Mr. K's assigned and
variable prices become price *schedules*. His assigned price schedule,
$\bar{p}_k$, is again subject to the constraint that the vertical sum of the assigned prices to him and all others add up to the cost of producing the
good, $\emptyset$. Mr. K's variable price schedule, p_k', is determined by subtracting the revealed demand schedule of all others from the marginal cost of supply.

Output is determined at that point where the sum of revealed
demand prices of Mr. K and all others, $RB_k + RB_0$, is equal to the marginal cost of supply, $\emptyset$. At this output, Mr. K's revealed demand price
must also be equal to his variable price, as must the revealed demand
and variable prices of each of the other participants.

If Mr. K wishes to maximize, he must reveal a demand price
equal, at the marginal unit of provision, q^*, to his true demand price,
B_k. In addition to his fixed charge, $\bar{p}_k\bar{q}_k$, he pays a variable charge equal
to the sum of the variable prices on increments of output between his
assigned and the actual output,

$$\int_{\bar{q}_k}^{q^*} p_k'$$

By revealing his true demand price at q^*, he maximizes benefit less his
contribution,

$$\bar{p}_k\bar{q}_k + \int_{\bar{q}_k}^{q^*} p_k'$$

However, Mr. K's variable price schedule, $p_k' = \emptyset - RB_0$, represents only one of any number of possible schedules, depending upon the demand revelation pattern of all others. Without knowledge of RB_0 and, in turn, p_k', Mr. K must reveal a locus of points such that, at each point on the locus, his true demand price is equal to variable price, p_k', at the marginal unit of provision. The locus of points defines his true demand schedule.

My more extended treatment of the proposed system demonstrates that incentive is also lacking for an individual to misreveal his demand by altering the demand revelation pattern of others in a way that will improve his own opportunity set. (Problems of strategic behavior, common to all arrangements for public-choice decisions and at the heart of the free-rider dilemma, are not addressed directly here.) In particular, individuals have no influence directly or *indirectly* over the determination of their own fixed charges. Nor do problems which might disturb otherwise Pareto-efficient results arise from a possible excess of contributions over cost.[4]

In both this and the preceding chapter (A), the relevance of the so-called Samuelson dilemma to the efficient provision of public goods has been sharply called into question. Yet this in no way suggests that the new approaches are themselves the most efficient mechanisms for public choice. Instead, it suggests that the relative efficiency of existing and proposed institutional arrangements must be considered in terms of all the *relevant costs*—costs of inefficient output equilibria, of transactions, and of information. In any realistic setting, the conventional assumption that an individual can specify his own preferences without costs must be set aside. Then it becomes necessary to consider whether the potential gains from knowledge of individual preferences is worth the cost to individuals in determining and specifying these preferences.[5]

NOTES

1. The discussion is adapted from two other works by Edward H. Clarke, "Introduction to Theory for Optimum Public Goods Pricing," *Public Choice*, IX (Fall 1971), and "A Market Solution to the Public Goods Problem" (un-

published doctoral dissertation, University of Chicago). On the free-rider problem, see Paul Samuelson, "The Pure Theory of Public Expenditure," *Review of Economics and Statistics*, 36 (November 1954), 387–389.

2. Mr. K's revealed demand price must, in this case, also be greater than his assigned price. If $\bar{p}_k + \bar{p}_0 = \emptyset$ by rule, $p_k' = \emptyset - RB_0$ by definition, and $RB_0 < p_0$ by assumption, then $p_k' > \bar{p}_k$. If $RB_k > p_k'$ by assumption, then $RB_k > \bar{p}_k$. If $\bar{p} < RB_k < p_k'$, then, because of discontinuities, the example becomes less interesting, with the result being similar to the previous case where the revealed demand price of *each* participant is less than his variable price and the contribution of each for a zero output is also zero.

Note also that, as a result of discontinuities inherent in the discrete output case, there are inequality relationships between revealed demand and variable prices. In the more general nondiscrete case considered later, each participant's revealed demand price will be equal, at the marginal unit of provision, to his variable price.

3. A numerical example is helpful here. The sum of Mr. K's assigned price, $\bar{p}_k = \$1$, and the assigned prices to all others, $\bar{p}_0 = \$10$, adds up to the cost of production, $\emptyset = \$11$. The sum of the revealed demand prices of all others, $RB_0 = \$9$, is less than the sum of their assigned prices, $\bar{p}_0$. Mr. K's revealed demand price, $RB_k = \$3$, is greater than his variable price, $p_k' = \emptyset - RB_0 = \$2$. Therefore, a positive output, q_1, is produced because $RB_k + RB_0 > \emptyset$. Mr. K's assigned output, $\bar{q}_k$, is zero because $\bar{p}_k + RB_0 < \emptyset$. Mr. K's fixed charge, $\bar{p}_k \bar{q}_k$, is zero and his variable charge, $p_k' = \$2$. Total contributions, always equal to or in excess of production cost, will be, assuming that the assigned outputs to all others are equal to actual output, q_1, the sum of Mr. K's variable charge, $p_k' = \$2$, and the fixed charges to all others, $\bar{p}_0 \bar{q} = \$10$. The excess of contributions over production cost is $\$1$.

4. As illustrated in the previous examples, the sum of the fixed charges paid by all individuals will be equal to or in excess of the cost of producing the good. Total contributions, the sum of fixed and positive or negative variable charges, will also be equal to or in excess of production cost, depending on whether individual revealed demand prices are equal to or differ from individual *assigned* prices at the marginal unit of provision.

5. Costs of the proposed system and alternative nonmarket arrangements, aspects of strategic behavior, and the distribution of surplus contributions under the proposed system are considered in "Introduction to Theory for Public Goods Pricing" and "A Market Solution to the Public Goods Problem" (see note 1, above).

PART TWO
The State of the Art

Discharge Capacity of Waterways and Effluent Charges

ETERIORATION of water quality is not a new problem. In recent decades, however, with the increasingly rapid growth of the economy, the problem has become so large and complex that water quality management must be regarded as a critical problem calling for bold initiatives. Basically, it is a problem of how to allocate most efficiently a resource service that has become scarce: the assimilative capacity of water. A distinctive feature of this modern problem is the fact that the economic institutions on which we customarily rely to balance costs and returns—the interaction of market forces in a private enterprise system—do not perform this function satisfactorily for waste disposal.

Thus the problem of environmental pollution and congestion in general and of deteriorating water quality in particular is in large measure the result of inappropriate and uneconomic incentives. In turn, the existence of uneconomic incentives (incentives that encourage an inefficient allocation of resources) is the result of two fundamental factors: (1) the limited capacity of environmental resources relative to the growth-induced demands for their services, and (2) the technical and economic characteristics of environmental resources that require deliberate collective action to alter the incentive structures to which private users of resource services respond. The persistent disparity between existing and optimal incentive structures represents a serious

Allen V. Kneese is Director, Quality of the Environment Program at Resources for the Future, Inc., Washington, D.C.

Author's Note: Without implicating them, I wish to acknowledge the help of Blair T. Bower and Robert Haveman in the preparation of this chapter.

shortfall in the nation's willingness (or ability) to see the problem as one of uneconomic incentives and to muster the resolve to undertake a deliberate alteration of the incentives that influence private use of these resources. The latter implies removal of an implicit social subsidy to those interests making the heaviest demands on the services of the nation's resources.

This chapter focuses primarily on the use of economic incentives as a means to improve water quality. The discussion will touch briefly on the issues of water quality management and on ways of improving quality. Next the problem of externalities or common property resources will be introduced, followed by proposals for public intervention to control use of waterways. The latter section emphasizes effluent charges and points out some problems that arise in determining them. Regional water quality management systems are also discussed as the most efficient administrative device to buttress a system of effluent charges and to implement improved water quality use.

The Issues

The issue of effluent charges has to be posed against problems of water quality management. These problems raise three main questions.

1. How do we determine the quality of water we want to maintain in our watercourses, both surface and underground? As part of this problem, we must decide the degree of certainty with which we want the specified level of water quality, i.e., 100 percent of the time (which is virtually impossible in most cases), 98 percent of the time, or 95 percent of the time.

2. What is the "best" system of management measures for achieving the specified pattern of water quality? Research has shown that there is a wide variety of alternative measures potentially available to improve water quality. The best system must be devised within the context of overall water resources management.

3. What are the best institutional or organizational arrangements for managing water quality? What sort of organizational form and range of authority should a management agency have in order to use information on alternatives provided by engineering-economic analysis and to implement an effective and efficient management program?

All these issues are related. For example, the choice of quality level must depend on the cost of achieving that level, and the cost largely depends on how effective the management agency is.

Improving Water Quality

There are numerous ways to manage the waste loads discharged into the nation's waterways.[1] The quality of water bodies can be improved by reducing the waste loads discharged to them, by increasing or making more effective use of their assimilative capacity, and by combinations of the two.[2] If the focus is on water quality management in streams, and if there is no problem with floating materials, reducing waste loads and changing assimilative capacity are technical substitutes for one another. Assimilative capacity can be increased by altering the time patterns of streamflows, by altering the time patterns and/or locations of waste discharges, by artificial reaeration, or by some combination of these measures. Flowing streams, of course, are much more amenable to procedures for changing assimilative capacity than are ground water aquifers or even reservoirs and lakes.

Improving the water quality of receiving waters by reducing waste loads can be accomplished in two broad ways: by reducing the generation of wastes, and by modifying the residual wastes. Within these two broad categories various techniques are available, as indicated in Table 6.1. The dividing lines between methods that reduce waste generation and those that affect the residual wastes are not always as clear cut as implied in the table. Materials recovery, for example, is in a sense a change in production processes because it involves a change in the mix of raw product inputs; process change may be necessary before inplant water recirculation is possible, and product output changes may require some changes in production processes. Nevertheless, the distinctions are worth preserving as a basis for discussion. Table 6.1 also indicates ways of managing the assimilative capacity of receiving waters. The various alternatives in both categories are depicted in the generalized flow diagram of Figure 6.1. For example, following generation, waste materials may be recovered, used for the production of by-products, reduced by waste treatment, temporarily stored prior to discharge, conveyed to another water user,[3] or discharged in various possible ways into one or more receiving water bodies.

Although Table 6.1 and Figure 6.1 are oriented primarily toward

136

TABLE 6.1

Methods for Improving the Quality of Receiving Waters

METHODS FOR REDUCING WASTE DISCHARGES
Methods for reducing wastes generation
    1. Change in type of raw material inputs
    2. Change in production process
    3. Change in product outputs
    4. Inplant recirculation of water
Methods for reducing wastes after generation
    1. Materials recovery
    2. By-product production
    3. Waste treatment
    4. Effluent reuse (including ground water recharge, waste water reclamation or renovation)
METHODS FOR INCREASING OR MAKING BETTER USE OF ASSIMILATIVE CAPACITY
    1. Addition of dilution water
    2. Multiple outlets from reservoirs
    3. Reservoir mixing
    4. Reaeration of streams
    5. Saltwater barriers
    6. Effluent redistribution (including regulated discharge)

SOURCE: Allen V. Kneese and Blair T. Bower, *Managing Water Quality: Economics, Technology, Institutions* (Johns Hopkins Press for Resources for the Future, 1968), p. 42.

industrial plants, they are also relevant to municipalities and urban areas. Thus, "municipality" could be substituted for "production process" in Figure 6.1. This would require only slight modification of the diagram, i.e., elimination of the line to "materials recovery, etc.," and of the line indicating direct recirculation.

Industrial wastes play a large role in water quality management. An understanding of the factors that influence the generation of these wastes is extremely important because these are the factors that we are seeking to change by new incentives. This is not to say that the magnitude of wastes generated by domestic and commercial users is insignificant; on the contrary, with expanding population, particularly in urban areas, the absolute quantity of domestic wastes generated is bound to increase. And with the widespread adoption of garbage grinders, there may also be an increase in the generation of wastes per capita within the home. Treatment is the only general method for reducing waste discharges from households, barring significant changes

Fig. 6.1   *Waste Loads and Assimilative Capacity*

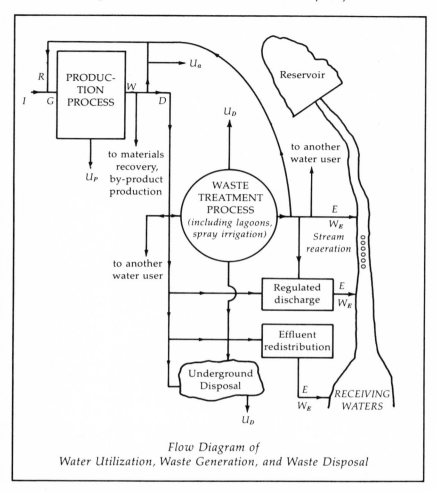

Flow Diagram of
Water Utilization, Waste Generation, and Waste Disposal

I = Intake water.
R = Recirculated water.
G = Gross water applied for all in-plant uses.
U = Consumptive use or net depletion of water. $U = U_P + U_D + U_R$, where U_P = consumptive use in the production process, U_D = consumptive use in the wastewater disposal system, and U_R = consumptive use in the recirculation system.
D = Wastewater discharge from the production process.
E = Final effluent from the production unit (available for reuse). Where a lagoon or spray irrigation system is involved, the final effluent (if any) consists of seepage, lagoon discharge, and/or surface runoff.
W = Waste load generated in all operations of the production process, for example, pounds of BOD, Btu's of heat.
W_E = Waste load in the final effluent, ie., pounds of BOD, Btu's.
Degree of recirculation = $R/G \times 100\%$.

SOURCE: Allen V. Kneese and Blair T. Bower, *Managing Water Quality: Economics, Technology, Institutions* (Johns Hopkins Press for Resources for the Future, 1968), p. 43.

in consumption patterns. However, industrial waste discharges currently account for the greater share of the residual materials discharged to receiving waters in the United States, and their control is a complex, multifaceted process.

Ways to reduce wastes generation

The generation of industrial wastes per unit of raw product processed or per unit of final product is a function primarily of the type of raw materials used in the production process, the technology of the production process, the product mix, and sometimes the extent of inplant water recirculation.

Shifting to a different grade or type of raw material is one way of reducing waste loads, but changes in production processes have the major impact on wastes generation. It should be emphasized, however, that technological changes have not usually been instituted because of water quality problems; most changes in production technology have been stimulated by factors unrelated to water problems. On the other hand, when management is stimulated by sewer charges, for example, the result is often process modification. As more systematic means are developed to bring to bear on industry the broader social costs associated with the discharge of waste materials into the environment, the generation and control of wastes will probably receive more consideration in regard to the raw materials used, process design, and perhaps even in product development. Studies of several industries make clear that even comparatively small incentive changes can have a substantial effect.

Methods for reducing wastes after generation

Materials recovery and by-product generation are two methods for reducing wastes *after* generation. They form a logical pair because the types of processes are often very similar. We differentiate between them on the basis of the final destination of their outputs. In materials recovery the output is reused within the same production unit as an input to the production process. By-product production yields consumption goods or intermediate goods used in other production processes.

Materials recovery includes, for example, the recovery of chemicals in black liquor recovery systems in the production of sulfate pulp and the utilization of save-alls in paper production. In steel production, sedimentation to eliminate mill scale from waste discharges has resulted in the recovery of iron that can be used in the production process. Waste liquor from citrus peel processing, normally a waste disposal headache, is concentrated to syrup and returned to the process. This procedure saves fuel in addition to reducing the waste.

By-product generation includes, for example, the conversion of cottage cheese whey into protein food supplements. In canning apples, the use of the "waste" segments of the apple for vinegar production has reduced the waste load per ton. Bran waste from milling has been used to make inexpensive plates, casseroles, and trays. Coffee grounds have been used to produce discs and shelves.

Even after such processes are used, there are often residual waste loads that must be reduced or otherwise handled prior to final discharge. Some common methods for treating residual industrial wastes (for the most part also applicable to municipal wastes) are the following: disinfection, incineration, screening, sedimentation, and stabilization lagoons.

Increasing Assimilative Capacity

The more water flow there is, the greater the natural dilution of wastes. Providing water for dilution by greater use of available streamflow is one possibility. Low streamflows often coincide with heavy concentrations of waste loads, as well as with high temperatures. Where the waste loads consist of oxygen-demanding wastes, the dissolved oxygen level of receiving waters is thereby depressed.

Dilution of wastes beyond that normally provided by natural streamflow during low-flow periods can be provided by modifying the pattern of streamflow, by modifying the time pattern and/or locations of waste discharge, or by some combination of the two. The most common practice to increase flows during low periods is to control waste releases by temporary storage. Flow can also be increased by drawing on ground water and releasing it into surface watercourses. In general, however, these methods have little effect on waste loads as such, and do not modify the receiving water. New research on chemical methods of accelerating streamflows needs to be encouraged.

The assimilative capacity of streams and lakes can be increased by artificial reaeration with either air or oxygen. Mobile or fixed aerating devices can be installed in reaches of streams where the dissolved oxygen supply needs to be replenished to prevent anaerobic conditions.

Common Property Resources

The concept of a common property resource encompasses those valuable attributes of the natural world that cannot be, or can be only imperfectly, reduced to individual ownership and therefore do not enter into the processes of market exchange and the price system. It should be noted that this is inherently a social concept, but that the resources to which it relates are normally attributes of the natural world rather than artifacts created by human beings to be of service to human beings. Notable among such resources are the air mantle, watercourses, complex ecological systems, and certain attributes of space— e.g., the nearby landscape or the far-out radio spectrum.

All these "environmental" resources have one main feature in common: they are subject to congestion. At some low level of use, an additional user of the resource would probably impose virtually no cost on others. However, a point is reached where an additional user will cause others to incur additional costs or suffer disutilities associated with congestion. An externality impact occurs or, in other words, a particular user does not take account of the cost he imposes on others when he decides to use the common property resource. And our present system of allocating resources through the exchange of private property provides no incentive for the user to take account of the cost. Also, past efforts by government to control the use of common property resources by direct regulation have had limited success. These points are directly applicable to the discharge of waste waters into our common property watercourses.

Public intervention in use of common property

It is now clear that the main basis for collective action in our society is shifting from the need for cooperation in the realization of collective benefits to the urgent need for generating private incentives in regard to the use of common property resources. Undoubtedly this need will continue to grow in the future. Economists have long held that external effects can be efficiently counteracted by levying a tax on the unit generating the external effect. As I later argue in greater detail, one of the most promising means of public intervention is a system of charges. First, however, some of the problems involved in charge setting and damage measurement are briefly discussed.

Charges and the "damage cost function." The system of effluent charges is based on the concept that efficiency and equity require payment for the use of valuable resources whether they happen to be privately or collectively owned. These prices will be reflected in the industrial producers' decision to install treatment equipment and otherwise reduce the generation of residuals. They will also be reflected in the price of intermediate and final goods so that a broader incentive will be provided to shift to goods with a lesser environmental cost.

The charge system works economically when the addition of cost is equal to the damage done. Basic to an understanding of an optimum system of effluent charges, or for that matter any procedure aimed at achieving an economically optimal level of water quality, therefore, is delineation of the "damage cost function," which is the functional relationship between the amount of a waste discharged and damages.

The simplest situation occurs when this damage cost function is linear, i.e., each additional unit of waste discharge results in an equal increment of damage. (In general, the discussion here will assume linear damage functions.) Such a situation is illustrated in Table 6.2, where it is assumed that five plants are arrayed along a stream, that streamflow increases along the course of the stream (say, because a tributary enters), and that the discharged waste is nondegradable (say, chloride). (The nondegradability assumption does not change the analysis in any way, but it simplifies the example.)

Since damage per day is assumed to be in direct proportion to concentration, a level of charges equal to incremental damage costs can be worked out for each level of flow and for each plant. For example, at flow condition I, the charge for plant 1 is \$4.25 per pound of waste discharged, which is the sum of the damages caused by plant 1 to plants 2, 3, 4, and 5. (At flow condition II, the charge for plant 1 is \$8.50 per pound, because the same waste discharge results in a doubling of the concentration.) The charge for plant 1 is the same regardless of the level of discharge of the other plants. If plant 1 reduced its discharge by half in response to the charge levied on it, its assess-

TABLE 6.2

Simple Illustration of Damage Distribution

Plant no. (serially located along stream)	Chloride load discharged (1,000 lb. per day)	Chloride load at plant intake (1,000 lb. per day)	Flow Condition I				Flow Condition II			
			Stream-flow (mill. gpd)	Chloride concentration (1,000 lb. per mill. gpd)	Damage per day ($1,000)	Total damage per day ($1,000)	Stream-flow (mill. gpd)	Chloride concentration (1,000 lb. per mill. gpd)	Damage per day ($1,000)	Total damage per day ($1,000)
1	1.0									
2	0.5	1.0	1.0	1.0	1.00	1.00	0.5	2.0	2.00	2.00
3	1.5	1.5	1.0	1.5	3.00	4.00	0.5	3.0	6.00	8.00
4	1.0	3.0	2.0	1.5	3.00	7.00	1.0	3.0	6.00	14.00
5	0.5	4.0	2.0	2.0	1.00	8.00	1.0	4.0	2.00	16.00

Flow Condition I

Damages caused at	Damage caused by:				Sum of damages caused to stream
	Plant 1	Plant 2	Plant 3	Plant 4	
	(------------------------------ $1,000 ------------------------------)				
Plant 1	0.00	0.00	0.00	0.00	0.00
Plant 2	1.00	0.00	0.00	0.00	1.00
Plant 3	2.00	1.00	0.00	0.00	3.00
Plant 4	1.00	0.50	1.50	0.00	3.00
Plant 5	0.25	0.125	0.375	0.25	1.00
Sum of damages:	4.25	1.625	1.875	0.25	8.00

Flow Condition II

Damages caused at	Damage caused by:				Sum of damages caused to stream
	Plant 1	Plant 2	Plant 3	Plant 4	
Plant 1	0.00	0.00	0.00	0.00	0.00
Plant 2	2.00	0.00	0.00	0.00	2.00
Plant 3	4.00	2.00	0.00	0.00	6.00
Plant 4	2.00	1.00	3.00	0.00	6.00
Plant 5	0.50	0.25	0.75	0.50	2.00
Sum of damages:	8.50	3.25	3.75	0.50	16.00

SOURCE: See Source for Table 6.1.

ment would drop by half to $2.15—the amount by which downstream damages are reduced. This "separability" characteristic of linear damage functions is important since it greatly reduces the amount of information a regulatory authority must have to implement an efficient effluent charge system.

The manner in which a plant maximizing its profits (or minimizing its losses) will respond to an effluent charge levied on it at a given level of streamflow and the effect of this response on costs associated with its waste disposal are shown in Figure 6.2. Under the circumstances pictured, the plant will reduce its waste discharge from point D to point E, thus minimizing the costs associated with its waste disposal.

The marginal cost of withholding wastes in an optimal manner in-

Fig. 6.2 *Industrial Plant's Response to Effluent Charges*

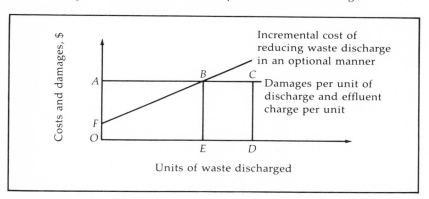

OD   = Units of waste discharge if no charge levied on effluent.
OA   = Damages per unit of waste discharge and effluent charge per unit.
OACD = Total damages associated with unrestricted waste discharge, i.e., no effluent charge levied.
OE   = Reduction of waste discharge with effluent charge OA.
OFBE = Total cost of reducing effluent discharge to ED.
OFBDC = Total cost associated with waste disposal with ED waste discharge, i.e., residual damage costs plus cost of reducing discharge.
OABE = Total damages avoided.
ABF   = Net reduction in waste disposal associated costs by reducing waste discharge by OE, i.e., OABE minus OFBE. This also equals the total cost of *not* reducing the effluent discharge.

SOURCE: Allen V. Kneese and Blair T. Bower, *Managing Water Quality: Economics, Technology, Institutions* (Johns Hopkins Press for Resources for the Future, 1968), p. 110.

cludes, for example, in the case of chlorides, such alternatives as temporary storage, process adjustments, and reduction of production. The marginal-cost function rises after some point because it becomes progressively more expensive to withhold production (say, as inventory is run down), or to adjust production processes.

A system of effluent charges based upon linear damage functions is relatively simple, because each waste discharger's damage costs can be determined separately. In contrast, nonlinearities are associated with interaction between waste discharges in the sense that the incremental external cost associated with one cannot be determined unless the level of discharge of the other is known. To put this in another way, there are cross product or congestion terms in the damage function. Thus, instead of merely needing to know damage functions and being able to achieve an optimal solution by imposing damage costs on the waste dischargers and letting them respond, we must also know the cost-functions for waste reduction at each interdependent point of waste discharge. And the optimum level of waste reduction for each point *before* charges are assessed on effluents must be determined if an optimal solution is to be obtained.

Additional theoretical problems in determining optimal charges are present when "separability" problems are involved. A *separable externality* is defined as one that occurs when the total cost of a productive process is affected by the level of output in another process but marginal cost is not. Even when damage functions are linear, such problems may arise if waste disposers impose damages on a series of downstream units and the waste discharge of one firm affects the marginal production cost of another.

For example, if factory A discharged a waste which caused factory B to put in a water supply treatment plant, the new total cost function becomes a vertical displacement of the old, and marginal costs are not changed. The effect of the externality is intramarginal and thus merely affects the firm's profit position and the decision whether to continue production or to stop. In this instance, the appropriate effluent fee is simply a lump sum equal to the increase in total cost, and is essentially a fee levied for the privilege of discharging at all. The only question involved is whether to discharge or not.

A *nonseparable externality* is defined as occurring when the marginal cost in a productive process is affected by the level of output in another process. For example, assume that petroleum refinery A, which expels a hot effluent, locates upstream from petroleum refinery B, which is operated by a different firm and which uses the stream for cooling water. Cooling efficiency for plant B will drop, and for the purpose of our example we assume it will have to pump more water for cooling per unit of output. The marginal costs of plant B *for a given level of output* will be affected by the externality.

Still other problems arise if different waste dischargers and water users impose external costs on multiple production units. Assume an initial equilibrium along a stream where a number of water users and waste dischargers impose external diseconomies on one another seriatim. Assume that a regulatory authority imposes the incremental costs of Z, the last one of these users, upon Y, Z's next neighbor, and so on back up the line. When the charge is levied upon Y the outputs of both Y and Z change. As the cost imposed by X on Y is levied on X, the output of Y changes again; accordingly so does that of Z. We have an interdependent system, and a simultaneous solution is necessary for the entire system. The problem clearly is analytically complex, and requires detailed information on the costs of reducing waste discharges as well as damages imposed.

Measurement of damages. One aspect of damage measurement importantly related to the problem of levying appropriate effluent charges (as well as establishing standards) is the probabilistic character of damages. As already explained, the damaging effect of a given waste discharge is heavily dependent upon the natural environmental conditions that prevail when the discharge is made. Most important are conditions of water availability and temperature. Although records are often short, methods have been devised which permit analysis of the characteristics of frequency distributions of streamflow and temperature. In general, they rely on chainlike statistical sequences.[4]

An effluent charge that does not vary over time should ideally reflect the *expected* value of damages avoided when waste discharge is reduced incrementally. The waste discharger would then have an economic incentive to plan and design his waste reduction facilities in a way that should minimize the overall costs associated with his waste discharge, given that his waste reduction facilities are to operate at a constant level regardless of the variation in flow and changes in the concentration of waste at the points of downstream use. This cost would be affected, under both the assumption of continuous rate operation and variable rate operation, by his own waste disposal facilities and the resulting concentration throughout the stream.

Some empirical information is now available concerning the possible cost savings for variable rate operation of waste treatment works. One study by Frankel explored the hypothesis that significant cost savings might be achieved in connection with a waste management system based upon streamflow conditions in the Eel River in California.[5] Frankel began by estimating the cost of achieving stream standards based upon continuous rate operation of conventional waste treatment plants. Next, by varying the degree of treatment just to maintain the standard, he found that operating costs could be reduced by about 15 percent per year. He also explored the possibility of storing wastes during low flows and discharging at higher flows, and found that this produced a saving in costs of about 30 percent over continuous rate operation of treatment plants to maintain the minimum standard.

So long as improved water quality does not itself induce water-based activities, an effluent charge based upon shortrun variations in external costs and provision to the waste discharger of information concerning the expected value of future charges and their duration at various levels for planning and design purposes would tend to produce optimum results. The latter would of course reflect any expected growth of water use in the region, and the general level of charges would be increased over time as the external costs of a given level of waste discharge rose. However, improved water quality itself may induce adjustments that affect external costs. For example, if the water quality were improved and maintained at the higher level, this might induce additional water use. To illustrate, it might lead to the development of such skills as water skiing, along with the associated investments in equipment. In these instances a certain promotional element must enter into the level at which the effluent charges are set.

If long periods of adjustment are involved, the present worth of the future benefits at various levels of control need to be assessed to determine whether they are equal to (or greater or lesser than) the present worth of the costs which would be needed to achieve these levels. The costs associated with waste disposal have been considered broadly as damage costs and waste-reduction costs. But damage costs also relate to aesthetics and recreation; these costs must also be assessed.

Proposals for a Strategy

Effluent charges

Precise damage assessments, as this discussion suggests, are not likely to be attained. Despite the lack of precision, effluent charges, as a strategy that would be alternative or complementary to regulation and standard setting, would improve the quality of our national waters (which implies a kind of rough damage estimation). I believe if this strategy had been adopted earlier our efforts to improve that quality would be substantially further advanced than they now are, and we might be moving into a position to achieve justifiable or desirable levels of water quality at the least cost to society.

The federal government's greater insulation from powerful local interests provides an opportunity for public leadership. One use of this leadership might be to levy a national effluent charge on all waste dischargers above some minimum amount of discharge. The charge could be based on a formula similar to those that are used in the Ruhr area of West Germany, or one of those used by certain cities in the United States in levying sewer service charges upon industry.[6] The national charge could be considered a minimum, and a state or regional water quality agency could, at its own discretion, impose a higher effluent charge.

The proceeds from effluent charges would yield a rent on a scarce resource to society that could be used in various ways, including further measures to improve water quality. The "rents" or revenues obtained by the federal government could be made available for purposes of general jurisdiction, or the revenues could be used to establish regional water quality management agencies.

Also, and even more important, the effluent charge would provide an incentive to restraint in the use of the watercourses for waste discharge. Careful industry studies have shown that industries can often reduce waste discharges enormously, usually at low cost, if they are given a proper incentive to do so.[7] In many instances, as we have noted, the most effective means for reducing waste discharges is internal process change, and recovery and recycle of materials that would otherwise be lost.

Our present policies put heavy emphasis on the construction of plants for the treatment of waste, with little or no followthrough on operations. Experts have pointed out that most treatment plants are operated far below their capabilities. The effluent charges system focuses on what is put in the stream, and thereby offers an incentive for effective operations of existing waste treatment facilities.

Some persons have seen fit to dub the effluent charge "a license to pollute." In my view this mindless cliché has certainly not contributed to the cause of effective water quality management. It is also sometimes said that effluent charges cannot be implemented because industries do not know what they discharge to watercourses. The latter part of this statement is, unfortunately, frequently true, but only through a system of charges could this situation be remedied.

Regional systems

The fundamental task with respect to water quality improvement is how best to accomplish it. But it is also true that the task itself needs to be clearly defined. The job is not simply to "clean up" the nation's water bodies; rather it is to manage continuously the quality of these waters over time in the dynamic context of a growing and affluent urban-industrial society. Therefore our strategy would include not only effluent charges but also the implementation of a systematic and well-integrated water quality management plan on a regional basis. The latter would contain elements other than the mere reduction of waste generation and treatment of waste waters at particular outfalls.

Research on water quality management over the past several years has clearly shown that major efficiencies can be obtained by the implementation of water quality management systems on a regional basis. In addition to the standard control of waste waters, such management systems could include a number of other alternatives closely articulated in planning and operation. These could, for example, include riverflow regulation; air being put directly into streams; or brief periods of high-level chemical treatment during adverse conditions. Studies of the Potomac, the Miami of Ohio, the Delaware, the San Francisco Bay region, and of other areas have shown beyond question the economies to be realized from this kind of regional approach. It appears that such an approach can only be effectively implemented by a regional river basin agency having the authority to plan, construct, and operate the necessary facilities.[8] Again, there is a role for federal leadership in the establishment of such agencies. So far, however, tendencies to support such an approach at the federal level have been minimal.

The federal government could, of course, take direct action. It could set up regional water quality management agencies or regional water resource management agencies. These could be separate entities, such as TVA, or regional units of federal agencies, such as proposed by the first Hoover Commission. There has been so much opposition to arrangements of this nature that it is questionable whether the federal government should or would be willing to move in this fashion. An alternative would be for the federal government to establish incentives and guidelines for the organization and operation of regional management agencies, either under state law or through interstate compacts.

An agency with adequate authority to plan and implement a regional water quality management system would be eligible for a grant of funds to support a portion of its budget to help staff the agency and to make the first data collections, analyses, and formulation of specific measures for water quality management. If the federal government is satisfied that the proposed program and the plan for its implementation satisfy criteria for its efficient operation, the agency might be eligible for a grant to assist it with actual construction and operating expenses. Such a system might appropriately be limited to the early implementation—say, five years. During this period, it would be necessary to work out long-term arrangements for financing the agency. Clearly, the proposed effluent charges system could play a major role in this.

Presumably, administration of the effluent charges system would be turned over to the regional agencies with the federal level of charges continuing to be regarded as a baseline. In this manner, regional scale measures would be financed while at the same time providing appropriate incentives to waste dischargers to cut back on their emissions. Special provisions might be included in the federal law toward marginal industrial plants that might go under and those in which there is a broader social interest in protection. It should be noted that where serious efforts to implement regional water quality management have been undertaken (as in the Delaware and the Miami), one of the most serious problems has been to set up adequate financing arrangements.

Conclusion

The effluent charge can be used to achieve a steam water quality standard efficiently, i.e., at lowest economic or resource cost. It tends to induce the least costly combination of measures for waste reduction at each outfall, and the least cost distribution of waste reduction among outfalls, thereby minimizing the real resources cost of attaining a stream water quality standard. In the process, it will normally yield a net revenue as well.

What happens is that each waste discharger is charged in proportion to the use he makes of a resource—the resource being the waste-assimilating and carrying capacity of the watercourse. The waste discharger can compare his marginal costs and marginal charges and decide whether it pays him to reduce his waste, and to what degree. The revenue that accrues to the agency from the charges can be viewed as a rental return on a natural resource. How much this will be depends on the scarcity of the resource, i.e., how small the natural flow is, how high the standard is, how highly developed the basin is. It is as though parties wishing to use other parts of the public domain—public land, for instance—were competing for its use and thereby establishing its rental value, and the rental return was accruing to the public. This seems equitable.

In my theoretical development of charges, I have focused on actual waste discharge. In principle, of course, charges should be levied on all activities that reduce water quality sufficiently to justify imposing external costs. This may not be administratively feasible in some instances, but it should be possible, for example, to assess a hydropower plant that draws water from the oxygen-depleted strata of reservoirs in the summer months, discharges it into a stream, and causes a reduction in the dissolved oxygen content of the stream. Similarly, other activities that divert or deplete water in such a way as to reduce assimilative capacity should be subject to charges.

My analysis leads me to the conclusion that systems of charges may properly be viewed as a central tool of water quality management.

I feel that regional water quality management agencies should be provided with this tool.

NOTES

1. Allen V. Kneese and Blair T. Bower, *Managing Water Quality: Economics, Technology, Institutions* (Johns Hopkins Press for Resources for the Future, 1968). These authors provide a more thorough discussion.

2. *Environmental Quality*, the First Annual Report of the Council on Environmental Quality, transmitted to the Congress August, 1970 (Government Printing Office), and Louis Klein, *River Pollution* (Academic Press, 1959). These sources provide helpful references for this chapter's discussion.

3. For example, sewage effluent from a city may be treated in a waste treatment plant, and subsequently used to irrigate golf courses or be conveyed to some industrial plant where it may be used directly in cooling or some other operation.

4. Maynard M. Hufschmidt and Myron B. Fiering, *Simulation Techniques for Design of Water Resource Systems* (Harvard University Press, 1968), particularly Chapter 2. These are known as Markov processes.

5. Richard J. Frankel, "Water Quality Management: Engineering-Economic Factors in Municipal Waste Disposal," *Water Resources Research*, 1 (Second Quarter, 1965) : 184.

6. More recently, various effluent charge schemes have been produced in Czechoslovakia, France, and England. A law is pending that would bring such a scheme into being in Canada.

7. George Löf and Allen Kneese, *The Economics of Water Utilization in the Beet Sugar Industry* (Resources for the Future, 1968).

8. See footnote 1 above. Kneese and Bower provide a more thorough discussion of this point.

Air Pollution Control:
Benefits, Costs, and Inducements

*A*IR pollution control as carried out by federal, state and local governments relies exclusively on direct regulation and enforcement of regulations by court actions, fines, and other penalties. Proponents of regulation claim that the process has been at least moderately successful and that further refinements will make it even more so. But questions remain: Can the regulatory process do the whole job of pollution control? Is there a place for economic incentives? If so, what is that place?

This chapter explores further the role of economic incentives as one element in a system of inducements for the control of air pollution.[1] It deals primarily with market-type incentives as distinct from fines, threats of shutdowns, jail sentences, outright grants, and other accouterments of direct regulation enforcement. Recognizing that economic incentives can only be part of a system of inducements that is dominated by regulation, the question addressed here is what kind of market-type economic incentives can be useful supplements to the regulatory process.

Potential Gains and Costs

At the beginning of the 1970s the economy of the United States was producing close to a trillion dollars worth of goods and services a year. In terms of air pollution alone, it was also producing more than 200 million tons of pollutants and $15 to $20 billion worth of ill effects.[2]

Paul H. Gerhardt is Chief, Standards Research Branch, Office of Research and Monitoring, in the Environmental Protection Agency.

To a large extent, the production of air pollution is a function of the fuels we burn and the production of the goods and services we consume. The principal air pollutants are carbon monoxide (CO), hydrocarbons (HC), nitrogen oxides (NO_x), particulate matter, and sulfur oxides (SO_x). National emissions of these pollutants totaled about 214 million tons in 1968. Of these emissions, 42 percent came from transportation sources, including automobiles, trucks, busses, trains, and aircraft; 21 percent came from fuel combustion in stationary sources such as public utility and industrial power plants and from commercial and residential space heating. The remainder was from industrial processes, solid waste disposal, and miscellaneous sources such as open burning and forest fires (see Table 7.1).

TABLE 7.1

Estimates of Nationwide Emissions, 1968
(Millions of tons/yr.)

	CO	Particulates	SO_x	HC	NO_x
Transportation	63.8	1.2	0.8	16.6	8.1
Fuel combustion in stationary sources	1.9	8.9	24.4	0.7	10.0
Industrial processes	9.7	7.5	7.3	4.6	0.2
Solid waste disposal	7.8	1.1	0.1	1.6	0.6
Miscellaneous	16.9	9.6	0.6	8.5	1.7
Total (1968)	100.1	28.3	33.2	32.0	20.6

SOURCE: Based on data from the Division of Air Quality and Emissions, assembled by the Air Pollution Control Office, Bureau of Criteria and Standards.

Cost of damages

A number of studies of the economic effects of air pollution have been undertaken to develop defensible estimates of the effects of pollutants on human, plant, and animal health, physical materials, property values, soil, and aesthetics.[3]

The most important category of damages from an economic point of view is probably in the area of human health. Air pollution has been linked with both respiratory and cardiovascular diseases, and with excess mortality and morbidity. The economic dimensions are obvious in nature—early death and reduced productivity—but obscure in terms of fact and "scientific" proof. This is a most difficult area to investigate because of conceptual and data problems. Nevertheless, some good statistical analyses have been undertaken and present indications are that the economic cost of mortality and morbidity because of air pollution is probably in the neighborhood of $6 billion annually.[4]

Other studies attempt to determine the effects of various pollutants on agricultural productivity, including the ability of the soil to support various types of plant and animal life. The results of such studies will help us understand the long-term environmental and ecological significance of air pollution. The Office of Air Programs (OAP) staff has underway the study of the distribution of estimated costs of damage among the various pollutants, based on a combination of documented effects studies and considerable judgment. A similar approach can be used to distribute estimated damage costs among the major source categories.

The estimate of gross economic damage for any one year is a function of the pollution levels that prevailed in that year. Presumably, damages will be reduced as pollution levels are reduced. To date, however, no functional relationships between pollution levels and the economic costs of damage have been firmly established.

Obviously, the whole subject of the economic costs of pollution damage would benefit considerably from further research efforts. As control programs and public and private expenditures grow, questions of potential benefits will come under closer scrutiny.

Costs of control

OAP estimates that a billion or more dollars will be spent on air pollution control programs between 1971 and 1975 by federal, state, and local governments. The additional annual capital and operating costs to industry of controlling particulate and sulfur oxide air pollution from fuel combustion and industrial processes in major manufacturing activities and power generation is estimated at about $2 billion. The annual cost of motor vehicle emission control could add another $2 billion a year. Thus, the additional public and private annual cost of air pollution control could be in the $4 to $5 billion range by 1976.[5] These costs will be additional to whatever costs are currently being incurred. The limited information available suggests that current costs range from $500 million to $4 billion per year on an annual basis.

Table 7.2 shows projected costs of control of stationary sources of air pollution for 298 metropolitan areas containing most of the nation's population and economic activity. Investment and annual costs are indicated on the assumption that implementation plans as called for by legislation will materialize. Compared to the current level of annual costs of, perhaps, $0.5 billion, a projected $5.0 billion could represent a ten-fold increase. It would amount to about one-half of 1 percent of the present GNP.[6]

Society, to the extent that it wants cleaner air—and is willing to pay for it—has three basic choices. One is to continue to enact new legislation and to strengthen legal enforcement procedures. A second is for government to find some way to make private control efforts profitable by altering economic incentives. A third choice is to seek to combine the best features of both regulation and economic (or market-type) incentives.

Regulation

The road of direct regulation and enforcement with fines and other penalties has generally been seen as the best way to abate and control pollution.[7] Land-use controls and nuisance laws have been used by municipalities. The Clean Air Act with its several amendments was designed to help states and the designated air quality control regions implement plans for the attainment of air quality standards. In the field of motor vehicle pollution control, the federal government, in accordance with provisions of the 1965 amendments to the act, is empowered by Congress to set emission standards for new motor vehicles. This approach is based on the philosophy that little can be accomplished through efforts to apply controls to the motor vehicle population within specific geographic areas because automobiles can move freely across boundary lines. Furthermore, automobiles are comparatively homogeneous, and the internal combustion engine and exhaust appear to be amenable to control with a common technology. Consequently, a federal emission standard approach has been accepted as sensible.

With the 1970 amendments to the Clean Air Act, the federal government is adopting new and more stringent requirements. The automobile industry will be required to produce a virtually pollution-free

TABLE 7.2

Emission Levels and Associated Costs
Stationary Sources (298 Metropolitan Areas[a])

Source	Quantity of Emissions[b] (thousands of tons per year)						Control Costs (millions of dollars)	
	Part.	SO_x	CO	F	Pb	HC	Investment	Annual
Solid Waste Disposal								
Without Clean Air Act[e]	1,500	—	5,450	—	—	2,020	$201	$113
With Act[d]	185	—	414	—	—	293		
Stationary Fuel Combustion								
Without	3,867	14,447	—	—	—	—	2,432	1,006
With	930	4,697	—	—	—	—		
Industrial Processes								
Without	6,053	6,229	10,040	73	30	1,736	3,877	1,095
With	453	1,720	539	9	10	849		
Total								
Without	11,420	20,676	15,490	73	30	3,756	6,510	2,214
With	1,568	6,417	953	9	30	1,142		

[a] Metropolitan areas are defined as APCO Air Quality Control Regions and are similar to Standard Metropolitan Statistical Areas.
[b] Emission abbreviations are: particulates (part.), sulfur oxides (SO_x), carbon monoxide (CO), hydrocarbons (HC), fluorides (F), and lead (Pb). Blanks in the table indicate that emission levels meet applicable regulations or that emissions are negligible or do not exist.
[c] Estimates without implementation of the Clean Air Act; afterward referred to as "Without."
[d] Estimates with implementation of the Clean Air Act; afterward referred to as "With."

SOURCE: Adapted from Air Pollution Control Office, *The Economics of Clean Air*, Third Annual Report to the Congress of the U.S., Government Printing Office, Washington, D.C., March, 1971.

vehicle by 1976. Naturally, this goal is meeting some opposition and a bargaining process has begun in which the government emphasizes pollution reduction in the interest of human health and welfare while the industry claims technical and economic difficulties.

For stationary sources, regulations relating specifically to the control of emission through application of best available methods are being developed under the Clean Air Act Amendment of 1970, in the form of national performance standards. Such point source control standards have advantages of understandability in comparison with air quality standards, which individual polluters often find difficult to relate to. However, with the improvement of capabilities to track damages from receptor points back over the topography and through the atmosphere to a specific emitter, emission control regulation in relation to air quality requirements will become increasingly defensible. This new technology would also help solve problems that now arise when regulatory agencies try to discriminate between point source emitters in terms of differences in air quality requirements.

From the point of view of economic efficiency, a totally uniform and inflexible control approach leaves much to be desired. Some flexibility is, in fact, built into the new federal legislation, which establishes a method for designating air quality control regions on a priority basis in relation to air quality improvement needs.

Economic efficiency further requires that controls be adopted in direct relation to each polluter's contribution to receptor point damages. Precise implementation of this approach would demand a capability not only to identify specific point sources but also to measure both quantitatively and qualitatively the nature of the pollutants and the damages they produce.

In fact, however, point source emission measurements today are mainly the result of direct stack gas sampling, in which a team of technicians physically probe the stack to extract a sample of the exit gas for analysis. Certain physical problems of access and construction have to be overcome, and in some cases, legal difficulties are encountered. To be most effective, measurements should be continuous, or at least on a reasonably periodic basis to assure a representative sampling.

In the absence of complete measurement capability, most regulations have relied on even simpler approaches involving direct visual observations by pollution control inspectors and citizens with photo-graphic records and special air samplers to supplement evidence gained in other ways. The accumulation of evidence is used in the construction of prima facie cases against polluters. The courts have shown a willingness to accept prima facie evidence to support fines and other penalties for offenders.

A principal feature of the regulatory approach to air pollution control is that it requires inspection and enforcement procedures that rely on court actions. The incentive effect is in direct proportion to the enforcement effort, including the probability of detection and the potential economic impact of fines and other court action. Low fines in relation to control costs may tend to be taken as a fee for pollution.

At the state level, an interesting approach to control is being developed in New Jersey, where a stationary source polluter may be fined up to $2,500 per day for each day he is found to be in violation of the state's regulation. To achieve compliance, the offender must first obtain a permit from the state, giving evidence that his corrective actions are acceptable to state air pollution control engineering standards. Before beginning operations again, the offender must obtain another permit, this time an operating permit, which in effect tells the public that the offender has actually taken the corrective actions on which the permit was based. If the corrective action has been completed within a reasonable amount of time, the offender may be forgiven up to 90 percent of his total fines. The offender must pay for the corrective action and recover his cost as best he can, presumably through adjustments in prices and costs.

Sulfur dioxide, caused by combustion of fossil fuels, especially bituminous coal and residue oil, constitutes a serious pollution control problem. At the present time, there is no completely satisfactory technology for the removal of sulphur dioxide from power plant gases. Many states now have regulations to control the amount of sulfur in fuels burned within their boundaries. This approach may work well for one or two states, but as more and more states and regional agencies try to adopt such regulations, the limited supplies of natural low-sulfur fuels begin to pose increasing difficulties.

A possible direct advantage of regulations limiting sulfur content is that they tend to force substitution of lower-sulfur for higher-sulfur fuels of the same type. Later, a fuel user may switch from coal to oil or to natural gas to accommodate to the requirement. Fuel suppliers are induced to reduce the sulfur content of the fuel they sell. Higher fuel costs required in the interest of sulfur reduction are passed along to customers as cost-of-service adjustments. As low-sulfur fuels become harder to find, however, the sulfur content limiting requirement will have to be abandoned in favor of alternative approaches, which will place the focus where it belongs—on reducing emissions.

If restrictions on sulfur content hinder the development of emission control systems, this particular regulatory approach is not neutral from a technological standpoint. A simple adjustment would relate the regulation to the equivalent sulfur content of the fuel and allow each plant to adopt whatever control measure or combination of measures it found to be most cost-effective for its own situation.

Economic Incentives

Lowered levels of air pollution must be paid for. The payment may be direct, in terms of product-price adjustments, or indirect, in terms of tax adjustments. If regulations are enforced, costs of control will be reflected in prices of products and in factor shares. Some prices will rise and some profits will fall in the polluting industries, while suppliers of pollution control technology will be experiencing growth. One way or another, resources will be reallocated.

If regulations require economically efficient solutions, the case for market-type economic incentives must be that they can attain such solutions with a smaller commitment of administrative and enforcement effort than the regulatory process. We don't know that the market type of economic incentive would be more efficient in terms of resource allocation, but we do know that it has not been tried. At least, it might be possible to incorporate some system of market-type incentives as a worthwhile supplement to the regulatory process.

Economic incentives include emission charges or taxes (provided that they are geared to the full additional costs of control) and full-cost subsidies or payments of any kind, including tax credits that cover the full additional costs of control.

Several technical considerations are important in evaluating the possible use of economic incentives. Pollution may be reduced through

(1) use of substitute fuels or materials, (2) the practice of processing fuels and materials to clean them of pollutants prior to use, (3) modifications in production process, or (4) proper treatment of wastes before final discharge or disposal. Because the costs of the several methods are apt to vary widely from plant to plant, it is of great importance that each polluter be free to choose the method or combination of methods that is least costly for him to apply in relation to the standards he must meet. Should an economic incentive alter the relative costs of available methods of control, it could lead to adoption of more rather than less costly methods. Furthermore, to the extent that a promising means of abatement may involve action by a supplier of fuels or raw materials, an economic incentive should be structured to encourage such actions. The desulfurization of fuels prior to use would be an example.

If new incentives are to be considered, it is important to consider them in relation to their prospective efficiencies in abatement. Furthermore, the effects of any new proposed system of incentives must be evaluated in relation to alternatives—one of which is to rely on regulation, an alternative that is favored by many experts familiar with the technical, economic, and administrative aspects of pollution control.

Pollution control taxes

Essentially, a pollution control tax system would recognize the social costs of pollution. This approach reserves to individual polluters a considerable amount of decision-making as to control method and places the direct costs of control on the polluter himself, allowing him to find the method or combination of methods that best suits his own particular situation. He then shares the costs of control as he can with customers, suppliers, and equity holders. Such a tax system, if properly structured, would tend to work in the direction of efficient resource reallocation.

The primary requirement for air pollution control is detailed knowledge of how receptor point damages relate to point source emissions over time. The optimum tax system would require a system of charges for individual point source emitters based on how much each one contributes to all individual receptor point damages. The application of such damage-related charges to polluters would induce additional control applications up to the point where additional control costs exceeded incremental damages.

This approach could also incorporate a system of payments to receptors to provide them compensation for uncontrolled pollution. Ideally, the control authority would be able to vary the tax system in accordance with changing patterns of pollution production, transport, and damage.

Past considerations of this solution have found it to be impractical for at least four reasons: (1) the economic extent of damages at individual receptor points has not been clearly established; (2) the exact responsibilty of individual emitters for the pattern of damage has not been established; (3) the administrative and legal difficulties of damage assessment are many; and (4) the required discretionary taxing authority would be difficult to legislate.

As with any new and untried approach, a general system of emission charges would present a number of problems. In the first place, implementation could add, at least temporarily, to the administrative costs of government. Administrative costs would be minimal, however, if the charges could be levied in rough proportion to damages and control costs and if existing governmental tax collection agencies could be relied on. Second, any system of emission charges based solely on the output of pollution would obviously require an emission measurement capability that, in the case of air pollution, may not be available or would be extremely costly and difficult to provide. Consequently, proxies for actual emissions may have to be relied upon until appropriate emission measurement capability is provided. An example of a proxy would be an engineering calculation based on established relationships between input, processes, and the efficiencies of control methods.

An efficient fee schedule must be constructed to bring about the desired level of pollution reduction. Theoretically this could be accomplished by setting the taxes at (1) levels equal to the damages of emission or (2) levels exceeding the expected additional costs involved in reducing the damages of emission. Application of the fee schedule requires detailed knowledge of the functional relationships between damages, control costs, and the levels of control attainable. While much research needs to be done, there is a considerable body of knowledge regarding the technological alternatives available for some air pollution control problems and at least some understanding of the costs of applying alternative degrees of the various methods of control. Such information could be used in the structuring of a system of emission control taxes.

Taxes on fuel and material inputs

Because charges relating directly to pollution damages or to emissions encounter serious measurement problems, taxes on fuel and other material inputs have been considered as alternatives. The recently proposed tax on leaded gasoline is one example. A variant of the proposal would be to levy a tax directly on the volume of tetraethyl and metraethyl lead produced and sold by that segment of the chemical industry. This would place the direct burden of the tax on a few companies operating a limited number of plants. Such a tax could be varied over time to produce a variety of results in terms of the use of lead in automobile fuels. It would obviously circumvent the need to measure the lead oxide emissions of some 100 million tailpipes.

Another material input substitute for an emission tax might take the form of a unit tax per pound of the equivalent uncontrolled sulfur in power plant fuels. Any sulfur recovered in the ash or collected from the stack gas would be deducted from the tax liability. The recovered sulfur would be valued at the tax rate applicable at the time. Alternatively—and depending on ease of measurement—the actual gaseous emissions of SO_2 and SO_3 could be used in calculating the tax liability. Such a tax would encourage sulfur removal through stack gas cleaning and the preprocessing of the sulfur-bearing fuel. The tax rate would be related to the marginal costs of sulfur oxide control and set in such a way that the total savings available as control methods are applied would noticeably exceed the extra costs of abatement. This potential excess of available tax savings over costs of control (appropriately discounted, of course) should provide an effective economic incentive. The tax might also be structured to include a system of credits to stimulate private research, development, and demonstration activities.

The key to the success of any tax as an emission control device is that the tax be set so that the total obligation is seen by the polluter as noticeably higher than (or at least equal to) the full additional costs of control. Taxes set at less than the full additional costs of control, in the absence of regulations, would encourage polluters to pay the tax rather than to undertake additional control efforts. The question of who finally pays the tax depends on the ability of firms to share costs with customers, suppliers, and equity holders. This in turn depends on elasticities of demand and supply and on cross-elasticities and substitution possibilities, as well as the competitive cost structure of the industry. One clear effect of a pollution control tax would be to discourage consumption of polluting products.

Subsidies

In the field of air pollution control, where direct-cost offsets to polluter control efforts seem to diminish rapidly as control efficiencies and costs rise, it is especially useful to distinguish very clearly between incentives and subsidies. An incentive may be employed with or without regulation, but a subsidy requires existence of an enforceable regulation as a precondition to expanded control efforts.

Some subsidies that have been tried or suggested include investment tax credits, accelerated depreciation, or partial payment approaches and performance award payments. From the standpoint of pollution control, however, these subsidy approaches raise a number of problems. To the extent that they do not provide full-cost offsets, they are not apt to constitute effective incentives because they will not make air pollution control investments competitive with alternative investment opportunities. Also, in determining the amount of tax credits or subsidies, it may be difficult to decide how much of a given investment should be charged to pollution control and how much to a process change undertaken primarily for increased efficiency and only incidentally to reduce pollution. The effect of capital equipment purchase subsidies (such as investment tax credits) may be to subsidize economic inefficiency rather than to encourage more effective and lower-cost approaches such as fuel or material changes, process modification, and better operating and maintenance practices. To the extent that the net costs and economic burdens of pollution control will be relatively low for most industries, financial aid subsidies may be more trouble than they are worth.

The Need for Criteria

Regulatory approaches have been criticized by some as arbitrary and inflexible. Proposals to tax firms for pollutants emitted to the environment have been labeled licenses to pollute. Permits and other legislative requirements have posed difficult administrative problems. Clearly, we need a set of criteria that will help guide the development of new inducement systems. Efficiency considerations would require adoption of those inducements that promise maximum present value of net benefits. But what does this mean with respect to the evaluation of specific proposals? If efficiency demands that polluters be treated with selectivity depending on whether they are large or small, old or new, in city or country locations, how will equity be served?

Any criteria selected will result in differences of opinion, if only because those who would be disadvantaged by the application of particular criteria will, on that basis alone, disagree with the criteria chosen. And differences of opinion will be augmented by uncertainty regarding the nature and meaning of air quality criteria, the extent and possible resolution of the problem in the future, and the relationship of air quality to other environmental and social issues.

An incremental approach to the selection of an initial set of all-encompassing criteria may have some advantages. The intent would be to find procedures that yield criteria which can be agreed upon by many groups and individuals, and to limit the number of program alternatives that are assessed. While no policy is likely to be best in terms of all criteria, some will be so obviously disadvantageous in terms of one or more of the criteria that they will be discarded. One set of criteria against which policy approaches may be evaluated is presented in Table 7.3. A few comments on the major headings follow.

Equity

Any new strategy alternative, no matter what its theoretical advantages, will be difficult to implement unless its principles and expected results are believed to be fair by those involved in the decision. As long as a strategy is considered too complex or too abstract, there will be difficulty in understanding its impact and further difficulty in convincing decision-makers to adopt it. "When in doubt, don't" is a

TABLE 7.3

Grading Sheet for Evaluation of Air Pollution Regulations or Incentives

Equity considerations
1. Equal or equitable treatment of:
    a. Polluters
    b. Geographical areas
    c. Methods of control
2. Consideration of polluters in various financial positions

Efficiency considerations
1. Importance of pollutants controlled
2. Approach technologically comprehensive
3. Understandable
4. Technically feasible
5. Administrable
6. Supportable politically
7. Flexible
8. Revenue productivity

Compatibility considerations
1. Primary air quality standards
2. Secondary standards
3. National performance standards
4. Regional priorities with other federal programs

common response, and it applies strongly to public innovations where a large number of individuals and organizations must be persuaded before a new idea can be adopted. The queries here are: "What quality of air and at what price?" and also, "Who will pay and how much?" The basic question involves the range of difficulties of establishing equity or fairness: will the different individuals and groups in society concede that the costs of air pollution control are borne fairly and equitably in relation to the long-term distribution of benefits, with respect to damages, geography, and technology available?

Efficiency

To win support, a program must demonstrate that it is superior to other programs over the long term in the efficiency of resource allocation. Policies must be capable of control to the degree required by society. A policy must be considered in terms of its costs to different groups: polluters, monitors, and the public at large.

Compatibility

Alternatives that involve great changes from present procedures, systems, and structures are less likely to be successful than those that involve minimal changes. The federal role in air pollution is currently directed more toward research, advice, and supervision. The state role is primarily concerned with actual implementation of policy. Because of these two distinct roles, proposals that would radically change this situation will be more liable to failure than those which can be integrated into an existing framework.

Alternatives not compatible with present systems and procedures result in transitional costs. Disruption means that benefits are delayed. A decision must be made whether a new approach is worth the disruptions. Since future benefits are uncertain while present costs are relatively certain, the chance of implementing radical changes lessens. Finally, those who find change upsetting will oppose it even if no substantial reasons can be given.

Stimulation

Any strategy, especially where existing control technology is known to be inadequate, should make a substantial provision for the stimulation of research, development, and demonstration programs. Various approaches to encourage R&D are feasible. Tax credits, for example, might be allowed for activities designed to produce new control methods and/or reduce the cost of existing methods. The financing of research, development, and demonstration projects might be facilitated to the extent that it could be made available out of a special, governmentally administered "environmental quality fund." Such a fund might be established and financed initially through revenues from taxes on polluting activities. However, it might not be wise to make R&D totally dependent on such taxes, especially where they are designed to reduce pollution and thus may be eliminated as a source of revenue.

Subsidy criteria

To the extent that subsidies may qualify as an incentive, there is a need for criteria to limit their application to the stimulation of pollution control. Otherwise, the general application of a subsidy could well result in considerable waste and very little additional control effort.

The basic and admittedly difficult test would involve the effect of a control effort cost on a firm's long-term financial position. A related test would involve whether or not this long-term financial position would be seriously harmed by the incurrence of control cost commitments in the short run. For example, a small, relatively profitable firm simply might not be able to marshal the financing to meet immediate capital needs. Such a firm would be a logical candidate for some assistance, perhaps by being given access to an available pool of funds. It may or may not make a big difference whether the funds were made available at regular or low rates of interest. The danger involved in low-interest financing is simply that firms would tend to seek such financing as an alternative to other, more economic, pollution control measures.

In the process, an otherwise justifiable program could result in subsidizing economic inefficiency along with some worthwhile pollution control efforts. The pollution controller might tend to be swayed too easily by firms using the "I'll have to go out of business" argument. It must be remembered that firms go out of business every day and that it is not the job of pollution control to interfere with normal economic processes. Nevertheless, if a firm can show a good long-term market position along with its claim of limited cash or other liquid assets, some special treatment might well be in order to avoid undue hardship and the possible loss to the community of a productive enterprise.

Table 7.3 represents one approach to grading alternatives. A grading scheme of one to five could be used as a basis for preliminary evaluation and screening. Follow-on analyses would obviously be in greater detail.

Conclusions

Recent cost studies suggest that a maximum air pollution control effort may possibly require annual expenditures of $5 billion per year by 1976. Even at this rate, the annual resource commitment would still be less than 0.5 percent of the gross national product that, as of 1971, was already over $1 trillion per year.

The expenditures required should be manageable within the framework of cost-price-profit adjustments. Some polluters would undoubtedly be hard hit; others would be able to share cost increases in various ways with customers, suppliers, and equity holders. For some, new economic opportunities would be created. A review of the major incentive and cost-sharing alternatives seems to point away from those who would require substantial additions to government budgets. This would tend to eliminate most subsidy approaches (as well as cost-plus-profit contracts to buy pollution abatement). If regulations need to be supplemented, the approaches that appear most promising are those that would use a small governmental effort along with a potent economic incentive for leverage. Pollution control taxation approaches designed to utilize existing taxes, such as those on motor vehicles, gasoline, and tobacco, have some obvious advantages over new taxes.

There has recently been considerable discussion in government and academic circles regarding the proper role of pollution taxes. Emission taxes for air pollution control could be related to costs of control or to damages done. The latter alternative is probably not a realistic one, given the nature of the problem. Without good damage functions the setting of pollution taxes can only be justified in one of two ways: because society wants to gain a measure of control over pollution reduction, or because society wants a source of revenue to help fund pollution control programs.

In air pollution, significant control (i.e., 98 percent or more) is possible for particulate matter from stationary sources. The incremental costs of such high levels of control are also high. If a tax is to achieve a control objective it must either: (1) provide an incentive in the form of tax savings net of control costs, or (2) provide a regulatory body with needed information and enforcement muscle.

There may be special circumstances, however, where immediate compliance with pollution control regulations could make a specific and otherwise viable firm's market position untenable. Equity suggests that financial aid be made available to such firms in the form of loans to offset immediate pressures and undue loss of liquid assets.

Current policy recognizes that economic efficiency considerations can be served effectively by allowing individual polluters to choose their own best method of control and pay the initial costs of application. It also recognizes that costs of control will ultimately be shared with the customers, suppliers, and equity holders.

To the extent that they may be unwilling to bear the generally small increase in cost, customers may choose other products, suppliers may find other markets, and equity holders may shift funds to other less-polluting enterprises. Not only will an economically efficient pattern of resource allocation tend to be preserved, but—even more importantly—a vital set of social values will have been introduced into the economic calculus.

The basic choices are now clarified. We can continue on the road of regulation and enforcement or we can begin to introduce economic incentives as potential substitutes for regulation. But a much more realistic and practical alternative would be to combine the two, creating a set of economic incentives that will provide effective and complementary support for the regulatory objectives already provided by law.

NOTES

1. For an earlier summary see Paul H. Gerhardt, "Incentives to Air Pollution Control," in *Law and Contemporary Problems* (Duke University Press, Spring, 1968).

2. There are no official estimates of damages at the national level. The figures contained in this chapter are judgmental, based on a survey of a number of pertinent studies.

3. R. J. Anderson, Jr., and T. D. Crocker, "Air Pollution and Housing: Some Findings," Paper 264, Institute for Research in the Behavioral, Economic, and Management Sciences, Krannert Graduate School of Industrial Administration, Purdue University (December, 1969), p. 34.

4. Thomas D. Crocker, "Air Pollution and Residential Property Values in Chicago, Illinois," study for the Air Pollution Control Office, Environmental Protection Agency, December, 1970; also Lester B. Lave and Eugene Seskin, "Air Pollution and Human Mortality," for Resources for the Future, published in part in *Science* (July 1970).

Health and ecological studies suggest that the effects of air pollution may be more serious than the estimates cited.

5. Air Pollution Control Office, *The Economics of Clean Air*, Third Annual Report to Congress, Environmental Protection Agency (Government Printing Office, March, 1971).

6. Since GNP measures the final output of goods and services at market prices, it includes the value of products and services devoted to cleanup and control of pollution. Government and private outlays are included, but many social costs are not.

7. See J. Clarence Davies, III, *The Politics of Pollution* (Pegasus, 1970), for an excellent discussion of recent regulatory developments.

Further references are:

Battelle Memorial Institute, "A Survey and Economic Assessment of the Effects of Air Pollution on Elastometers." CPA–22–69–146. Final Report (June, 1970).

R. Ferrando and G. Milhad, "The Biological Effects of Air Pollution on Animals" (abstract translated by PHS from French). *Rev. Med. Soc.* 17 (3) (1969): 295–306.

Paul H. Gerhardt, "An Approach to the Estimation of Economic Losses Due to Air Pollution," *Ohio's Health* (November–December 1970).

C. C. Havighurst, "A Survey of Air Pollution Litigation in the Philadelphia Area." CPA–22–69–112. Final Report (December, 1969).

F. H. Haynie, "Estimation of Cost of Air Pollution as the Result of Corrosion of Galvanized Steel." Unpublished Report, Division of Economic Effects Research, National Air Pollution Control Office.

Irving Michelson and Boris Tourin, "Comparative Method for Studying Costs of Air Pollution," *Public Health Reports* 81 (6) (June 1966): 505–511.

Midwest Research Institute, "Systems Analysis of the Effects of Air Pollution on Materials." CPA–22–69–113. Final Report (January 1970).

H. Miessner, "Damage to Animals Caused by Industry and Technology" (translated by PHS from German). *Deut. Tieraerzti. Wechschr* 39 (1931): 340–345.

Dorothy P. Rice, *Estimating the Cost of Illness.* (Department of Health, Education, and Welfare, 1966.)

Ronald G. Ridker, *Economic Costs of Air Pollution.* (Frederick A. Praeger, 1967), pp. 12–29.

Ronald G. Ridker, "The Problem of Estimating Total Costs of Air Pollution, a Discussion and an Illustration." Unpublished Report to U.S. Public Health Service (July, 1966), p. 21.

M. Rubay, "About the Fog Observed in the Meuse Valley in December, 1930 and Its Noxious Effects on Animals" (abstract translated by PHS from French). *Ann. Med. Vétérinaire* 77 (March 1932): 97–110.

V. S. Salvin. "Survey and Economic Assessment of the Effects of Air Pollution on Textile Fibers and Dyes." PH–22–68–2. Final Report (June, 1970)

Stanford Research Institute, "Inquiry into the Economic Effects of Air Pollution on Electrical Contacts." PH–22–68–35. Final Report (April, 1970).

Thomas E. Waddell, "The Economic Effects of Sulfur Oxide Air Pollution from Point Sources on Vegetation and Environment." National Air Pollution Control Office, unpublished (June, 1970).

Economics of Solid Waste Handling and Government Intervention

SOLID waste handling and environmental quality are intimately connected. The increasing concern with the latter, the rapid growth of solid waste generation, and the high cost of even the current inadequate waste treatment all add to the crisis atmosphere surrounding decisions on the "waste problem" and point to the need to abandon a limited view of solid waste and pollution control options.

Despite an enormous engineering literature from the 1960s on, there is still very little known of the basic statistics of waste generation (composition, sources) and the direct and indirect costs and benefits of waste processing. Economic literature on the efficient provision of environment-related services is growing but still with little attention to solid waste as a source of pollution.

The use of market incentives to influence waste creation and handling will be analyzed. But first, solid waste management will be defined and elements of the cost and demand conditions will be examined.

Solid Wastes and Solid Waste Handling

The waste cycle

The processes of production and consumption yield solid, liquid, and gaseous residuals; those residuals that are not recycled become

Judith M. Guéron recently completed the requirements for her Ph.D. in economics at Harvard University. She is currently employed by the Human Resources Administration of New York City.

"wastes." A material is thus a solid waste, not because of any intrinsic physical properties, but because for it "at a given point in time, there is no *economic* use" (emphasis added), where what is "economic" depends on the cost, technology, and market for the direct reuse of mixed residuals or for the separation and recycling of waste components.[1]

Figure 8.1 summarizes the possible paths traveled by material resources from their extraction to their return in some form to the environment. Table 8.1 shows the components of solid waste.

TABLE 8.1

Solid Waste Components

Category[a]	Source	Amount (million tons/year)[b]
Garbage	Household and	
Rubbish	commercial	
Ashes		
Street refuse		250
Dead animals	Municipal	
Abandoned vehicles and junk		
Sewage sludge		
Industrial wastes		
Demolition wastes	Industrial	110
Special hazardous wastes		
Mineral wastes		1,100
Agricultural wastes		2,000

[a] "Refuse" includes all of the solid waste components listed except mineral and agricultural wastes.
[b] Estimated, United States, 1967.
SOURCE: R. J. Black, A. J. Muhich, A. J. Klee, H. L. Hickman, Jr., and R. D. Vaughan, "The National Solid Wastes Survey, an Interim Report," presented at the Annual Meeting of the Institute for Solid Wastes of the American Public Works Association (Public Health Service, Solid Wastes Program, October 1968), p. 48. Also American Public Works Association, *Municipal Refuse Disposal* (Chicago: Public Administration Service, 1966), p. 12.

The traditional approach to solid waste management takes waste generation as exogenous and limits policy decisions to collection and disposal (stages 3 and 4 of Figure 8.1). This remains the context of most studies.[2] However, the tools of solid waste management have been increasingly recognized as including all the instruments of intervention

Fig. 8.1 *Flow Diagram of Solid Waste Generation and Treatment*

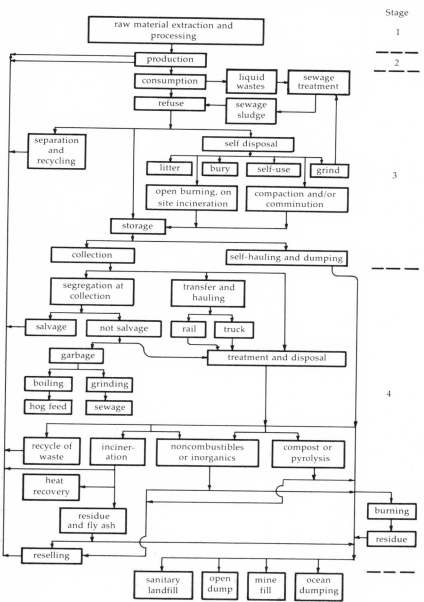

at any point in the waste generation cycle.[3] Only the comparison of net benefits of changes at all stages in Figure 8.1 can lead to longrun efficient resource allocation to environmental quality. In fact, most of the needed information is currently unavailable.

Collection and disposal defined

The services of collection and disposal are the mechanisms by which solid wastes are aggregated and redistributed into different environmental media as pollutants in solid, liquid, or gaseous forms.[4] They are multidimensional services, each aspect of which is relevant both to the nature and number of beneficiaries and to the costs incurred.

The quantity dimension measures the amount of solid waste handled. The quality variables can be expressed in terms of any of the three stages in the transformation of residuals into disservices (shown in Table 8.2). That is, on the cost side, the quality parameters of a unit of output can be expressed directly in terms of the service technology variables and the accompanying specific pollutant emissions at level *b*.

TABLE 8.2

Residual Damage Transformation

Level	Form	Agents that generate the quantity at the level indicated by operating on the quantities at the directly preceding level
a.	Solid residuals	Production and consumption decisions; direct recycling
b.	Pollutants	Collection technology and decisions on the level and type of service; disposal technology and the use of alternate disposal methods and equipment
c.	Pollution	Service conditions that relate pollutant to pollution: environmental absorption ability (meteorology, hydrology, climate, existing pollution); time rate of pollutant emission; interaction among pollutants
d.	Specific damages to users of environmental resources	Technical conditions and preference functions

Or, if the technical relationship between pollutants and environmental deterioration is known, we can transform cost-pollutant into cost-pollution functions at level c. The damages at level d are the dimensions of the consumption mix that are directly perceived by environmental users. If total knowledge were available—of the disposal and collection production functions, including pollutant emissions, of the technical transformation of pollutants to pollution, of the social costs from changes in environmental quality, and of the interaction among pollutants—the total cost and total benefit of variations in service equality could be expressed at levels b, c, or d, which are then just alternate stages in the waste flow and describe the same influences on consumer welfare.[5]

Residential refuse collection

We include under collection the quantity-quality parameters of the action, or lack of it, on storage, pickup, and local haul of the residuals of household consumption. Quantity or amount is measured in weight (tonnage, gross vehicle weight) or volume (containers, cubic feet, vehicle volume). The amount of refuse generated by reference individual i is A^i. The amount, in tons, etc., of solid waste collected from individual i is $C_{j_i}^i$. Subscript j_i is the vector with components, each of which is an environmental attribute of collection options (e.g., noise, odor) and can take values in accordance with the existing collection possibilities; we assume that there is a finite number of such vectors, i.e., $j = 1 \ldots n$. $A^i - C_{j_i}^i = L_{k_i}^i$ is the amount of own disposal by i. Subscript k_i, where $k = 1 \ldots m$, refers to a vector of environmental qualities resulting from available combinations of own disposal by i (litter, dumping, own burning, etc.) of that part of A^i which is not collected. Table 8.3 shows some examples of quality parameters in vector j expressed as level b service features, which enter directly into the collection cost function, giving the kind of level c pollution, level d damages, and other service aspects that result from decisions in each of the eight groups of service features listed.[6]

Residential refuse disposal

We include under disposal the processing and release into the environment of solid wastes. Implicit in the Table 8.2 relationship between pollutants and pollution, and in the earlier statement that

TABLE 8.3

Quality Parameters of Solid Waste Collection

Level *b*, service features	Level *c*, pollution	Level *d*, damages

Household treatment required:
   household comminution
   household garbage grinding
   other
	Landscape pollution
	Air pollution
	Acoustic pollution
		Own and community
		   health
		Nuisances: aesthetics
		     odors
		     disturbance,
		      loss of
		       sleep,
		     traffic inter-
		      ference

Storage container:
   metal can
   plastic can
   plastic bag
   paper bag
   other
		Own effort (sorting,
		   storing refuse;
		   transporting
		   containers)

Nature of collection:
   separation of rubbish and
      garbage required;
   separation not required
		Own expense (installing
		   house equipment,
		   purchasing storage
		   containers)

Location:
   curbside
   backyard
   other		

Frequency:
   daily
   once-a-week
   twice-a-week
   other		

Handling-qualities of pickup:
   degree of quietness
   degree of cleanliness
   reliability
   courtesy		

Type of equipment:
   open truck
   compaction truck
   other		

Haul route		

solid residuals must either be recycled or become wastes and pollutants, is the concept that there is no such thing as solid waste "disposal." A "disposable" means to the housewife an item she can throw away; similarly, to a locality "disposal" traditionally meant hauling and dumping wastes beyond the populated area or burning them and letting the air transport the gases away. All of these actions substituted "out of sight, out of mind" for actual residual elimination. Interjurisdictional redistribution of residuals was mistaken for residual destruction. When this mistake is recognized, it is clear that the aim of a solid waste "disposal" program can be characterized as determining "the optimum way to sequester wastes in the earth."[7]

The elements of disposal that influence individual welfare and production costs could theoretically be described on any one of the three levels of Table 8.2. Preferences for parameters at stages c and d are, indirectly, valuations of technologies and pollution control equipment that cause pollutants at level b. However, the technologies and options of disposal are not divisible into components and stages that can be varied independently and combined in many ways as was the case for collection. Rather, the complex alternative disposal systems result in packages of pollutants, disservices, and valuable byproducts.

Table 8.4 indicates some of the quality parameters at level c that may result from disposal choices. The table shows the media affected and the major pollutants. Table 8.5 indicates the pervasive damages from deterioration in environmental qualities. It points to the components of, and thus problems in, computing any dollar value for total damages.

Collection and Disposal as Impure Public Goods

The services of collection and disposal are neither pure "public goods" nor "private goods."[8] While both services are impure public goods, they differ significantly in the nature and importance of the externalities they produce.

Collection

The service of collection to individual i substitutes for his own effort and expense on his own disposal and/or haul. It has a private

180

TABLE 8.4

Quality Parameters of Solid Waste Disposal: Environmental Pollution

Air quality[a]
    particulate matter (settleable solids)[b]
    suspended dust
    sulphur oxides
    carbon monoxides
    hydrocarbons
    nitrogen oxides
    aldehydes
    other gases and vapors[c]

Water quality[d]
    biochemical oxygen demand
    suspended solids
    hardness
    total dissolved solids
    other

Land quality
    soil pollutants
    landscape pollutants

[a] The emissions of pollutants to the atmosphere from incineration and refuse burning, the amounts of each pollutant, and the proportions of the pollutant coming from refuse disposal, as opposed to all other sources, are listed in Russell J. Peterson and Richard G. Glenn, "Collection and Disposal of Solid Waste for the Des Moines Metropolitan Area," prepared by Henningson, Durham, and Richardson, Inc., and Veenstra and Kimm (U.S. Dept. of Health, Education, and Welfare, 1968), pp. 126–128; Regional Plan Association, *Waste Management: A Report of the Second Regional Plan* (New York, March 1968), pp. 30, 93; and C. G. Golueke and P. H. McGauhey, *Comprehensive Studies of Solid Wastes Management, First Annual Report* (Sanitary Engineering Research Laboratory, University of California, Berkeley, May 1967), pp. 81–85. Refuse disposal pours a total of 3.3 million tons of pollutants into the atmosphere per year, 2.6 percent of the total atmospheric pollutants.

[b] Smoke, soot, fly ash, grit, and dirt. Particulates are solids temporarily suspended in the air.

[c] Organic acids, chlorine (mainly from polyvinyl plastic).

[d] The damage from and nature of leaching of substances and gas migration from landfills into ground water are discussed in *Waste Management* (see [a] above), pp. 30, 94–97; Golueke and McGauhey (see [a] above), pp. 86–88; and American Public Works Association, *Municipal Refuse Disposal* (Public Administration Service, 1966), pp. 123–129.

component. Consumption of the *quantity* parameter of solid waste collection is rival: more for i is less for h and the marginal cost, for an additional quantity for any individual, is positive. There is no externality in the amount of waste removal; collection in this sense is divisible, and exclusion is possible.

However, this is not the only way in which i is affected by collection service in the community. There are externalities in the *quality* parameters (see Table 8.3), since individuals are jointly damaged by deteriorations in the environment resulting from their own or another person's actions on solid waste collection. The marginal cost of supplying this disservice to an additional consumer is zero, as is the marginal cost of servicing an additional consumer in the benefiting area for a given pollution abatement program. Exclusion is not possible.[9]

Disposal

As distinguished from collection, there is no direct or rival consumption of quantities of production units of solid waste disposal. There is no individual purchase of solid waste disposal in municipal or private collective disposal facilities, since individual benefit is insufficient to cover total unit costs.[10] The amount of disposal is determined by the collection decision—that is, all solid waste collected has to be disposed of in some manner. Aside from this exogenous determination of the amount of the service, this is a typical impure public good.[11] Given the agents linking levels b and c in Table 8.2, a decision on the amount of waste treated, the allocation of wastes among specific quality disposal technologies (including pollutant-control mechanisms) and sites, and the operation of such facilities determine the environmental quality changes with their mix of negative consumption components to each individual. The marginal cost of the consumption by an additional individual in the "benefiting" area of the change in environmental quality is zero.

Thus solid waste collection and disposal differ in the type of externalities, the importance of direct and indirect benefits, and the geographic benefit range. However, they are similar in their possession of public good qualities, which means that isolated market decisions on collection or disposal will result in an oversupply of the external diseconomy, pollutants.

182

TABLE 8.5

Quality Parameters of Solid Waste Disposal:
The Damages to Users of Environmental Resources from the
Amount and Nature of Air, Water, and Land Pollution

Human health
Animal health (livestock, fish, wildlife)
Nuisances: odors, smoke, visibility, psychological factors,
    unsightliness, fire and other hazards, insects
Material damages: metals, fabrics, rubber, paint, glass,
    building stone, electric current elements, etc.[a]
Crops and vegetation[b]
Recreation facilities
Loss of rare ecology, natural vegetation
Production costs and quality[c]

[a] Mostly from air pollution; different pollutants damage different materials.
[b] Agricultural solid wastes, depending on their distribution, can either be landscape pollutants or improve soil quality.
[c] The presence of unwanted pollutants in air, water, or land as production inputs can lead to increased costs (to remove the pollutants or maintain industrial equipment) and a loss in product quality.

SOURCES: *Air pollution:* For a general discussion of all the damages of air pollution, see Committee on Pollution, National Academy of Sciences—National Research Council, Waste Management and Control, *Report to the Federal Council for Science and Technology:* Publication 1400 (Washington, 1966), pp. 127 ff. (Hereafter referred to as NAS-NRC, *Report.*) Also see Harold Wolozin, "The Economics of Air Pollution: Central Problems," *Law and Contemporary Problems,* 33 (Spring 1968): 227–238. For the health effects, see NAS-NRC, *Report,* pp. 51 ff., pp. 77–84, and elsewhere; C. G. Golueke and P. H. McGauhey, *Comprehensive Studies of Solid Wastes Management, First Annual Report* (Berkeley: Sanitary Engineering Research Laboratory, University of California, May 1967): 82–86; and Eris J. Cassell, "The Health Effects of Air Pollution and Their Implications for Control," *Law and Contemporary Problems,* 33 (Spring 1968): 197–216. For an analysis of air and water quality as industrial inputs and their importance to economic development, see NAS-NCR, *Report,* p. 58.

Water Pollution: See NAS-NCR, *Report,* pp. 42–48, 70–76, 136–144; American Public Works Association, *Municipal Refuse Disposal* (Chicago: Public Administration Service, 1966), pp. 121 ff.; and for the difficulty in estimating health effects, see NAS-NCR, *Report,* p. 60.

Land Pollution: See NAS-NCR, *Report,* pp. 84–87, 130–136. Landscape pollution had been held inevitable for any disposal facility. Some recent evidence suggests this may no longer be true: compare George S. Blair, "Interjurisdictional Agreements in Southeastern Pennsylvania" (Fels Institute of Local and State Government, University of Pennsylvania, 1960), p. 92 and "Solid Wastes Pile Up While Laws Crack Down and Engineers Gear Up," *Engineering News-Record,* 182 (June 12, 1969): 31.

The "Demand" for Collection and Disposal

The private demand for collection

That there is a private demand for collection was pointed out earlier. The direct benefits must be substantial, since individuals do purchase this service: on a population basis, 32 percent of household solid wastes are collected by private collectors; 56 percent by public collectors; 12 percent by the individual himself.[12] Table 8.6 shows some further statistics for the solid waste industry.

TABLE 8.6

Solid Waste Statistics for the United States

	Pounds per person per day[a]
Waste generation	
household, commercial and municipal	7
industrial	3
Waste collection[b]	
household, commercial and municipal	4.73
industrial	.59

Expenditure on solid waste collection and disposal	$ Billion/year
municipal	1.7[c]
private waste management industry	1.8
individual or industrial	1.0
Total	4.5

[a] National averages, 1967.
[b] Does not include waste transported or disposed of by the waste generating individual or firm.
[c] Of which municipalities spent an average $1.42 per person per year for disposal and $5.39 per person per year for collection services.
SOURCE: R. J. Black, A. J. Muhich, A. J. Klee, H. L. Hickman, Jr., and R. D. Vaughan, "The National Solid Wastes Survey, An Interim Report," presented at the Annual Meeting of the Institute for Solid Wastes of the American Public Works Association, October, 1968 (Public Health Service, Solid Wastes Program), pp. 13–14, 48–50.

Even for this component of demand for collection, there is little information beyond an indication that pricing can affect the amount collected. A study by the American Public Works Association of twelve United States cities in 1959 shows a great range of quantities collected per capita from all sources, which the APWA attributes to collection practices, disposal regulations, and manner of disposal rather than differences in waste generation. In only one of the cities, San Francisco, were householders and commercial establishments charged for collection on the basis of quantity.[13] The figure of 794 pounds collected per capita per year in San Francisco was substantially below the next lowest value and the median figure of 1,430 pounds per capita per year. This suggests that there is probably some price elasticity, but we do not know how much—and that information is, of course, vital in evaluating the efficiency loss of pricing in excess of marginal social cost.

The APWA study assumes this price elasticity reflects a change in the size of and subscript to $L_k{}^i$, i.e., more own burning, littering, dumping, grinding, salvage. But there is another way in which price policy could alter $C_{j_i}{}^i$ that goes beyond the limitation to stages 3 and 4 in Figure 8.1. The individual could respond to pricing based on the quantity of waste by reducing his consumption of residual intensive goods (goods having a high ratio of residuals to service flow) that are made more expensive. If collection rates were based on disposability, these substitution effects could be even greater and more beneficial.

Additional problems in isolating price elasticity from information on waste generation, collection, and price rationing arise because (1) all variation in the difference between A^i and $C_{j_i}{}^i$ cannot be attributed to price, since some own disposal results from convenience,[14] and (2) the data that include statistics on collective purchases (apartment house, other "clubs") will reflect amount generated (need) and not "demand," unless the collectivity requires individuals to pay according to the amount of waste contributed.

There is no quantitative data on income elasticity. However, it seems reasonable to assume that income elasticity is positive throughout, i.e., that collection is a superior good.

Individual i rarely has the opportunity to specify the quality of collection desired. He purchases varying amounts of the available service quality, although the existence of several private collectors may modify this. The amount of service purchases, $C_{j_i}{}^i$, only reveals i's preferences for that quality service; his and the community's preferences for quality variations are unknown.

Even if we could determine private demand, the individual cost/

benefit calculations that are reflected in this function neglect the external benefits and damages that accompany private purchases or the absence thereof. Unless direct benefits greatly outweigh indirect benefits, allocation according to private demand will be suboptimal.[15] The aggregate demand for amount and quality consumption of collection by each i is the "sum" of private and public components. The total net benefit for an additional unit of collection of a specified quality from an individual i is positive as long as the marginal benefit of a unit reduction in own disposal by i exceeds the marginal direct and indirect costs of the unit charge in collection.

Inelastic demand: a waste generation model

Efficient allocation would require the knowledge and comparison of the cardinal welfare changes resulting from each discontinuous alternative with its distinct vector of environmental qualities. Empirical work on estimating total benefits is, however, very limited.[16] The output dimension does not present the same problem.

For many regions the social cost of any unrestricted own disposal (litter, burning, etc.) exceeds the direct collection and disposal cost for a wide range of options. Where this is true, efficiency requires that all solid waste generated be collected. The community demand function for the *amount* of collection from each household becomes a waste generation function: demand is replaced by need with no price elasticity in the relevant range.[17] This assumption of exogenous amount reduces the number of alternatives, though it doesn't help the calculation of total benefits from quality variations.

For an individual, one can write

$$A^i = f(U^i, Y^i, H^i, p, R, V, Y, G) \tag{1}$$

where

$A^i =$ a vector whose components are the amounts of different types of solid wastes generated by individual i

$U^i =$ the utility function of individual i

$Y^i =$ disposable income of individual i

$H^i =$ relevant personal characteristics (cultural background, etc.)

$p =$ a vector of final prices (including taxes) for the m goods and services available for consumption to individual i

$R =$ a vector whose components measure the amount of solid residual per unit service flow for each of the m goods and services. This summarizes the whole production decision on inputs, process technology, product innovations, and disposability

$V =$ a vector of salvage or recycling of waste components

$Y =$ the community income level, economic development, habits, and living standards, as well as current economic conditions

$G =$ local geography: weather, seasons, special community characteristics

Aggregate household waste production in a community of s individuals is of course the sum of individual waste generation:

$$A = \sum_{i=1}^{s} A^i$$

The empirical evidence on the importance of these variables is minimal. The APWA study observes that geography is important for composition but not for quantity and that seasonal variations may be substantial.[18] The literature supports the presumption that waste generation is a superior good. The income and substitution effects of growing affluence that increase waste generation especially include (1) the reduced need for salvage, thrift, and any effort at waste separation, and (2) the increased consumption of leisure-related products designed for convenience and rapid disposal.[19]

Costs of Solid Waste Handling

The paucity of data on all aspects of solid waste problems is evident throughout the literature.[20] The NAS-NRC study, for example, states that "a major shortcoming in solid waste management is the lack of accurate quantity and meaningful cost data, making it virtually impossible to evaluate alternative methods, thus perpetuating archaic practices."[21]

Some limited time-series and cross-section data exist; there are also engineering studies for certain processes and equipment, but not for all the available technology.[22] Both of these approaches have weaknesses in estimating industrywide cost functions because of (1) the extremely local character of the relevant variables, (2) rapid techno-logical change, which means that ex post statistical data or previous engineering studies will not indicate all the opportunities available,[23] and (3) the ex post data that do not distinguish supply and cost functions, which are unlikely to be identical.[24]

What can we say a priori of the cost function facing the solid waste manager? Hirsch examines the probable shape of the shortrun, quasi-longrun, and longrun average unit cost functions for horizontally and vertically integrated services as output expands with government growth or consolidation. He classifies collection as horizontally integrated, for which services he finds reasonable horizontal longrun and flat-bottomed U-shaped quasi-longrun average cost functions. He does not discuss disposal; however, the fact that existing facilities are often costly, used up, or illegal means that, for disposal, the decision-maker is more likely to face the longrun cost function. The literature on the costs of quality parameters is very limited.[25]

Collection

About 70 to 80 percent of total solid waste management costs is collection cost. The survey of solid waste practices coordinated by the Bureau of Solid Wastes gives some national statistics on collection practices and average costs (see Table 8.6). Another study contains cross-section data on collection costs from 166 cities throughout the United States and indicates constant or decreasing returns to scale with an average cost per ton of $17.60.[26] (See Table 8.7).

This is in line with the cost range in other reports.[27] These costs refer to the collection of controlled waste. In contrast, the average cost

TABLE 8.7

Collection Costs

Population (1,000's)	Cost per ton for median city ($)	Average cost per ton ($)
10–100	9.90	9.50
100–500	10.64	10.20
500 and over	12.78	24.05

SOURCE: Ralph Stone and Company, Inc., *A Study of Solid Waste Collection Systems Comparing One-Man with Multi-Man Crews*, Public Health Service Publication No. 1892 (GPO, 1969), p. 61, Table XVIII.

of collecting *an item* of waste discarded on a highway is estimated by Hershaft at $.32.[28] This enormous difference is important in evaluating any rationing of collection services that might result in increasing the amount of uncontrolled litter.

Existing statistical data are for a mix of service qualities, conditions, and factor costs. The evidence on scale economies for collection is inconclusive and the costs of environmental quality vector *j* are undetermined.[29]

Disposal

The data are also limited with respect to disposal. Table 8.8 summarizes the distribution of solid waste handling among different disposal technologies in 1966. Table 8.9 shows rough estimates of the relative operating and capital costs of the different options.

Disposal costs, too, are very dependent on such local conditions as: the availability, quality, and prices of scarce inputs (land and capital); the waste amount and composition, and thus the waste-creating sectors serviced by the facility and the local geography, industry, and climate; other service conditions, e.g., environmental qualities,

TABLE 8.8

Distribution of Solid Waste Processing Among Different Disposal Methods, 1966

Disposal Method		Percent of solid waste tonnage handled
Incineration		14.0
municipal, commercial, industrial		
and apartment house incinerators	6.0	
backyard household burners	8.0	
Sanitary landfill[a]		5.0
Open dumping[b]		77.5
Composting		0.5
Salvage[c]		3.0

    [a] Strictly defined: waste is covered daily.
    [b] Including open dumping, ocean dumping, and litter.
    [c] Including all salvage (from incineration, composting, sanitary landfill, collection, etc.).

    SOURCE: Arsen Darnay and William E. Franklin, *The Role of Packaging in Solid Waste Management, 1966 to 1976*, Public Health Service Publication No. 1855 (GPO, 1969), p. 120.

TABLE 8.9

*The Operating and Capital Costs of Different
Solid Waste Processing Technologies*

	Operating cost	Capital cost
	(estimated $/ton)	
Open dumping	$0.96	
Sanitary landfill	1.25– 2.50[a]	1,000– 2,000
Incineration	3.00– 8.00	3,500–10,000
Composting	3.00–10.00	3,500–10,000
Pyrolysis	3.00–10.00	5,000–10,000
Rail haul	4.00– 7.00	

[a] The cost ranges indicated are national averages. For a given locality, costs may be much higher. For example, in the Boston area, sanitary landfill costs range from $1.80–$5.72 and incineration from $3.42–$12.13. See Metropolitan Area Planning Council, Commonwealth of Massachusetts, "Solid Waste Disposal Program for Metropolitan Boston: Volume 1" (Boston, n.d.), p. viii.

SOURCES: R. J. Black, A. J. Muhich, A. J. Klee, H. L. Hickman, Jr., and R. D. Vaughan, "The National Solid Wastes Survey, An Interim Report," presented at the Annual Meeting ing of the Institute for Solid Wastes of the American Public Works Association, October, 1968 (Public Health Service, Solid Wastes Program), p. 29; Committee on Pollution, National Academy of Sciences–National Research Council, *Waste Management and Control. Report to the Federal Council for Science and Technology:* Publication 1400 (Washington, 1966), p. 196; D. G. Wilson, ed., "Summer Study on the Management of Solid Wastes: Final Report, Vol. 1" (Urban Systems Laboratory, M.I.T., September, 1968), p. 27; and Alex Hershaft, "Solid Waste Treatment," *Science and Technology* (June 1969), 38.

reliability required, present and future pollution emission or ambient standards, etc.; the market for disposal of by-products—site, heat, incinerator residue, etc.; the existing collection practices; and the available utilities, access roads, etc.

Sanitary Landfill. Land disposal is unique in that, while the degree of compactability, degradability, and density of solid wastes affects their suitability for such disposal, all forms of solid waste from all collection methods can be handled.[30] All other disposal methods require some land disposal to accept the wastes inappropriate to the method and/or the process residues.

In recent years, burial has been increasingly recognized as an inadequate way to remove materials from possible further influence on the environment; thus, site selection and operating procedures have grown in importance. It is possible to eliminate and control the potential negative externalities of land disposal: air pollution (dust, smoke, odors); disease breeding; insects; fire hazards; noise; unsightliness;

blowing litter; surface or groundwater pollution by leaching or gas migration, etc. However, this depends on meeting certain site characteristics (which requires knowledge of hydrological conditions that may be undeterminable or demand costly site investigation) and operation practices (daily cover, adequate compaction), the cost of which varies with local conditions (availability and quality of cover material, climate, drainage) and previous waste processing.[31] While scale economies do appear to exist, the range and amount are uncertain.[32]

Sanitary landfill is the cheapest disposal method (low capital and operating costs); its use suggests regional cooperation among localities of less than 50,000 to 100,000 population. However, the total costs of a disposal option include processing, disposal, and *haul* costs, even if, in fact, private collection charges cover haul costs. Above a specific length (which depends on local traffic, costs, etc.), the consideration of haul costs will add a region of increasing costs to the total unit cost curve and eventually will make sanitary landfill more expensive than alternate disposal technologies.[33]

The case for sanitary landfill disposal thus depends on the proximity of a suitable site, and the increasingly severe requirements for suitability point to the need for interlocal cooperation to permit the fullest utilization of this cheap and high-quality disposal method. High costs of land and/or haul result in cost advantages for technologies that reduce waste prior to land disposal or avoid it entirely by complete recycling.[34]

Incineration. Incineration changes solid wastes through combustion to varying amounts of some or all of the following: gases and odors; fly ash; water pollutants; heat; residue; salvage. The waste input and the design and operation of the incinerator, air pollution, and heat utilization equipment will determine the amounts of each item, which, given the price vector P, will allow the determination of the unit cost per ton of refuse processed net of by-product sales.

Refuse composition is important in determining the proportion that the incinerator can accept and the cost of the different outputs (amounts and qualities). Unfortunately, this basic datum is largely unknown, although it is evident that solid waste is changing in the direction of increasing incineration difficulty, defined in terms of combustibility, resulting amount of solid residue, potential damage to incinerator equipment, BTU value, and sulfur content.[35] (The last two are important in determining heat recovery and air pollution equipment possibilities, respectively.)

Since waste composition, on which potential air and water pollutant emission depends, is uncertain, incinerator outputs are not known with precision. Incineration has to cause some air pollution; what comes out of the incinerator must equal what goes into it, and it is illogical to transform all incinerator effluents back into solids. What the literature claims, however, is that adequate design and operation can reduce the potential negative externalities of air pollution (water vapor, toxic gases, odor, particulate matter) and of water and thermal pollution to tolerable amounts. Pollution reduction, however, depends on the sophistication and design of costly control equipment. There are pronounced economies of scale favoring cooperation among municipalities to create a minimum of waste handled of 1000 or more tons per day.[36]

The lack of knowledge of waste composition and the rapid changes in market conditions and in the technology of incinerator design, air pollution control equipment, by-product generation and utilization—all compound the estimating difficulty and the danger of relying on an industrywide cost function. A further problem results from the fact that statistical cost data cannot be assumed to represent optimum decisions, since the financing method often results in poor decisions. That is, as incinerator capital costs are met by bond issues, voters make selections about incinerators and other disposal technologies according to initial capital costs. This can lead to expensive and inefficient operation, because there is an inverse relationship between capital costs and operating costs.

Incinerator costs are high and uncertain. Nonetheless, increasing land scarcity points to the use of incinerator technology and therefore to the importance of clarifying unit costs and outputs of alternate equipment.

Recycling. Our earlier definition of solid wastes points to an alternative to waste creation and disposal that was partially included, without elaboration, in the discussion above of by-products of disposal. Solid residuals can be recovered and recycled, or they can be dispersed into some environmental media, causing unknown and possibly unknowable damage. The amount of waste and resulting pollution thus depends on the economics of recycling. The alternatives facing the solid waste manager or the longterm government policymaker therefore include not only recommendations on collection and disposal or production itself but also salvage and reclamation at many points in the waste creation-absorption cycle.

The logic of partial or complete recycling is based on the facts that: (1) solid waste "disposal" or processing technologies involve some environmental pollution and land utilization; (2) the value of environmental quality increases as income rises; and (3) there are limitations to the ability or benefit of reducing residual generation and composition at the source (the producer). The report by the Committee on Pollution of the NAS-NRC (National Academy of Sciences—National Research Council) therefore argues for an ultimate goal of a closed system with no waste and no pollution (i.e., an unbroken cycle from resource to user to reuse as a resource).[37]

The ways in which residuals can be converted into economic "goods" include recycling processed wastes, salvage and separation, and mining solid wastes.[38] While recycling techniques appear a promising alternative or complement to solid waste processing, information on costs and benefits on which to evaluate such choices is very deficient.

Government Intervention

A strategy to deal with the "solid waste pollution problem" includes not only local-regional decisions on solid waste management options but also national determination of the longrun least cost method of environmental improvement. Most of the literature on negative externalities and public goods assumes continuous functions and examines the success of alternate tax/price policies in reaching a static contract curve. However, for solid waste disposal and environmental pollution, it is vital to define longrun allocative efficiency to include welfare changes, not only from the operation of collection and disposal facilities and equipment and the excess burden of policy instruments, but also from competitive and discontinuous changes in variables at all points in the raw-material-extraction-production-consumption-reuse-waste-handling cycle.[39]

The large number of "beneficiaries" from improvements or deterioration in environmental quality creates the familiar "free rider" situation where one cannot expect private trade and negotiation to cause movement to optimality. "Bargaining" mainly takes the form of voting and otherwise selecting coercive taxes, regulations, etc.[40]

Government action to minimize the welfare loss from residual generation and absorption includes instruments to influence variables and functions throughout the waste generation-dispersal cycle shown in Figure 8.1 and abbreviated in equations (2) to (5) below, where equation (5) covers all the production-consumption decisions that influence the size and components of the vector A and assumes given preference functions and income distribution. See equation (1) on page 185.

$$W = f_W (J, \ldots \ldots) \tag{2}$$

$$J = f_J (Q, E) \tag{3}$$

$$AC = f_C(Q, A, B, P, I, F, S, T) \tag{4}$$

$$A = f_A (p, R, V, Y, G) \tag{5}$$

Where W = social welfare

f_W = the total benefit or damage function relating welfare to environmental quality

J = a vector of environmental effects whose components are positive or negative changes in pollution levels

Q = a vector of the quality parameters of waste handling whose components are the quantity of different pollutant emissions

E = environmental absorption ability and other agents that transform Q into J

f_J = the pollutant-pollution transformation function

AC = the longrun average unit cost for waste handling operations

A = a vector of waste quantities

B = a vector of by-products to handling A

P = a price vector whose components are the prices $\geq$ for the by-products and ≤ 0 (effluent charges) for the pollutant flows

I = a vector of input factors

F = a vector of input factor prices

S = the legal, political, financial, and physical service conditions affecting input requirements

$T =$ the given technology

$p =$ a vector of final prices for the m goods and services

$R =$ a vector of residual/service flow for the m goods and services

$V =$ a vector of salvage or recycling of waste components

$Y =$ the community income level, economic development, habits, and living standards

$G =$ local geography

The tools for intervention include: government operation, regulation and standards, incentives and subsidies, tax and price policies, education, research, and public relations.

From among the competing and complementary changes, the optimum policy is that for which the longrun net benefit is a maximum and from the equilibrium of which there could be no additional benefit from further expenditures on waste elimination and processing and absorption.[41] The range of noncomplementary strategies and of the information required indicates both the difficulty of action and the importance of the complete consideration of available alternatives. It is clear that the costs of, and time required for, information-gathering and the cost of inaction require decisions on one or several lines of attack under conditions of imperfect knowledge.

To see more clearly some of the difficulties in designing and enforcing an efficient policy and to distinguish the solid waste problem from the general pollution discussion, several possibilities for market intervention to influence waste creation or ration waste handling will be considered in the rest of this chapter. User taxes on environmental assimilative capacity will be examined first. Support for such taxes draws from several assumptions, including the following three concepts:

An equity concept: that the basis for the Pigouvian tax on a factor or product equal to the external diseconomy caused thereby is the placing of legal responsibility on the parties causing pollution and purchasing pollution-creating products for the cost of abatement to a non-Pareto relevant level or the compensation of the damaged parties.[42] An alternative concept (for example, the diverse group of damaged parties bribing the pollution producer to change behavior) could technically be efficient but leads to a different final distribution.

An efficiency concept: that the addition of a tax to production cost will, in forcing the producer to consider own and social costs, create an economic motive for his elimination of pollution and that he will respond to this by actions moving the economy toward the utility frontier.

A financing function: that user-tax revenue can be employed to finance waste processing and environmental improvement with less excess burden and redistribution than alternate revenue-generating schemes.

Pollution added tax on direct pollutant emission

An efficiently designed pollution added tax (PAT_E)—a set of effluent charges for the use of environmental resources to absorb pollutant emissions—would add a cost to industry (including solid waste disposal facilities) for marginal pollutant emissions equal to the present value of the additional social cost or damage such an emission would create. Ideally, the polluter would respond to the internalization of all costs by a continual search for a new least cost solution that would now count the external diseconomies as a production cost. Pollution would continue, but Pareto-relevant externalities would not.[43]

The enormous practical problems in designing and enforcing PAT_E include:

1. *Polluter response.* An effluent tax can lead to efficient allocation only if industry voluntarily responds to such charges by profit-maximizing behavior, selecting among alternate methods to reduce emissions (changes in production processes, raw material inputs, investments in pollution abatement equipment and by-product utilization, etc.) the least cost solution, including the payment of effluent taxes.[44] Profit-maximizing behavior is especially doubtful when the polluter is a publicly owned disposal facility. For solid waste disposal facilities, an efficient response to such effluent charges is unlikely, also, because of the lack of knowledge of the cost function, specifically the costs and effectiveness of pollution abatement equipment.

2. *Determining the actual charges, PAT_E.* Calculation of marginal social cost involves completely unavailable prior knowledge of ex post values for Q, E, f_J, f_W. Variations in each of these mean that efficient charges should change with regions, weather, technological change, economic conditions. There should be no uniform national charges.[45]

3. *Determining the redistribution.* The efficiency criteria only cover marginal payments. Charges on intramarginal emissions involve a value judgment on the desired distribution of costs and the amount of pollution at equilibrium. The windfall gains to beneficiaries of environmental improvement constitute another problem.

4. *Imperfections elsewhere in the economy.* Recent literature on second-best problems points to the need to modify marginal pricing requirements when imperfections exist elsewhere in the economy or in the industry generating the externality.[46]

5. *If the PAT_E does not correctly estimate social costs or does not cover all media and types of pollution (i.e., the whole Q vector).* This could result in decreases in some pollutant emissions and costly increases in others. In fact, most actual proposals cover only some air and water pollutants and not the more vague idea of landscape or soil pollution. Industries or solid waste managers might be induced to shift inefficiently from air polluting technologies (e.g., incineration) to land polluting ones.

6. *Elimination of Pareto-relevant externalities.* This involves the actual payment of compensation to the damaged parties.

7. *Monitoring problems (especially if mobile sources are included) and legal problems.*

However, even if the marginal opportunity cost could be calculated and would cause private firms and public disposal facilities to alter their behavior to cause "optimal" pollutant emissions, a more profound problem results from limiting calculations of negative externality to direct pollutant flows. Such limits neglect the future social cost of pollutant emission from handling the solid residuals that also result from production decisions. A new concept of externality to include pollution potential is required that recognizes, as in equation (5), that the amount and composition of solid waste is not exogenous.

Pollution added tax equal to disposal cost

To achieve longrun efficiency, a user charge must be applied in a discriminatory way at the interface of production and consumption decisions.[47] Such a set of user taxes, PAT_D, should add to the produc-

tion cost of a good or service that creates wastes in an amount equal
to the total direct and indirect cost of their processing, disposal, and
absorption by environmental media. That is,

$$p' = p + PAT_D$$
$$= p + MC + D$$

where

$p =$ a vector of final prices before the imposition of tax
PAT_D for the m goods and services.

$p' =$ a vector of final prices including PAT_D.

$MC =$ a vector of the marginal costs of direct waste handling (collection and disposal), net of revenue from
reuse, salvage, sale of by-products, for residuals from
each of the m goods and services.

$D =$ a vector of the damages (social cost) from any change
in J that results from the changes in Q that accompany waste handling for each of the m goods and
services.

Final prices would thus include discriminatory excise taxes that varied
with the good and locality. If firms responded as profit maximizers,
this change from vector p to p' would result in minimal residual generation through changes in R, specific products, raw material use, production processes, and residual recycling. Recent proposals hint at
such an efficiency tax.[48]

Such a PAT_D scheme has the further advantage of providing revenue to finance environmental improvement and solid waste disposal
at the same time it is changing waste generation.[49] However, all of the
problems in the design and enforcement of PAT_E noted earlier exist to a
greater extent for the more comprehensive PAT_D. Specific difficulties
include:

1. *The ex ante determination* of a unique MC, accompanying Q,
and resulting change in pollution vectors, from the disposal of each
product at each location;[50] of the marginal welfare loss, D (and thus
the local damage function, f_W); of the response pattern of individuals
and firms to the change in final price vector from p to p', given the fact
that MC and D depend on the final equilibrium production output

decisions, the actual disposal practices, and the final resulting aggregate J vector.

2. *Even a PAT_D accurately calculated to cover local direct and indirect residual costs will not be efficient when the purchase and disposal locations are not identical.* This, in addition to the political-legal problems of and producer objections to the uncertainty from implementing regionally discriminatory taxes, points to fixing PAT_D for each product on some form of national average MC and D.

3. *The actual loss in efficiency from $p' \neq$ marginal social cost.* This depends on the price elasticity for the products. In the extreme case of inelastic demand, suboptimal PAT_D would only affect distribution.

If the difficulty or cost of data collection, problems in the response and design, or political-legal facts hindering discriminatory sales taxation mean that any comprehensive pollution added tax based on total disposal cost would inevitably create a whole new set of excess burdens, an alternate way to finance disposal costs would be a general revenue tax on initial sale, PAT_F. Such a financing tax could be justified by vague user pay equity criteria, though it would not be efficient, having only income and not substitution effects.

However, PAT_D, PAT_F, or other revenue taxes should not be used to finance solid waste handling facilities without a simultaneous effluent tax or regulations on the quality of collective and individual waste disposal. Thus, only a combination of pollution added tax on disposability and emission, PAT_D and PAT_E, can correctly minimize A and the social and direct costs of its handling, given the available production, waste processing, by-product utilization, and salvage technology.[51]

This discussion has pointed out the requirements and problems in the use of price incentives to generate efficient behavior changes. A selection among, or combination of, market and other intervention is a complicated second-best problem requiring the evaluation of relative information cost, welfare gain, excess burden, political feasibility, inflationary impact, the availability of and need for additional local and/or national budget finance, the possibility for the sale of solid waste collection and disposal services, the cost of tax assessment, and the resulting final income distributions.

Other forms of intervention are not examined here in detail but several comments will be made to point out the equivalence in information required and allocation changes from either tax or regulatory measures and possible elements of a more piecemeal antipollution policy.[52]

Complete industrial regulation is an alternative to a PAT_D tax, but its efficient design requires no less information and lacks the advantage of decentralizing decisions and somewhat revealing preferences that can then be used to confirm or deny ex ante benefit calculations. If a PAT_D on all goods (or extensive government industrial regulation) is rejected as a means to influence R, product changes, and A, an alternative could be a system of selective rewards to industry based on product characteristics such as durability, separability, and reuse potential, or the quantity and disposability of the solid residuals of production and use.[53]

Equal knowledge and flexibility is required to design efficient effluent taxes or emission standards. Given the obvious difficulty in so doing, a suboptimization policy could be substituted for a welfare maximizing goal: for example, the objective function could be minimum cost to achieve or surpass a minimum environmental quality.[54]

Alternatives to general legislation are selective taxes or regulations applied locally or nationally on reuse, disposal, consumption, production, or raw material usage in situations where estimated social cost clearly exceeds "private" gain. For example, legislation might enforce, or tax incentives effect: reuse of soft drink containers, replacement of "tin" by steel cans, limitations on the use of polyvinyl chlorides, restrictions on certain fuel inputs, improvement of disposal practices by individuals, municipalities, and manufacturing industries (no open dumping, low quality incineration, backyard burning, litter, open collection trucks, etc.), and the elimination of abandoned automobiles.[55] The choice of taxes or standards depends on the positive model of individual and industrial response, the legal-political questions, and the ability to enforce standards rigorously, with more than token fines for infractions.

Uncertainties, high costs, and external benefits point to the continued need for direct federal support or conduct of research and/or first generation facilities in: solid waste disposal technology, waste reuse and salvage, by-product usage (e.g., heat generation), new products (e.g., degradable containers), monitoring technology, means to change E or f_w, data collection on the functional relationships in equations (2) to (5), including the environmental effects of new products.

Selling Collection and Disposal

User charges to individual consumers

It is crucial, in considering public utility pricing of solid waste services to individual consumers in a locality, to recall the distinction between collection and disposal, as noted earlier. Solid waste *collection* is a mixed good that has private benefits from which exclusion is possible, an increase in the amount or quality of which causes positive externalities to other consumers, from which exclusion is not possible, of an amount that depends on the alternative own disposal practiced by each consumer. Price rationing is possible, but the good should be subsidized to be efficient. Solid waste *disposal* is a public good: once an individual's refuse has been collected, he will not purchase its further processing since he receives no private benefits and cannot be excluded from the benefits and damages of the collective disposal operation. The price mechanism thus cannot be used for disposal alone.

User charges are clearly appealing as a means to solve the allocation, distribution, and financing decisions simultaneously. The efficiency of selling units of $C_{j_i}{}^i$ to each individual i depends on three economic relationships: the price elasticity of demand for collection; the social cost of the alternative to collection, $L_{k_i}{}^i$, for each i; and the excess burden of alternate financing methods.

If the demand for solid waste collection is price-elastic, and if this represents an increase in litter, burning, etc., and not a reduction in waste generation, then the pricing of solid waste per container or pound collected would lead to an increase in pollution and social damages from own disposal.[56] Given current United States conditions, it seems reasonable to assume that the social cost of any unrestricted own disposal exceeds the direct cost of collective handling, at least for some quality services. When this is true, overlooking the problem of actual compensatory payments, any policy that encourages an inequality between waste generation and collection results in additional welfare losses.

These two assumptions mean that collection should not be sold; an efficient price is a zero marginal price.[57] Thus, the sale of units of collection is not advisable; however, the rationing of service quality does not present the same problem. Individuals could be given the option to purchase variations in collection frequency, location, handling, etc. Unlike our assumption for quantity variations alone, quality components can be raised to a point at which the sum of the marginal private and public benefits equals the marginal cost of the quality change. The efficient price ($p = MC - MSB$) is positive. However, the information is not currently available to allow the determination of this price.

This discussion points to the use of taxes or nonmarginal charges as the means to finance the (minimum quality) collection of all waste generated and all disposal costs.[58] Depending on the availability of adequate cost information, the revenue projection, and the costs of implementation, a system of user charges for collection quality improvements can supplement such tax financing.[59] The actual provision of collection and even of disposal can be public or by a regulated private utility as long as the total cost is not met through charges on marginal purchases and all waste generated is collected.[60]

Rejecting the use of the price mechanism simultaneously to allocate and finance collection and disposal services leaves us with no decentralized mechanism to select among service quality options. As noted earlier, existing technology can, at a cost, eliminate all negative externalities; there is, however, no a priori reason to favor such expenditures. In the discussion below we will see how the fact of interlocal negotiation can help in selecting and financing decisions; however, for each locality there remain the problems of financing the local contribution to the joint activity, and of using a political mechanism to express aggregate preference functions.

In cases of clear inefficiencies and perverse "free rider" behavior, communities should enact and enforce a set of ordinances (varying with local conditions) against litter, unrestricted dumping and burning, and minimum collection and disposal regulations (on collection equipment, permissible noise, container types, storage location, unsanitary land disposal, permissible incinerator effluents, etc.).

User charges to municipalities

The efficiency of user charges to cooperating local governments for waste handling services depends on the same elasticity and externality criteria as those for individual sales discussed above. There are, however, significant differences in the interlocal situations that make pricing both an attractive and less essential allocation mechanism.

While voluntary cooperation limits the outcome to Paretian changes for each locality, the existence of a large area of potential gains from trade—especially for solid waste disposal, with its substantial Pareto-relevant pollution spillovers, possible savings from scale economies, and advantages to pooling scarce sites—means that municipalities have a great interest in creating conditions for their own and others' participation. The small-number negotiation increases the possibilities of determining a price and total cost-sharing policy such that those localities participate whose alternative behavior would cause a social loss to the cooperating group, and of collectively setting and enforcing service conditions that affect local production functions to assure desired marginal and total behavior. The small-number negotiation also increases the possibilities of approaching the desired investment for the area.[61]

The purchase of disposal by a community is comparable to the purchase of collection by an individual: the community has a private gain and can be excluded; the aggregate demand is the horizontal sum of the communities' demands. The positive marginal social benefit to surrounding communities that accompanies the purchase of high quality disposal from the joint facility means that the efficient price (specific to each purchasing community) is less than marginal cost. However, when club behavior results in substantial savings in direct and indirect costs, it is probable that pricing in excess of marginal cost (for example, to cover average cost) would not affect government decisions on participation in the joint venture or on the amount of waste there processed. Any risk of social and private loss from pricing in excess of marginal social cost affecting the purchaser's behavior could be eliminated by including in the cooperating agreement a requirement that the joint disposal facility handle all waste collected in the participating communities.[62]

When either economic or legal conditions make government purchases of disposal from the collective facility effectively price inelastic, the choice of a particular price policy (discriminating or uniform among municipalities or over intramarginal units—covering total, variable, or marginal costs) will not affect efficient utilization but only the distribution of consumers' and producers' surpluses, which will reflect the relative bargaining strengths. And, as long as there is no a priori cost-sharing arrangement but instead a bargaining situation, there is the possibility for optimum utilization and investment.[63] Henderson in a different context points to this special quality of the small-number situation:

Suppose a bridge is being contemplated by a small group of farmers who will have to bear the whole cost. Each will make up his mind as to what it would be worth paying to prevent the scheme falling through, that is, he estimates his consumers' surplus. If the cost is less than the aggregate consumers' surplus it will be built, if not, not. The farmers will meet and bargain, so that if the gain is considerable, the division of costs will depend largely on ability at bluffing, while if the gain is small, the costs will be distributed nearly in proportion to each farmer's consumers' surplus from the bridge. In this way a bridge may be built which no practicable system of tolls would finance and no user is prevented from using it because of a toll. But such a method is only practicable where the community is small. Where it is large, the individual contribution cannot be fixed by negotiation, but must be determined by some authority on the basis of objective criteria.[64]

This zero elasticity and small-number situation mean that there is no short- or longrun efficiency reason to favor marginal- or average-cost pricing over lump sum cost sharing arrangements based on population, assessed valuation, etc.[65]

There is an efficiency reason to oppose decentralized decisions and financing of waste handling not indicated in the above discussion. The economics of current solid waste practices limits the region of gainful cooperation: for example, sanitary landfill disposal has no scale advantages above a minimum size, and haul costs can offset the substantial advantages to scale in incineration. When the set of cooperating communities does not cover the entire region or population damaged by their disposal decision, the mechanism of negotiation cannot eliminate all Pareto-relevant externalities.[66]

Thus a national policy should include both the encouragement of regional cooperation and, in specific cases, either incentives to select a disposal technology that eliminates damages that spill outside the cooperating region, or laws or effluent taxes to internalize the social costs. The choice depends on the prevailing opinion on who should pay for environmental improvement: the residents in the area causing the pollution (who may be poor or have low preferences for environmental quality) or the benefiting and nonbenefiting citizens elsewhere in the nation.

Conclusion

In this chapter I have sketched a framework in which to describe the mechanism of solid waste generation and the policy options available to influence the amount and nature of pollutant emission from this source. The procedure emphasizes the interdependence among environmental media and the complex evaluation of competing alternatives required for longrun efficiency. The need for innovative solutions is evident from the simultaneous increase, with rising living standards, in waste generation and in the demand for a halt to pollution.

Our present knowledge of the costs of or benefits from, or even the amount of, the outputs (pollutants and by-products) of different waste handling options and of the existence, range, or importance of scale economies is extremely limited. A detailed evaluation, beyond the discussion above of alternate policies for intervention and the advantages of interlocal cooperation, would require currently unavailable information on cost- and preference-functions and diffusion models.

The costs of both information gathering and the attendant inaction point to the replacement of a Pareto-efficiency goal with an eclectic attack designed to eliminate obvious social losses and provide the information and advanced technology necessary to the selection and design of a high quality solid waste management system. This might involve:

1. Action to encourage interlocal cooperation in collection and disposal.

2. Regional or national emission standards or a pollution added tax on direct pollutant emissions to raise the costs of low quality waste handling.

3. National or regional product standards or market incentives (including a pollution added tax equal to direct and indirect disposal cost) to alter waste generation through changes in production processes, product design, or consumption patterns.

4. Federal or regional action to influence the use of disposal by-products and the profitability of salvage operations.

5. Federal or regional grants to local disposal operations to improve the service quality in cases of capital scarcity or substantial spillovers beyond the cooperating area.

6. Federal support of research and development in sophisticated recycling, separation, disposal and collection systems, and in means of expanding environmental absorption.

7. Support of economic research on the social costs of chronic and acute pollution, the cost and demand functions for collection and disposal services (including the demand for products having high disposal costs), and the effectiveness of different pollution added tax systems in internalizing the externalities of waste handling or product design.

NOTES

1. Regional Plan Association, *Waste Management: A Report of the Second Regional Plan* (New York, March 1968), p. 13.

2. Russell J. Peterson, "Solid Waste Disposal for the Omaha-Council Bluffs Metropolitan Area Planning Agency," prepared by Henningson, Durham, and Richardson, Inc. (Omaha, 1969). (Hereafter referred to as Peterson: "Solid Waste Disposal for Omaha-Council Bluffs.") Office of Local Government, State of New York, *Municipal Refuse Collection and Disposal, A Guide for Muncipal Officials* (September 1964); Aerojet-General Corporation and Engineering-Science, Inc., *A Systems Study of Solid Waste Management in the Fresno Area, Final Report on a Solid Waste Management Demonstration*, Public Health Service Publication No. 1959 (GPO, 1969); "Solid Waste Disposal Study, Technical Report, Genesee County, Michigan," prepared by a Special Service Committee: D. L. Robinson, T. R. Johnson, W. C. Kingsley, Jr., T. P. Mansour, and L. Nichols, with consulting services by Consoer, Townsend, and Associates in Michigan (Cincinnati: U.S. Department of Health, Education, and Welfare, 1969); Russell J. Peterson and Richard G. Glenn, "Collection and Disposal of Solid Waste for the Des Moines Metropolitan Area," prepared by Henningson, Durham, and Richardson, Inc., and Veenstra and Kimm (Cincinnati: U.S. Department of Health, Education, and Welfare, 1968).

3. *Waste Management*, p. 23 (see note 1 above). Also, Committee on Pollution, National Academy of Sciences–National Research Council, *Waste Management and Control, Report to the Federal Council for Science and Technology,*

Publication 1400 (Washington, 1966), pp. 22–23. (Hereafter referred to as: NAS-NRC, *Waste Management and Control*.) This total view of waste management is evident in the general equilibrium model described in Robert U. Ayres and Allen V. Kneese, "Production, Consumption, and Externalities," *American Economic Review* 59 (June 1969): 282–297. Also see Arsen Darnay and William E. Franklin, *The Role of Packaging in Solid Waste Management, 1966 to 1976*, Public Health Service Publication No. 1855 (GPO, 1969). Further information may be found in the extension of research sponsored by the Solid Waste Disposal Act of 1965 from the operation and development of disposal programs and facilities to techniques to increase waste recovery and reduce waste generation.

4. D. G. Wilson, "Rethinking the Solid Waste Problem," *Science Journal* 5A (September 1969), pp. 68–75. I use D. G. Wilson's definition of a "pollutant" as "any matter not at equilibrium with its environment" (p. 71). This includes not only liquid, gaseous, and solid pollutants but also thermal and acoustic ones. The conversion of solid wastes to solid, liquid, or gaseous pollutants points to the fact that one cannot talk of "a" quantity of "solid" wastes: for example, as a by-product of waste reduction, incineration converts solids to gases and suspended particulates; garbage grinding introduces solids directly into the watercourses; sanitary landfills may result in pollutants leaching into groundwater. This interdependence among quantities of wastes in different states is a reason to reject partial analysis, limited to one environmental medium or waste state.

5. Let us say an individual has preferences for clean furnishings and good health. With perfect knowledge, this could be converted to a preference for clean air (the absence of specific air pollutants) and no land pollution (no accumulated refuse with the attendant insect and rodent breeding). With perfect information this could be viewed as a derived preference for land disposal and/or air pollution control equipment and frequent refuse collection and/or better storage containers. This equivalency between production and consumption units is discussed by James M. Buchanan, *The Demand and Supply of Public Goods* (Rand McNally, 1968), p. 60. The problem remains, however, that the mechanisms linking the different levels are unknown and the functional relationships undetermined and perhaps undeterminable.

6. Werner Z. Hirsch, "Cost Functions of an Urban Government Service: Refuse Collection," *Review of Economics and Statistics* 47 (February 1965): 87–93. Hirsch discusses some of the service-quality features listed here.

7. C. G. Golueke and P. H. McGauhey, *Comprehensive Studies of Solid Wastes Management, First Annual Report* (Sanitary Engineering Research Laboratory, University of California, Berkeley, May 1967), p. 5. "Disposables" are really "discardables." See Darnay and Franklin, p. 109. Also, see NAS-NRC, *Waste Management and Control*, which develops the concept of the earth as a closed system, where liquid, gaseous, and solid by-products are stored or recycled, with some environmental media acting as transport systems of limited reservoir capacity for pollutants (fresh water, atmospheric resources) and others as sinks for quality factors (land, ocean).

8. There is no economic literature integrating solid waste collection and disposal services into this recent public goods theory, although Hirsch (see note 6

above) has briefly discussed the public good nature of these services. A "pure public good" is nonrival in consumption: any change in the size of the consuming group will not change the benefit received by anyone in the group resulting from some given level and quality of service; the marginal cost of servicing an additional consumer is zero. Exclusion is therefore not desirable, even if possible. All individuals need not receive the same flow of homogeneous quality consumption units, but the relationship between the similar or dissimilar consumption components is fixed.

9. This is what Buchanan (see note 5, p. 67) has called a type 2 externality in which *"each person's consumption or utilization of the service* must be considered separately, as an independent public good." Spillover per unit of collection depends on the specific consumer, since the damages of noncollection depend on the form of own disposal—the disposal vector k_i—which can vary among the s consumers.

10. This is not entirely true. Individuals sometimes pay a price for collection that includes a charge covering the operation of disposal facilities; however, this does not mean that the amount purchased reveals a demand for disposal. In addition, they pay to install home garbage grinders and may pay to use collective facilities for own disposal. There is some private benefit in the change in land values for properties located near new or changed disposal sites. While individuals do not consume quantities of disposal directly, the aggregate of individuals that form a community does. If a locality has the option of exporting wastes to another community's disposal facility, it replaces collective own disposal with the collective purchase of collection and haul. The community and its residents benefit in relation to the amount transported and the negative externalities of own disposal versus collection-haul and interlocal spillins. "Demand" in the economic sense for disposal is not to be confused with political pressure or the lack of it, as is done in the Omaha-Council Bluffs study; see Peterson, "Solid Waste Disposal for Omaha-Council Bluffs," p. TS–1, which notes that sanitary nuisance-free disposal is available "when the public demands proper service."

11. In Buchanan's terminology, it is a type 1 good in which the act of producing the good supplies benefits jointly to a number of individuals, in contrast to the type 2 good defined in note 9. Richard M. Musgrave describes these type 1 and 2 externalities, labeled "social goods with limited spillovers" and "interdependent utilities," in "Provision for Social Goods," paper presented at the meeting of the International Economics Association, Biarritz (1966).

12. R. J. Black, A. J. Muhich, A. J. Klee, H. L. Hickman, Jr., and R. D. Vaughan, "The National Solid Wastes Survey, An Interim Report," presented at the Annual Meeting of the Institute for Solid Wastes of the American Public Works Association, October, 1968 (Public Health Service, Solid Wastes Program), pp. 10, 19. The share of solid waste collected by private contractors is much higher for commercial and industrial wastes—62 and 57 percent, respectively. A description of various collection arrangements (municipal, contract, private) can be found in Peterson, "Solid Waste Disposal for Omaha-Council Bluffs," pp. I–14, I–15. In using private collection to indicate elasticity, I am assuming that all such purchases are voluntary, though this is probably not the case.

13. American Public Works Association, *Municipal Refuse Disposal* (Chicago: Public Administration Service, 1966), pp. 25–28. In NAS-NRC, *Waste Management and Control*, p. 132, it is noted that, when collection service is private, as much as 25 percent of the population may refuse purchase.

14. APWA, *Municipal Refuse Disposal*, pp. 22–23. Thus household and yard rubbish may be burned to avoid the unsightliness of accumulation until collection day; apartment houses burn some garbage and rubbish for convenience. See Peterson, "Solid Waste Disposal for Omaha-Council Bluffs," p. II–7, for estimates that 6 percent of residential solid waste is burned on site.

15. This inefficiency is often incorrectly diagnosed as resulting from the insufficient moral sensibility of the consumer. Thus in Peterson, "Solid Waste Disposal for Omaha-Council Bluffs," p. I–15, it is noted that the private system is deficient since it "places the responsibility for the collection of waste with the individual property owner who may or may not have a conscientious concern for the problem." However, the fault is not with private provision or individual selfishness but with distribution based on private purchase and the fact that the individual cannot correctly represent social benefit in his purchase decision. Government provision distributed with user charges would create the same inefficiency.

Estimates in the literature on the importance of externalities in collection range from "relatively minor" by Hirsch, p. 87, to the statement that storage and transportation create 50 percent of the environmental problems of solid waste management, 33 percent from storage alone (Aerojet-General Corporation and Engneering-Science, Inc., *A Systems Study of Solid Waste Management in the Fresno Area*, pp. A–1, IV–11, IV–14; see note 2 above.) (These two studies differ in that the former covers residential refuse collection and the latter industrial, agricultural, commercial, and municipal.) As an example of social costs, studies show that, in some cities, 90 percent of the insect population is bred in garbage cans.

16. Judith M. Guéron, "The Economics of Solid Waste Management: the Provision of Public Services with Interindividual and Interlocal Externalities" (unpublished Ph.D. dissertation, Harvard University, 1970). On pp. 39–53 there is a discussion of total benefit functions, estimation techniques, and decision models.

17. The aggregate demand curve for collection from each individual i is a vertical line intersecting the quantity axis at A^i. The aggregate demand for C is vertical from A. For sufficiently costly collection-disposal possibilities, however, this curve will show some elasticity.

18. APWA, *Municipal Refuse Disposal*, pp. 27–28. Some of the other variables in the equation are also discussed in Chapter 2 of this source.

19. The relationship between the stage of development and industrial production and the amount of residuals requiring absorption, and the environment's absorption capacity, are discussed by Ayres and Kneese, pp. 82–83.

20. *Waste Management* (see note 1, p. 69). The list of areas of waste management that require further study in this report indicates the very limited current knowledge. The lack of basic quantitative information on even the amount of

waste treated is evident in many empirical studies, which therefore include lengthy sections on the amount and composition of solid wastes; see, e.g., Russell J. Peterson and Richard G. Glenn, "Collection and Disposal of Solid Waste for the Des Moines Metropolitan Area," prepared by Henningson, Durham, and Richardson, Inc., and Veenstra and Kimm (Cincinnati: U.S. Department of Health, Education, and Welfare, 1968). The total absence of the information necessary to any calculation of the costs of handling different waste components is recognized in Darnay and Franklin, pp. 110 ff. Darnay and Franklin show disposability to be determined by qualitative judgments and information on the technical difficulty of processing various waste materials in present facilities. And the NAS-NRC study points to the lack of information of the pollution from different waste management options, and the lack of adequate data to determine diffusion models (see note 3 above, pp. 51–52 and 172).

21. See note 3 above, p. 177.

22. Engineering Foundation, "Solid Waste Research and Development, II," Engineering Foundation Research Conference, Wayland Academy, Beaver Dam, Wisconsin, July 22–26, 1968 (New York: Engineering Foundation); *Proceedings of the 1968 National Incinerator Conference* (New York: American Society of Mechanical Engineers, 1968); and *Proceedings of the 1966 National Incinerator Conference* (New York: American Society of Mechanical Engineers, 1966). Many of these engineering studies of different solid waste processes and equipment point to the limited current information.

23. D. G. Wilson, ed., "Summer Study on the Management of Solid Wastes: Final Report, Vol. 1" (Urban Systems Laboratory, M.I.T., September, 1968). This study exemplifies the fact that longrun solid waste handling recommendations often, unlike those for many public services, emphasize the development of new, or reorganization of existing, technologies, due to land scarcity, increasingly severe legal restrictions on output quality, and high costs.

24. H. S. Perloff and L. Wingo, Jr., eds., *Issues in Urban Economics* (published for Resources for the Future, Inc., by The Johns Hopkins Press, 1969), pp. 487–490, 495–496, 512–522. Hirsch's discussion of supply functions in this essay points to the questionable validity of the production function as a positive model of the decision-maker's options.

25. Harold Wolozin, "The Economics of Air Pollution: Central Problems," *Law and Contemporary Problems* 33 (Spring 1968), pp. 230, 237. Wolozin, in a discussion of the costs of air pollution abatement, supports a presumption of non-linearity, with areas of increasing and decreasing costs; however, he notes contrary assumptions elsewhere in the literature.

26. Ralph Stone and Company, Inc., *A Study of Solid Waste Collection Systems Comparing One-Man with Multi-Man Crews*, Public Health Service Publication No. 1892 (GPO, 1969), pp. 59, 61, Table XVIII.

27. Darnay and Franklin, p. 113; and Aerojet-General Corporation and Engineering-Science, Inc., *A Systems Study of Solid Waste Management in the Fresno Area*, p. II–10. Darnay and Franklin estimate national average cost of collection and disposal at $9/ton with local variations as high as $25/ton. The Fresno study reports a median range of collection costs of $10 to $16 per ton.

28. Alex Hershaft, "Solid Waste Treatment," *Science and Technology,* (June 1969), p. 36.

29. On the one hand, many writers assume scale economies and cite examples from engineering studies and actual interlocal cooperation. Thus, F. L. Heaney, in discussing the advantages of regional cooperation, notes that "savings in collection costs through the formation of intermunicipal solid waste districts often are greater than those obtained in connection with disposal." See *Proceedings of the 1968 National Incinerator Conference,* pp. 123–124. An example is Oyster Bay, New York, where twelve separate garbage collection districts were consolidated into one town-operated collection system. Substantial savings resulted from the more efficient use of crews and vehicles. See New York State, Joint Legislative Committee on Metropolitan Area Study, "Metropolitan Action: A Six-County Inventory of Practical Programs" (Albany, January, 1960), p. 33; also, Peterson and Glenn, pp. 3–34, 40. On the other hand, Hirsch's statistical study of the St. Louis area found no scale economies for communities ranging from 200 to 225,000 pickup units (see note 6 above).

30. Darnay and Franklin, pp. 124, 133–134, discuss in detail the importance of these three characteristics and the extent to which they are met by different waste materials. The degree of compaction, for example, determines land requirements, future land use, and the possibility of disease breeding. This study points to the lack of information and the weakness of laboratory measurements. Ralph Stone (see note 26 above) also discusses the relationship between compaction and landfill costs and benefits. Normal landfill facilities cannot handle very bulky objects or radioactive or chemically hazardous substances.

31. APWA, *Municipal Refuse Disposal,* pp. 91, 121–132; Golueke and McGauhey, pp. 86–89; and NAS-NRC, *Waste Management and Control,* pp. 135–136. These sources contain discussions of the possibilities of leaching and gas migration. The APWA book describes and classifies disposal sites and the wastes they can accept without causing pollution. See also Peterson, "Solid Waste Disposal for Omaha-Council Bluffs," pp. I–9, I–12.

32. Office of Local Government, State of New York, *Municipal Refuse Collection and Disposal, a Guide for Municipal Officials* (September, 1964), p. 42; APWA, *Municipal Refuse Disposal,* p. 118; Metropolitan Area Planning Council, Commonwealth of Massachusetts, "Solid Waste Disposal Program for Metropolitan Boston: Volume 1" (Boston, n.d.), pp. 5–6. These studies all indicate mild economies of scale but differ as to whether the point at which such economies cease is at 250 or 500 tons per day.

33. New York, *Municipal Refuse Collection,* pp. 43–46; Massachusetts, "Solid Waste Disposal Program," pp. 12–15.

34. Sanitary landfill is land intensive, requiring approximately 70 percent more land than open dumping or incineration. In addition, when all wastes are so handled, site characteristics are more stringent than for landfill of previously processed waste.

35. An example of a study of refuse composition is E. R. Kaiser's "Chemical Analyses of Refuse Components," pp. 84–88. See *Proceedings of the 1966 National Incinerator Conference.* A discussion of the change in solid wastes over

time can be found in Golueke and McGauhey, pp. 35–38. Incinerators can accept 80–90 percent of the total volume of municipal refuse and reduce it in volume by 70–80 percent and in weight by 60–80 percent. Ideally, noncombustibles (25 percent) would be separated prior to incineration. Unsuitable refuse includes large objects that clog hoppers, hazardous materials, large metal appliances, and tree trunks.

Darnay and Franklin, pp. 121–143, have a very useful discussion of the importance of the five characteristics noted above and their use to calculate a disposability difficulty index for incineration and other disposal methods for different waste components, given the absence of direct cost information. Certain materials (glass, plastic, aluminum) damage incinerators, which points to the need for advances in separation technology.

36. Fernandes, "Incinerator Air Pollution Control," in *Proceedings of the 1968 National Incinerator Conference*, pp. 101–116, has a most thorough discussion of efficiency and relative capital and operating cost of different pollution control equipment. See also Stephenson and Cafiero, "Municipal Incinerator Design Practices and Trends," in *Proceedings of the 1966 National Incinerator Conference*. An example of the elimination of pollution and nuisances sufficient to allow the location of an incinerator in an expensive residential area is given in "Solid Wastes Pile Up While Laws Crack Down and Engineers Gear Up," *Engineering News-Record* 182 (June 12, 1969): 28–32. The relationship between air pollution control equipment and resulting increase in water pollution is discussed in *Waste Management*, p. 15, and D. G. Wilson, "Rethinking the Solid Waste Problem," *Science Journal* 5A (September 1969): 69.

Discussions of the optimum region served by an incinerator emphasize large savings from cooperation. Wilson in "Summer Study" (M.I.T.), p. 13, urges the formation of cooperative units processing a minimum of 1000 tons per day. Additional discussion of the extent and range of scale economies can be found in Heany, "Regional Districts for Incineration," pp. 123–28, in *Proceedings of the 1968 National Incinerator Conference*.

37. NAS-NCR, *Waste Management and Control*, p. 89.

38. The following sources contain descriptions of composting: APWA, *Municipal Refuse Disposal*, pp. 279–315; Wilson, "Summer Study" (M.I.T.), pp. 12, 16, 42; "Solid Waste Disposal Study, Genesee County, Michigan," pp. II–27, II–41 (see note 2 above); and Golueke and McGauhey, pp. 100–104.

Descriptions of pyrolysis may be found in Wilson, "Summer Study," and Golueke and McGauhey.

Descriptions of wet oxidation and other methods of indirect recycling may be found in Golueke and McGauhey.

Descriptions of current salvage technology and profitability for specific materials may be found in Golueke and McGauhey, and Darnay and Franklin.

A futuristic description of mining solid wastes may be found in Bernard J. Eastlund and William C. Gough, "The Fusion Torch, Closing the Cycle from Use to Reuse" (Division of Research, U.S. Atomic Energy Commission, May 1969).

39. I assume that the goal of government intervention in externality generating industries is improved efficiency and not redistribution per se.

40. The welfare loss and redistribution from "free rider" behavior are defined and examined in James M. Buchanan, "A Behavioral Theory of Pollution," *Western Economic Journal*, 6 (December 1968): 347–358; and Buchanan, *Demand and Supply*.

41. The rigorous definition of this policy would require ex ante knowledge of potential costs and benefits for all individuals and regions from all changes in equations (2) to (5).

42. F. Treney Dolbear, Jr., "On the Theory of Optimum Externality," *American Economic Review* 57 (March 1967): 90–103. Dolbear discusses the importance of legal responsibility in determining the amount of pollution and the distribution of gains from trade. More general arguments for user taxes versus other financing methods can be found in William S. Vickrey, "General and Specific Financing of Urban Services," *Public Expenditure Decisions in the Urban Community*, H. G. Schaller, ed. (published for Resources for the Future, Inc., by The Johns Hopkins Press, 1963); Alexander M. Henderson, "The Pricing of Public Utility Undertakings," *Manchester School of Economics and Social Studies*, 15 (1947), pp. 223–250; and Buchanan, *Demand and Supply*. Of course, the employment of such a tax assumes that environmental absorption capacity is an "economic good."

43. Wolozin, "The Economics of Air Pollution" (see note 25 above); George Hagevik, "Legislating for Air Quality Management," *Law and Contemporary Problems* 33 (Spring 1968): 369–398; and Ayres and Kneese. These sources give examples of the arguments for and against effluent taxes. $PATE$ is not a sumptuary tax on environmental resources since, though discriminatory, the aim is not to charge in excess of marginal social cost. However, like sumptuary excise taxes, it is designed mainly, not to produce revenue, but to discourage use.

44. Wolozin, pp. 235–236, reviews the meaning of alternative assumptions of management response for the efficiency of effluent taxes. The welfare loss from the lack of response to market incentives varies for the environmental media. See Paul Gerhardt, "Incentives to Air Pollution Control," *Law and Contemporary Problems* 33 (Spring 1968): 265. Gerhardt points out that for water pollutant emissions the revenue from the payment of the effluent tax as an alternative to treatment at point sources can be used to finance subsequent river purification. For air pollution, however, there is no secondary offsite treatment option.

45. The argument against regionally discriminating standards or taxes could be justified if efficiency were not a national goal, if designing a Pareto-efficient effluent tax were considered impossible, if the redistribution pattern from a more efficient tax were considered undesirable, or if the negative effects of discriminating taxes on firm location, decision-making, etc., were considered excessive.

46. James M. Buchanan, "External Diseconomies, Corrective Taxes, and Market Structure," *American Economic Review* 59 (March 1969): 174–177; and R. Rees, "Second-Best Rules for Public Enterprise Pricing," *Economica*, 35 (August 1968): 260–273.

47. Darnay and Franklin, p. iii, point out the need for action at the production-consumption level, in a discussion of what results from the current absence of market or other forces that relate manufacturing and purchasing decisions to disposal cost in the packaging industry. "To a large extent the aims of packaging and of solid waste disposal are mutually exclusive. The packager wants—and technology

is developing—a container that won't burn, break, crush, degrade, or dissolve in water. The waste processor wants a package which is easy to reduce by burning, breaking, compaction, or degradation." While this industry is extreme in the positive relationship between the value of package design and disposal cost, the same elements exist elsewhere. Various means and aims of government intervention are discussed by Darnay and Franklin, pp. 157–160, including the pros and cons of a general use tax and selective deterrent taxes; they note, among other things, the political and legal problems and the absence of disposal cost data.

48. The "use tax" in Darnay and Franklin, pp. 147–148, is not our PAT_D, since the social cost of the externality (waste generation) is limited to the direct disposal cost. Recent government proposals mention a form of environmental use tax. See President Nixon's State of the Union Message to Congress: "[Concern for limiting the abuse of common property resources] requires that to the extent possible the price of goods should be made to include the costs of production and disposing of them without damage to the environment." (New York Times, Jan. 23, 1970, p. 22.)

49. Of course, the efficient user tax does not specify intramarginal payments. Given this and the tendency toward increasing returns in solid waste handling, actual tax revenues could be less than, more than, or equal to total direct disposal costs. An alternative PAT_D could be $PAT_D = D + AC$, where AC is the average cost of waste handling for the specific product.

50. That is, considering local variations in cost elements (F, P, etc.) and variables determining F_J (local meteorology, existing pollution, etc.).

51. Charles Plott, "Externalities and Corrective Taxes," Economica 33 (February 1966): 84–87. Plott's argument that, in the absence of rigid joint production of a good and an externality, one must be sure to place the corrective tax on the externality itself, points to the need for simultaneous product and effluent taxation.

52. Once one decides where to act in the flow chart (Figure 8.1), i.e., on which variables in equations (2) to (5), one can in theory use taxation or regulations to induce the desired changes. However, a positive model of the economy's actual reaction to different stimuli may mean this is not so. Some of the arguments for legal and economic intervention are discussed in NAS-NCR, Waste Management, pp. 203–221. Examples of piecemeal recommendations can be found in the same source and in Darnay and Franklin, pp. 170–171.

53. Wilson, "Summer Study," p. 19, includes suggestions for legislation to require companies that introduce new materials above a certain volume either to dispose of these materials themselves or be able to recommend an acceptable ultimate disposal procedure.

54. Cassell argues against a fixed emission standard and defends a maximum quality regardless of cost policy that cannot be supported on efficiency grounds. Thus he states that air pollution requirements should specify control "to the greatest extent feasible employing maximum technological capability." See Eric J. Cassell, "The Health Effects of Air Pollution and Their Implications for Control," Law and Contemporary Problems 33 (Spring 1968): 215.

55. An example of a financing and incentive scheme for abandoned automobiles is described by Goddard in Engineering Foundation Research Conference,

1968. High taxes or regulations banning the use of certain products contain the risk that they will be maintained when such usage no longer results in a welfare loss. In calculating the marginal opportunity cost of the use of polyvinyl chlorides, for example, one must continually review developments in the cost of hydrochloric acid separation in incinerators, the ability to add a material to PVC so that it will not cause HCl when burned, and the costs of substitute materials. (See comments by Robert Vaughan and Austin Heller, *New York Times,* Oct. 28, 1969, p. 49.)

56. If the elasticity were zero, the choice of a price policy would affect only distribution and not marginal decisions, and thus allocation.

57. Even if one could, without excessive expense, determine the amount collected from each pickup unit and household, the assumption that marginal social benefit (*MSB*) exceeds marginal cost for all units of collection until $C = A$ means that a 100 percent subsidy is an efficient price. However, this need not be the unique efficient price and, if the marginal evaluation were positive at $A^i = C_{ji}^i$ for all i, positive prices would exist that would not reduce collection.

It would seem that enactment and enforcement of legal measures to change the social cost of the price elasticity (i.e., laws against littering, dumping, burning) would eliminate the undesirable effects of price rationing. However, if such measures were effective in eliminating the own disposal option, the "price" becomes a unit user "tax." Decisions to use such a tax depend on the cost of the enforcement of these regulations and whether it would lead consumers to change waste generation.

Another possibility—the sale of collection and the simultaneous provision of a public disposal facility that individuals can use at no charge—could solve the problems of price rationing if it was successful in eliminating any other own disposal. Of course, insofar as solid waste collection cannot be efficiently sold to individual consumers, disposal costs cannot thus be financed.

58. Examples are: general taxes (property and income taxes); specific taxes (head tax, dwelling tax, the combination of a uniform lump sum payment with a levy based on elements of cost incurred, e.g., distance); federal grants. For solid waste services, the special element of general usage and roughly equal per capita waste generation means that financing through general taxation does not have the usual disadvantages of redistribution from users to nonusers. Seventy percent of U.S. cities pay for disposal out of general tax revenue. Property taxes have the advantage of making empty land share in the financing of disposal facilities whose improvement is capitalized in the land value. The advantages of different tax and price schemes for public services are discussed in Vickrey and Henderson (see note 42 above).

59. However, the revenue from such a user charge would not even cover the total cost of the quality improvements it allowed, given the positive externality and subsidization.

60. A decision between the two would depend on the comparative efficiency of the two management systems; the existence of and ability to take advantage of scale economies; the desired system of charges; the investments required; the value given to and ability to offer service variability (the present system of pri-

vate firms with overlapping jurisdictions does this, at a cost); the importance of joint management or coordinated decisions on collection and disposal.

61. In this section, I do not detail the common financing tools or the available forms of cooperation, the most common of which are joint agreements to finance disposal facilities serving several communities or to establish joint authorities or special districts and service contracts for the sale by one municipality of the use of its disposal facilities by another. See Advisory Commission on Intergovernmental Relations, *A Handbook for Interlocal Agreements and Contracts*, Report M–29 (GPO, March, 1967), pp. 53–57, 109, 166; and George S. Blair, "Interjurisdictional Agreements in Southeastern Pennsylvania" (Fels Institute of Local and State Government, University of Pennsylvania, 1960), pp. 108–113, for a general discussion of financing procedures and examples of such agreements and contracts. Of course, the arguments in the section above on individual consumers are directly relevant when a joint authority or special district considers selling collection or disposal services directly to individual consumers in the participating communities; only now there are additional problems of interlocal redistribution and further limitations on financing any gap between total costs and revenues, since joint authorities rarely have tax power.

62. Peterson, "Solid Waste Disposal for Omaha-Council Bluffs," p. IV–1, recommends that each locality grant the regional solid waste agency exclusive operating authority. Such regulations are enforceable in sales to governments but not in sales to individual consumers. An alternate procedure would be to include in the agreement a set of standards for each participating locality's own disposal behavior and thus eliminate negative spillouts.

63. In fact, negotiation costs and the uncertainties in the costs and the nature and distribution of benefits of disposal operations hinder the possibility for efficient negotiation. Additional inefficiencies can result from incorrect representation by local governments of aggregate community preferences for environmental quality. To allow rational voter decision-making, the costs and damages of the expensive noncomplementary options should be presented as fully as possible, indicating the annual direct and indirect costs as well as the initial capital expenditures. The specific way a locality chooses to finance its share of the joint cost will of course determine the distribution and excess burden in that locality.

64. Henderson, p. 232.

65. I.e., in this specific case, a zero price would not result in excess "consumption" of disposal processing services, since a community's demand for disposal is given by individual waste generation that is independent of such community price policies.

66. When spillovers are contained within the cooperating region, federal aid can create inefficiencies, since the cooperating municipalities will not have to "bear the whole cost." Federal aid to, or interference in, cooperative disposal projects can be justified if benefits spill out of the cooperating region, if local capital scarcity would lead to undesirable decisions on disposal quality, or if the interlocal distribution resulting from unrestrained negotiations conflicts with national equity goals.

Chapter **9**   STEPHEN L. FELDMAN

Waste Collection Services:
A Survey of Costs and Pricing

POPULATION growth and concentration of population in congested areas make public provisions for waste disposal a necessity. Economic growth and higher incomes mean more production, more consumption, and hence more waste. Although estimates vary as to the amount of refuse, the total production of refuse has been rising exponentially, and a further rise has been projected.

Production of refuse in 1965 was estimated at about 4.5 pounds per capita per day (lb./cap./day) or 1,650 lb./cap./year. If we assume that the trend from 1955 to 1969 will continue, the annual increase of wastes will be about 0.07 lb./cap./day or 25 lb./cap./year. Superimposing the projected population growth on the per capita increase in wastes gives an increase in anticipated total refuse production in the United States from 150 million tons in 1963 to about 260 million tons per year in 1980, i.e., by more than 73 percent. Of this increase of 110 million tons, about half will result from the per capita increase in amount of refuse produced and about half from the expected total population increase. By 1985, total refuse production is expected to double its 1963 amount.[1]

New processes, products, and technology have altered the nature of refuse. Wet garbage was formerly a much more important collection and disposal problem for sanitation workers than it is today. In many towns and cities one of the familiar solutions to the problem was to

---

Stephen L. Feldman was a summer student intern when he wrote this chapter. He is now a graduate student at The Johns Hopkins University and is Visiting Lecturer in Geography at Towson State College, Baltimore.

allot garbage to farmers for hog feed at no cost. In recent years, in cities where garbage grinders are allowed, the percentage of garbage has decreased from its former 25 percent of total refuse to 10 percent.

Among the new products and processes that increase the amount of household solid wastes are plastic containers, metal and plastic wrappings, disposable bottles, and other disposable products.[2] Industrial wastes have been increased by new methods of construction and demolition.[3] Some of the new products and processes have created especially costly disposal requirements; the outstanding example is, of course, disposal of radioactive materials.

Waste Collection

Collection services, whether municipal or private, depend on frequency of pick up, the degree of separation of materials required, the types of onsite burning permitted (outdoors, in fireplaces and furnaces, and in domestic and apartment house incinerators), the extent of use of food waste grinders, and restrictions in the amounts or types of refuse collected. Since the mid-1950s there has been a per-capita decrease in quantities of garbage and ashes collected, but an increase in combustible rubbish, particularly paper and plastics.[4] The decrease in collections of ashes is traceable to greater dependence on oil, gas, and electricity rather than coal and wood as fuels for heating and cooking. Increased packaging by food companies and less extensive culling, trimming, and food preparation by the housewife have offset the decrease in garbage. On balance, these changes have resulted in a great increase in the volume of refuse, but a much lesser increase in its weight. Refuse has less weight per volume in the 1960s than it had in the preceding decade.

Collection services are variously supplied: by municipalities, by private contractors for a municipality, or by private firms contracting directly with private customers. Municipal services are provided directly as a responsibility of the government. However, a number of local governments exercise their responsibility for refuse collection through contracts with one or more private firms. Many of the contracts are made for five-year terms, although the period is sometimes as short as one or two years or as long as ten years. In practice, contracts lapse more often than they are renewed, with the result that cities are faced with successive periods of adjustment to new contractors. Of the cities using the contract method, 78 percent employed only one contractor, according to a survey of 995 cities made by the American Public Works Association (APWA) in 1964.

Private collection of refuse involves arrangements between the consumer of the service and the provider of the service, without the mediation of the governmental unit. In this case consumers can, of course, act individually or collectively. Private collection fills an important need where no publicly managed or financed system is in operation, or where municipal or contract collection service is not provided for certain kinds of properties or certain classes of refuse.

Of the cities reporting in the 1964 APWA survey, 45 percent had complete municipal service, and 20 percent had partial municipal service. Larger cities frequently used combined municipal and private collection; 44 percent of the cities with populations over 100,000 fall in this category. An additional 34 percent of the larger cities reported municipal collection only, whereas only 8 percent provided the services under contract, and 6 percent had private collection only. Municipal services in some places are restricted to residential households; in other places commercial establishments and sometimes even industrial firms are included. There has been in recent years some increase in private collection privately arranged. In the 1955 APWA survey of cities, 11 percent reported using this method exclusively, and an additional 11 percent reported private arrangements in conjunction with either municipal or contract collection. By 1964, the survey indicated that 13 percent of the cities used private collection exclusively, and 21 percent used some combination of private and municipal or contract collection. Most noticeable was the increase from 6 percent to 15 percent for cities employing both municipal and private collection.[5]

Within each category of service there is considerable variation in the nature of wastes and in the scope of the collection service. Table 9.1 classifies refuse materials and the originating household, commercial establishment, or industry. Table 9.2 shows the class of refuse collected as reported for 1964 by the 1,142 collection systems in the 995 cities.

As an additional index of service quality, the frequency of municipal collection is shown for residential and commercial areas. In residential areas over 95 percent of the collections were made once or twice a

TABLE 9.1

Classification of Refuse Materials

Refuse (solid wastes)	Garbage		Wastes from the preparation, cooking, and serving of food Market refuse, waste from the handling, storage, and sale of produce and meats	From: households, institutions, and commercial concerns such as: hotels, stores, restaurants, markets, etc.
	Rubbish	Combustible (primarily organic)	Paper, cardboard, cartons Wood, boxes, excelsior Plastics Rags, cloth, bedding Leather, rubber Grass, leaves, yard trimmings	
		Non-combustible (primarily inorganic)	Metals, tin cans, metal foils Dirt Stones, bricks, ceramics, crockery Glass, bottles Other mineral refuse	
	Ashes		Residue from fires used for cooking and for heating buildings, cinders	
	Bulky wastes		Large auto parts, tires Stoves, refrigerators, other large appliances Furniture, large crates Trees, branches, palm fronds, stumps, flotage	From: streets, sidewalks, alleys, vacant lots, etc.
	Street refuse		Street sweepings, dirt Leaves Catch basin dirt Contents of litter receptacles	
	Dead animals		Small animals: cats, dogs, poultry, etc. Large animals: horses, cows, etc.	
	Abandoned vehicles		Automobiles, trucks	
	Construction & demolition wastes		Lumber, roofing, and sheathing scraps Rubble, broken concrete, plaster, etc. Conduit, pipe, wire, insulation, etc.	
	Industrial refuse		Solid wastes resulting from industrial processes and manufacturing operations, such as: food-processing wastes, boiler house cinders, wood, plastic, and metal scraps and shavings, etc.	From: factories, power plants, etc.
	Special wastes		Hazardous wastes: pathological wastes, explosives, radioactive materials Security wastes: confidential documents, negotiable papers, etc.	Households, hospitals, institutions, stores, industry, etc.
	Animal and agricultural wastes		Manures, crop residues	Farms, feed lots
	Sewage treatment residues		Coarse screening, grit, septic tank sludge, dewatered sludge	Sewage treatment plants, septic tanks

SOURCE: All tables in this chapter are based upon reports and statistics of the American Public Works Association.

TABLE 9.2

Class of Refuse Collected

(Class of refuse collected in 1964 by 1,142 collection systems including
municipal, municipal-contract, and private collectors)
(in percent)

Class of Refuse Collected	Yes	No
Combined refuse	76.0%	24.0%
Garbage	94.6	5.4
Combustible rubbish	93.1	6.9
Noncombustible rubbish	93.3	6.7
Abandoned automobiles	7.6	92.4
Industrial refuse	34.5	65.5
Contractors' building or demolition wastes	16.9	83.1
Ashes	78.0	22.0
Dead animals	42.5	57.5
Tree debris	35.5	64.5
Bulk refuse	43.0	57.0
Evictions	35.9	64.1

week with almost an equal division in the number of communities
having twice-a-week and once-a-week collection. Commercial collections tended to be far more frequent (Table 9.3).

TABLE 9.3

Frequency of Collection

(Frequency of combined refuse collections from residential and commercial
areas during the summer by municipal collection agencies in 1964[a])

Frequency of collection[b]	Residential	Commercial
Once a week	46.7%	8.1%
Twice a week	48.5	11.4
Three times a week	3.6	3.6
Four times a week	0.0	1.1
Five times a week	0.0	11.7
More than five times a week	0.0	29.3
Fortnightly	0.5	0.0
Monthly	0.0	0.0
Variable	0.7	34.8
Cleanup drives	0.0	0.0
	100.0	100.0

[a] The frequency of collections during the winter varies only slightly from that in the
summer.
[b] Number of communities responding: 418 residential; 359 commercial.

A 1965 survey by the APWA's Solid Wastes Committee found that residential refuse varied from 1.1 lb./cap./day to 3.2 lb./cap./day, with a median value of 2.0. Commercial and industrial refuse collected ranged from 1.3 lb./cap./day to 2.6, with a median value of 2.0 also.

Cost of Refuse Collection

A basic requirement in assessing the feasibility of prices or user charges as devices to ration, guide investment in, and finance refuse collection services is a full understanding of costs. Ideally, the costs to be counted should measure the opportunity cost of using resources in the productive activity of providing refuse collection. These costs will cover the direct operating costs of collection and disposal as well as the appropriate capital costs.[6] Use of capital costs requires that an appropriate price or value has to be chosen for assessing the actual opportunity cost of capital. If the capital costs are not measured properly or if they are ignored, then the resulting total cost figures will be misleading. For instance, if land fill is used for disposal, the cost equation should include a measure of the rental the land could obtain in its next best alternative. If the costs are to be measured over several time periods, an appropriate rate of social discount needs to be determined.[7]

Emphasis should be placed on deriving the total cost function. From the total cost function, the incremental costs, the marginal costs of varying the service level or the quality variables, can be determined. If user charges are to be cost determined, then incremental or marginal cost is the appropriate cost concept to use. For instance, if different groups in the city prefer a different level of service and a higher quality of service, then by knowing the appropriate marginal cost, we can specify a user charge that will reflect these differential costs and lead to an efficient allocation of resources.

Because of the variety and diversity of refuse collection services among cities, it is difficult to present an actual cost function. The variables that seem most important, however, are quantity and types of waste; quality such as frequency and the pickup location; service conditions such as the pickup or population density and land-use mix; factor prices, and technology. These are discussed in turn.

Output: measures and types

For many purposes, the measure of output (or the basic service unit) can be tons (or some other measure of weight) per time period. Measurement procedures differ from city to city, making comparison difficult. The most common measure is pounds per capita per calendar day. Data may also be kept on a volume basis. But the measure of volume (cubic yards) varies greatly with the type of truck (compactor, non-compactor), the loading crew method, and the completeness of loading. In a modern compactor truck, the density of refuse can vary from 150 lb./cu. yd., if the crew neglects to load it properly, to more than 500 lb./cu. yd., if the refuse is properly loaded and compacted. A load of noncombustible rubbish with high ash content, in contrast, may weigh as much as 1,000 lbs./cu. yard.

The quantities of total refuse collected per capita among cities ranged from 856 lbs./year to 2,373 lbs./year, the latter including demolition wastes. The general trend of median values for the annual total refuse collected is as follows: 794 lbs. per capita in 1939; 834 lbs. per capita in 1955; 1,430 lbs. per capita in 1957–58; and 1,435 lbs. per capita in 1965.

Seasonal variation. Variations in the quantities of various classes of refuse produced within a community are affected by seasonal changes.[8] For example, yard rubbish may account for an appreciable part of total refuse in spring and summer, and cities in cooler climates may have large quantities of ashes during winter.

A Purdue University study for 1959–62 of combined residential refuse collected in Milwaukee, Indianapolis, and Bloomington found, for example, that the peak monthly quantity varied from spring (April) to fall (October). The maximum quantity varied from 14 to 31 percent above the mean. Seasonal lows occurred in winter or spring (December to March) and were 9 to 27 percent below the mean. Similarly, research at the Department of Geography and Environmental Engineering at The Johns Hopkins University on the monthly variation of refuse production for Baltimore City revealed that June and February deviations are approximately +7 percent to −9 percent respectively. The data were compiled over the eight-year period 1962–69.[9]

Daily fluctuations in the amount of refuse collection usually exceed seasonal variations. The largest collections occur after weekends and holidays. Increased tonnage may also be a result of weather variations, with snow, rain, or frost adding considerable weight to loads. When collection occurs more than once a week, the daily amounts during the first half of the week may be as much as double those of the last half. This reflects not only the scheduling with uneven number of days between, but also the greater amount of refuse discarded over weekends. Daily variations in Baltimore City's refuse collection system indicate a 50 percent difference in wastes collected on Mondays through Wednesdays over that collected on Thursdays through Saturdays.

Density. Knowledge of the density of various classes of refuse is needed as a guide for the selection of proper collection equipment. Refuse is usually weighed in the collection vehicles, and the influence of the type of vehicle on the density can be very significant. The density of uncompacted refuse is continually decreasing; however, the better compaction technology being attained in modern trucks appears to have more than offset this up to now. According to the APWA 1965 survey, the density of combined refuse after compaction varied from 300 to 750 lb./cu. yd., with the median being 475 lb./cu. yd.

Classification of the physical components of refuse. Refuse may be classified into two major categories: organic wastes (mostly combustible) and inorganic wastes (mostly noncombustible). The APWA has broken down these two general classes into such physical components as (1) garbage, paper, wood, plastics, grass and trimmings, and (2) metals, glass, ashes, ceramics, stones, and dirt. The type of refuse will of course affect the type of equipment and handling procedures.

The Purdue University study cited earlier found the composition of "average municipal refuse" to be rubbish (combustible) 64 percent, garbage (including fats) 12 percent, and rubbish (noncombustible) 24 percent. Paper was the predominant subcategory, accounting for 42 percent of the total.

How refuse should be classified and what the measure of output should be are questions that can be resolved only when a particular cost analysis is to be done. To compare intercity costs, for instance, weighted indices of output would have to be used. For an investigation of costs in a specific city, finer analysis would be appropriate.

The amount of refuse collected is, of course, less than the amount produced. The difference depends on the amount of self-disposal by industry and residents; the efficiency, intent, cost, and timing of the service; and the amount of refuse salvage before the regular collection. The amount of material salvaged from household or business refuse is closely related to the market value of the materials.

Service quality

Refuse collection has a variety of quality dimensions that may be defined and identified. These quality dimensions vary greatly among cities. Diversity in practices can be illustrated by examining the broad service patterns of the 1,142 collection systems for which the data were summarized in Table 9.2.

Limitations of service. Cities may collect garbage only, or they may collect everything except garbage, counting on the use of household and commercial grinders for garbage disposal. Likewise, commercial rubbish and ashes are sometimes included. In addition to excluding entire *classes* of refuse from municipal service, cities may exclude certain *kinds* of materials from the classes of refuse that are collected. Yard rubbish, grass cuttings, tree branches, furniture, building materials, cartons, boxes, market refuse, and dead animals are typical of the kinds of refuse that various municipal agencies may decide not to handle.

Another limitation on service is the denial of refuse collection to certain classes of property. This is most often applied to commercial properties or multiple dwellings, but other forms of property-class limitations are also found. Such limitation will obviously affect the output and will consequently complicate attempts at cost analysis among cities. In general, *quantity* limitations are uncommon.

Frequency of service. The character of collection service also varies with the frequency with which the several classes of material are removed from a householder's premises (see Table 9.3). When refuse is removed often, fewer or smaller containers are needed, garbage does not putrefy and is less likely to harbor flies, other vectors of disease, or rodents.

Studies of the Chicago collection system suggest that an increase in frequency of collection from one to two times per week produces increases in per capita refuse production. These increases ranged from 21 to 63 percent, and were shown to be independent of seasonal variations.[10]

Different districts or classes of property within a single city may receive service with varying frequencies. For instance, commercial areas will usually be visited five or six times a week for garbage pickup. On the average, because of increases in the rate of putrefaction, summer months require more frequent collections.

In his cross-section cost analysis of the St. Louis urban area, Hirsch found that the frequency of pickup was a significant variable affecting the average cost of collection and disposal per pickup. Approximately 60 percent of the variation in the average cost (given the level of other variables) could be explained by the variation in the frequency of service.[11]

Pickup location. The location of the refuse container at the time of collection is an important factor in the quality of the collection service. In some cities the refuse is picked up from back doors, back porches, or even basements, to be carried by the collectors to the street or to the alley for loading. Other cities demand that householders do a part of the work themselves by placing the containers on the curb or in the alley before the scheduled pickup time. Such local decisions on division of work between the householder and the collection agency are of considerable importance in judging the relative quality and the costs of service. Those cities that remove ashes and other refuse from basements have been shown to spend somewhat more than those giving less complete service. The tradeoff between cost and better quality is indicated in Hirsch's study, which shows a significant positive effect on costs as well as quality if the location for pickup is changed from the curb to the back of the house.[12]

Other quality variables can be defined. Hirsch, for instance, includes the type of equipment, the disposal method, and the nature of the pickup. For purposes of analysis, the type of equipment and the disposal method would certainly seem to affect the service inputs.

Effect of service conditions

Various physical, legal, and political factors may affect the refuse collection services. One such factor is population density, i.e., the pickup density of a given jurisdiction. The closer the pickup locations

to each other, the shorter the distance the trucks have to drive between locations.[13] Pickup density results in economies of scale, although for collection services such economies are hard to define and
measure because of the degree of variation in services rendered.

Density also influences methods of collection and the types of
equipment used. The full range of methods and procedures may be
available to the large, dense community. However because of congestion costs and the fact that the haul from collection routes to disposal
or transfer sites is generally longer, the methods that go best with
short hauls become uneconomic. For the smaller city, in contrast, there
is a definite limit on the methods and equipment that can be economically and effectively used; the total amount of work to be done may
be too small for some technology that is highly efficient in a larger city.

Zoning and the resultant land-use mix affect collection services.
The composition of the refuse to be collected is different for residential
units than for nonresidential units, and there are variations in the
type of collection between industries, e.g., the refuse of a chemical
plant is different from that of a retail store. The land-use mix also has
a feedback on the pickup density. For instance, if there is no public
service provided to commercial establishments in an area with both
residential and commercial activities, the collection crews would have
to travel greater distances between each residential pickup. The haul
after pickup to the refuse disposal site might become longer, the route
of trucks more roundabout, the density and nature of the traffic encountered greater.

Pronounced differences among intracity personal income groups
produce large differences in per capita waste production and collection services. Based upon 1970 Baltimore data, a total cost curve
(linear) was calculated utilizing a sample of 10 percent of the total
number of the city's refuse routes. Total cost and quantities of refuse
were determined on a per capita basis. Quantities of refuse in high-
income areas of the city (average family income—$10,000–$14,000)
ranged from 120 to 230 lbs./cap. per month. In contrast, low-income
routes (average family income—$3,000–$5,000) produced 30 to 60
lbs./cap. per month. Collection and disposal costs in high-income outer
city areas for mixed refuse were roughly estimated to be four times
more than those of low-income inner city areas.[14]

Management activities of the city also affect cost. Supervision will be affected in part by political factors and in part by the internal organization of the refuse service itself. Some elected officials may fear that any real effort to enforce regulations might cause them to lose political support, consequently regulations dealing with such matters as the separation of refuse, the provision of containers, and the placing of refuse for collection may go unenforced. Most administrative officials, however, are fully aware of the added costs and decreased effectiveness that inevitably stem from a lack of proper internal organization and the neglect of modern techniques for personnel administration, planning and programing, scientific job analysis, route determination, field reporting, and cost analysis.

Hirsch's study suggested that costs may be affected by the "nature of the contractual arrangement"—that is, whether the service is provided under contract by a private firm, or by the city, or through any number of other arrangements that result from limitations and restrictions placed on the refuse collection, although his empirical analysis did not find this variable significant.

Price of inputs or factors

Factor prices will affect costs in several ways. Among communities, the relative differences in factor prices will be crucial for comparison. The mix of labor and capital inputs will affect costs and in turn be affected by relative prices. A decrease in capital costs relative to those of labor will cause cities to substitute capital for labor (and vice versa) in the absence of technological change.

Labor expenses (for collectors, truck drivers, and helpers) normally account for 60 to 80 percent of the total cost of refuse collection. Data from 995 cities (APWA, 1964) show hourly wages ranging from under $1 to more than $3, with wages in most cities (411) being in the $1.75 to $1.99 range. Thus, even ignoring all other cost differences, differences in wage rates alone can easily account for a two-to-one intercity differential in expenditures. The size of labor costs and the intercity difference of labor costs suggest that for any cost analysis, particularly one that is designed to consider the implementation of a user charge, careful specification of the labor input is required.[15]

State of technology and productivity

The state of technology determines for a given level and quality of refuse collection the set of inputs required. The state of the art is changing and careful analysis is needed to isolate the impact of new methods on costs. For a city considering optional refuse collection services, the state of technology must be investigated explicitly because of the different input requirements as well as future changes that may occur. For instance, garbage grinders in homes represent a technological change in refuse collection. Home trash packaging is a still more novel technological change.

Experience shows that the installation of home garbage grinders, which are substitutes for collection services, must be regulated through local building codes or other ordinances. For instance, the installation of home grinders may be prohibited by ordinance until adequate sewers are available or capacity of the local sewage treatment plant is enlarged to a level sufficient to accept and process the additional sewage that would result.

The cost of installing a grinder in a house under construction may be as little as $75, but installation in a house already built may cost $125 to $200 or more. Average annual costs to a householder for a $150 garbage grinder with a 20-year life expectancy installed when the house is built are approximately $17. For the same installation in an old house costs are probably about 50 percent more, so that annual costs are about $22. In either case, the cost is somewhat higher than that of an efficient garbage collection and disposal system, so that home grinders must be justified on grounds other than direct cost.

Financing Solid Waste Collection

Financing the collection of refuse cannot be considered apart from the financing of disposal operations. From the perspective of the user, the two processes, collection and disposal, are part of a single service. Or, stated differently, the retailing in this instance runs prior to the processing phase.

If prices for refuse collection are to be imposed, they must be set at the retailing phase, except as intermediate transactions take place between collections and transfer or disposal operations. Several local governments may join together for disposal operations, for example, or government units may carry out the disposal from some central point for private collectors.

According to the APWA, refuse collection at present is financed by the following methods:

1. *General fund taxes.* Regular appropriations are made from general revenues obtained from annual property taxation, from state-collected, locally shared sales taxes, from local income taxes, or similar sources.

2. *Separate property taxes.* Separate ad valorem taxes are levied, usually on the same basis as general property taxes, for a specific purpose such as refuse collection.

3. *Service charges or fees.* Charges made to householders and other producers of refuse are on the basis of the measured, estimated, or presumed amount of waste removed, or assessments of time and costs accrued to remove such wastes.

4. *Can and container rental charges.* These are rates or charges that provide refuse producers with municipally owned receptacles, including paper or plastic bags. They cover the cost of emptying, servicing, maintaining, and replacing such containers.

5. *Miscellaneous revenues.* These may include proceeds from fees for private collection licenses, fees for salvage privileges, sale of salvaged material, sale of collection privileges, etc.

General revenue financing through the property tax or other general tax sources is the most common procedure. Such financing is justified by the benefits to the neighborhood that accrue in reduction of health hazards and in the maintaining of land and property values as a consequence of waste collection. Thus, general financing helps to ensure that such neighborhood effects are not impaired by individual user preferences. However, the handling of commercial and industrial wastes is often separately financed. And, in general, the wide variation in volume and kind of industrial wastes, and the concomitant difficulties in their handling, suggest privately financed collection, or at least a system of special public charges.

Service charges for waste collection are increasingly coming into use. In general, municipal fees and charges are based on the measured, estimated, or presumed amount of waste material removed from the premises. Such charges are established, to the extent practicable, according to the amount and kind of service rendered, and in proportion to the benefits derived by individuals and businesses producing the refuse. Often, service charges do not cover full cost but are used in conjunction with general revenue. In 1964, at least 425 cities were known to be using service charges to finance all or part of their refuse collection. This represented a rise of 75 cities within a decade.

Table 9.4 shows the methods of financing solid waste collection in 850 communities in 1964. Service charges were reported by about

231

TABLE 9.4

Methods of Financing Refuse Collection Services,
by Size of Community, 1964

Population Size of Community	Total No. of Communities in Sample	Per Cent	Distribution of Financing Methods			
			General Tax	Service Charge	Tax and Serv. Chg.	Other
5,000–9,999	180	100.0	47.2%	39.0%	13.4%	0.6%
10,000–24,999	307	100.0	46.0	38.0	16.0	0.0
25,000–49,999	190	100.0	51.5	32.7	14.2	1.6
50,000–99,999	93	100.0	58.0	28.0	12.9	1.1
100,000–999,999	74	100.0	59.5	27.0	13.5	0.0
1,000,000 and over	6	100.0	66.6	0.0	33.4	0.0
Total Sample	850	100.0	50.1	34.9	14.4	0.6

two out of three communities responding to the survey; in about one out of three, service charges were the exclusive method of financing. Smaller communities made more extensive use of service charges than larger jurisdictions. In none of the municipalities with populations of one million or over were service charges used exclusively.

Refuse collection by contract is more frequently financed by straight service charges than municipal collection itself. The municipal services, on the other hand, often use a combination of tax and service charge financing. Collections are financed through service charges or general tax, plus service charge arrangements, in 47.6 percent of the communities removing refuse by contract.

Charge setting

Cities have adopted many different methods of setting fees for refuse collection service. Some are based on the estimated or average cost of conducting the collection and disposal, others on the benefits received by the individuals or properties serviced. Most of the rate structures are relatively simple, and in many cases it has been contended by the APWA that the rates are so simplified that they do not provide an accurate measure of cost-of-service or of benefit. However, the actual charges may be too small to justify the greater expense and overhead cost of applying more accurate but much more complex measures such as different intracity billing.

Various methods of measuring service are employed by cities in setting service charges for refuse collection.[16] Though a single base is sometimes used, it is more common to find two or three different measures used in combination. Not infrequently the base or combination used in the residential district differs from that in the commercial or industrial district. The rate structures include:

1. Uniform charges for each residential household, or each service.
2. Rates based on the number of rooms, which approximate in a very rough way the benefit derived or the difference in the cost of collection.
3. Number of dwelling units or apartments in the structure.
4. The number of containers, which provides a reasonable estimate of

TABLE 9.5

*Examples of Residential Rates Charged for Collection
of Unrestricted Quantities of Refuse*

City	Service Charge Period	Single Unit Rate	Each Added Unit in Building
Little Rock, Arkansas	Year	$12.00	—
Camden, Arkansas	Year	9.00	—
Burbank, California	Month	1.00	0.75
Compton, California	Month	1.00	—
Pomona, California	Month	1.50	0.50
Alhambra, California	Month	1.35	0.50
Fort Collins, Colorado	Year	5.00	—
Springfield, Illinois	Quarterly	4.50	—
	Semiannually	8.00	—
	Annually	14.00	—
Perry, Iowa	Month	1.50	—
Salina, Kansas	Month	1.50	—
Monroe, Louisiana	Month	2.50	—
Sidney, Nebraska	Year	18.00	3.00
Albuquerque, New Mexico	Year	21.00	12.00
Grand Forks, North Dakota	Month	1.55	1.30
Warren, Ohio	Quarter	4.50	—
Oklahoma City, Oklahoma	Month	2.50	2.50
Shawnee, Oklahoma	Month	1.00	0.75
Corpus Christi, Texas	Month	1.35	—
Midland, Texas	Month	2.00	2.00
Rock Springs, Wyoming	Quarter	2.25	1.50
Quebec, Quebec, Canada	Year	9.00	9.00

TABLE 9.6

Residential Rates Based Primarily on Quantity of Refuse Collected

City	Where Collected	First Container[a]			All Over Base Amt.		
		Cap.	Rate	Per.	Ea. Addl.	Rate	Per.
Santa Clara, Calif.		30 gal.	1.25	Month	30 gal.	.45	Month
St. Petersburg, Fla.[b]	Alley, rear house line	30 gal.	2.25	Month	30 gal.	.40	Month
Sterling, Colo.		20 gal.	1.00	Month	20 gal.	.25	Month
Spokane, Wash.	Alley or 25' from curb	30 gal.	1.25	Month	30 gal.	1.00	Month
	25' to 125'	30 gal.	2.00	Month	30 gal.	2.00	Month
Tacoma, Wash.[c]	25' or less	30 gal.	1.10	Month	30 gal.	.80	Month
	25' to 75'	30 gal.	1.50	Month	30 gal.	1.05	Month
	75' to 120'	30 gal.	1.85	Month	30 gal.	1.25	Month
	Over 120'	30 gal.	2.20	Month	30 gal.	1.50	Month
Edmonton, Alberta	Alley	1 cu. yd.	Free	Week	cu. yd.	1.00	Week

[a] The first container, or the basic quantity, is usually charged at a higher rate in order that certain expenses, such as readiness to serve and route travel will not be duplicated.
[b] Second 30 gallons, 65¢ per month.
[c] 25¢ added for each flight of stairs.

the quantity of the material removed and may, therefore, be a good index of volume of service.

5. The size of containers, which permits a fairly accurate measure of the quantity of refuse collected.

6. The measured volume of refuse, which provides a fairly accurate measure of quantity.

7. Time consumed in making collections, which might include loading and haul time.

8. The amount of floor space in the building served, which approximates the extent of service rendered.

9. Frequency of collection.

10. Distance from collection vehicles to containers.

11. Topography.

12. "Readiness to serve" charges are usually associated with bulky wastes, leaves, or commercial refuse when the quantity of wastes produced varies from time to time.

Service charge rates for residential properties. Residential refuse collection fees tend to be highest in private collection systems, and lowest for municipal collection systems; fees for refuse collection by contract tend to be in the middle. The main characteristics of the rate structures now in effect for residential properties in typical cities have

TABLE 9.7

Monthly Residential Rates Based on Quantity and Frequency of Refuse Collection

City	Quantity or Size of Container	Collections per Week				
		1	2	3	5	6
Berkeley, California[a]	30 gallons	$ 1.00	$ 2.00	$3.00	—	$ 6.00
	40 gallons	1.10	2.20	3.30	—	6.60
	50 gallons	1.75	3.50	5.25	—	10.50
Fresno, California[b]	30 gallons	19.20	33.00	—	—	73.20
	30 gallons	13.80	17.40	—	—	61.20
Eugene, Oregon	1 can	1.60	3.20	4.20	—	—
	2 cans	2.75	5.50	7.50	—	—
	ea. addl. can	1.00	1.00	1.00	—	—
Paducah, Kentucky	96 gallons[c]	1.00	3.40	6.00	—	—

[a] For District No. 1. Other districts slightly higher.
[b] Per year.
[c] Three cans.

been tabulated and are presented in Tables 9.5, 9.6, and 9.7[17] In numerous cities the rates established for residential areas do not take into account the quantity of refuse presented for collection. Some cities have flat rates in combination with other measurement bases, such as the number of rooms or apartments or the kind of material collected (see Table 9.5).

Rates based primarily on the quantity of refuse normally set out for collection in residential areas are shown in Table 9.6. Some cities offer residential properties an option of two or more different frequencies of collection. These frequencies may range from once a week to daily. Rate structures within four cities charging on this basis are shown in Table 9.7.

Service charge rates for commercial properties. Rate structures for commercial collections, because of greater variation in the service demanded and the kind and quantity of refuse produced, are usually more complicated than those for the residential sector. The main characteristics of various rate structures for commercial properties are listed here with references to the appropriate following tables:

1. Commercial rates based on quantity (Table 9.8).
2. Charges based on frequency of collection and quantity collected (Table 9.9). Quantities are, in some cases, simply estimated by city officials.
3. Some cities establish rates on the basis of the nature of the business involved. Two examples are shown in Table 9.10.
4. Commercial charges based on square footage (Table 9.11).
5. Flat rates (Table 9.12).
6. Commercial rates for large container service (Table 9.13).

TABLE 9.8

Commercial Rates Based Primarily on Quantity of Refuse Collected

| City | First Container | | Second Cont. | | Ea. Added Cont. | | |
	Capacity	Rate	Capacity	Rate	Capacity	Rate	Period
Coral Gables, Florida	60 gal.	13.00	—	—	30 gal.	6.50	Quarter
Rochester, Minnesota	32 gal.	0.50	32 gal.	0.40	30 gal.	2.00	Month
Tacoma, Washington[a]	30 gal.	1.50	30 gal.	1.15	30 gal.	1.00[b]	Month

[a] Stairs, 25¢ per month per flight extra.
[b] Third can no charge. $1.00 for each can over three.

TABLE 9.9

Monthly Rates for Commercial Collection Based on Quantity and Frequency

City	Quantity, Number or Size of Containers (Gallons)	Collections per Week						
		1 Rate	2 Rate	3 Rate	4 Rate	5 Rate	6 Rate	7 Rate
Berkeley, Cal.	30 gal.	$ 1.00	$ 2.00	$ 3.00	$ 4.00	$ 5.00	$ 6.00	$7.00
	40 gal.	1.10	2.20	3.30	4.40	5.50	6.60	7.70
Fullerton, Cal.	1st cu. yd.	2.00	2.00	3.00	—	—	4.00	—
	Ea. addl. cu. yd.	1.00	2.00	3.00	—	—	6.00	—
San Angelo, Tex.	5 cu. yd.	—	—	4.00	—	—	6.50	—
Eugene, Ore.	1 can	1.75	3.25	4.75	5.50	7.75	9.00	—
	2 cans	3.10	5.50	7.50	9.00	12.50	14.50	—
	3 cans	4.25	7.50	9.75	13.00	17.75	20.00	—
Longview, Wash.	1 cu. yd.	5.35	8.80	10.40	—	—	18.40	—
	2 cu. yd.	8.85	14.40	17.40	—	—	31.00	—
	3 cu. yd.	10.95	18.90	23.00	—	—	41.50	—

TABLE 9.10

Commercial Rates for Refuse Collection Based on Kind of Business, 1961

Westerville, Ohio			Monthly Charge
Churches and lodge halls			1.50
	large	medium	small
Retail food 35.00	35.00	20.00	5.00–10.00
Restaurants 30.00	30.00	20.00	10.00–15.00
Mercantile 35.00	35.00	20.00	5.00–10.00
Drug stores 15.00	15.00	20.00	7.50
Industrial ....:40.00	40.00	25.00	5.00–10.00
Auto service stations & commercial garages.................			7.50
Barber shops, beauty salons, laundries, funeral homes.........			5.00
Hospitals, clinics, nursing and rest homes...................			15.00
Theaters, bowling alleys, skating rinks, billiard parlors.........			10.00
Schools, libraries, public buildings........................			10.00

Oklahoma City, Oklahoma	Monthly Charge
Restaurants	4.50– 45.00
Hot tamale and ice cream stands...........................	4.50– 15.00
Drug stores..................................	4.50– 40.00
Hospitals and sanitariums................................	6.00– 60.00
Butcher shops...	4.50– 30.00
Retail grocers...	4.50– 60.00
Retail fish stores..	4.50– 20.00
Wholesale grocery stores.................................	10.00– 60.00
Retail poultry stores.....................................	4.50– 20.00
Wholesale poultry stores.................................	10.00– 60.00
Wholesale fish stores....................................	10.00– 60.00
Hotels	6.00–100.00
Miscellaneous establishments.............................	4.50– 60.00

Success in using service charges for refuse collection depends, in large measure, on the ability to collect the charges regularly and inexpensively so that there will be no interruptions in collection service. Cities utilize various devices and methods to assure this and to enforce the payment of delinquent accounts. One successful device has been the collection of fees in advance, a method which is probably used wherever practicable and legally possible. With such a system, if the bills are not paid by the designated time, action is started at once (e.g., stopping the refuse pickup service). Penalties for failure to pay bills on time also have proved effective, and discounts for prompt

238

TABLE 9.11

Collection Rates on Square Foot Basis in Fort Worth, Texas

The collection of refuse from commercial premises is divided into 16 classes.

Six collections per week		Three collections per week	
Class	Monthly Charge	Class	Monthly Charge
I	15.00	Ia	7.50
II	10.50	IIa	5.25
III	7.50	IIIa	3.75
IV	6.00	IVa	3.00
V	5.25	Va	2.65
VI	4.50	VIa	2.25
VII	3.75	VIIa	1.85
VIII	3.00	VIIIa	1.50

Each of the classes has its own active business area value, and these vary according to their general occupancy class, i.e., commercial buildings, such as garages.

Class I and Ia	100,000 sq/ft
Class II and IIa	70,000 sq/ft
Class III and IIIa	50,000 sq/ft

or, in case of hotels, the areas are computed at ½ those of "commercial" buildings.

payment may have a similar effect. The APWA survey shows that the current trend is definitely in the direction of continuing regular refuse service rather than stopping it for nonpayment of charges. In such

TABLE 9.12

Flat Rates Charged for Refuse Collection from Commercial Properties

Billings, Montana		$60.00 annually, each place of business
Topeka, Kansas .... Inside	Fire Dist. #1—Garbage	$2.00 a month
Outside	Fire Dist. #1—Garbage	.75 a month
Outside	Fire Dist. #1—Trash	1:00 a month

TABLE 9.13

Rates Charged for Refuse Collection by Large Container Service[a]

	Rate Terms
Tuscaloosa, Alabama ..	More than once daily, 8 cubic yards, $37.50 per month
	Not more than once daily, 8 cubic yards, $22.50 per month
	Not more than once daily, 6 cubic yards, $15.00 per month
Paducah, Kentucky	10 cubic yards

10 cubic yards

1 day a week, $26.80 per month
2 days, $35.45
3 days, $45.10
4 days, $52.75
5 days, $61.00
6 days, $70.00

8 cubic yards

1 day a week, $22.80 per month
2 days, $31.45
3 days, $40.10
4 days, $48.75
5 days, $57.00
6 days, $66.00

6 cubic yards

1 day a week, $18.80
2 days, $27.45
3 days, $36.10
4 days, $44.75
5 days, $53.00
6 days, $62.00

[a] Service consists of transporting large detachable refuse containers to disposal sites for emptying. Full container is replaced with an empty one at time of pickup.

cases the collection of delinquent accounts is enforced by other legal means, such as shutting off water service.

Service to properties outside the city. To compensate for possible longer hauls or greater travel distance between pickups, municipal refuse collection rates are often set higher for outside customers. Four cities reported to the APWA that outside properties are regularly served and their outside rates are compared with the regular city rates (Table 9.14).

TABLE 9.14

Rates Charged by Four Cities for Refuse Collection
Service Outside City Limits, Compared with City Rates

City		Rates
Montgomery, Alabama.....		Rates slightly higher outside city
Roseville, California.......	Outside:	$1.75 a month for 30 gallons collected once a week. Each added 10 gallons, 40¢
	Inside:	$1.00 a month for 30 gallons collected once a week. Each added 10 gallons, 15¢
Traverse City, Michigan....	Outside:	$1.25 a month for 1st dwelling unit. 70¢ added units
	Inside:	$ .95 a month for 1st dwelling unit. 50¢ added units
Marion, Ohio.............	Outside:	$5.25 a quarter for 10 gallons of garbage and 3 bushels of rubbish collected once a week. Excess at commercial rate
	Inside:	$3.75 a quarter for 10 gallons of garbage and 3 bushels of rubbish collected once a week. Excess at commercial rate

NOTES

1. Unless otherwise noted, all statistics cited and all tables in this chapter are derived from the 1964 and 1965 surveys of the American Public Works Association. These excellent surveys appeared in *Refuse Collection Practice* (APWA, 1966) and provided the basic data for much of this chapter.

2. *The Role of Packaging in Solid Waste Management, 1966 to 1976* (U.S. Public Health Service, Solid Waste Bureau, 1969) provides considerable data on packaging materials.

3. However, most cities reporting did not include demolition or construction wastes in their collective services.

4. Information on a further breakdown of paper and plastics (and other "packaging") into composition and quantities can be obtained from the Packaging Institute, Inc., New York, N.Y.

5. The extent of private refuse collection operations in a community (and especially in a large city) is sometimes very difficult to determine, particularly when the city does not operate or control all disposal facilities. The largest city served by private collection for which the APWA has compiled statistics is San Francisco.

6. Werner Z. Hirsch, "Cost Functions of an Urban Government: Refuse Collection," *Review of Economics and Statistics*, 47 (February 1965): 87–92, in-

cludes both operating and capital costs, but how the capital costs were measured is not specified. However, researchers at Johns Hopkins have used equipment rental charges as a proxy for capital costs in an analysis of Baltimore City's refuse collection system.

7. W. J. Baumol, "On Social Rates of Discount," *American Economic Review*, 58 (September 1968): 788–802; also S. A. Marglin, "The Social Rate of Discount and the Optimal Rate of Interest," *Quarterly Journal of Economics*, 77 (February 1963): 92–112.

8. A cost analysis can avoid problems of seasonal and daily variation if the system is designed to carry the peak loads and to calculate the costs on this basis. However, such a procedure may not take into account what the shortrun variations in cost may be.

9. M. Gordon Wolman and Stephen Feldman, *An Evaluation of Solid Waste Collection Services in Baltimore City* (Department of Geography and Environmental Engineering, The Johns Hopkins University, forthcoming).

10. Jimmie E. Quon, et al., "Refuse Quantities and Frequency of Service," *Journal of the Sanitary Engineering Division, Proceedings of the ASCE*, 94 (April 1968): 403–420.

11. Hirsch. See note 6 above. The variation is actually the partial correlation coefficient of the average cost of frequency, given five other variables.

12. Hirsch's partial correlation coefficient of the average cost per pickup to the pickup location was 0.551. Put another way, Hirsch found that the average annual costs for residential refuse collection would increase by $3.97 (in 1960 prices) if the pickup location was changed from the curb to the back of the house.

13. Hirsch concluded that the population density, or pickup density, is one of the important variables affecting residential refuse collection costs.

14. Wolman and Feldman. See note 9 above.

15. Jimmie E. Quon, et al., "Efficiency of Refuse Collection Crews," *Journal of the Sanitary Engineering Division, Proceedings of the ASCE*, 96 (April 1970): 437–453. Quon discusses costs in the Chicago refuse collection system.

16. Aside from the APWA surveys, the most detailed information on refuse collection and disposal service charges in 380 American and Canadian communities is contained in a survey published by the Municipal Finance Officers Association of the United States and Canada in 1961.

17. These tabulations by the APWA are intended primarily to show the methods of establishing service-charge rate structures. Given the selectivity of the data, caution must be exercised in using the information for any other purpose.

Congestion Toll Pricing for
Public Transport Facilities

*E*CONOMISTS, policy-minded administrators, and planners have increasingly been suggesting congestion toll pricing as a practical and efficient instrument for solving the traffic congestion problem. However, advocacy of shortrun marginal-cost pricing as a replacement for the present method of roadway pricing (which for the public highway system approximates shortrun average variable cost pricing) has generally relied on an oversimple theoretical world in reaching conclusions about the efficacy of marginal-cost pricing. Briefly, the case and, particularly, the public arguments for marginal-cost pricing have sometimes failed (1) to view shortrun marginal-cost pricing within a longrun context and thus to view our pricing *and* investment policies as an inseparable package, (2) to consider properly some money and nonmoney costs and effects that will stem from the abandonment of our existing pricing system in favor of a marginal-cost pricing system, and (3) to consider the incidence of one pricing system versus another (in the sense of "who gains and who loses," and so forth).

Although the problem of traffic congestion in urban areas is too often viewed myopically as confined solely to highways and affecting just the users of autos, trucks, and busses, in fact, it affects all users of all transit systems, whether underground, surface, or overhead. It confronts these users not only as they wait in queues when entering or exiting from subways, rapid transit stations, or busses, but also as they are crowded into and thus "congested" within transit cars or

Martin Wohl is Director of Transportation Studies at The Urban Institute.

busses. This "inside" congestion, unlike highway traffic snarls, will not add greatly to the passenger's travel time but can, and often does, markedly affect his level of discomfort.[1] Furthermore, in these crowding situations (just as in highway congestion) each additional individual transit user, for a given time period, is causing the total "costs" to all transit users to increase more than the private "cost" he faces. (If I jam into a subway car, I not only suffer the discomfort of the "crush" but also cause the other occupants of the car to suffer additionally from my entrance.) In summary, then, the argument that a highway user causes congestion for all other highway users is applicable to the transit user situation.

Some supporters of marginal-cost pricing (often referred to as "congestion pricing") assume that traffic congestion is intolerable and thus that "the problem" is nothing more or less than to reduce congestion. Therefore, any measure to reduce traffic congestion—whether it is the imposition of tolls to reduce traffic flow or to shift users from autos to transit modes or to shift their travel hours from the peak to offpeak periods—is, a priori, deemed better than existing conditions. Nevertheless, looking at the matter more rationally, there are three choices open to society: (1) continue to endure congestion, whether on jammed highways or in crowded transit vehicles; (2) reduce the traffic flow or passenger ridership, whether through pricing mechanisms, administrative controls, or physical barriers; or (3) expand the highway system capacity or the number of transit lines, vehicles, or trains. The wisdom of the second or third alternative, relative to the first, will depend principally on the extent to which congestion will thereby be reduced; on the value of this reduction to those enjoying faster travel or reduced crowding; on the disbenefit, should the second alternative be adopted, to those "forced off" or to others affected by those "forced off" the facilities; on the extra travel benefit accruing to new users; and on the cost or resource commitments necessary to expand the system capacity should the third alternative be adopted, and so forth. Further, there will be equity and income redistribution considerations that should enter the decision-making process.

The remainder of this chapter examines the consequences of different pricing policies in the nonbackward-bending or nonreducing capacity case for transport facilities.[2]

Shortrun Considerations

Most economists argue that shortrun marginal-cost pricing will lead to maximization of net benefits. This argument is generally founded on the assumption that marginal-cost pricing prevails throughout the economy, and that the costs of implementing such a pricing scheme and of countering any averse effects on employment and income distribution are negligible. But these assumptions hardly describe the "real" world, and other objectives might be ill served by a sharp reversal of the existing average-cost type of pricing policy and a move to marginal-cost pricing.[3]

To explore some of these points, we make use of the cost, price, and demand relationships shown in Figure 10.1. Assume that the variable-cost curve includes not only the variable supporting-way and vehicle operating and maintenance costs (and other like expenditures that vary with the flow rate) but also the costs for travel time, effort, discomfort, and safety hazard incurred by travelers; assume further that under the pricing policy now practiced for highway and transit systems the traveler, in deciding whether to travel and how much to travel, perceives his trip payments to total and be equal to the short-run average variable cost. More specifically, we assume the following: (1) that, for a given highway trip, users perceive the variable user gas, tire, and parts taxes equally and as part of their complete money-time-effort payment,[4] and that the unit variable user gas, tire, and parts taxes are just equal to the unit variable costs for operating and maintaining the highway and are constant for all levels of flow, and (2) that, for transit travel, the fare is perceived by transit users and is just equal to the unit variable costs for operating and maintaining the transit systems.[5] Also, for highway travel, the complete money-time-effort variable costs increase at an increasing rate due to the increase in congestion and travel time with increases in flow q, while for transit travel the increasing rate stems from increases in congestion and passenger discomfort (due to crowding) with increases in flow q.[6]

Looking at Figure 10.1, it is evident that if we switched from the present average variable-cost type of pricing policy to marginal-cost pricing (while ignoring the costs of implementing a workable marginal-cost pricing system) some of the existing q_1 travelers (or q_1 minus q_2

Fig. 10.1 *Shortrun Cost, Demand, and Pricing Relationships*[a]

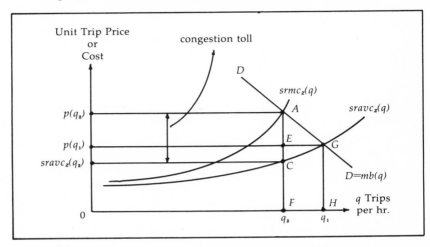

[a] These curves can be applied with equal validity to both highway and transit travel. In the highway case, q can be regarded as the hourly vehicular flow on a particular highway; the increase in variable costs with increases in q stems mainly from increased travel time. In the transit case, q can be regarded as the hourly passenger flow arriving at a particular bus stop or rail transit station; the increase in variable costs with increases in q stem partially from increased travel time but mainly from increased crowding and discomfort as busses or trains become overloaded (relative to the number of seats). In the shortrun, the highway vehicular and transit passenger capacity should be regarded as fixed.

$srmc_z(q)$ = Shortrun marginal costs for flow q on facility z
$sravc_z(q)$ = Shortrun average variable costs for flow q on facility z
DD = Demand function for facility z = $mb(q)$
$p(q)$ = Price for flow q (for certain pricing policies)
$sratc_z(q)$ = Shortrun average total costs for flow q on facility z
$mb(q)$ = Marginal benefit for flow q on facility z

travelers) would be unable or unwilling to pay the toll *AC* that would be required to bring about marginal-cost pricing. And, in the shortrun, these q_1 minus q_2 users would suffer a loss as they switched to a less preferable mode, a less preferable hour of travel, a less preferable route, or finally less travel. For example, they could decide to travel less often or not at all. Furthermore, *all* of the q_2 users (even though able and willing to pay the toll of *AC*) would suffer a unit loss of *AE* with marginal-cost pricing (relative to an average variable-cost pricing policy); that is, while their unit congestion costs would be reduced by an amount of *EC* when the volume was reduced from q_1 to q_2, their money payments would be increased by AC, an amount that would exceed the reduction in congestion costs by a unit amount of AE. Thus in the shortrun all of the users, both those continuing to use the facility and those forced off it, are worse off.[7]

The obvious question arises: How can net benefits to society be increased when the benefits to *all* users of the facility are decreased by a switch to marginal-cost pricing? The problem is simply that the increases in net benefit have been extracted from the q_2 users in the form of tolls and (presumably) have been transferred to other groups, and so on. Thus the users have suffered a loss, individually and in aggregate, but those receiving the tolls and society in aggregate have received a greater gain. Imposing marginal-cost pricing would be most unlikely to induce users to look upon the results as "optimum" or "efficient"; rather, they would probably view the matter as highly inequitable, at least in the shortrun. Finally, there could be other "losers." That is, some of the users who were unwilling or unable to pay the toll required by marginal-cost pricing would shift to other routes, other modes, or other times of day. In the process, they would usually increase the travel time, congestion, and/or crowding on those other routes or modes, both for themselves and for the longer-established users of the routes and modes.

Practicalities and Costs of Pricing Policies

When considering the wisdom of abandoning average variable-cost pricing in favor of marginal-cost pricing, we need to develop a system that will inform users, in advance of their making a trip, about the marginal-cost prices they *will* face *if* they decide to travel. To develop a system in which the prices would be hidden, or which bills users later in some aggregate fashion (e.g., by sending monthly bills), might (or would tend to) defeat a major purpose of marginal-cost pricing, namely, to make users aware of the costs stemming from additional trip-making. Ideally, of course, the pricing system would be pervasive for all facilities, modes, times of travel, and so forth. Prices for given facilities would change from hour to hour and from day to day, as the equilibrium flows and marginal costs changed in response to fluctuations or changes in demand. And certainly the system should reflect the demand relations for each mode of travel during each hour of the day as well as the cross relations with respect to other modes and times of day for trip-making. However, the situations of the two facility modes that we consider specifically here—highway and transit—differ somewhat from each other.

The highway case

Were such a flexible and pervasive pricing system to be instituted for roadways—and one can hardly argue otherwise if the case for marginal-cost pricing is to have a solid basis—quite evidently an extensive and expensive toll collection system would also be required. Though many types of electronic systems have been talked about, their efficacy in practice remains to be proved, as does their cost effectiveness. Until this practicality gap is bridged, the usual toll gate type of system could be used to implement marginal-cost pricing. On the one hand, the toll gates on roadway systems would ensure that all users are confronted with the actual shortrun marginal costs, and that the marginal benefit for all users is not less than the marginal costs for volume rates of that magnitude. On the other hand, instituting *de novo* a toll gate (or other) system would not only require resource expenditures for the system's construction and operation but would also cause the system users to suffer additional travel-time delays and other time costs while waiting to be serviced at the toll gates.[8]

The *full* marginal costs, to include the variable costs of implementing and being delayed by a marginal-cost pricing system, may be represented somewhat as shown by the $srmc_z'(q)$ curve in Figure 10.2: $srmc_z'(q) =$ shortrun marginal cost, including pricing implementation and delay costs, for facility z at volume rate q. These costs together with the extra fixed costs required for the toll gates can be compared with $srmc_z(q)$, the shortrun marginal costs for "costless" marginal-cost pricing, and with the shortrun average variable costs both with and without the costs of implementing the pricing system, $sravc_z'(q)$ and $sravc_z(q)$ respectively. Relative to "costless" marginal-cost pricing, the full marginal costs will cause the peak and offpeak period costs and prices to be increased, thus reducing the hourly flow from q_p to q_2 during peak periods and from q_o to q_1 during offpeak periods.[9] (This assumes, of course, that the hourly demand throughout the day can be represented by hourly demand functions for just two time periods; this representation also ignores the cross relations between peak and offpeak time periods, two obvious oversimplifications.)

Fig. 10.2 *Shortrun Cost, Demand, and Pricing Relationships for Marginal-Cost Pricing*

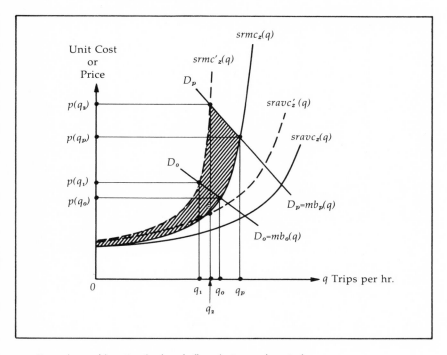

D_p = *demand function for hourly flow during peak periods*
D_o = *demand function for hourly flow during offpeak periods*

At this stage of the analysis it is appropriate to ask whether, in light of the additional travel delays and toll collection costs, marginal-cost pricing still appears to be the most efficient pricing policy. Obviously, the answer depends on what other alternative pricing schemes and pricing policies are available. But it is of utmost importance to note that, given these broader and more realistic conditions accompanying the advocacy of marginal-cost pricing, one can no longer argue a priori that marginal-cost pricing is or is not better than average-cost pricing or quasi-average-cost pricing.

Alternatively, the present pricing policy for most public roads might be looked upon as a quasi-average total cost pricing scheme in which the perceived roadway price is equivalent to the uniform user tax plus the shortrun average variable cost.[10] For these assumptions, the price to the user would be represented by the $srtvc_z(q)$ curve shown in Figure 10.3. The costs of administering this pricing policy for highways and of collecting the user prices (uniform tax plus the user's expenditures of time and effort, etc.) are virtually nil, particularly since travel-

Fig. 10.3 *Shortrun Cost, Demand, and Pricing Relationships for Uniform User Tax Pricing Policy*

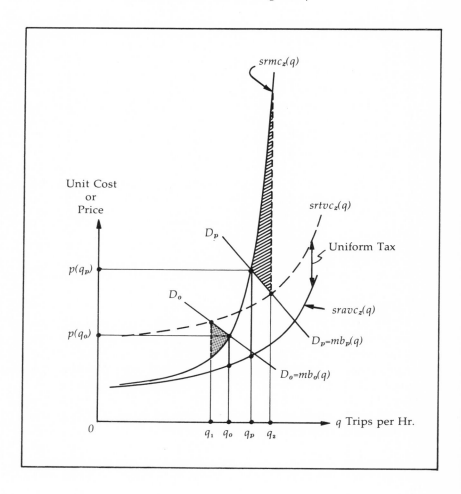

ers are not delayed because of the collection scheme. Thus, as a practical matter, the average variable cost plus uniform tax pricing policy for highways is costless. Relative to "costless" marginal-cost pricing, as represented by $srmc_z(q)$, we would usually find that hourly flows and congestion during peak periods would be too high and during offpeak periods too low.[11] Relative to "costless" marginal-cost pricing, this average variable plus uniform tax cost pricing scheme would cause *hourly* losses in net benefits during the peak and offpeak periods roughly as shown, respectively, by the right and left shaded areas in Figure 10.3.[12] These losses can be compared to the losses stemming from full marginal-cost pricing that are represented by the shaded areas below the peak period (D_p) and offpeak period (D_o) demand functions in Figure 10.2, plus the extra fixed costs required to install the toll gate or other pricing system.

On balance, which pricing policy will result in the smallest net benefit losses is not clear. Thus only a full-scale benefit-cost analysis will indicate which of these (or other) pricing policies will be most efficient economically or will be better on other grounds. A second but equally important conclusion can be drawn with respect to pricing highway travel. That is, since the costs of administering uniform user taxes are nil, or virtually so, *some* user tax is preferable to *no* user tax or to "free" highway travel. For example, referring to Figure 10.3, it can be seen that a uniform tax set high enough to bring about a price of $p(q_0)$ and an hourly flow of q_0 during offpeak hours will result in lower peak *and* offpeak hourly losses in net benefits—relative to "costless" marginal-cost pricing—than would a zero uniform tax.

The transit case

For transit facilities, other than "free transit," there is no way of administering either a uniform or differentiated price that will (1) be "costless" (or virtually so) and (2) prevent delay of passengers during collection. If a uniform rate (plus shortrun average variable costs) type of pricing policy were to be used for the transit system, the situation would be as depicted in Figure 10.4.

The $srmc_z'(q)$ curve in Figure 10.4 represents the shortrun marginal costs for facility z operating at hourly flow q, to include the variable costs of implementing the collection system and of delaying passengers while collecting fares; curve $srfvc_z(q)$ represents the price

Fig. 10.4 *Shortrun Cost, Demand, and Pricing Relationships for Uniform Transit Fare Pricing*

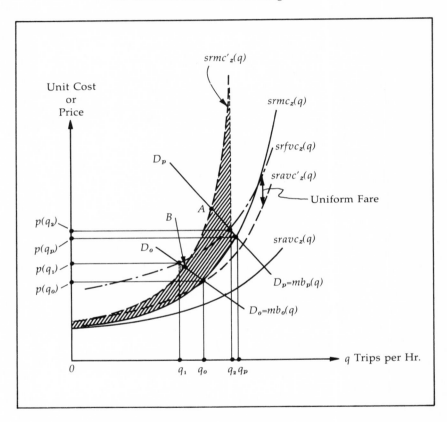

function faced by travelers and is the sum of the uniform fare and shortrun average variable costs (to include those caused by more and more crowding and the resultant discomfort). During peak periods, the hourly flow would be q_2 and the price would be $p(q_2)$ for this uniform fare policy and, relative to the net benefits resulting from "costless" marginal-cost pricing as represented by the $srmc_z(q)$ curve, the resulting hourly losses would be equal to the entire *dashed* shaded area plus the fixed costs for the collection facilities. During offpeak periods, the hourly flow would be q_1, the price would be $p(q_1)$, and the hourly losses (again, relative to the net benefits obtainable with "costless" marginal-cost pricing) would be equivalent to the entire *dashed and dotted* shaded area lying below D_0 (the off-peak demand curve) plus the fixed costs for the collection facilities.

One should ask whether the use of differential peak and offpeak transit fares would help to reduce the above losses in net benefits. The answer, almost certainly, is yes.[13] If the peak-period fare were increased so as to bring the total user price up to point A on Figure 10.4, the loss in net benefits lying between D_p (the peak-period demand curve) and $srmc_z'(q)$ could be eliminated. Although differential prices would almost certainly be more efficient than a uniform fare policy for transit facilities (in contrast to the case for highway facilities in which such a result may or may not be true), one may not assert that such a pricing policy is definitely preferable to "free transit" (that is, to a zero transit fare policy). For the "free transit" case, the hourly loss in net benefits relative to the "costless" marginal-cost pricing case would be equal to the dashed shaded area in Figure 10.5 during peak periods and to the dotted shaded area during offpeak periods. On an a priori basis, we cannot argue that the sum of these shaded areas is either larger or smaller than the combined sum of fixed costs of the collection facilities and the shaded areas for either the uniform or differentiated transit price policies that were discussed earlier and depicted in Figure 10.4.

Longrun Considerations

Some practical aspects of pricing and facility expansion

Considerable attention should be devoted to the efficacy of imposing marginal-cost pricing in situations when further expansion of the roadway system is regarded as "impossible," for whatever reasons and regardless of whether its expansion is economically efficient or not.[14] Or, to put the matter in more technical terms, one should consider pricing in broader perspective, as just one of several links in the investment-pricing-operating chain rather than as a matter for short-run consideration at the present time.[15] Innumerable studies and articles on the subject of roadway and congestion pricing suggest that a fundamental purpose of pricing is to reduce congestion, to lessen peaking, or to shift people from auto to transit. More pertinently, however, pricing is a mechanism to guide consumers in making decisions among

Fig. 10.5 *Shortrun Cost, Demand, and Pricing Relationships for "Free Transit" Pricing*

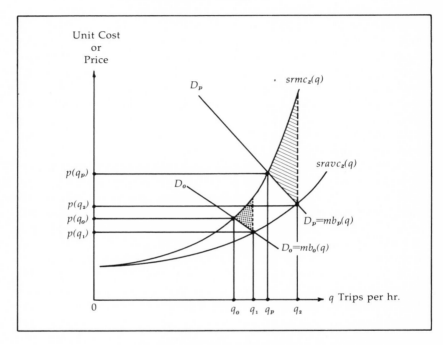

the choices open to them, to help establish the values of products or services, and thus to aid private or public firms or agencies in their decisions about investments, operations, products, and services.[16] Pricing is merely one of the instruments available to help determine how many and which kind of modal services should be provided, the extent to which the services should be offered, and the appropriate levels of operation and congestion (or, say, performance) for those modal systems.

For highways, the appropriate use of pricing and the concurrent analysis of the additional costs of expansion and the extra value of increasing trip-making and reduced congestion can serve to guide decisions about the amount of highways and number of lanes needed. Similar tradeoffs should be employed in making decisions about the wisdom of direct pricing mechanisms, about the number of toll booths (should they prove to be warranted), and so forth. For transit systems, good pricing and incremental benefit-cost analysis can aid significantly in making decisions not only about the feasibility of various modal systems, together with their route coverage and trackage requirements, but also about schedule frequency and train lengths. For the latter, transit operators can more sensibly make tradeoffs between different crowding levels within busses or trains (and the associated loading/ unloading times) and different bus or train frequencies, bus sizes, and train lengths rather than rely on arbitrary load factors or operating rules of thumb to make such decisions.

Pricing *is* a shortrun proposition and a matter of determining day-to-day prices, *given* the market (as represented by appropriate demand functions), *given* a pricing policy, and *given* the actual day-to-day variable costs stemming from operation and usage of a particular facility. And it is a problem of determining which pricing policy will result in the most efficient (defined as maximization of net benefits) day-to-day operation and usage or volume (and thus congestion) levels. And, from day to day, one can do no better than maximize the daily efficiency (i.e., net benefits) of the system that is in place and in operation. However, of equal clarity and importance is the all-too-obvious fact that the system's size and its service and operating characteristics can be altered over time, thus changing the cost functions and the resultant usage, prices, net benefits, and so forth. As a consequence, our concern with pricing should include, not only the present shortrun operating circumstances of a given facility or system, but also the effects of longrun changes on the facilities and their operations.

To view this problem more directly, we must note that many economists, when analyzing the roadway pricing problem, have concluded that present uniform user tax levels and pricing policies have led to pricing highway travel (particularly in core areas of cities) far below shortrun marginal costs and thus have also led to economic inefficiency. Crucially, though, not all of these economists have appropriately analyzed either the more longrun implications of the conclusion or the practical considerations and costs stemming from the implementation of a marginal-cost pricing system (the costs in the sense discussed in the opening paragraphs of this chapter). And it is here that the contradiction seems most apparent. Much to the point, economists have continually concerned themselves with economic inefficiencies stemming from poor shortrun pricing policies, but they have sometimes failed to examine and pinpoint the manner and extent to which economic inefficiencies also can and do result from poor investment and expansion policies. Inefficiency with respect to pricing is no more onerous than inefficiency with respect to expansion.

Further, we are inescapably led to conclude that economists, by arguing for the institution of congestion tolls (set equal to the shortrun marginal costs) without specifically considering the longrun possibilities and implications as well, are (unwittingly, perhaps) lending support to the usual contentions that traffic congestion must be abated; that traffic is strangling and choking the downtown and central city core areas; that the construction of more highways will only lead to more traffic, more congestion, and more strangling; and that the urban highway expansion program (particularly the Interstate Highway links) should be slowed if not halted;[17] and that more rapid transit should be constructed in place of highways. It should be obvious, of course, that most economists would hardly endorse such bald and unqualified contentions, and certainly not without having been provided the appropriate benefit-cost analyses to validate the views.

It may be, for example, that traffic is strangling and choking the central business district or the central city. But such a conclusion must rest on deeper consideration of many aspects other than the mere existence of traffic congestion on streets and expressways. In the first place, the fact that workers or shoppers will actually put up with traffic congestion during certain times of day and will continue to travel by auto—rather than forgo trips altogether, rather than use mass transit (where it is available), or rather than travel at some less congested time of day—is ample proof that auto trips during those times of day are highly valued, both in an absolute sense and relative to other available opportunities. It is also proof that reduction of auto travel will lead to a reduction in benefits, as well as congestion costs. A related matter of considerable importance is that auto and mass transit can hardly be regarded as highly or even reasonably substitutable services for either work or shopping trips and that significant shifts from auto to mass transit are not in the offing.[18] As a consequence, a shift to congestion toll pricing (at shortrun marginal cost) for highways would, in all likelihood, reduce traffic and its congestion but would also reduce the number of person trips (and the associated benefits). Thus, a mixed blessing may result—and the city may well be crippled more by the loss of workers and shoppers (and their expenditures and contributions) than by the reduced congestion for those willing to pay the tolls. In fact, it is difficult to envision how any significant gains—aside from less noise and air pollution—will accrue to the city itself or to its businessmen merely from having traffic congestion reduced, *unless*, of course, there are excess toll revenues that will be distributed to the city and its businessmen or used to reduce their taxes.

Consider the latter point about excess revenues: If the highway travel demand produces heavy congestion *and* results in equilibrium flows above the level corresponding to that at which the shortrun average total costs are at a minimum point (i.e., if equilibrium flow q is above the level q_0 shown in Figure 10.6), to adopt marginal-cost pricing will result in excess money revenues being generated; referring to Figure 10.6, the revenues in excess of total costs to society would be equal to q_A times the difference between $p(q_A)$ and $sratc_x(q_A)$. Also, if the situation as depicted in Figure 10.6 is representative of urban-core

Fig. 10.6 *Shortrun Cost and Demand Relationships for a Fixed Facility and High Demand*

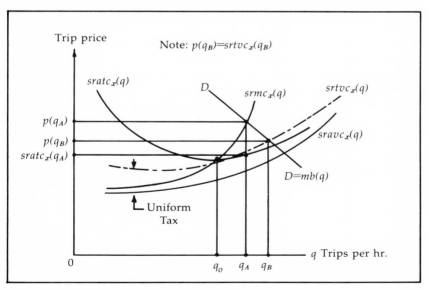

highway conditions at present, then, so long as facilities are not improved or expanded, we can expect the excess revenues or profits to increase continually over time. These increases in profits will occur, of course, so long as demand shifts (upward and to the right) in response to population shifts, to income increases, and so forth. The excess revenues alone should induce the economist and the engineer (and the "city fathers") to consider the obvious question: Should the facilities be expanded?

Clearly, to talk about the necessity or economic wisdom of instituting marginal-cost pricing and to ignore government policies with respect to investment planning is tantamount to being negligent or unobjective. Putting the matter more strongly, I suspect that some planners and analysts would (for noneconomic and subjective reasons) be delighted to see shortrun marginal-cost pricing instituted and to have the urban highway program halted even if longrun considerations indicated that expanding the highway system would be more economically efficient. In a sense, this suggests that they feel it is "impossible" or would do irreparable harm to expand the highway system within urban/core areas, and thus they forgo consideration of this possibility.

Effects of Expansion Under Nonconstant Returns to Scale

In a rough way, the short- and longrun effects of following different pricing and investment (or, say, expansion) policies can be examined by making reference to the cost and demand relationships that are illustrated in Figure 10.7. (Of course, even these situations and functional relationships are oversimplified, particularly with respect to the characterization of demand as static, both during the day and over the years; on the other hand, cases of both increasing and decreasing returns to scale are represented.)

Given cost and demand functions such as those shown in Figure 10.7, we can determine which facility size or capacity will maximize net benefits over the long run by noting the specific facility associated with the intersection between the demand and the longrun marginal-cost curves. (And, if the demand function intersects the longrun average total cost curve, we may be sure that net benefits will be positive, fixed costs included.) Or, in other terms, facilities and in turn the output should be continually expanded so long as the incremental benefits

Fig. 10.7 *Longrun Cost and Demand Relationships for Other than Constant Returns to Scale*

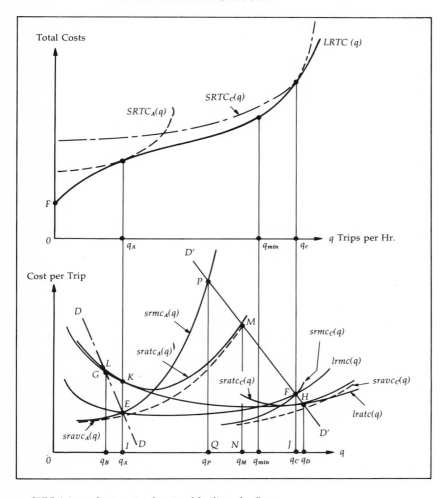

SRTCx(q) = shortrun total costs of facility x for flow q
LRTC(q) = longrun total costs for flow q
lrmc(q) = longrun marginal costs for flow q
lratc(q) = longrun average total costs for flow q

are larger than the additional fixed and variable costs stemming from increased capacity and output (these costs being represented by the longrun marginal-cost curve). Similarly, facilities and output should be contracted so long as the loss in benefits is less than the reduction in fixed and variable costs. At the point when the marginal benefit just equals the longrun marginal cost—or point E for demand curve DD in Figure 10.7 and point F for demand curve $D'D'$—the longrun marginal cost will also equal the shortrun marginal cost for the proper facility, i.e., the facility of lowest total cost for that output or q level, and will determine the "most efficient" day-to-day operating price.[19]

To follow the criteria outlined above, and to adopt facility A and output level q_A (with a price equal to EI) when the demand is DD, or to adopt facility C and output level q_C (with a price equal to FJ) when the demand is $D'D'$, will result in maximizing net benefits to the public at large—regardless of whether a public or private facility is involved.[20] However, such idyllic planning and operating decisions will not always be forthcoming, because of the lack of competition (both in the private and the public sectors), or because of financial feasibility and pricing constraints, or because demand is not really so static and predictable.

Were the demand level to be at Figure 10.7's DD, for example, no firm or public authority could build facility A, price its usage so as to maximize net benefits (i.e., set its toll so that the total user price was equal to shortrun marginal cost or EI), and cover its total costs. (In fact, and even with some competition, firms or public authorities operating under these demand conditions would tend to build the minimum total cost facility for an output level of q_B or less, rather than facility A.) But if facility A were built by a firm or public authority and if total costs had to be recovered (i.e., if financial feasibility were a require-ment), a high toll—equal to the difference between the shortrun aver-age total cost and shortrun average variable cost—would have to be charged. The total user price would correspond to the level indicated by point L and the flow would be reduced to an amount slightly below q_B. Clearly, from a public point of view (i.e., a view that attempts to maximize net benefits to the public, regardless of who incurs the costs and who accrues the benefits), it would be in the interest of society to subsidize either public or private firms or authorities faced with like demand and cost conditions (the classic increasing returns-to-scale case, as illustrated in Figure 10.7 and indicated by demand DD) to the extent required to encourage proper planning and pricing.

More specifically, both private and public firms and agencies should be encouraged to build facility A—for the DD demand case—and to set the toll equal to marginal cost minus average variable cost. In this instance, the total user price would be EI; the toll would be equal to EI minus $sravc_A(q_A)$; the subsidy per trip would be KE; and the total (hourly) subsidy to the firm or agency would be equal to the product of KE and q_A. More realistically, certain—though not many—low-usage and high-fixed-cost turnpike and bridge authorities (such as the Massachusetts Turnpike Extension) are likely to find themselves in this increasing returns-to-scale situation and required (because of commitments to bondholders) to set a price to cover total costs, thus causing the public at large to forgo the extra net benefits accruing from a lower toll and higher usage. In such instances, the local, state, or federal government would do well to consider a subsidy (assuming, of course, that the authority had decided to adopt marginal-cost pricing).

The shortrun facility A cost and $D'D'$ demand relations shown in Figure 10.7 are probably more representative of present-day conditions for public highways in many dense urban-core areas and thus can be used to focus attention more generally on the pricing and investment policy questions. Also, the shortrun average variable cost curve for facility A can be regarded as the price function *now* being faced by travelers. As a result of these assumptions and conditions, usage of and congestion on facility A are high, with an equilibrium flow of q_M and a total user price of MN. Clearly, this pricing policy and the resultant flow level cause serious shortrun economic inefficiencies, since some of the tripmakers (those represented by the demand function between flow q_P and flow q_M) will have marginal benefits that are less than the marginal costs attendant with an increase in hourly flow rate from q_P to q_M. Clearly, considerable longrun economic inefficiencies also result, because for these conditions (i.e., facility A and demand $D'D'$) capacity is in short supply and grossly underexpanded. For this case and the relations shown in Figure 10.7, expansion to the level of facility C would bring about the following:

1. More trip-making would be permitted and thus total travel benefits would increase.

2. Total (fixed and variable) travel and facility costs would increase with expansion, but to a lesser extent than the travel benefits would; thus *net* benefits would increase.

3. The price of travel—to an individual trip-maker—would de-

crease, whether the present-day user tax plus shortrun variable-cost pricing policy were to be continued or marginal-cost pricing were to be adopted.

4. Congestion would be markedly reduced, even though the (hourly) volume rate would be increased.

At this point it is worth indicating an anomaly that can result from considering only the effects of pricing policy changes rather than those of pricing *and* investment changes. Again, let us assume that facility A is presently in existence and that the $D'D'$ demand curve is representative of the market for travel. On one hand, if the present pricing policy and its price function can be typified by the shortrun average variable-cost curve, and if attention is restricted to the efficiencies stemming from a switch to shortrun marginal-cost pricing and if facility expansion is regarded as "impossible" for whatever reasons, the result will be to increase the total price of a trip from MN to PQ and to reduce the (hourly) volume rate from q_M to q_P. On the other hand, if both pricing and investment (or expansion) policy changes were to be adopted, thus switching to marginal-cost pricing and expanding the capacity level to that of facility C, opposite longrun effects would result. After expansion, the trip price would be reduced from MN to FJ and (hourly) volume rate would be increased from q_M to q_C. Obviously, during the expansion period, prices—if adjusted to marginal cost—would fluctuate considerably. In the early years before new capacity becomes available, congestion, and thus trip price, would be high and flow would be reduced considerably (from the flow now witnessed with shortrun average variable-cost pricing). Later, after new capacity was made available and congestion dropped, the price would fall markedly and flow would increase.

The price fluctuations noted above and the resultant shifts in trip-making (to other modes, to other routes, to other times of day, or to less trip-making) could, of course, cause numerous anxieties for the traveling public, as well as for the business and employment groups the public deals with, either directly or remotely. Among the numerous arguments against price fluctuation, particularly where the differences are large and facilities have been seriously underexpanded, two are worth noting.

1. It should be recognized that certain individuals have taken jobs and businesses have established locations based upon many factors

including an expectation of the continuation of existing highway pricing policies. Given a switch in pricing policy, many of these individuals or firms might find themselves in untenable economic circumstances even though they were not (or were only partially) responsible for the bad predictions about policy changes. Thus, it seems wise to ask whether it is "fair" for them to suffer the costs stemming from the switch in pricing policy.[21]

2. Boiteux, among others, has argued the desirability of maintaining steady rates over periods of changing demand and expansion and of setting a constant price equivalent to one that would result if the facility capacity were always in "perfect" adjustment.[22] This would seem particularly important when facilities have been seriously under-expanded.

Conclusions About the Feasibility of Different Pricing Policy Options

We have reviewed above the major pricing systems available for public option: (1) a marginal-cost pricing type of system (with peak and offpeak period differentials); (2) a uniform fare or toll pricing system (common to that now practiced on transit systems or highway toll facilities); (3) a uniform user tax type of pricing system (common to that now utilized on the bulk of our public streets and highways); and (4) a "zero" toll, fare, or tax pricing system. On balance, with respect to these systems, the following conclusions can be drawn.

1. For public highways not now having toll facilities already in place, some user tax price *is* clearly preferable to having no (i.e., a "zero") user tax price.

2. For public highways not now having toll facilities already in place, it is not clear whether it is preferable to continue with uniform user tax pricing or to change to a differential peak and offpeak price and toll system; a full-scale benefit-cost analysis is required to determine which pricing system is more feasible.

3. For highways that will continue to operate as toll facilities or for those that will be converted to toll facilities (for whatever reasons and whether it is, economically speaking, in the public interest to do so or not), it will be more efficient and in the public interest to adopt marginal-cost type pricing (i.e., to use differential peak and offpeak tolls) than to use a uniform daily toll.

4. For public transit systems, it is not clear whether it is more efficient to adopt a "free fare" policy or to charge a uniform fare as is presently common; a full-scale analysis is required to determine which is in the public interest.

5. For public transit systems that will continue to operate with some fare, it will be more efficient and in the public interest to adopt marginal-cost type pricing (i.e., to use differentiated peak and offpeak fares) than to use a uniform daily fare as is now common.

6. In deciding among the various pricing alternatives and their benefit and cost circumstances, and thus feasibility, the analyst must take account of present and future benefits and costs (all properly discounted), and he must take account of both fixed and variable costs.

In sum, the analyst and economist cannot say a priori whether or not prices should tend in the direction of marginal cost and thus peak and offpeak differentiated prices. Nor can he say whether a "free fare," "free tax," or "free toll" pricing system is or is not better than other pricing policy alternatives. Intensive analysis must be undertaken before firm conclusions can be enunciated about the efficacy of one policy or another. Unfortunately, the nation's support for such analysis is so weak that definite answers appear to be a long way down the pike.

NOTES

1. Clearly, his travel time will be increased to some extent—as his wait to get into and off transit cars or busses is increased, and as the time for intermediate station stops is increased. (In the short run the vehicle fleet, and thus train length and train or bus schedule frequency, are fixed.)

2. A. A. Walters, "The Theory and Measurement of Private and Social Cost of Highway Congestion," *Econometrica*, 29 (October 1961): 678–681; M. Wohl and B. V. Martin, *Traffic System Analysis* (McGraw-Hill, 1967), sec. 10.2.3.; and M. Wohl, "Development of a Rationale for Transportation Investment" (unpublished thesis, University of California, Berkeley, 1966), sec. 4.3. These sources consider the "bottleneck" or backward-bending case.

3. M. Wohl, "The Short-Run Congestion Cost and Pricing Dilemma," *Traffic Quarterly*, 20 (January 1966); also see R. Zettel and R. Carll, "The Basic Theory of Efficiency Tolls: The Tolled, the Tolled-Off, and the Untolled," *Highway Research Board Record No. 47* (1964).

4. These taxes are assumed to be variable with respect to the quantity and length of trips but uniform per vehicle-mile.

5. These assumptions are made mainly for convenience and may do some violence to the actual facts: i.e., the highway user tax in some instances may well more than cover the highway maintenance and operating costs; in other cases it may not cover these costs. Similarly, transit fares may sometimes cover more than the transit maintenance and operating expenses and sometimes may not. For many dense urban situations, however, I suspect that my assumptions are not far from the truth.

6. In the latter case, as busses and the cars of a rail transit train become more and more crowded with increases in the passenger load (that is, with increases in q), crowding and discomfort will increase; so will travel time, because longer stops are required.

7. Throughout the chapter, I have presumed that motorists were homogeneous with respect to time and congestion values and costs.

8. Delays at toll gates could of course be reduced to virtually nothing if enough extra toll booths were provided and operated; there is an obvious tradeoff between shortrun travel delays, operating costs, and longrun toll gate costs, though it is presumed that even the most efficient gate capacity would result in some queuing delays.

9. The comparisons between hourly flows and between net benefit totals for different pricing policies will be made by using the "costless" marginal-cost curve and pricing policy as a base; this base simplifies the graphic illustrations of the changes in total net benefit.

10. This view is somewhat different from that adopted earlier for the general comments about the effects of different pricing policies. Here we imply that the present highway user taxes cover more than the variable facility operating and maintenance expenses. In fact, many would estimate that for the highway system in aggregate or for the system within central cities (again, taken as a whole) user taxes in total cover both the fixed and variable costs for the highway facilities. See L. Fitch and Associates, *Urban Transportation and Public Policy* (Chandler, 1964), pp. 32 and 129; also G. P. St. Clair, "Congestion Tolls—An Engineer's Viewpoint," *Highway Research Board Record No. 47* (1964), pp. 93 and 95.

11. The uniform tax level *could* be set high enough to result in a marginal-cost price being charged during peak periods—with an overall price of $p(q_2)$ and flow q_2 as shown in Figure 10.2; however, flow during offpeak periods would be far too low. On an a priori basis, no conclusion can be reached about the "best" or "better" level for the uniform tax.

12. The losses in net benefits are equal to the difference between the total net benefits for the pricing policy in question and those for the "costless" marginal-cost pricing policy. Total net benefits for any given pricing policy are defined as the difference between total benefits and total costs, the latter to include any fixed costs. (The total benefits may be calculated by summing the marginal benefits—or integrating under the demand curve—up to the equilibrium flow level; total costs may be calculated by summing marginal costs up to the equilibrium flow level and then by adding them to any fixed costs, where applicable, for new or existing facilities.)

For further discussion of the above points and of the mathematical expressions for the losses associated with the pricing policies illustrated in Figures 10.2 and 10.3, see Wohl and Martin, sec. 10.4, and Wohl (1966, thesis), sec: 5.1.

13. This conclusion would need no qualification if the costs of administering and collecting differential fares (including delays to users) were equal to those for a uniform fare system. While differential fares may entail slightly higher collection costs, the remarks that follow assume that the increase is negligible.

14. Gabriel Roth, for example, seems to adopt this attitude in saying: "In most cases access is provided by one road only, and the provision of further roads is impossible because of the technical layout of built-up areas. In these circumstances competition in any area is effectively impossible. Any firm or individual owning an access road would be in a monopoly position." See Roth, *A Self-Financing Road System* (Institute of Economic Affairs, 1966), p. 31.

15. To simplify the discussion of this point, the costs of implementing pricing systems are ignored.

16. These comments are made in the context of maximizing the public's economic welfare and aside from matters of equity and income redistribution.

17. The unrest with respect to this contention probably stems less from matters of pricing and longrun investment policy than it does from past failures to recognize and take account of certain externalities and income redistribution problems (for those dislocated or affected by specific highway locations), from failure to compensate nonusers for their social costs, from poor aesthetic designs, and from inability (or failure) to trade off these social and external costs with higher highway location or design costs.

18. The evidence on these matters is far from complete and is, of course, limited to the presently available set of modal opportunities. However, the few competent studies thus far conducted bear this out. See, for example, the auto and transit demand elasticities (with respect to auto and mass transit times and costs) tabulated in Charles River Associates, "An Evaluation of Free Transit Service," Report for Office of Policy Development, Department of Transportation (August 1968), Tables 3–1 and 3–2.

19. At output level q_A, facility A is the facility having lowest total cost and at output level q_C, it is facility C.

20. Admittedly, idealized conditions are embodied within these cost and static demand functions and the costs and other effects of implementing workable marginal-cost pricing systems are not included. Using the same assumptions as before, the price is the combined time, effort, and money expense the user must forgo to make a trip; further, it is assumed that—aside from any toll—users perceive their time, effort, and money expense to be equivalent to the shortrun average variable cost. Thus, for shortrun marginal-cost pricing, the toll for facility x and flow must be set equal to $srmc_x(q)$ minus $sravc_x(q)$.

21. This argument is somewhat analogous to an argument of J. R. Meyer, et al., in *The Economics of Competition in the Transportation Industries* (Harvard University Press, 1959), Chapter I.

22. M. Boiteux, "Peak Load Pricing," in J. R. Nelson, ed., *Marginal Cost Pricing in Practice* (Prentice-Hall, 1964).

Urban Transport:
A Survey of Some Pricing Aspects

*P*RICES in urban transportation services and facilities provided by governments (mass transit, highways, airports, parking, and harbor facilities and terminals) serve a many-faceted role. User charges in transportation influence the efficiency of transportation services, the socioeconomic environment, and the achievement of "socially efficient" solutions. Total transportation charges per capita in the 43 largest U.S. cities ranged in 1966–67 from a low of less than 50 cents per capita in Newark, New Jersey, to a high of $67 per person in New York City. Excluding New York, these cities collected an average of $11 per capita in transport charges, an amount equivalent to 10 percent of their collective tax revenue.

In total, $316 million was collected as transportation user charges in 42 cities (excluding New York); a third of the total was from airports, a third from mass transit, and the remaining third from highways, parking facilities, and water transport and terminal facilities. New York City alone collected $523 million, considerably more than all the other cities combined, and equivalent to 21 percent of its tax revenues. Some $436 million of this charge revenue was from the mass transit system; the remainder was from highways, parking facilities, and water transport and terminal facilities. Over 75 percent of the $417 million expended for transportation by the 42 cities was covered by transportation charge revenue. Only highway expenditures were

John G. Duba is Vice President, Airport Facilities of the Air Transport Association of America, Washintgon, D.C.

Duba wrote the rapid transit and airport section; various Urban Institute staff contributed to preparation of the waterfront section.

greater than charges recovered. For nonhighway transport functions, charges were equal to 156 percent of expenditures.

Rapid Transit Pricing

The only U.S. cities now served by rail rapid transit are New York, Chicago, Boston, Philadelphia, and Cleveland.[1] New York City alone accounts for four-fifths of all rail rapid transit and almost one-third of all transit riding in the United States.

With the exception of Cleveland, where the rapid transit service was inaugurated in the 1950s, the subway and elevated systems now operating in the U.S. were developed before the automobile became a popular mode of transportation. Conventional transit systems lost their market to the automobile because of its originally assumed convenience, flexibility, and speed, despite its recognized higher cost of operation (including parking fees). Of all daily passenger trips in urban areas of over 50,000 population, about 96 percent are made by automobile; 3 percent of the trips are made by motor bus and 1 percent by rail transit.

New patterns of urban land development brought about by the automobile resulted first in a decline in transit use and then in a build-up of great congestion on highways and streets. Thus cities are again considering the necessity of new or enlarged transit systems.

New rapid transit systems

The Bay Area Rapid Transit System in San Francisco has been the first of many proposed new systems in the nation to reach the development stage. A new subway system is also under construction in Washington, D.C. New systems are under consideration in a number of cities, including Atlanta, Baltimore, Columbus, Los Angeles, Memphis, Miami, Milwaukee, Minneapolis, St. Paul, New Orleans, Pittsburgh, Portland (Oregon), Seattle, and St. Louis. Being considered are rail facilities, rapid busways, and various combinations of such facilities.

Most of the new systems now under construction stress relatively high line-haul speeds with stations spaced up to two miles apart. Provision is made for bus transfers, for "kiss-and-ride" dropoff points where a wife can drive her husband to the station, and for parking.

This concept contrasts with earlier developed systems where it was assumed the transit passenger would walk to the station.

Economic feasibility studies for proposed new rail transit systems have generally indicated that estimated volumes of potential riders would be insufficient to meet minimum costs for maintenance and operation and would never be able to generate revenues to meet the capital costs of roadway construction, stations, service facilities and rolling stock. For this reason, and also because few cities have more than a few miles of routes where new rail systems would be required to accommodate extremely high peak hour patronage forecasts, cities considering new or improved transit systems are favoring busways or a combination of busways and rail rapid transit. The rail system generally is designed to serve the high density routes.

Bus rapid transit evolved from satisfactory experiences in the operation of express busses on freeways in such cities as Atlanta, Chicago, Dallas, Los Angeles, and New York, and from the concept of reserved bus lanes on streets and freeways, which resulted in greatly improved service. For example, a test of reserved bus lanes conducted by the U.S. Department of Transportation and the Virginia State Highway Department, beginning in September, 1969 on a five-mile section of Interstate 95 leading into Washington, D.C., resulted in a time saving of 12 to 18 minutes per trip.

Where reserved bus lanes can be used, bus rapid transit is economical. Even where special sections of rights-of-way are required, extra costs of development are only a fraction of the cost of a rail system. However, as patronage grows, bus operating costs increase faster than costs for a rail system. In this event, higher operating costs may overcome the initial advantage of lower system installation costs.

Pricing policies

Pricing policies of various transit companies are difficult to compare because of: (1) the inherent differences between public and private operations and (2) the varying public policies practiced by government transit owners. For example, New York City, as a matter of policy, has subsidized transit fares for subways, busses, and the Staten Island ferry. As the demands on New York's city treasury for a wide range of services increased, the city could not afford to meet the continually rising operating costs of the transit system. Hence, an increase in fares became necessary. The original 5-cent fare became 10 cents. Subsequently fares were raised again and again, despite continued subsidy by the city. In 1969, the subway and bus fares were raised from 20 to 30 cents, but the ferry fare remained at 5 cents. Early in 1972 the subway fare was increased to 35 cents.

The New York City government recognizes the value of good transit service, believing that the entire population should have the opportunity to be mobile. The poor, the young, and the old who cannot use the automobile are beneficiaries of the subsidy. An effective transit system is intended also to combat traffic congestion, another objective high on the list of the city's priorities. New equipment and planned extensions and improvements to the system should guarantee a continued high level of ridership but will not obviate the need for subsidies. Thus new sources of revenue are constantly being sought.

The enabling legislation that authorized creation of the Chicago Transit Authority stipulated that costs of maintenance and operation must come from the farebox. As a result, fares in Chicago have been consistently higher than those in New York City. Chicago's most recent change (1970) resulted in an increase from 35 to 45 cents for rapid transit service, plus an increase from 5 to 10 cents in the charge for transfers. This was, however, still deemed insufficient to generate revenue to cover operating expenses. Thus a subsidy from the State of Illinois was sought and obtained.

The City of Chicago has been providing a subsidy by financing needed capital improvements with general obligation bonds. The most recent extensions to the system were made possible by federal grants of some $46 million, representing two-thirds of the actual cost. Federal funds are also being sought for proposed additional improvements.

In 1970, Chicago voters approved the establishment of a Downtown Rapid Transit District. This was an innovative method of raising the local share of proposed improvements for the central business district transit system. Property owners within the district will pay the local share of development costs on a special assessment basis. However, despite the subsidy provided by the city and federal government for capital improvements, another fare hike will be required in Chicago unless some further form of subsidy for operation is provided.

In large and small cities across the country, similar transit problems are found. Proposals have been made to use portions of revenues from gasoline taxes or sales taxes and to obtain state and federal subsidies. The need for assistance is not limited to municipal systems. Some cities, for example, contract with private companies, guaranteeing to cover costs in excess of farebox revenues.

Because the history of transit in the United States has been adversely influenced by the impact of the automobile, pricing policy for transit has necessarily become related to the extent of subsidization. Transit proponents argue that ridership will grow and companies will prosper, given an efficiently managed system. Further, they point out, routes must be conveniently located so that equipment can operate at frequent intervals and on reliable schedules.

Experience indicates that so long as the automobile driver has the convenience of parking close to his place of employment, not even the high costs associated with commuting will lure him back to travel by mass transportation. Some planners suggest that a combination of good transit service and extremely expensive or very limited central-area parking will attract new riders and reduce or eliminate the need for subsidy. To date, however, the trend appears to be toward transit pricing policies that are not related either to the quality of service or to the cost of providing service but instead depend upon the attitudes of specific governments toward the value of transit service to the community.

Pricing and Urban Waterfronts

Urban waterfronts are valuable resources with substantial potential for helping achieve the economic and social goals of persons living in an urban area. However, many waterfronts have been allowed to deteriorate and are thus failing to contribute to the best interests of the cities and metropolitan areas of which they are parts. Recently, a number of cities—among them New Orleans, Baltimore, and Philadelphia[2]—have begun urban renewal projects that involve rebuilding of waterfront areas.

The various types of economic activities found on urban waterfronts include: (1) shipping terminals: cargo (bulk, general, or containerized) and passenger traffic; (2) transportation: airports, highways, rail and bus terminals, truck terminals, hovercraft and ferries, tour boats; (3) commercial establishments: retail stores, office buildings, restaurants, hotels and motels, tourist attractions; (4) wholesale markets; (5) warehouses; (6) recreation facilities: beaches, pleasure boat marinas, fishing piers, parks; (7) commercial fishing: marinas, markets, canneries; (8) industrial plants: shipbuilding, other manufacturing; (9) residences; (10) waste disposal and land fill activities; (11) wildlife preserves and undisturbed scenery; (12) natural resource exploitation: mines, oil wells; and (13) military bases and shipyards.

Prices associated with waterfront activities

Prices associated with the various activities on urban waterfronts include charges for output goods and services, prices on input resources (including land), and rents on the use of equipment and facilities. Other charges include tolls on transportation facilities (and conceivably on waterways) and taxes (sales and property). These diverse levies have their individual incentive effects with respect to the location, production, and resource use of the set of economic activities in the urban harbor area.

Fees and charges for terminal services. These levies fall into two main groups—charges against the vessel (ship), and charges against the shipper (cargo). Within each group there is a long list of specific fees. Services charged against the vessel include: dockage—using wharf or pier; vessel demurrage—leaving a vessel overtime at pier; pilotage—taking aboard a pilot to navigate a ship into port; tug boats; supplies and services—receiving fuel, electricity, provisions; and stevedoring—loading and unloading cargo from a ship (sometimes charged against cargo). Services almost always charged against the shipper (or cargo) include: wharfage—storing and moving cargo on a pier; handling—loading and unloading from piers to rail cars and to trucks; and demurrage—allowing overtime cargo usage of pier.

Leases and rentals. Shipping terminals and auxiliary equipment are leased by owners (private, local government, or port authority) to steamship companies, railroads, etc. The charge is assessed on a time contract basis, and operation of the facility is the responsibility of the lessee. (In some instances railroads own piers.)

Price of land and other input factors. In addition to the purchase price of shoreline and backup land along the waterfront, these factors include the prices of capital equipment, utility services such as water and electricity, labor, and other services and materials required for the operation of terminal facilities and ships in port.

These charges all affect port industry production and resource use. If the value of inputs and outputs to the port industry and its clientele does not correspond to the *social* cost that the output production and use of input factors by the port industry entail, the charges could be modified to bring about a more desirable level of production and resource use. The effective price for the use of land by a particular activity, for example, could be changed by specialized property taxes or surcharges on the sale of land parcels to encourage more intensive use of land by the port industry.

User charges might also be geared to encourage more socially desirable use of waterways and to curtail socially undesirable levels and patterns of shipping and waterway exploitation. In particular, waterway tolls could be designed to compensate for the external costs (from pollution or congestion, for example) imposed on other economic activities whose use of water has been inhibited or excluded by shipping.

One important way in which charges, rentals, tolls, and prices of land and other factors affect resource use in the port is through their effect on *locational* incentives of activities on the waterfront. Locational decisions are influenced by prices to the extent that prices affect the relative attractiveness to various activities of particular sites within an urban waterfront area, or among different urban areas. For example, elevation of shipping terminal fees in Baltimore might divert some activities to Norfolk; or elevation of rental charges on terminal facilities near the city center may encourage the terminal activity to move into the outer harbor area. Similarly, tolls on inland waterways leading to a particular port city might depress shipping in that city to the point of relocation to a port whose access is not so dependent on such waterways. Finally, land costs will influence locational incentives, particularly with respect to alternative sites in a given urban port area.

Spillover benefits and costs

Waterfront activities produce externalities or spillover benefits and costs. These are manifested in two ways: (1) geographical spillover of benefits and costs from the locality of the port to the hinterland, and (2) interactivity spillovers, or direct interactions, that inhibit or enhance the efficiency of one activity as a result of the output of another, and cause prices to diverge from the optimal to the extent that they encourage output or resource use that inhibits achieving the urban goals. Geographical spillovers occur when the beaches and parks of a locality are used by people from outside of the area, or in the spoilage of water downstream from pollution at the port. Since the activities are often provided on a local basis, they may be undervalued or overvalued (priced) if no account is taken of the benefits and costs external to the locality.

Activity interactions are of two kinds. The first, complementarity of activities (pecuniary externalities), is taken into account by the market. For example, activities such as cargo shipment and warehousing are complementary in that one activity's output is the other's input. The market will encourage these activities to locate near one another to reduce costs. The second type, technological externalities, consists of direct interference with one activity's efficiency by another's output outside the domain of the market. For example, water pollution may result from shipping and from pleasure boating, and there is some belief that dredging may upset the ecological balance of an area.

Public goods characteristics

The principal outputs of some urban waterfront activities resemble public goods. Since prices cannot be used as exclusionary devices to facilitate collection of revenues for these services, private investment in these activities is unlikely. How does one price the value, for example, of scenic views, enjoyment of the outdoors, and climate and ecology maintenance?

The spillover and public good aspects of the waterfront activity pattern cause market prices to be inadequate measures of value with which to allocate resources and produce outputs. These phenomena may be identified in detail, and in some cases compensated for by developing a set of "shadow prices" to replace market prices. Such shadow prices would reflect the social purposes that are served by the outputs and resources to which they are attached. These prices could be implemented by modifying the existing structure of fees and charges and other levies used in conjunction with waterfront activity. Any attempt to thus alter the price structure of urban waterfronts, however, must take two additional factors into consideration—technological change and the institutional context.

Technological developments

The revolution in cargo handling and shipping technology is indicated by the advent of containerization and supersized ships, which are significantly increasing the productivity of the port and shipping industries.[3] For example, a single container berth is on the order of ten times as productive (in terms of tons that can be handled per unit time) as a conventional cargo handling terminal facility. The size of tankers, dry bulk carriers, and general cargo ships has increased dramatically since 1950, and is expected to more than double before the year 2000. Some implications of these developments are that: (1) less waterfront area is needed by the port industry, since piers may be used more intensively than before; (2) more backup land area is required for cargo storage; and (3) harbor channel deepening (or widening, or increasing the clearance under bridges) is required to accommodate larger ships.

New concepts for shipping, such as the offshore port and land-bridge, could also significantly affect port activity in the future.[4] The offshore port is a facility for unloading ocean cargo (oil, in particular) out at sea and distributing it to points on the mainland. This type of facility has the advantage of avoiding expensive dredging to deepen existing ports and preventing oil spills near the shore. However, an offshore port, or even the deepening of one or two large conventional ports, would seriously affect the pattern of trade and threaten the commercial status of smaller ports.

The land-bridge concept involves containerized transhipment of cargo from ship to train to ship as, for instance, across the Pacific, the American continent, and the Atlantic. This development, too, has the potential to transform the pattern of trade and the importance of some ports relative to others. In the United States, proposed land-bridge plans include: (1) a Penn Central–Santa Fe unit train consisting of 80 cars that would make a minimum of 25 continental round trips a year; and (2) a train of varying lengths (composed of ten-car segments) linking California and North Atlantic ports.

Institutional context

There are at least five major institutional factors that must be considered in proposing changes in the existing patterns of prices and port activity: (1) ownership of facilities; (2) the functional and legal nature of authorities that administer ports; (3) price regulation through regional conferences and federal review; (4) governmental jurisdiction; and (5) legal precedents.

Ownership. The following is a breakdown (as of 1966) of the ownership of port terminals (not including waterfront manufacturing sites that receive and ship materials by water).[5]

Type of ownership	No. of terminals	Percent of total
Private (profitmaking)	1349	64.1%
Local government agencies	499	23.5
State government agencies	214	10.1
U.S. Government agencies (nonmilitary)	43	2.0
Private (nonprofit)	6	0.3

Ownership clearly affects the range of options available for changing the price structure. Government ownership allows direct modification of fees, charges, and rentals. Activities at privately owned facilities must be influenced more indirectly, e.g., by surcharges or taxes on output services and resource use.

Functional and legal nature of port authorities. Ports are administered along a number of different functional, political, and organizational lines.[6] As with ownership, the strategy for achieving changes in the pattern of prices and activities is clearly dependent on the nature of port administration. Slightly fewer than one-third of the 95 major U.S. ports are administered by agencies on the local level, and only fifteen of these by municipal or county government departments. In addition, the functional responsibilities of the local departments vary considerably among themselves. Thus, the port is available for direct local manipulation in comparatively few instances, and the range of fees and charges under local management is not necessarily a wide one.

Price regulation. Two interrelated factors—regional pricing agreements among terminal operators, and Federal Maritime Commission (FMC) overview—regulate the level of charges for port services. Under the Shipping Act of 1916, steamship companies, terminal operators, and other interested parties are permitted to enter into agreements or conferences for fixing uniform rates and practices in connection with port terminal services. These agreements are voluntary among parties and are submitted to the FMC. If and when the agreements are found to be subject to Section 15 of the Shipping Act, they are approved or modified as necessary. Although the FMC does not control terminal rates, the schedules of charges for all ports are filed with it.

In the North Atlantic region (from Norfolk north) each port has conferences among pier operators or terminal representatives in each port area. The South Atlantic Marine Terminal Conference is the principal terminal agreement for that area. In the Pacific region, including Alaska and Hawaii, the major terminal operators belong to the Northwest Marine Terminal Association, or the California Association of Port Authorities.

Government jurisdiction. In the existing framework of federal, state, and local authority, urban waterfronts are subject to several jurisdictions. Waterways fall within the federal domain; port development may be the responsibility of states, local governments, or interstate semiautonomous port authorities; and shoreline land uses may be the responsibility of many different local governments. For this reason comprehensive approaches to port problems, which are essentially regional in nature, are extremely difficult to implement. Trends toward regional studies and the instituting of metropolitan government offer some promise of progress in this regard.

Legal precedents. Well-ingrained legal traditions sometimes inhibit change in economic structures. The Northwest Ordinance Act of 1787 and the "commerce clause" of the U.S. Constitution prohibit waterway tolls on navigable domestic waterways and harbor and channel entrances, except as they are necessary for operation, maintenance, and improvements. However, the Rivers and Harbors Act of 1882 prohibits, with no exceptions, the imposition of user charges for these waterways. In recent years several studies have been made suggesting charges for the use of federally assisted waterways. As proposed for federal legislation, waterway tolls would be instituted to recover investment costs for harbor and waterway improvements and to pay for navigation services such as lighthouse operations provided by the federal government. The most recent waterway user charge bill was introduced in Congress in 1961, although fuel taxes on tugs and towboats have been proposed since then.

Need for research

This discussion of urban waterfronts has served merely as a broad outline of the relationship of prices to urban waterfront activity. Substantial further research is clearly needed before the production characteristics and interactions associated with waterfront activities can be identified in sufficient quantitative detail to permit development of specific pricing policy recommendations.

Pricing Air Transportation

Airports, although built by local governments, are part of a national airport plan, and the airway system as such is the exclusive responsibility of the federal government. Local governments receive federal grants-in-aid for construction of airports. In 1968–69 local governments spent $634 million on air transportation facilities and the states spent an additional $89 million. In the same year local governments collected $400 million in charges connected with air transportation, while current operating expenditures amounted to $214 million.

Local airports

The operation of most airports in the United States is a community enterprise undertaken for the community's convenience and economic benefit.[7] In capital requirements, operation and maintenance costs, and monopolistic character of business, these airports closely resemble public utilities.

The primary functions performed by a commercial airport are: (1) to supply and manage facilities for landing, servicing, and takeoff of aircraft; and (2) to assemble, process, and dispatch passengers and cargo. The facilities that accomplish these objectives can be divided into two categories—airfield and terminal buildings. Prices charged for these services affect the total cost of public air transportation and are reflected in airline fares.

The costs of airfield facilities are priced to the air carrier through the imposition of landing fees. In recent years, revenue from these fees has been used to guarantee local airport revenue bonds issued for the improvement of facilities. This has been accomplished at many major airports through the implementation of longterm user agreements under which the air carriers agree to reimburse payments annually by the airport on its revenue bonds. The payment of landing fees to airports by the commercial air carriers has risen from $20.6 million in 1960 to $104.4 million in 1969 (see Table 11.1).

Actual contractual agreements for the use of airfield facilities are generally the result of negotiation between air carriers and the airport management. Facilities are leased to the carriers on a square footage basis and to concessionaires on the basis of a percentage of gross income. Generally, the carriers pay a rental fee that is adequate to cover operating and maintenance costs and debt service of the facilities utilized, plus costs allocated for the general public areas supporting those facilities.

There are many secondary or nonaviation services supplied by an airport that provide revenue to the airport. This revenue can reduce the revenue required from aviation sources, and ultimately from the air traveler. Efficiently managed airports maximize concession and rental revenue as a means of generating income for expansion and improvement without increasing air carrier charges. Since communities receive substantial benefits from the presence of an airport (e.g., economic activity generated by the airport's employment and expenditures and access to rapid, convenient, and efficient air transportation), these benefits must be carefully considered in the formulation of airport pricing policy.

Federal user charges

Under the Federal Aviation Act, the Federal Aviation Administration (FAA) has responsibility for planning, administering, and operating the airways. Historically, the costs of maintaining the nation's airways system have been financed from general federal tax revenues, supplemented by a 5 percent tax on airline passengers.[8] This tax has produced about $1.6 billion since 1960.

On July 1, 1970, the Airport and Airways Development Act of 1970 became law, under which direct federal charges for use of the airways were imposed on commercial air carriers, the traveling public, and general aviation. The charges are in the form of an 8 percent tax

TABLE 11.1

Air Transport Industry's Support to the Nation's Airports and
Airways System, Decade of the 1960s

(In thousands of dollars)

| | DIRECT SUPPORT | | | INDIRECT SUPPORT | | | |
Year	Tax on Passengers[a]	Other Taxes[b]	Total	Facility Rentals	Landing Fees	Total	Total Industry Support
1960	$ 158,131	$ 21,976	$ 180,107	$ 55,623	$ 20,592	$ 76,220	$ 256,327
1961	165,877	19,356	185,233	62,792	25,553	88,345	273,578
1962	172,722[c]	17,227	189,949	80,376	33,607	113,983	303,932
1963	100,912	16,762	117,674	92,519	39,147	131,666	249,340
1964	106,062	16,258	122,320	92,020	40,407	132,427	254,747
1965	125,890	15,565	141,455	111,520	45,512	157,032	298,487
1966	139,624	13,690	153,314	119,784	52,688	172,472	325,786
1967	170,323	13,957	184,280	136,736	74,077	210,813	395,093
1968	185,531	12,313	197,844	167,317[d]	89,040	256,357	454,201
1969	259,233	14,759	273,992	180,400[d]	104,407	284,807	558,799
Total 1960–69	$1,584,305	$161,863	$1,746,168	$1,099,092	$525,030	$1,624,122	$3,370,290

[a] About 15 percent of total passenger revenues are not subject to tax because government agency personnel traveling on official business are exempt.
[b] Includes federal and state tax on fuel and other miscellaneous taxes on aircraft operations.
[c] Tax rate 10 percent through November 15, 1962, 5 percent thereafter.
[d] Estimated

on each ticket for domestic travel, a $3 charge on international travel, a 5 percent tax on air freight waybills, a use tax on airline aircraft, and a fuel tax applicable to general aviation airplanes. The revenue generated by these taxes is placed in an Airports and Airways Trust Fund to be used for the expansion, modernization, and improvement of airways and airport facilities throughout the United States.

For the first time in U.S. history, users are now being charged directly for making use of both airways and airports. The user taxes are, of course, reflected in the pricing of the public service rendered by the air transportation industry. In the case of airways, the user charge principle assumes that a user should pay for a government service only to the extent that it provides a special benefit to him and that additional costs should be absorbed by the general taxpayer.[9] It is equally important that the users be charged equitably, i.e., no user should be required to pay more than his own share based on actual use of airways facilities. The 1970 Act directed the Secretary of Transportation to conduct a study to determine the proper allocation of costs to users. The final report of this effort was scheduled for 1972.

The 1970 Act also authorizes funds, on a matching basis, for developing new and expanded airport facilities. These funds, generated by the previously mentioned user taxes, are limited to airfield projects, excluding terminal area projects. The construction of terminal facilities also requires large amounts of capital; this is supplied through the issuance of general obligation bonds, revenue bonds, or private investment.

Pricing air transportation

Three separate management groups are involved in pricing air transportation: airports, which comprise a community enterprise; airways, which are the exclusive responsibility of the federal government; and air carriers, which are corporate entities financed by private capital and subject to utility-type pricing. There are innumerable factors that enter into the airline fare and ratemaking process: air carrier taxes, airport landing fees, facilities lease costs, and equipment amortization and depreciation are but a few. However, the actual pricing of air transportation services to the public is controlled by the federal government through its regulatory agency, the Civil Aeronautics Board (CAB), which must approve all rates and charges of the air carriers.

Under the Federal Aviation Act, the CAB is charged with the economic regulation of commercial air transportation. It regulates fares, rates, route structures, accounting procedures, and establishes what it deems to be a fair and reasonable return on investment for the industry.

Far more research is needed to establish more ideal air transport pricing practices, including pricing to reflect airport and airway congestion costs.

NOTES

1. Systems utilizing vehicles operating on exclusive rights-of-way are referred to as rapid transit. The right-of-way may be elevated, in a separate busway, or at grade. A rapid transit system is sometimes composed of a combination of types of right-of-way. For instance, in Chicago subway trains also operate on elevated tracks and on rails laid in the median strips of expressways. Historically, "rapid transit" vehicles have operated only on fixed rail systems but now the term is recognized to include any vehicle that operates at a high average speed with a high degree of schedule dependability. Busses operating in reserved bus lanes on highways or on specially constructed busways at an overall average speed of twenty miles per hour or more would be considered rapid transit.

2. *Waterfront Renewal* (Report of Wisconsin Department of Resource Development, 1966).

3. R. O. Goss, "Port Investment," in Denys Munby, ed., *Transport* (Penguin, Modern Economics Series, 1968); also U.S. Army Corps of Engineers, *Harbor and Port Development: A Problem and an Opportunity* (July 1968).

4. H. J. Marsden, "The Regional Approach to Port Development Planning," paper delivered to National Meeting on Transportation Engineering, American Society of Civil Engineers, July 1969, pp. 14–15; also, "Land-Bridge," *World Ports* (May 1969):22.

5. *State and Local Public Facility Needs and Financing* (U.S. Congress, Joint Economic Committee, December 1966), Vol. 1, Chapter 15.

6. U.S. Maritime Administration, *United States Seaports*.

7. Washington's Dulles International Airport and National Airport are the only U.S. airports owned and operated by the federal government.

8. Prior to Nov. 15, 1962, a 10 percent federal transportation tax was levied on all modes of common carrier transportation. This tax was discontinued after that date on all modes of transportation except commercial airlines, which were required to pay a 5 percent tax.

9. The general public benefits from the airway system's contribution to the national defense, and there is clearly an economic benefit to the nation at large accruing from a safe and efficient airways system that permits goods and services to be brought to all parts of the nation as swiftly as possible.

Pricing
Urban Water

*I*N 1652 Boston instituted the first municipal water supply in the United States, an exceedingly small operation providing domestic water and fire protection for a single street. As late as 1850 there were only 83 public water systems. By 1900, however, the number was approximately 4,000, and by 1963 the industry consisted of some 19,236 utilities providing 20 billion gallons of water a day to some 150,000,000 people.[1] As indicated in Table 12.1, most of these utilities were relatively small, with 79.2 percent of them serving only 12.5 percent of the population.

Since the 1890s, urban water service has been primarily provided by a department of a municipal government, although regulated private water companies and special districts retain a significant role (Table 12.2). In 1963 approximately 71 percent of all utilities were publicly owned. The private companies are characteristically smaller than the public utilities: a private company served an average of 3,900 persons while the public utility served an average of 9,500.

The supplying of water may be divided into three phases: acquisition, treatment, and distribution. The degree of complexity associated with systems varies widely and is dependent on such factors as local topography, hydrologic conditions, distance from the source of water

Steve H. Hanke is Assistant Professor in the Departments of Geography and Environmental Engineering and of Political Economy at The Johns Hopkins University.

Author's Note: I wish to thank John J. Boland, Paul Bugg, Robert K. Davis, Louis De Alessi, and Charles W. Howe for their helpful comments on earlier versions of this chapter.

TABLE 12.1

Water-Producing Facilities by Size of Population, 1963

Customers served	Number of facilities	Percent of facilities[a]	Population served	Percent of population served[a]
Under 500	5,433	28.2%	1,724,981	1.1%
500–1000	3,751	19.5	2,901,512	1.9
1000–5000	6,054	31.5	14,269,131	9.5
5000–10,000	1,503	7.8	10,150,890	6.7
10,000–25,000	1,225	6.4	16,707,415	11.1
25,000–50,000	573	3.0	14,791,755	9.8
50,000–100,000	298	1.5	12,900,250	8.6
Over 100,000	399	2.1	77,156,210	51.2
Totals	19,236	100.0%	150,602,144	100.0%

[a] Percentages may not add to 100 percent due to rounding

SOURCE: *Statistical Summary of Municipal Water Facilities in the United States, Jan. 1, 1963* (U.S. Public Health Service, Publication No. 1039), Table 5.

to the treatment plant, density of urban development, the quality of raw water intake, and the kinds of demand being placed on the system.

In spite of their physical complexity and variability, urban water systems do possess several pervasive economic characteristics. For example, their fixed costs are large relative to variable costs. In most periods, the utilities operate at levels of output well below their capacity. Demand approaches capacity only during a few hours of the day in months of peak seasonal demands; hence, shortrun marginal costs are below average costs in most periods. Moreover, the demands show a strong seasonal pattern. The water utilities, therefore, have a low load factor, i.e., a low ratio of peak-load sales to average sales.

Joint or common costs also characterize water utilities, since the same physical plant is used to provide service during periods of peak and offpeak demand. The same system is also used to supply customers located at various distances from the sources, at various elevations and at various housing densities. An understanding of the economic problems associated with these characteristics is fundamental to an analysis of water pricing and investment policies.

In the 1955 to 1965 period $10.2 billion, or an average of $258 per additional consumer, was invested in new water supply facilities. By 1968, this figure had risen to $300, with approximately 60 percent of

TABLE 12.2

Ownership of Water Facilities by Size of Population, 1963

Population size	Total	Publicly Owned		Privately Owned		Dual owner- ship
		Number	Percent[a]	Number	Percent[a]	Number
Under 500	5,334	3,245	24.1	2,078	37.8	11
500–1000	3,695	2,762	20.5	922	16.8	11
1000–5000	6,017	4,692	34.8	1,315	23.9	10
5000–10,000	1,487	1,113	8.3	372	6.8	2
10,000–25,000	1,218	876	6.5	340	6.2	2
25,000–50,000	567	362	2.7	204	3.7	1
50,000–100,000	296	173	1.3	123	2.2	
Over 100,000	392	245	1.8	147	2.7	
Total	19,006	13,468	100.0%	5,501	100.0%	37
Percent of Total	100.0%	70.9%		28.9%		0.2%

[a] Percentages may not add to 100 percent due to rounding

SOURCE: *Statistical Summary of Municipal Water Facilities in the United States, Jan. 1, 1963* (U.S. Public Health Service, Publication No. 1039).

this amount related to residential consumption.[2]

One reason for the large investments in water utilities is that streamflows are negatively correlated with seasonal demands. Hence, over-the-season storage is needed as demands increase. Table 12.3 summarizes estimates of capital costs that were assembled by questionnaire in 1966 from 188 water supply facilities in the United States. Acquisition costs, which are associated with over-the-season storage, account for almost 39 percent of all capital costs. Lof and Hardison have provided evidence that this percentage will increase in the future. They have determined that arid regions require storage equal to mean annual streamflow to facilitate a uniform draft equal to only 10 to 20 percent of the mean annual flow.[3] Storage costs increase sharply when storage is developed beyond these levels as the better sites are pre-empted. Moreover, external costs associated with reservoir development, which Lof and Hardison did not include in their calculations, appear to be increasing as society becomes more sensitive to the scenic and historic values that are lost through inundation.

TABLE 12.3

Percent Distribution of Capital Cost Among System Components, 1966

Acquisition	38.7%	
Source of supply		7.6%
Transmission		31.1
Distribution	35.5	
Mains		27.1
Booster stations		3.0
Storage in distribution system		3.9
Hydrants		1.5
Treatment	14.3	
Screening		0.5
Chemical handling		2.6
Softening		2.1
Sedimentation		2.2
Filtration		4.6
Disinfection		0.8
Plant storage		1.5
Meters	2.3	
Unassigned	9.3	
Pumping		3.9
Lab equipment		0.1
Flow measurement		0.1
Instrument and control		0.6
Other		4.6

SOURCE: *Water and Wastes Engineering* (April 1966): 34–39.

Pricing and the Water Utility

If the demand for water were totally inelastic, an analysis of pricing policies would be irrelevant in determining the efficiency with which water resources are used, since price would then not affect the rate at which water is consumed. The demand for water, however, is not totally inelastic; therefore, this analysis is important.

Water utilities, whether private or public, base their pricing practices on a long-accepted principle: a "fair return" on invested capital. The widespread adoption of this principle can be attributed to two factors: (1) in the case of private water companies, the legal and economic principles of public utility regulation, which include a "fair return" concept, are directly imposed by state regulatory commissions; (2) municipal water utilities, even though they may not be directly regulated, generally adopt the policy recommendations of the American Water Works Association, which are similar to those made by formal regulatory agencies. The AWWA's *Water Rates Manual,* for example, recommends that "every water works should receive a gross revenue in an amount that will suffice to provide adequate service and assure the maintenance, development, and perpetuation of the system."[4] The pricing policy compatible with this principle equates price to average costs.

In addition to charging prices that yield a fair rate of return, water companies generally adopt a corollary policy—a uniform pricing system, in which the same price is charged for water over a given area and over a given time, even though the cost of supplying customers varies from one part of the area to another and from one time in the period to another. Both the fair return and the uniform pricing systems have significant effects on the ways in which water and land are used.[5]

For water to be used in an economically efficient manner, consumers should be charged a price equal to the shortrun marginal opportunity cost. Marginal opportunity cost is the value which the resources used to produce the marginal unit of a given good could command in their most productive alternative use. If water is sold at prices that exceed marginal opportunity costs, buyers purchase less than the optimum quantity. Consumers would be willing to pay more than the opportunity costs of the resources that are required to produce slightly more water, and society would benefit from having users consume more water, since the incremental benefits would exceed the associated incremental costs.

Uniform pricing over time

During a production cycle, the quantity of water demanded at any given price varies over the cycle, i.e., a peak-load problem exists. A water enterprise's current pricing policies must, therefore, be evaluated in the light of this problem. The object is to choose the right capacity and structure of prices, a choice which also determines the level of output in each subperiod of the cycle. Given a peak-load problem, the determination of appropriate prices and capacity is much more complex than when the quantity demanded is uniform over time.

The major contributor to the peak-load problem is the residential water demand for lawn irrigation. This was documented in 1966 by a team of researchers at Johns Hopkins.[6] Their study included ten metered western areas in which the ratio of average summer to average winter use (reflecting the influence of sprinkling demands) ranged from 1.6 to 3.4, with a mean value of 2.2. The thirteen metered eastern areas that were studied had ratios ranging from 1.2 to 3.2 with a mean of 1.9. The maximum day ratios reflected even a larger divergence between winter and summer: the range in the western areas was from 2.2 to 4.7, and in the eastern areas 1.8 to 5.5.

Peak demands, although largely explained by sprinkling demands, cannot be fully understood until data on other urban water uses can be obtained. This was partially accomplished in 1966 in a study of commercial water use in the Baltimore region.[7] On the basis of their results, the Johns Hopkins group developed a synthetic hydrograph for a twenty-four hour period for a community with a population of 100,000. (See Figure 12.1.) This hydrograph demonstrates the demand variability that can exist in a water system.

A fair rate of return policy and attendant average cost pricing tend to encourage inefficiency in the utilization of existing facilities and of inputs. Under a fair rate of return on investment (the "rate base"), there is one clear avenue open to the utility to increase its total earnings: an expansion of its rate base. Therefore, the utility will find it profitable to employ more capital relative to other inputs than is consistent with minimization of cost for the quantity of water delivered.

In practice, when a peak-load problem exists, utilities will sustain their overcapitalized positions by encouraging peak-load consumption.[8] This is accomplished by the use of a uniform pricing system in which peak and off-peak rates are equal. As a result of this practice, peak-load rates, on the relatively elastic peak demands, will be less than their opportunity costs. Hence, these demands will be excessive. Conversely, the off-peak rates for the relatively inelastic off-peak demands, will exceed their opportunity costs. Therefore, these demands will exceed their opportunity costs. For that reason, these de-

Fig. 12.1 *Synthetic Hydrograph for Community with 100,000 Population (28,000 Owner-Occupied Dwellings)*

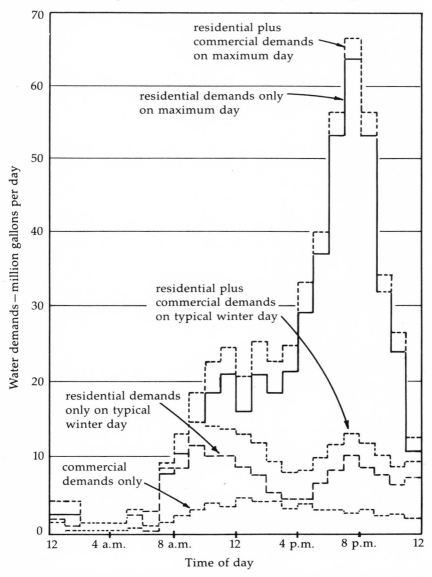

residential plus commercial demands on maximum day

residential demands only on maximum day

residential plus commercial demands on typical winter day

residential demands only on typical winter day

commercial demands only

Water demands – million gallons per day

Time of day

SOURCE: Jerome Wolff, F. P. Linaweaver, Jr., John C. Geyer, *Water Use in Selected Commercial and Institutional Establishments in the Baltimore Metropolitan Area: A Report on the Commercial Water Use Research Project* (Johns Hopkins University Press, June, 1966).

mands will not be large enough to use existing capacity efficiently. When the off-peak revenues generated by uniform pricing are equal to the additional investment costs and revenue loss from peak sales, the rate of return will remain constant, and the fair rate of return criterion will be satisfied. Total profits, however, will be greater as the total investment (rate base) required to meet peak demands increases. Hence, uniform pricing, in the face of a peak-load problem, results in inefficient resource allocation and an involuntary subsidy to the peak users by the off-peak users.

Uniform pricing over space

Two types of system expansion, with markedly different effects on water system costs, have been distinguished by Gaffney.[9] First, a system may be expanded by enlarging a utility's service area and lengthening its distribution mains. This type of expansion increases longrun marginal costs. Secondly, a system may be expanded by serving more customers within an existing service area. This type of expansion decreases longrun marginal costs. Therefore, the type of system expansion may produce very different effects on system costs. Both economies of density and diseconomies of distance must be given due consideration when evaluating a water utility's pricing policies.

Uniform pricing over space, like that over time, leads to a social loss in efficiency if marginal opportunity costs vary over space. These efficiency losses are illustrated in Figure 12.2.

At a uniform price OC_2 that is equal to the weighted average of the separate marginal costs, low-density customers will purchase $OX_{ld,gd}$ units and high-density users $OX_{hd,sd}$ units. However, if the rates reflect marginal opportunity costs, the low-density consumers would take no water from the public system and would instead use individual wells and cisterns. On the other hand, high-density users would expand consumption to $OX'_{hd,sd}$. Opportunity cost-pricing generates efficiency gains as the incremental cost of expanding volume in the high density area is $EFX'_{hd,sd}X_{hd,sd}$ and the incremental gain is $DFX'_{hd,sd}X_{hd,sd}$. This results in a net incremental gain to high density users represented by the triangle *DEF*. There is also a net gain to society from not serving low-density users. The costs saved by not serving are $OC_3GX_{ld,gd}$, while the value of benefits to low-density users would be $OIHX_{ld,gd}$.

Fig. 12.2 *Uniform Prices and Welfare Loss*

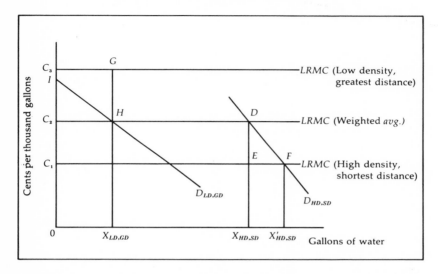

SOURCE: Adapted fom Ralph Turvey, *Optimal Pricing and Investment in Electricity Supply: An Essay in Applied Welfare Economics* (London: Allen and Unwin, Ltd., 1968).

The net saving is IC_3GH. Therefore, the total efficiency gain associated with appropriate pricing policy is DEF plus IC_3GH.

Even though all evidence indicates that costs increase as one moves farther from load centers to more sparsely settled areas, current pricing practices ignore these cost variations and are therefore inefficient. Consumers and society benefit from opportunity cost-pricing over space, but utilities prefer the uniform price under a fair return system, for this pricing policy tends to allow them to extend service over space and increase the capital intensity of the water system.

The effects of uniform pricing over space and time may combine to affect markedly the areal growth patterns of urban areas.[10] By charging uniform rates the utility imposes a "tax" on consumers who are located in high-density areas near the load center of the utility. In addition, these rates provide a subsidy for consumers who are in low-density areas located farther away from load centers. This process not only leads to an overinvestment of resources in the supply of water services, but also results in a premature development of land at the rural-urban fringe. Uniform prices thus subsidize population diffusion and urban sprawl.

Uniform prices over time further aggravate the problem of over-extension of service and urban sprawl. Users who live farthest from the water system's load center, in general, also live in low-density neighborhoods and have large sprinkling demands, which create most of the system peaking. Since uniform rates offer no special incentive for the lawn irrigator to alter his peak demands, current pricing practices tend to encourage the consumer to move away from load centers and to settle in low-density areas.

Peak responsibility pricing

Current pricing practices may be improved by adoption of a pricing system in which prices are varied over space. This requires a price schedule that increases as one moves farther from the water system's load center—assuming marginal costs increase as one moves away from the load center. Another improvement would be to vary prices among periods in the production cycle. This system has been referred to as the peak responsibility method of pricing.[11]

The motivation for peak responsibility pricing is to maximize welfare, i.e., to maximize the sum of producers' and consumers' surpluses. In its simplest form, the peak responsibility method is quite clear. Price should exceed marginal operating costs in periods when demand is high by amounts that will restrict demand to system capacity. In periods of low demand, price should be equated to marginal operating cost. There is a causal connection between the peak users and required capacity. The adoption of peak responsibility pricing makes this connection clear by making those who place demands on the system's capacity responsible for financing it.

Figure 12.3 illustrates the salient features of peak responsibility pricing. Consider the following simplified problem: there are two demand periods (summer and winter), and the demands in each are independent of one another. Let the shortrun marginal costs of supplying water, considered separately for each of the periods, be constant (OH) until capacity is reached, at which point they become infinite. Service beyond this point can be provided for any one of the periods at a cost of OI per unit. This represents the cost per unit ($OI - OH$) of provid-

Fig. 12.3 *Allocation of Capacity Cost and Peak Responsibility*

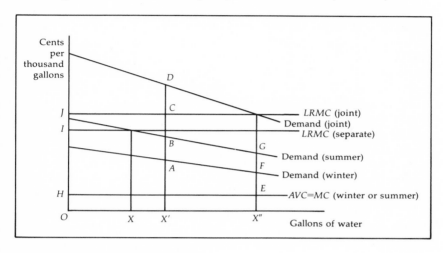

LRMC = long range marginal cost
AVC = average variable cost
MC   = marginal cost

ing new capacity plus the variable cost per unit of providing water in that period *(OH)*. Hence, the *LRMC* (separate) curve indicates the cost of increasing output for one period while the output of the other is held constant at some lower level. If the demands for both periods are combined, the shortrun marginal costs are twice those for one period considered separately (2 × *OH*) until capacity is reached. Service beyond that point can be provided for combined demands at a cost *OJ* per unit. This cost is represented by *LRMC* (joint) curve and is made up of a capacity cost per unit *(OI — OH)* plus two variable costs per unit—one for winter and another for summer. The combined summer and winter demands, Demand (joint), is a vertical summation of the summer plus winter demands. The vertical summation, not a horizontal summation, is appropriate in this peak-load problem, because the demand during the summer does not affect the quantity of water that can be consumed in the winter. Therefore, the separate demands placed upon capacity are complementary, not competitive.

Given this simple peak-load problem, the pricing investment rules that lead to an equilibrium and a welfare optimum are **quite clear.**

In the short run, the price, for both demand periods, should be equated to shortrun marginal opportunity cost. If the initial capacity is OX' (Figure 12.3), capacity is effectively rationed when winter users are charged $X'A$ and summer users are charged $X'B$. At these prices the marginal value of service is equal to the marginal opportunities foregone. If prices had not been equated to shortrun opportunity cost, there would have been both a disequilibrium and a loss of efficiency in the water market. Consider equating prices to average variable cost (OH). At this price, excess demands will exist in both periods and water will have to be rationed by administrative means. Another inappropriate pricing scheme, under the assumptions of this example, would be to charge winter consumers average variable cost (OH) and peak-load summer users variable cost plus capacity cost (OI). Under these conditions, the winter period would experience excess demands while the summer period would experience excess capacity (XX'). This is clearly inefficient, for the marginal values placed on additional units of water during the summer exceed the marginal opportunity cost (OH) throughout the range from zero to X'. Hence, the amount OX' should be provided in the summer.

In the long run, prices should still be equated to shortrun opportunity cost, and capacity should be expanded until the relevant longrun marginal cost is equated to the relevant vertical summation of demand prices.

The case illustrated in Figure 12.3 is that of the "shifting-peak," in which capacity acts as a constraint on demand in both periods.[12] Therefore, the relevant demand curve is Demand (joint), which is the vertical summation of summer and winter. The relevant cost curve for comparison is $LRMC$ (joint). This curve includes a per unit marginal cost for both the summer and winter and a per unit capacity charge. If capacity is still OX', then neither the summer nor the winter demands taken separately will justify an increase in capacity. But the demand price for the combined periods will justify an increase in capacity. The efficient price in the winter is $X'A$ while the summer price is $X'B$. Summing these demand prices vertically yields a joint demand price of $X'D$, which exceeds the joint longrun marginal cost $(X'C)$ by CD. Therefore, expansion is signaled, and will continue to be signaled until the optimum capacity is reached (at OX'') where joint demand equals joint longrun marginal cost. At this equilibrium level, efficiency is maximized and winter demand prices are $X''F$ and summer demand prices are $X''G$.

To implement more efficient pricing systems, utilities should determine rate zones that are based on cost differences in service areas. Within each zone, peak responsibility pricing should be practiced. It is not discriminatory, and it allows the utility to choose the correct capacity, structure of prices, and level of output in each subperiod of the production cycle. Moreover, it leads to a welfare optimum.

Demand Estimation and Pricing

Quantitative estimates of price elasticities and demand are essential in determining whether and how to put this analysis into practice. If the demand for water is inelastic, the impact of price changes on the quantity of water demanded will be relatively small, and so will the effects of alternative pricing policies on efficiency in the urban water market. As the price elasticities of demand increase, so do the misallocations resulting from prices that are not equated to marginal costs. Without reliable estimates of demand, utilities do not know whether resources are being allocated efficiently, and to what extent their pricing policies are appropriate.

The current practice in the water utility industry is to assume that the price elasticity of demand is zero. This assumption is demonstrably incorrect, but will continue to be held as long as a "fair return" can be earned on additional capacity since there is an incentive to develop more capacity. This can be more easily justified if projections of water "requirements" are made and not water demands that vary with price.

The typical requirements forecast simply assumes that the demand for urban water will increase proportionately or in some simple relation to the increase in population and economic activity:

$$Q = P \times q,$$
where
Q = total annual demand
P = projected population
q = averaged annual per capita demand

Projections that ignore the influence of price on demand invariably support conclusions of the following type: "Our forecasts indicate that we will face a critical water shortage in ten years, as our water needs will exceed our supplies. We, therefore, must expand our current water system."

A similar simplistic rationale underlies the minimum design standards of the Federal Housing Authority, which serve as the criteria for water systems serving properties insured by the FHA.[13] As Table 12.4 shows, water use data collected from flat rate areas for the FHA itself are not consistent with the FHA's design criteria.[14] For example, in the

TABLE 12.4

Comparison of Field Data with FHA Standards

Type of Demand	FHA Standards (gpd/du)	Field Data (gdp/du)[a]			Field Data Flat-Rate Average
		National Average	West	East	National Average
Average Daily	400	398	458	310	692
Maximum Daily	800	870	979	786	2,354
Peak-Hour Average Conditions	2,000	2,115	2,481	1,833	5,170

[a] For metered areas with public water and sewer gpd/du (gallons per day/dwelling unit)

SOURCE: F. P. Linaweaver, Jr., John C. Geyer, and Jerome B. Wolff, "Summary Report on the Residential Water Use Research Project," *Journal of the American Water Works Association*, 59 (March 1967): Table 3, 278.

thirty-nine areas studied, average annual demands were from 47 gpcd to 437 gpcd, the ratios of maximum day to average day use were from 157 percent to 541 percent, while peak-hour to average-hour ratios were from 247 percent to 1,650 percent. A number of studies of the price elasticity of the demand for water are summarized in Table 12.5. Almost all of these studies—which are of varying degrees of statistical sophistication—were based on aggregate cross-sectional data. Either all of the major classes of urban users (residential, commercial, industrial) are treated as one, or residential use is not disaggregated to inhouse and sprinkling uses. These studies suggest that the demand for water is relatively inelastic, so that price policies would have relatively little impact on allocative efficiency. However, this conclusion is not generally valid because the quality of the data used in these studies was inadequate.

Aggregate cross-sectional studies are static in nature and cannot be relied upon to predict the allocative effect of price changes. Projections based on these data must assume that the spatial effects of prices are synonymous with temporal effects. The aggregation of user classes creates additional problems that cast doubt on the validity of price elasticities derived from these data. When user classes have been aggregated, a single theoretical explanation of demand does not exist. The aggregate includes elements (domestic use and sprinkling) that must be explained by consumer demand theory. It also includes industrial and commercial uses in which water is viewed as an input into a productive process. In this case the demand is represented by a derived input demand and is studied in terms of water's objective dollar value in the productive process. Consequently, aggregate demand cannot be theoretically explained and its statistical estimation amounts to nothing more than an overall average of urban uses. This average is distorted as the proportionate importance of demand components varies from city to city. Therefore, the apparent influence of price on the quantity demanded will be influenced by the relative importance of the classes of users in the areas from which the demand data are gathered. This problem becomes particularly acute when considering rate changes for various classes of customers, because the specific price elasticities by user class are needed if accurate predictions of revenue changes and quantity adjustments that affect allocational efficiency are to be made. An average price elasticity, therefore, will not be suitable for most purposes.

In addition to averaging demand, these studies have used average prices, since different buyers, who are served by the same utility, purchase water at different prices per thousand gallons. The practice of using average prices is not a satisfactory procedure because the determining variable, average price, is not strictly independent of the dependent variable, the quantity of water demanded.

The Residential Water Use Research Group at Johns Hopkins has collected the most complete set of water use data to date. These data were collected on master meters that recorded flows every fifteen minutes. They are superior to the data mentioned above, because they were collected on a disaggregated basis by user groups.

The empirical results found in this study for *domestic demands* were: (1) a distinct daily cycle with morning and evening peaks, al-

TABLE 12.5

Estimates of Price Elasticity of Water Demands

Investigator	Demand sector	Data characteristics Year	Data characteristics No. Points	Remarks	Estimate of elasticity
Metcalf	Municipal	1926	30		.65
Seidel, Bauman	Municipal	1955	441	@ $.15/1000 g	1.0
				@ $.45/1000 g	0.12
Fourt	Municipal	1955	44		.39
Flack	Municipal less un-accounted	1955		Western cities:	
				@ $.15/1000 g	1.00
				@ $.25/1000 g	.61
				@ $.35/1000 g	.32
				@ $.45/1000 g	.12
				All cities:	
				@ $.15/1000 g	.28
				@ $.25/1000 g	.45
				@ $.35/1000 g	.49
				@ $.45/1000 g	.65
				@ $.55/1000 g	.41
				@ $.65/1000 g	.28
Gottlieb	Municipal	1952	68	Kansas	1.02
		1957	84	Kansas	.69
		1952	19	Kansas, Multiple Regression	1.24
		1957	24	Kansas, Multiple Regression	.68
		1958	24	Kansas, Multiple Regression	.66
		1947–9		Illinois, Multiple Regression	.27

TABLE 12.5 (Continued)

Investigator	Demand sector	Data characteristics Year	No. Points	Remarks	Estimate of elasticity
Renshaw	Residential	1955	21		.45
	Commercial	1955	36		1.04
	Industrial	1955	41		.80
Ware, North	Residential	1965	634 residences	Georgia, linear	.67
				Georgia, logarithmic	.61
Howe, Linaweaver	Residential, Domestic	1963–5	21	Public sewer	.23
	Residential, Sprinkling	1963–5	21	Public sewer	1.12
			10	Public sewer, west	.70
			11	Public sewer, east	1.57
	Residential, Max. Day Sprinkling	1963–5	21	Public sewer	.68
			11	Public sewer, east	1.25
Bain, Caves, Margolis	Municipal	a	41	Northern California	1.10
Gardner, Schick	Residential	a	43	Northern Utah Multiple Regression	.77
Boland (Hittman Assoc.)	Residential	1960	27	Multiple Regression	.44

a. Dates of inquiry not cited by authors.

SOURCE: Hittman Associates, Inc. "Price, Demand, Cost, and Revenue in Urban Water Utilities." (Report HIT–474, Columbia, Md., September 1970).

though these peaks were not severe and were not the major cause of system peaking problems (peak-hour to average ratios averaged 3.73); (2) no display of any seasonal cycle; (3) a price elasticity of approximately —.23 for metered areas with public sewers; and (4) an income elasticity, as measured by the surrogate of property value, of approximately 0.35.

The empirical results associated with *average summer sprinkling demand* were: (1) sprinkling demand exhibited significantly greater price elasticity than domestic demand; (2) sprinkling demand exhibited a much higher income elasticity than domestic demand; (3) price elasticity in arid regions of the West was less than that of the humid East; and (4) the income surrogate, property value, was a major factor affecting sprinkling demand in flat rate areas.

The empirical results associated with *maximum day sprinkling demand* were: (1) maximum day magnitudes of demand in the arid and humid regions did respond significantly to price changes; (2) the elasticities of these demands are lower than those of average demands; and (3) income elasticities measured by the surrogate of property value were lower than those of average day sprinkling demands. This measure of income elasticity was much lower in arid regions than humid regions. It should be noted that these results were obtained using the existing metering and pricing procedures. At present, higher prices provide an incentive for alterations in average sprinkling use, but there are no special incentives to avoid days of very high sprinkling uses; demand meters and appropriate peak-load pricing are not currently utilized.[15]

A time-series study

The first study based on disaggregated time series data was conducted in 1970 in the semi-arid West. Prior to 1961, the water utility managers of Boulder, Colorado, relied exclusively on alterations in the city's water supply to meet shortages caused by increased demands. In 1961, however, a major change took place. The utility, in an attempt to meet impending water shortages, looked to the demand side of the market. Water meters were universally installed, and an incremental commodity charge of 35 cents per thousand gallons was adopted. The 1970 study concluded that sprinkling demands were not only reduced by meter installation, but also subsequently continued to decline. Moreover, the rates of sprinkling application were greater than the calculated "ideal" application that would maintain a green yard by as much as 77 percent before metering, and less than "ideal" by as much as 37 percent after metering. This implies that consumers will substitute brown for green yards after commodity charges reach high enough levels. In the case of Boulder, Colorado, consumers made this substitution at the relatively low price of 35 cents per thousand gallons.

Domestic (inside the house) use represents the other component of residential water demand. The conclusions with regard to this component were similar to those with respect to sprinkling demand. As Table 12.6 shows, domestic consumption was reduced sharply upon the introduction of meters as people altered their activities in response to a positive water price. The average use in the metered-rate period for all the routes being considered was 36 percent lower than in the flat rate period.

The unexpected result of the time-series data is that the shift in use is very sharp and of such great magnitude. This implies much higher price elasticities for domestic use than have heretofore been calculated when cross-section data were employed. The reason for this disparity centers on the fact that the cross-section studies used price-quantity relations for many price ranges, while the time-series study concentrated on the switch from flat to metered rates (a zero incremental price to a positive price).

The major explanation for the observed decrease in use appears to lie in such once-and-for-all changes as repairing leaks in the domestic plumbing systems and altering basic consumption within the home, e.g., using a stopper or dishpan when washing dishes instead of using a constant flow.[16] These types of changes are available only to a limited degree to consumers once they have made the first and most basic of alterations. Such significant responses of domestic demands to further increases in incremental commodity charges will probably not occur, unless price changes are very large.

The trends both in sprinkling and domestic use were similar. After the introduction of meters (1962–1968), demands stabilized at their lower levels.

Studies such as these reinforce the standard postulates of demand theory and refute the requirements approach to forecasting and sys-

TABLE 12.6

Domestic Water Use

Year	Consumption PDU northern routes[a] (1000 gal. per month)	Consumption PDU southern routes[b] (1000 gal. per month)	Consumption PDU TOTAL (1000 gal. per month)
1955	8.6	8.6	8.6
1956	8.7	8.7 ·	8.7
1957	9.2	9.2	9.2
1958	10.9	10.9	10.9
1959	9.9	9.9	9.9
1960	9.2	9·2	9.2
1961	9.3	9.3	9.3
1962	9.5	7.4[d]	8.1[d]
1963	4.4[c]	6.1[c]	5.4[c]
1964	4.9[c]	5.7[c]	5.5[c]
1965	4.9[c]	6.3[c]	5.9[c]
1966	4.9[c]	6.5[c]	6.0[c]
1967	4.9[c]	6.5[c]	6.0[c]
1968	4.2[c]	6.0[c]	5.5[c]
Ave. flat rate	9.4	9.1	9.2
Ave. metered rate	4.7[c]	6.2[c]	5.9[c]

[a] Northern routes include: 16, 18, 53, and 54
[b] Southern routes include: 37, 70, 71, 72, 73, 74, 75, 76, 78, and 79.
[c] Totally metered
[d] Partially metered
SOURCE: Steve H. Hanke, "Demand for Water Under Dynamic Conditions," *Water Resources Research*, 6 (October 1970): Table 3, 1260.

tem design.[17] The evidence also suggests that a seasonal pricing policy in which summer rates are higher than winter rates would have a significant impact on consumption, because of the relatively high price elasticity coefficients for summer sprinkling.[18] Moreover, metering clearly has a marked effect on both inhouse and sprinkling uses. Pricing is thus a powerful tool that can be used by utilities to influence water use and, therefore, the efficiency with which resources are allocated. Prices that do not reflect the appropriate opportunity costs can account for significant misallocations of resources, as is clear from the price elasticity of the sprinkling demands that largely determine the design parameters of the system. Water managers must be aware not only of the principles of pricing, but also of the nature of the demands that they face if they are to be able to calculate the benefits that are forthcoming under efficient pricing.

What is needed now are more empirical studies of water use at locations where prices are varied over wide ranges. The water use data at these locations would ideally be collected individually for a number of households over a span of time, so that changes in the behavior of each household and of various groups could be traced over time and differences among units could be studied at any one time.

Summary and Conclusions

The water utility industry has historically been relatively free from pressing questions of technology, economics, or political judgments. But this situation is changing rapidly as the interplay between wants and water resources continues to be altered with the rapid growth of the industry in recent years. The pervasive economic problems associated with the industry are those of peak-load and joint or common cost.

Based on the analytical framework and empirical evidence presented above, let me now summarize several important points and inferences.

1. The provision of urban water fulfills the two necessary conditions for adoption of user fees. First, it is possible through the installation of water meters to identify the beneficiaries of this service without undue costs. Secondly, it is possible to exclude, without undue costs, those who are unwilling to pay for water service.

2. Even though most utilities impose user fees for the provision of water service, their method of doing so is inefficient, because their pricing policies are not based on sound economic principles. Rather, they adhere to the long accepted principle of a "fair return" on invested capital and the corollary policy of charging uniform prices over time and space.

3. The principle of a fair return, while limiting the rate of return earned on invested capital, does not limit the amount of capital employed. Hence, the aggregate profits earned by the utility can be in-

creased by extending both the intensive and extensive margins of capital. The fair return policy will, therefore, encourage an expansion of the water utility system beyond its optimal size.

4. This expansionist policy is implemented by adopting uniform pricing systems in which the uniform rates are set close to the monopolistic price for offpeak sales and below the opportunity costs for peak-load sales. Some of the revenues from offpeak sales can then be used to cover the losses of the uneconomic sales to peak users. This encourages an expansion of the water system designed to serve peak users.

5. Uniform rates over space also facilitate the expansion of water systems. Uniform rates are set close to the average costs of serving both high-cost users located in low-density areas farthest from the system's load center and low-cost users located in high-density areas closest to the system's load center. Some of the revenues gained from setting rates above the opportunity costs of the low-cost areas can then be used to cover the sales at below opportunity costs to high-cost users. This encourages expansion of the system to serve consumers farther from its load center.

6. The fair return policies in concert with uniform pricing systems tend to favor peak-load users who reside in low-density areas located at the greatest distance from load centers at the expense of offpeak users who reside in high-density areas located nearest to load centers. This results not only in an overinvestment of resources in the supply of water services, but also in a premature development of land at the rural-urban fringe.

7. The misallocations resulting from these uneconomic pricing policies can be potentially great, because the quantity of water demanded is sensitive to changes in its price. This is particularly true for sprinkling demands in all areas and at all prices that have been studied, and also for domestic demands at least when the switch from flat rate prices to metered rates is made.

8. Prices that take account of the opportunity costs of using economic resources will improve the allocation of water resources. As one moves farther from the system's load center, prices should increase to reflect the diseconomies of distance. As one moves to more densely settled areas, the rates should be lowered to reflect the economies of density. The rates should be varied over time to reflect the

peak responsibility associated with the use of the system's capacity. In practice, this can be accomplished by adopting both seasonal and zonal rates.

NOTES

1. American Water Works Association, "The Water Utility Industry in the United States," *Journal American Water Works Association*, 58 (July 1966): 771. Also see *AWWA Water Rates Manual* (1954).

2. Charles W. Howe, "Municipal Water Demands," in W. R. Derrick Sewell and Blair T. Bower, eds., *Forecasting the Demands for Water* (Ottawa: Policy and Planning Branch, Department of Energy, Mines, and Resources, 1968).

3. George O. G. Lof and Clayton H. Hardison, "Storage Requirements for Water in the United States," *Water Resources Research*, 2 (Third Quarter, 1966): 340–347.

4. *The American Water Works Association Water Rates Manual* (New York: The American Water Works Association, 1954): 2.

5. Jerome W. Milliman, "Beneficiary Charges and Efficient Public Expenditure Decisions," in *The Analysis and Evaluation of Public Expenditures: The PPB System, A Compendium of Papers Submitted to the Subcommittee on Economy in Governing*, 1 (Joint Economic Committee, 91st Cong., 1st sess., 1969): 291–318.

6. F. Pierce Linaweaver, Jr., John C. Geyer, and Jerome B. Wolff, *Final and Summary Report on the Residential Water Use Project* (The Johns Hopkins University Press, June 1966), Appendix A.

7. Jerome Wolff, F. Pierce Linaweaver, Jr., and John C. Geyer, *Water Use in Selected Commercial and Institutional Establishments in the Baltimore Metropolitan Area: A Report on the Commercial Water Use Research Project* (The Johns Hopkins University Press, June 1966).

8. Stanislaw H. Wellisz, "Regulation of Natural Gas Pipeline Companies: An Economic Analysis," *Journal of Political Economy*, 61 (February 1963): 30–43.

9. Mason Gaffney, "Replacement of Individual by Mass Systems in Urban Growth," *Proceedings of the American Real Estate and Urban Economics Association*, 4 (1969): 21–68. This argument is supported by the evidence in Paul B. Downing, "Extension of Sewer Service at the Urban-Rural Fringe," *Land Economics*, 45 (February 1969): 103–111; also Lawrence G. Hines, "The Long-Run Cost Function of Water Production for Selected Wisconsin Cities," *ibid.*, 133–140.

10. Mason Gaffney, "Land and Rent in Welfare Economics," in Joseph Ackerman, Marion Clawson, and Marshall Harris, eds., *Land Economics Research* (Johns Hopkins Press, 1962), pp. 141–167; and Gaffney, *op. cit.* (see note 9 above).

11. Jack Hirshleifer, "Peak Loads and Efficient Pricing: Comment," *Quarterly Journal of Economics*, 72 (August 1958): 451–462; also Hendrik S. Houthakker, "Electricity Tariffs in Theory and Practice," *Economic Journal*, 61 (March

1951): 1–25; Peter O. Steiner, "Peak Loads and Efficient Pricing," *Quarterly Journal of Economics*, 71 (November 1957): 584–568, and "Peak Loads and Efficient Pricing: Reply," *Quarterly Journal of Economics*, 72 (August 1958): 465–468; also Oliver E. Williamson, "Peak-Load Pricing and Optimal Capacity," *American Economic Review*, 56 (September 1966): 810–827.

12. Another possibility is the "firm peak," analyzed by Steiner.

13. Federal Housing Administration, *Minimum Design Standards for Community Water Supply Systems* (FHA No. 751, July, 1965).

14. F. Pierce Linaweaver, Jr., John C. Geyer, and Jerome B. Wolff, "Summary Report on the Residential Water Use Research Project," *Journal American Water Works Association*, 59 (March 1967).

15. Steve H. Hanke, "Demand for Water under Dynamic Conditions," *Water Resources Research*, 6 (October 1970): 1253–1261.

16. Steve H. Hanke, "Some Behavioral Characteristics Associated with Residential Water Price Changes," *Water Resources Research*, 6 (October 1970): 1383–1386.

17. The study of Boulder's metering experience has its limitations: e.g., only two prices were observed, so no explicit calculations of price elasticity were made.

18. Since this chapter was written, a study of the Washington, D.C., area has shown the probable effect of seasonal pricing. See: Steve H. Hanke and Robert K. Davis, "Demand Management Through Responsive Pricing," *Journal American Water Works Association*, 63 (September 1971).

Pricing Fire
Protection Services

THE provision of fire protection services by local governments in the United States cost $1.6 billion in 1967–68. In cities with population greater than 100,000, these costs constituted 5.9 percent of direct expenditures and amounted to $15.90 per capita. If financed by a special property tax outside of the general fund, these expenditures would require an annual levy in major U.S. cities ranging between $0.90 and $3.30 per thousand dollars of market value of property.[1] The figures, however, clearly fail to reflect the total costs of fire. Despite fire department and other efforts to limit damage, in 1967 fires killed 12,200 people, destroyed an estimated $1.7 billion of property, and prevented an unmeasured—but assuredly large—amount of industrial production through destruction of facilities and breaks in supply lines. The fire insurance purchased to protect property owners to some extent from fire-caused damage totaled $1.86 billion in 1967, yet that figure still understates the costs of the insurance because it ignores an additional $480 million of "extended coverage," which is largely for fire.

Numerous other public agencies as well as private firms and individuals incur further costs in attempts to reduce fire damage. Police departments control traffic and crowds in the area of a fire; water systems are geared to serve the instantaneous and reliable high-volume demands of firefighting; and municipal building and fire departments

William Pollak is an economist and member of the Research Staff of The Urban Institute.

Author's Note: I wish to thank Howard Chernick, a student summer intern, who made important contributions to the initial formulations of this material.

enforce codes designed to reduce damage and prevent outbreak. Property owners often provide their own supplemental protective devices: for example, fireproof materials and construction, and built-in detection, warning, and extinguisher systems. Putting a cost figure on these assorted contributions to fire prevention and suppression is very difficult, because in most cases the effort is inseparable from other activities that are not related to fire. For example, assessing precisely the extra building costs associated with special exit facilities, fireproof structural members, firewalls, etc., would be nearly impossible. Similarly, separating the costs of a police department's fire-related duties—such as enabling fire engines to get through traffic, rerouting other traffic, and controlling spectator crowds—from its other functions presents many problems.

However, estimates of water costs due to fire demands have been made. Because those demands are primarily for a maximum-flow capacity, their relative cost significance decreases as city size increases. Nonetheless, estimates presented by the International City Management Association suggest that approximately 20 percent of total water costs in very large cities is attributable to fire protection needs.[2] Since the dollar costs of water supply thus attributed to fire protection approximate 30 percent of total fire department outlays, it is clear that the total public sector costs of fire protection are well in excess of fire department budgets.

It is not surprising that a protective system with so many complex elements presents many opportunities for improvement of efficiency. Among the changes that have been proposed or tried are the following: combining police and fire departments into one department of public safety; merging small-jurisdiction fire departments to bring costs down and to improve effectiveness; assigning new tasks to fire companies so that their time, when not fighting fires, can be used more productively; and altering firehouse location and personnel response patterns, as wells as firefighting procedures, materials, and equipment. A number of organizations have been devoting significant effort to studying the efficacy of such changes and spreading information about them. Among these are the National Bureau of Standards, the National Fire Protection Association, and the RAND Corporation. RAND has also, in cooperation with the New York City Fire Department, been systematically studying the benefits and costs of several possible changes in department operations.

The changes noted relate directly to fire department operations, but the system might also be improved by alterations at other points. Although many fire departments and public fire protection agencies have made efforts to instruct householders and businesses about practices that would lessen fire hazards, little is known about the absolute effectiveness of such efforts or whether other possible educational or incentive efforts would have more impact. The practices of fire insurance firms do not directly affect fire damages but they can exert significant influence indirectly through their impact on fire department operations and private sector protection practices. The rates paid by residents of a given community for fire insurance are influenced by the grade given to their local department by insurance rating organizations. Similarly, the rates paid by owners of a particular property are influenced by the property's structural characteristics and protective measures. If insurance rates correctly reflect the actuarial value of reductions in damages caused by different protective measures, insurance practices will induce effective public and private protection behavior. However, insofar as insurance rates do not follow this pattern, they will induce behavior that results in lower insuree payments but that is inconsistent with effective protection. Fire insurance rate competition might force a correspondence between rate levels and damage probabilities, but the industry is heavily regulated and thus not very competitive, leaving considerable slack and room for productive change.

The protection measures installed in buildings and embodied in their structures are influenced, not only by insurance practices but also by building and fire code regulations (and the degree of their enforcement) and the practices of the suppliers of decorative and building materials. These suppliers are regulated to some extent by federal and state governments, and the flammability characteristics of materials are extensively studied by the National Bureau of Standards. Adjustments in any of these practices may reduce fire incidence or the spread of fire.

The production of fire department services also might be moved from the public to the private sector, or the manner in which public fire departments are financed might be altered. In Scottsdale, Arizona, for example, fire protection services are provided by a private firm under contract to the city; however, the financing, coming out of the city general fund, is conventional. The same firm also serves rural residents and businesses in other parts of Arizona on an annual fee or fee-for-suppression-services basis at the buyer's option.

Smaller changes in financing, however, are also possible. For example, the usual fees charged by fire departments could be greatly expanded. At present many cities levy charges for fire inspections and for permits for hazardous occupancies and processes. In general these charges bear little or no relationship to the cost of service provided, and it is likely that the fees could yield more revenue and be more equitable if redesigned. In addition, there are many cities that regularly or sporadically provide services to areas or individual properties outside of their legal jurisdictions and employ a variety of pricing rules in charging for service. For example, cities charge variously on the basis of the value of property in the outside area, the number of calls made, the number of calls adjusted for pieces of equipment dispatched, and so on. It is likely that the pricing policies could be improved to increase their revenue yield and to provide more useful incentives. This chapter focuses, however, on the potential for benefits from imposing fees on beneficiaries to finance the total firefighting operations of city fire departments.

Charging for Fire Protection: Possible Benefits

Efficiency benefits are generally viewed as following from the imposition of prices on a previously free service because fees place on users the social costs associated with the quantity and quality of service they consume. Since the individual will presumably purchase only those units of a priced service that yield benefits to him in excess of their costs to him, resources under pricing will be devoted only to the production of units of service whose output is justified by an excess of benefits over social costs. In contrast, users of zero-priced (free) public services will consume units if they have any value at all, and as a consequence will waste resources by using units of output whose value is less than their social cost. While this rationing effect is the most discussed source of allocative gains, such benefits might also arise if the introduction of pricing reveals a higher or lower level of public benefit (demand) than was estimated, at least implicitly, when output decisions were in administrative hands, completely isolated from the market.

This reasoning can be applied to fire protection: communities, by charging for protection, may reduce the level of fire service demand and thus the level of their outlay for fire departments. To discuss the implementation and benefits of pricing, we need to define (1) what the users of fire department services consume and (2) what they should be charged for. Although such information is easily found for most physical products where the unit is either self-defining (automobiles, combs, lathes) or of no operational or analytical significance (quart vs. liter, pound vs. ounce, etc.), definition is much more difficult in the area of services. Here the choice of units is complex and likely to affect market outcomes and the analysis of service outputs significantly. Does a patient who visits his doctor consume a particular cure or fifteen minutes of a doctor's time?[3] And to its users, is garbage service a "twice-weekly pickup" or pounds of garbage disposed?

In the case of fire protection, is a given property (1) "using" the service only in those instances when fire breaks out and the fire department is called in, or is it (2) "using," over a specified time period, the guarantee that extinguishment and other services of known quality will be provided?[4] Neither of these options is patently unreasonable. Therefore, some criteria must be specified to facilitate choices between them. The allocational consequences of the two options are considered here in order to select the specific charge unit that, when implemented, results in the most efficient use of fire protection resources.

Fire Protection Outputs: Units on Which To Base Charges

Option number 1: fire department turnout

If fire department turnout is the basis for charging a fee, those who observe the outbreak of fire, either as householders or property owners or as bystanders, must decide whether or not to sound an alarm. People in such circumstances, however, are unlikely to have the technical knowledge or to be in a state of mind accurately to weigh the benefits of fire department attendance against the costs of the fee. Therefore, though the fee may choke off some demands for fire department services, it is quite likely that the rationing thus achieved will have adverse allocation effects.[5] Furthermore, the individual who spurns fire department attention because he thinks the costs of its service may outweigh the possible reduction in risks to his own property may be ignoring the danger to neighboring properties— a decision that from society's point of view may be inefficient, to say the least.

Such arguments seem sufficiently damning to the case for charges on fire department turnouts, but still another argument arises out of the technical characteristics of fire department services. Virtually all fire department costs are a combination of personnel expense and depreciation of equipment and buildings. It is evident, therefore, that once a manned fire department is in place in an area, attending any specific fire imposes minimal additional cost on the department.[6] As a consequence, charging for fire department attendance at a fire would discourage use of valued fire service when, since it has no marginal cost, there is no reason to discourage it. In the language of economic theory, fire protection—at least in the short run—is like a public good; although exclusion is possible, the reduction of service through charges is irrational on economic grounds.[7] Whether or not the fire department turnout is a reasonable way to measure fire department output, it appears to be an inappropriate unit on which to base charges.

Option number 2: an annual fee to guarantee fire department service

This option would relieve individuals of making buy/no-buy decisions at the site of a fire. As long, however, as individuals are free to reject or to pay for annual service, the arrangement will also result in service being denied (to those people who do not subscribe) when the shortrun marginal cost of providing service is zero. Since this is inefficient, a system that guaranteed service to all and simultaneously *compelled* fee payment by all properties in the protected area might be more reasonable. A compulsory payment arrangement could clearly raise revenue, and at least would not have the negative effect of denying some people a service whose shortrun marginal cost is zero. Whether such a system would stimulate efficiency and, if the system were implemented, how charges should be varied for different properties are not clear. Let me consider these matters briefly.

Normally, the social costs of an individual's use of a product or a service are placed on the user by tying unit prices to unit costs and varying the user's financial cost on the basis of the quantity and quality of output that he consumes. This, as argued earlier, is desirable because users would be discouraged from consuming units whose benefits fell short of their social costs. If, however, the guarantee of a year of fire department services is the unit bought (under compulsion), users cannot independently vary the quantity or quality of their consumption. Instead, they are provided with whatever level of service is established in their area. All users in a particular area receive the same service, costs are not traceable to particular users, and it would seem that the institution of prices can serve no allocation objectives.

While these rather pessimistic conclusions about prices have some merit, they fail to reflect the significant influence that variable property characteristics have on the quality, extent, and therefore, costs of public fire protection. For example, high-incidence rates, dense population, and fire-prone structures all increase the benefits that stem from enhanced public fire protection, and thus would apparently justify greater department outlays. Such characteristics, since they influence public fire protection costs, might justifiably serve as the basis for fire service charges, even though the service provided to properties cannot be independently varied. In the absence of charges graded to the demands that properties make for protection, the fire department costs associated with properties do not fall on owners, who therefore will tend to underspend on those actions that could reduce the demands for fire service arising from their holdings—for example, installing protective devices, building more fire-resistant structures, and eliminating, altering, or creating safeguards for hazardous industrial processes. Fire department service charges proportioned to the service demands of properties would internalize the public benefits of enhanced owner-provided protection and prevention, and would constitute an incentive to expand that element of the fire protection system.

The above arguments suggest that allocation benefits may be achieved if the service unit is the year of available fire protection, and if compulsory charges are levied that vary according to the demands for fire protection made by a property.

Fire Department Charges: Analysis

If charges are based on the characteristics of properties that impose costs on the public sector, they would serve functions similar to those normally served by prices: i.e., they would finance fire department expenditures and, by creating incentives for owners to reduce the fire risks of properties, would discourage "use" of the fire service. In stressing these similarities, however, there is a risk of neglecting issues that are unique to a pricing scheme wherein charges are applied, not for use in the short run, but for certain aspects of longrun private behavior.

The rationale for the scheme derives (as pointed out earlier) from the influence of private behavior on public costs, which is but one example of public/private interaction in the fire protection field. The level of damages (or damages averted), for example, is determined, not by any one of the elements above—such as fire department quality, water service capability, or private structural or protectional efforts— but by the interaction of all of these and other elements in the fire protection system. Furthermore, while I have focused on the influence of private efforts on the level of public protection, the fact that public and private efforts *together* determine the level of protection suggests that the level of fire protection publicly provided may influence the level of protection that private units will choose to provide.

This suggestion may be damaging to the pricing argument, for I have assumed that, since private neglect of fire protection considerations could force uneconomic levels of public protection, some incentives (e.g., fire protection fees) were necessary to induce adequate private efforts. However, having just noted that the level of public protection may itself influence the level of private effort, I now must consider the possibility that the level of private effort may be appropriately influenced by the administratively determined level of public protection, without the additional incentive of prices. Put differently, my argument has posed fire protection prices as necessary to induce an efficient mix of public and private protection efforts, but I have not yet adequately considered the mix that would arise in the absence of prices.

The Fire Protection System: A Simple Behavioral Model

To facilitate the consideration here of zero pricing and its implications, a highly abstracted, simple model of the fire protection system has been set up so its workings may be examined. Those aspects of the system that are either unessential or irrelevant to user-charge concerns are eliminated from the model so that the focus can be on what appears to be the central relations and decisions in the system. The model is an economist's model: i.e., where behavior is involved, participants in the fire protection system are assumed to have specifiable objectives which they seek to maximize. Finally, because the model is presented at this stage for its heuristic value, I can proceed boldly, oblivious to the severe measurement problems which some of the variables might raise for an enterprising empiricist.

Public sector protection efforts are here regarded as uniformly blanketing the protection area of the community, while private efforts are regarded as specific to particular properties, whether household or business. Public fire protection expenditures (F) and private sector protection expenditures (O_i) for particular properties are assumed to determine the level of damage averted over the course of a year at those properties.[8] For any particular property, the expected value of damage averted (eda_i) is

$$eda_i = g_i(F, O_i),$$

and for the community the expected value of damage averted (EDA) is

$$EDA = G(F, O_i \ldots O_n) = \sum_{i=1}^{n} g_i(F, O_i).$$

This formulation implies that the damage averted in one property is independent of the private protection efforts of other properties—an oversight indulged in because that externality is not a concern here.[9] If the social objective is to minimize the sum of the expected value of fire damages and expenditures on protection or, in our terms, to maximize the expected value of damage averted minus expenditures on fire protection, then the optimal expenditure levels are those at which the marginal dollar of expenditure in each protection area yields an increase of a dollar in the expected value of damage averted.

Our concern, however, is with the determination of these different expenditure levels rather than with their optimal levels. In the following analysis, the public fire department is assumed to have the public interest in mind: given private efforts, F is therefore set at the level where an additional dollar of public effort yields a total—summing over all protected properties—of a dollar increase in the expected value of damages averted. Analogously, it is assumed that each owner seeks that level of own protection that, given the community level of protection provided by expenditure F, is optimal for him. That is, he will seek the level, given public protection, where an additional dollar spent on own protection will yield a dollar increase in damage averted. Because the individual's damage averted depends only on the level of his own (O_i) and the community's protection level (F), the analysis will not be altered by lumping all owners' protection into an aggregate O.

The "damage-averted" production function is assumed to be normal in that the marginal return to F declines with increases in F, but abnormal in that the marginal return to F also declines with increases in O expenditures. The marginal returns to O are assumed to behave symmetrically.[10] This function form seems more likely to describe the process than a more conventional form because we are dealing with a "protection" function rather than the economists' usual production function. By definition, the expected value of damage in the absence of protection becomes an upper bound to the value of protection output. As a consequence of this and the fact that either input alone can produce close to the maximum possible output, it becomes clear that, over some range, increasing one input lowers the marginal product of the other. These comments are included to introduce, rather than resolve, questions relating to "protection" functions and to justify the particular slopes adopted in Figure 13.1. The basic thrust of the argument would remain, however, if different slopes were employed.

The lines FF' (OO') in Figure 13.1 indicate for each level of $O(F)$ the level of $F(O)$ at which the marginal damage averted is one dollar. They also indicate, given the behavior pattern assumed above, the level of own and public protection that individuals and departments will seek, given the level of effort the other has set. If the optimal mix is indeed a mix and does not involve the elimination of either public or private protection efforts, then the two lines cross, since only if they cross can the two maximum conditions be simultaneously satisfied with positive F and O values.

It is evident that, if public protection is set at level F_A, owners will respond by spending level O_A, and the optimal mix of public and private efforts will be achieved—*without imposing user fees in fire protection*. This latter point deserves stress, since it suggests that allocative efficiency may be achieved while charging a zero price and without causing the shortage and rationing problems normally encountered

317

Fig. 13.1 *Damage Averted Through Private and Public Protection*

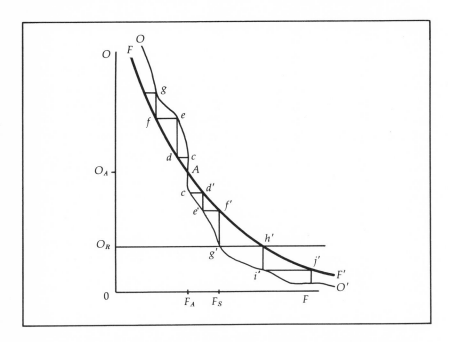

when an optimal level of output is produced but is distributed free of charge.

Before this conclusion is accepted, however, the model should be explored in a bit more detail. The two curves continually shift as new buildings are constructed and technology and prices change. Furthermore, adjustments in F and O take time, so that it is unlikely that the system will be in equilibrium.

If the system is above and to the left of *A*, fire departments would be seeking to reduce their efforts, and/or owners would be increasing their own efforts, with the system moving in the direction of no fire department and very significant levels of owner-provided protection. If fire departments and their owners each adjusted to the equilibrium appropriate to the other's previously set level of protection, the system would follow a pattern such as *cdef* and so on. On the other hand, if the initial position is below A, owners will be seeking to reduce their protective efforts, constantly increasing the quality of protection that the public sector is forced to provide. If adjustment here were in steps, the pattern would be from c' to h'.

Neither scenario "fits" the impressions born of casual empiricism: i.e., owners are not, through the quality of their own protective efforts, in the process of making public protection redundant (moving up and to the left), nor do they constantly reduce their efforts only to be bailed out by improved public fire department efforts. If, in fact, the system were below and to the right of A, it would not be unreasonable to prevent owners from reducing protection below some level so that a cumulative decline such as $c'-j'$ could be avoided.[11] The institution of such a limit in our model at O_R, for example, would leave the system at h', with owners chafing to reduce their efforts to a level consistent with the quality of public protection, and fire departments committed to the maintenance of standards that at least prevent complete shifting of protection efforts to them. The model thus provides a rationale for the real world phenomena of building codes and fire codes, which, as would O_R, require much effort for their enforcement.[12] The presence of these phenomena in the real world also suggests that points above and to the left of A, where owners seek ever higher levels of protection, are improbable.

Similarly, if the relative slopes of the two curves were such as to yield a stable equilibrium optimum at A (Figure 13.2), there would be no rationale, in the framework of the model, for minimum private protection standards. If the system were below A, owners would seek without external pressure what the codes try to force; if above A, codes could be justified only by a desire to force on the private sector an uneconomic share of the fire protection burden. Points below A in Figure 13.2 thus seem at odds with the real world, whereas points above A (for example at Z) are conceivable when municipal governments are strapped for funds.

In thus exploring the workings of this model, the intent is not to argue that the fire protection production function has a particular shape or to press the model's descriptive accuracy. Rather, our concern is to discover whether in a hypothetical fire protection system the achievement of an optimal mix of public and private efforts requires the institution of formal links (user charges, fire codes, etc.). Exploration with

Fig. 13.2 *Stable Equilibrium Optimum*

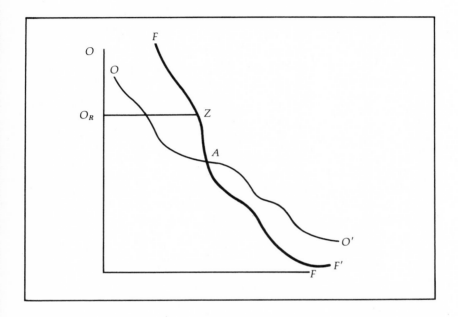

the model makes clear that, even with a well-intentioned and well-administered fire department, the dynamics of the system present significant obstacles to attainment of the proper fire protection mix. When the system is not at its optimum, user charges represent one way (though not the only way) of increasing private protection efforts by giving to owners, through a lower fee, the *public* benefit flowing from those efforts (or, conversely, placing on owners the fire department costs of neglecting private protection).

In sum, for certain publicly provided services, exclusion is impossible (or economically unjustifiable) because the individual's use of the service cannot (or should not) be varied in response to his payment. But since alterable behavior of individuals influences the provision level of the communally provided service, charges might be made so that private behavior does not require uneconomic levels of provision of the public good. Pursuit of this line of reasoning, however, has revealed that such manipulation of behavior through prices is unnecessary, since private behavior is appropriately influenced by the level of public good provision. While this conclusion is logically correct in a static model, it may be irrelevant in a dynamic context, where certain behavior patterns—e.g., optimization, given each other's position, by a public department and a private economic unit may move systems away from their optima. Furthermore, the costs of moving to the static optimum may prevent this solution. In this situation, allocation benefits may well flow from the institution of a user charge system.

Charges for Fire Protection: Pricing Formulas

If fees are charged they should reflect the costs imposed by users. In the case of fire services, this would involve charging individual properties a fee proportional to the demands they present for fire protection. As noted earlier, the guarantee of service over a specified period is probably the most useful unit on which to base charges. The most obvious dimension of this output is the quality of service provided.

The quality of service provided by a fire department has two basic aspects: (1) the time lag between the sounding of an alarm and the arrival of fire fighters, and (2) the effectiveness of the fire fighting units upon arrival.[13] Average response time clearly depends primarily on the average distance of properties from the nearest firehouse which, in turn, will be determined by the number and distribution of firehouses per unit area. Upon arrival, the effectiveness of extinguishment and related efforts will depend upon the quantity, type, and quality of equipment deployed, the waterflow available at the scene, and the operational skill and efficiency of the firefighting team. Itemizing the elements of fire department quality is rather easy, but aggregating them into a single index that measures quality is much more difficult. In fact, because an estimation of quality essentially depends, in part, on the characteristics of the properties to be protected, a unique index or measure would be needed for each specific community. These complexities may be avoided by using input value-per-unit-area as the quality measure. Given this input-oriented measure, the demand for quality units will depend on how a department's ability to prevent damage reacts to input increases, and on those characteristics of protected properties that influence the reductions in damages that will flow from given improvements in fire department effectiveness. These matters can be seen with the aid of Figure 13.3's conventional demand diagram, whose horizontal axis represents quality units (measured in dollars of expenditure per acre) rather than units of quantity. Since the demand curve is a marginal benefit curve, its height, at any quality level, indicates the benefit derived from a one-dollar-per-acre quality improvement. Such a curve can be drawn for each property in the department's protection area.[14] Furthermore, the protection area demand curve can be derived by vertically summing the demand curves of all of the properties in the area, since, as area service quality improves, it simultaneously improves for each property in the area.

The marginal benefit of quality increments can, as a first approximation, be regarded as the resulting reduction in the expected value of fire losses.[15] It should be noted that one may be able to identify this curve over relevant ranges without coping with the more slippery related total of damages averted. The actual shape and location of the marginal benefit curve, for any particular property, will depend on the

Fig. 13.3 *Marginal Benefit Derived from Quality Improvement*

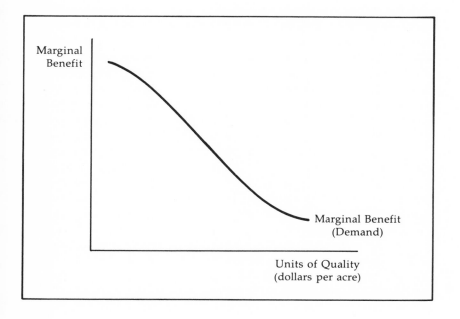

complex ways in which quality levels interact with property characteristics, fire incidence, and property values to determine fire losses. The overall height of the curve is clearly positively related to the probability of fire, the value of the property and of its contents, and the number of people at the property. The more.probable fire is, the greater will be the value of any given increase in service quality since that *quality increment* is more likely to be used. Increases in the value of property and contents and the number of people at the property will similarly shift the marginal benefit curve upward because such increases will enhance the *value* of any given reduction, caused by quality improvements, in the percentage of damage caused by fires in the protection area. On the other hand, increases in the fire resistiveness of structures, easing of exit, and provision of better automatic suppression devices will *lower* the marginal benefit curve because these are essentially owner-provided substitutes for public protection that reduce the latter's significance.[16]

If fire protection were a normal good, these conclusions would lead one to expect the quality of fire protection by properties to be positively related to their fire probability, value, and population, and negatively related to the extent and quality of protective measures in the property. However, as argued earlier, individuals cannot independently vary their purchase of fire protection; as a consequence, the significance of the individual property's demand lies in its influence on the community demand for protection, and thus on the level of community fire department expenditures.[17] Fees designed to reflect this influence in order to impose incentives to reduce fire protection demands would necessarily be related to those observable property characteristics shown above to be determinants of demand.[18] Thus, high-value, poorly protected, fireprone, and heavily populated properties would tend to pay more because their existence, relatively speaking, forces and justifies having high fire department expenditures. Insofar as properties eliminate these characteristics by, for example, providing better onsite protection measures, they would reduce their own fee payment and would facilitate lower public expenditure.

Finally, if fees are to reflect the influence of properties on department costs, they must also reflect the differing impacts that varied properties have on the size of the area a department is called upon to protect, since fire department costs are determined, not only by the quality of protection offered by the department, but also by the extent of area over which protection is provided.

Charges for Fire Protection: Implementation

Currently, fire services are in effect financed out of fees that are based on the value of properties and that require property assessments for their implementation. A pricing system based on the factors noted above could be based on either a direct rating of properties or a modification of the rating implicit in insurance rates. Under the first option it would be necessary to have, for each property, figures indicating property value, property area, and peak population, as well as some measure or rating of the probability of fire and the susceptibility to internal and external fire spread. Little difficulty would be encountered in collecting the first three figures, since property values are assessed for other purposes and area and population are simply physical characteristics. The last two figures are less straightforward but must be contemplated in the light of present fire and building code practices that already involve inspections of nonowner-occupied properties during the building process and periodically thereafter—a division that might justify different procedures and practices for the two property groups. Ignoring arson (which in fact is responsible for an indeterminate but significant percentage of fires), reasonable estimates can be made of incidence probabilities in properties, taking into account the number and type of occupancies and the population involved. It would probably be wise, given the inexactness of these estimates, to define four or five fire-probability classes rather than to make separate numerical estimates for each property. The difficulty of estimating firespread potential is reflected in the length and complexity of fire and building codes and fire insurance rating schemes, since every item recognized in these relates either to fire probability or the potential for firespread.

It would not, however, be impossible to create a reasonable scheme that takes into account structural, decorative, fire prevention, and occupancy characteristics of properties as a basis for rating the susceptibility of properties to extensive damage should fire occur. Nevertheless, while such a rating method could be worked out, its creation as a truly accurate instrument involves various problems. The difficulty arises partly from the complexity of the operation and partly from the weakness of our knowledge concerning the efficacy of the varied ways of reducing fire damage and loss—reductions such as those that come through fire sprinklers, fire detection devices, "fireproof" construction, layout, automatic-closing fire doors, and so on. But once a rating scheme was designed, its administration would not be too difficult or expensive, for the actual collection of facts would add little to the tasks involved in periodic inspection, while the accounting job of ratings and billings could be computerized to keep costs down.[19]

A British researcher concerned with the pricing of fire services has contended that the fire service fees charged for different properties should be in proportion to their fire insurance premiums.[20] Since the premiums are presumably designed to cover the expected value of (insured) fire losses plus insurance company administrative expenses and profits, they will clearly reflect property value, fire probability, and susceptibility of the property to extensive damage should fire occur. However, are such premiums, in addition to reflecting relevant variables, likely to correspond roughly with the demands that properties make for public protection? In the process of considering this question, certain ambiguities in my demand notion will be revealed—and may be resolved.

Figures 13.4 and 13.5 were constructed to assist the discussion of the matter. The horizontal axis of Figure 13.4, like that of Figure 13.3, measures fire department quality; the vertical axis indicates the expected value of property damage for the property or properties being considered. If fire department quality is at M, properties I and II clearly should pay identical fire insurance premiums if both are fully insured. Figure 13.5 shows that the corresponding demand (marginal damage reduction) curves and the demand for fire services of the two properties for fire department quality are different. While this example demonstrates that properties paying similar premiums may impose very different demands for fire services, examples can also be created to demonstrate that properties that pay different premiums under protection make similar demands for service. It may seem that a direct rating of properties would be subject to the same criticism, but that is not necessarily so. For example, given a particular level of protection, a fire-prone structure and a well-fireproofed and sprinklered structure may have similar levels of expected damages and, as a consequence,

Fig. 13.4 *Fire Insurance Premium Costs*

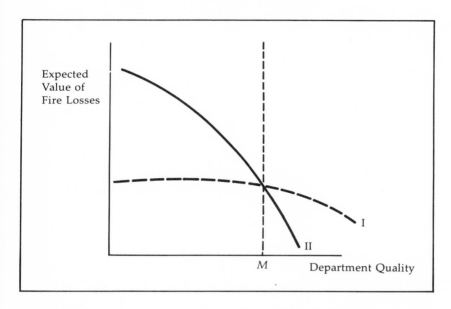

pay similar premiums. It would not, however, be difficult for a rating scheme to discriminate between the fire protection demands presented by these properties.

While formally correct, this analysis, which stresses the differences between actual fire risk (i.e., expected value of fire damage as reflected in premiums) and the damage reduction attributable to fire departments, may be splitting hairs in an area where factual knowledge is still not equal to such conceptual distinctions. More important in considering a distribution of fire service charges in proportion to insurance premiums are the things that are and are not covered by insurance. First, risks to life clearly are a significant component of fire department demand and strongly affect fire department operations. Nonetheless, because fire insurance is *property* insurance, premiums do not reflect risks to life. It is also true that many properties are underinsured or completely uninsured. Where the failure to insure results from insurance companies' refusals to serve (as often occurs in low-income areas of large cities), premiums paid clearly bear no relation to fire

Fig. 13.5 *Differences in Demand for Fire Department Quality*

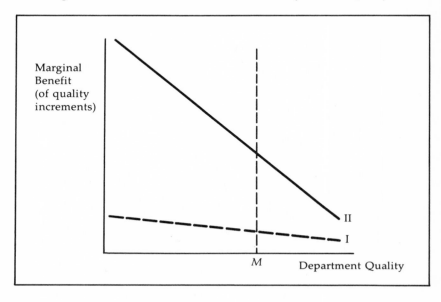

service demand. Where properties are voluntarily underinsured or un-insured, owners' tastes toward risk may result in a felt low fire service demand. The observer of the process is forced, therefore, to consider whether "demand" for fire service should mean the demand inferrable from the damage reduction it fosters or the demand owners might express. My preference, as reflected in the demand analysis, has the virtue of revealing a demand for a public good that otherwise might be with-held. It is also probably more consistent with fire department practice—i.e., it seems improbable that fire department service levels are related to the insuring pattern among protected properties.

In summary, apportioning fire service charges according to insur-ance premiums might be a fair proxy for the service demands arising out of property risk but would ignore demands for protection of life. In addition, insofar as area is a significant component of fire service demand, premiums are a faulty guide to pricing since they are inde-pendent of area.[21]

Under either plan for administering fees, two issues require further discussion. Much of the fire-incidence variation among prop-erties can be explained (in a statistical sense) by variations in per capita incomes of the areas in which the properties are located. However, the implication here is that fire service fees may well follow a regressive pattern on rental or owner-occupied residential properties. This may be objected to on the grounds that such distributional impacts are un-desirable and that property owners and residents are being inequitably charged for matters that, to some extent, are beyond their control. While a consideration of these distribution effects should certainly be included in any further study, I also suggest that relatively high fire service charges in high-incidence areas may have virtues. In particular, depending on the fee formula, it is likely that, where other factors lead to a high fee, the fee reduction flowing from automatic fire fighting or warning systems may be correspondingly great. This would strengthen the incentive for such built-in measures in areas where they may in fact be the wisest social response to a significant fire problem.

Any fee system chosen must obviously not be so complex as to baffle property owners. Failure in this respect would defeat the purpose of the fee scheme, which is to induce changes in behavior. But one might question whether the incentive coming from variations in so small a figure as the fire service fee can be counted upon to induce real changes in private fire protection behavior. Since we have been arguing for a cost-based fee, the response here really depends on whether more private protection is economically wise. If it is, the reduced fees (over a period of years) flowing from reduced public protection should be sufficient to induce—by compensating for the costs of—added private effort. More will be said on this below, but it is worth pointing out here that the present effective "fee" for fire services runs between 0.1 and 0.44 percent of market property values per annum (.13 and .57 percent including water costs attributable to fire protection needs).[22]

Identification of Costs Imposed by Users

A price scheme designed to pursue allocation goals must be based on some understanding of the costs that different users of the service impose. For normal commodities, this understanding is gained by identifying the relation between costs and output quality and quantity, and then discovering the quantity and quality of service that different users employ. In the case of fire services, however, users are not free to vary the quantity and quality of their individual "consumption" on their own; the level of service provided to them has been established by administrative decision in their area. In this case, an assignment of costs to particular users can be achieved only through identification of the influence that users (properties) have on the decision concerning the level of service provided in that area.[23]

Cross-section studies among cities and within individual cities may indicate the influence that different property characteristics have on the quality of the service that is provided. Such research might also yield interesting information on fire department behavior. It might reveal, for example, how resources are allocated in a field where "best possible" is the objective claimed for service to all areas. It might also turn up new information, interesting for its own sake, concerning the quality of service provided to different parts of urban areas.

Owner-Provided Protection and Fire Department Costs

Assume, for the purpose of this discussion, that a fire service fee structure based on the costs attributable to properties results in the following charge for individual properties:[24]

$$\text{Fee} = F(V, P, A, I, R)$$

where
$$\frac{\partial F}{\partial V}, \frac{\partial F}{\partial P}, \frac{\partial F}{\partial A}, \frac{\partial F}{\partial I} > 0 > \frac{\partial F}{\partial R}$$

$V =$ Property value
$P =$ Property population
$A =$ Property area
$I =$ Incidence probability
$R =$ Measure of resistiveness of property to fire, given structural characteristics, protective devices and measures, etc.

The only allocation benefit that could possibly flow from the application of such a fee would come through the increase in R (or possible decrease in I) that it might stimulate. It seems highly improbable that property owners will ration their "consumption" of fire service by reducing the value, area, or population of their properties to secure a slight fee decline that is dwarfed in importance by the other forces that determine the values of these variables.[25] And, although equity might be served by using this fee, which reflects benefits received more accurately than does the property tax (of which a share goes to finance fire department services), equity gains alone are not likely to justify so severe an alteration of the financing of fire department services.

Conversations with several fire protection experts suggest that those in the field believe that a relative shift from public to owner-provided protection would be wise. It also is apparent—given the high labor intensity of public protection, the relatively low labor intensity of owner-provided protection, and the rates of productivity change in the area—that the cost of protection through fire department operations is rising relative to the cost of protection through other means. (Labor costs constitute 90 percent of the costs of professional departments.) Neither the casual opinion of experts nor an apparent bias in the direction of relative cost changes, however, is solid evidence that a major shift in the protection burden would be economically wise; furthermore, pursuit of more "solid" evidence is rather complex. The complexity is inherent in the protection process, for departmental fire extinguishment operations and owner protection are multi-dimensional and their design is dependent upon the characteristics of properties protected. It is thus very difficult to state in what specific ways a given reduction in fire department expenditure would affect department operations and therefore damages, and certainly no easier to identify the optimal mix of owner-provided measures that should flow from a given increase in expenditures on them.

There is need for research on the allocation of benefits that might flow from financing fire departments out of fees proportioned by the fire department demands of different properties. Such fees would encourage property owners to take on a greater share of the protection burden and would be desirable only if such a shift resulted in a more efficient sharing of the burden.

NOTES

1. The expenditure figures are derived from U.S. Bureau of the Census, *City Government Finances in 1967–68* (1969), Table 3. The property tax estimates are

based on data in *Local Government Finances in Selected Metropolitan Areas in 1966–67* (1968), Table 3, and in *1967 Census of Governments, Taxable Property Values* (1968), Table 21.

2. International City Management Association, *Municipal Fire Administration* (Chicago, 1967), p. 114. The percentage of water costs attributable to fire protection needs is significantly greater for cities smaller than the very large cities to which these figures apply.

3. Conventions vary here. The unit of psychiatric output tends to be the fifty-minute hour, whereas a surgeon "produces" a tonsillectomy, etc., and an obstetrician, a nine-month care-and-delivery package.

4. As will be shown later, selection of either option raises more questions about unit definition. For example, is the fire department turnout measured by time on the scene, the value of damage averted, the number of men dispatched, or something else? Or, if what consumers receive is the assurance of protection, does one measure the individual user's consumption by the value of property, the probability of fire outbreak, the area of property, or the expected value of fire damage?

5. For example, where the existence of a fee delays but does not ultimately prevent an alarm, the fee is certain to have had a negative allocation effect. Evidence, even from cities not using fees, suggests that fees on fire department turnouts would in fact choke off at least some calls. For example, in New York City, where fees are not used, people phoning in alarms will frequently inquire into the costs of calling out different numbers of trucks so that they can adjust their requests accordingly.

6. A detailed consideration of fire department operations would reveal several cracks in this argument. For example, where a fire department is busy, attending one fire may impose a real (though not fire department) cost by delaying, making less adequate, or preventing attendance at another fire. For most departments in most places, however, these objections are not felt sufficient to invalidate the assertion that the marginal cost of department attendance approximates zero.

7. Milliman makes this point in the following words: "For public goods, then, not only is it technically impossible (or difficult) to exclude or to ration service, *it is also unnecessary and undesirable to do so.* The marginal cost of an extra consumer is zero (or nearly so) and there is no excess demand, and therefore, there is no need to ration. Even if it were possible to ration use, the correct price would be zero." See Jerome W. Milliman, "Beneficiary Charges and Efficient Public Expenditure Decisions," in *The Analysis and Evaluation of Public Expenditures: The PPB System*, Vol. 1 (U.S. Congress, 1969), p. 311.

8. Damage averted refers to the difference between damages (to property and people) that *would* occur if there were no fire department and if owners proceeded as if there were no risk of fire and those damages that *do* occur. The costs of owner-provided protection are any costs of structural change, process alteration, or equipment attributable to the existence of the fire risk.

9. We are, however, concerned with the effect on public expenditures of the

private neglect of the impact of the O decisions on F—an externality of a kind, but not the one ignored above.

10. The function employed here is not strictly a production function, since it relates output levels to input expenditures rather than to input quantities.

11. The same objective could be achieved with less administrative effort by setting public protection below the level appropriate to existing private efforts and refusing to increase it—e.g., set F at Fs. While this would prevent a cumulative decline, it would leave the fire department in an embarrassingly exposed position providing protection that may appear to be, and in fact is, inferior to what "ought" to be provided. The same argument would apply, a fortiori, to "farsighted" attempts by the fire department to achieve the optimum position by reducing its protective efforts in order to stimulate increased private effort.

12. Other rationales are not, however, hard to find. For example, lowered owner protection may, in addition to imposing higher costs on the public protection agency, increase the fire risk to adjacent properties. This externality, though ignored by the model, might also justify the imposition of minimum standards.

13. One might push the sequence back further and refer to the time lag as beginning when there is a desire to sound an alarm, since one aspect of quality is the way in which departments facilitate the sounding of an alarm.

14. We define "protection area" as the area that is benefited by a fire department quality improvement. It corresponds to part of a city or the whole city, depending on the nature of the quality improvement.

15. It is only a first approximation because of risk. A person may value a one dollar reduction in the level of his expected losses at more or less than one dollar. Assuming that insurance premiums are actuarially accurate, the reduction in premiums might be a useful proxy for damage reductions. They have the virtue of accounting for the risk factor but neglect all loss reductions not covered by fire insurance—most notably, lives, business disruptions, and underinsured and uninsured properties.

16. While these inferences about the impact of different factors on the location of the benefit curve are significant for our pricing concerns, it is clear that they do not illumine the forces determining the *shape* of the curve. Very little is known about these forces, although it is easy enough to specify the relevant relationships. For example, the relationship between the outbreak-to-fire-fighting time lag and the percentage of damage that occurs is crucial, since reducing response time through increased fire company concentration is one of the most important ways of improving quality. This means that the relationship between departmental expenditure and average response time will strongly affect the shape of the community demand curve. Similarly, the types of structures and the time pattern of firespread in them will affect the shape of the individual and community demand curves. These matters, which are also clearly relevant to the determination of departmental size and the distribution of department resources over its protection area, do not appear to have been analyzed theoretically or empirically. Insurance grading rules specify requirements that presumably re-

flect grading associations' notions of demand, but these requirements seem based more on traditional rules of thumb than on analysis.

17. The community demand curve is the vertical sum of the individual demand curves in the community. The optimal fire department quality level is at the intersection of this community demand curve with the marginal cost curve for community fire protection (a horizontal line at $1, given our quality measure). See Paul Samuelson, "Diagrammatic Exposition of a Theory of Public Expenditure," *Review of Economics and Statistics*, 32 (November 1955): 350–356.

18. Those familiar with the "public good" literature will recognize that I am proposing fees to induce allocation benefits which simultaneously will (at least roughly) capture the benefits received by different "users" of a public good. Such fees have traditionally been held to be unworkable, since beneficiaries will understate their own demands to minimize their fee payment, knowing that the good's publicness guarantees that their benefit will be virtually independent of their stated demand. That difficulty has been explicitly avoided here by tying fees to observable property characteristics rather than owners' statements concerning the level of their demand. This assumes that demand is determined by characteristics which were observable and independent of such unobservables as tastes and varying attitudes toward risk and the value of life, etc. Though ignored in the demand discussion, these other influences on demand do exist and have significance. My position is that demand as inferred from observables may be a better concept than felt demands (if they could somehow be identified) on which to base public fire protection policy because of owners' lack of knowledge about fire risks and the income-induced variations in life valuation which public policy may well wish to ignore.

19. Conversations with people in the fire protection field confirmed my surmises in this regard. These experts argued that inspections, already justified on other grounds, would be forced by a pricing system. Furthermore, in connection with a different problem, Harry Hickey, of the Fire Curriculum at the University of Maryland, is developing a method to rate the fire protection demands of structures and modules within structures.

20. R. L. Carter, "Pricing and the Risk of Fire," in *Essays in the Theory and Practice of Pricing* (The Institute of Economic Affairs, London, 1967), pp. 25–53.

21. Although we argued earlier that area was a significant component, an accurate view of this must await empirical exploration.

22. These figures impute to fire protection a percentage of property tax rates equal to the percentage of total property tax revenues that fire department expenditures represent. If to this one adds a water-for-fire fee, the figures rise by about 30 percent in large cities.

23. Standards of a sort exist in the schedules the insurance industry uses to grade departments for premium-setting purposes. It has been proposed that, by comparing increased fire department expenditures with the premium reduction they induce, one might arrive at a kind of optimal sized and designed department. There is reason, however, to question the effectiveness of such schedules in accurately capturing departmental improvements. In any event, such a procedure would ignore reductions in risks to life and uninsured risks.

24. As indicated elsewhere, the utility of the scheme would decline as the fee formula's complexity increased.

25. William Vickrey, "General and Specific Financing of Urban Services," in Howard Schaller, ed., *Public Expenditure Decisions in the Urban Community* (published for Resources for the Future by The Johns Hopkins University Press, 1963). Vickrey, in this article concerned almost entirely with allocation benefits, argues that fire department costs are determined by area covered, and that as a consequence charges should be based on area. Even if Vickrey is correct in his cost assertions, the *allocation* benefits he seeks will accrue only if area decisions are actually affected by the existence of the fee. Given the probable magnitude of the fee and the strength of other forces acting on a property owner's decision, it seems unlikely that the area decision will be much affected, or allocative efficiency stimulated, by this measure.

Chapter **14**   PHILIP I. MOSS

Pricing Recreation Services

EMAND for recreational activities has been increasing rapidly over recent years in response to growth in population, leisure time, and affluence. The response has also resulted from a greater sensitivity to the interactions between recreation, health, and well-being. The demands have been partially reflected in private and public production of recreational services, facilities, and equipment. Between 1960 and 1967 private expenditures for recreational services increased from $18.3 billion to $30.6 billion, and, as a percentage of consumption expenditures, from 5.6 to 6.2 percent. Over the same period, local government spending on parks and recreation remained at approximately 2.2 percent of total direct general local government expenditures, but absolutely it rose from $0.86 billion to $1.41 billion. Fees and charges financed approximately 13 percent of these public expenditures.

The total figures fail to reflect, however, the relatively more rapidly growing demands and recreational burdens that fall on the governments of large municipal areas with substantial numbers of low-income citizens. Low-income families can afford very few private recreational services. Furthermore, their poverty puts distant federal and state recreation facilities out of bounds, so that recreational facilities, if any, must be designed for them near their neighborhoods. High land costs in inner-city areas compound the problem. It is significant that city governments serving cities with populations greater than

Philip I. Moss was a summer student intern at The Urban Institute when he wrote this chapter. He is now a graduate student at the Massachusetts Institute of Technology.

300,000 spend about 45 percent more per capita on recreation than smaller cities do.

Until fairly recently, city recreational programs have been developed without explicit assessment of citizen preferences among the various types of recreation, and without much attempt to mesh programs with the characteristics of user groups. The increased outcry from inner-city residents for a better standard of living and a more adequate level of public services has tended to focus attention on the need for recreational facilities for young people in the ghetto. All of this—climaxed by the sporadic riots in many cities—has underscored the urgency of identifying present service needs and what additional, or different, services are required. In addition, it suggests the importance of distribution in any consideration of user-fee financing.

Outputs

Allocation decisions involve a comparison, from society's viewpoint, of relative outputs of, or benefits from, alternative activities. Although recreation outputs are difficult to quantify, they may be considered as being in three categories: utility of own consumption; long-term individual benefits; and community benefits.

The first category reflects the fact that recreation activities are primarily wanted because people enjoy them. A major output of recreation is, therefore, its immediate utility to the consumers of such activities. In this sense, recreation is a private consumption good. The second category reflects the assumption that access to recreation activities adds to the overall quality of the individual user's life—i.e., he can improve his physical and mental health throughout his life span. In this sense, recreation is an investment in human capital. The third category involves an accrual of benefits to third parties—i.e., to people living near or adjacent to attractive outdoor recreational areas or to a valuable resource such as a museum, and to members of society as a whole. In other words, people may derive utility indirectly from knowing that natural recreational facilities exist even though they do not actually use them. Thus there is an option demand for such facilities. Moreover, the society as a whole may benefit, to the degree that recreation contributes to the health and welfare of its citizens, particularly those citizens who do not have private means for satisfying their recreational needs. Thus, recreation generates both pecuniary and nonpecuniary external economies.

The services that produce these outputs are extremely varied. Recreation facilities within a city can be defined (as is done in the case of the Governments Divison of the Bureau of the Census) to include parks, playgrounds, playfields, swimming pools, bathing beaches, and special facilities such as auditoriums, museums, stadiums, zoos, auto camps, recreation piers, and boat harbors. The relative amount of each type of service provided by cities differs from case to case, depending on the cost of land acquisition, the natural geographical endowment of the city itself (i.e., whether it is on a lake or the seacoast, or near ski mountains, camping-type land, or unique natural areas), and the way in which land was "set aside" for recreational facilities many years ago (in some cases well over a century) when the city was developing.

Measuring the benefits of various facilities generates problems. One categorization of possible benefit measures includes:[1]

1. The gross volume of business generated as a result of the availability of recreational facilities.
2. The gross expenditures added to local business.
3. The demand, in terms of the willingness to pay a cost for traveling to the facilities.
4. The consumer surplus resulting from the fact that people are not charged for recreational services for which they would otherwise pay.[2]

To this list can be added the increase in property values in areas adjacent to or near attractive parks or other recreation facilities. Though some attempts have been made to estimate this effect, the results are not conclusive.[3]

The private market provides a variety of recreational services— country clubs, tennis and golf facilities, swimming pools and beaches, amusement parks, ski resorts, campsites, and so on—that are comparable to public recreation services. It might seem, therefore, that the first type of public recreation output, i.e., utility of own consumption, could be measured by referring to amounts other individuals are willing to pay for private services. However, several other problems arise.

1. The provision of free public facilities is likely to depress the price that might be asked and obtained for the use of comparable private facilities.

2. On the other hand, if we use the prices paid for private facilities as a measure of value for all analogous facilities, we are assuming that the private service is worth the same as a similar service that might be consumed free of charge. But an individual who uses private facilities may be paying for what he regards as the added value of exclusivity. Thus, we must separate the portion of the price that reflects the consumption of exclusivity from the portion that reflects the pure value of recreation. This is an important distinction to make in measuring benefits.

3. For some types of facilities—e.g., urban parks and playgrounds—there are really no exact private counterparts. The whole nature of the public facility would be changed if access or admission were restricted by charging even a nominal amount.

Estimating the amount people are willing to pay for public services is a classic problem. An individual has an incentive to understate his willingness to pay, provided he cannot be excluded from use of a facility such as a neighborhood park. Recognizing the difficulties with dollar measures of benefits, Mack and Myers have suggested employing merit-weighted user days as a measure.[4] This may help in establishing investment criteria among various kinds of recreation, but it offers much less help for comparisons between recreation services and many other public services, when scarce resources play a part in decision-making. It also seems deficient as a criterion for pricing recreation services.

The Users

In discussing the introduction of user charges for recreational output, we need to know whether the beneficiaries can be identified. For the first type of benefit, i.e., utility of own consumption, the benefits accrue to the immediate users. It seems fair to say that a significant portion of the output of such facilities as tennis courts, golf courses, swimming pools, picnic areas, and beaches is of this type. These facilities have private counterparts for which people pay a price; and, even more convincing, they are also the types of public facilities that now may often have some kind of charge for use. On the other hand, to the degree that total benefits fit into our other two general categories— long-term individual benefits and benefits to the community or nation —the balance is tipped away from user charges.

Even if city dwellers do not steadily use public recreation facilities, they may find it of more value to live in a city that provides more such services than in a city with less. Similarly, the nation as a whole may benefit from conserving its natural wild lands for recreation and "breathing space" even if not all citizens make use of these areas.

External benefits to third-party nonusers of recreational facilities complicate the problem of establishing an efficient set of charges. Residents and businesses may profit, without paying directly, by occupying land adjacent to or near a recreational facility. To some degree such benefits can be internalized through higher property taxes paid by the owner; even so, significant locational benefits may remain. In addition, people located near these facilities may enjoy increased levels of real consumption without paying directly, because the facility reduces noise and air pollution and perhaps helps the water drainage.

If we assume that the beneficiaries of public recreational facilities can to a large extent be identified as the specific users, the next task is to identify the characteristics of the users and to ask what implications these have for the nature of efficient prices. Ideally, users should be identified in terms of income, age, residence, and travel distance from, or cost incurred in getting to, the service facility.

To know whether or not users are in a position to pay for the service is essential. If they have reasonable incomes and are paying, or willing to pay, for some comparable privately provided service, it seems fair to say that the distributional issue is irrelevant and that the price of the public service should measure, in some way, the value of the service provided. If, however, the users are from lower-income groups and could not or would not pay a charge for use of a facility from which they are now benefiting, free provision then becomes a form of income distribution directed toward the lower-income groups, and a new set of questions arises. If income redistribution is considered desirable, is the provision of free recreational services an efficient or socially respectable way to accomplish it? Many of the freely provided urban facilities are probably used by people whose low income would not permit them to substitute private recreation consumption. Should there be no charge at all, or should there be a charge with some preferential pricing—e.g., no charge for low-income people? Or should there be a standard charge, but, in the case of some low-income groups, some type of income maintenance or supplement to enable them to afford the charge?

Another aspect of equity and income redistribution questions concerns the significant portion of publicly provided recreation services that involves more than an easy stroll to an urban neighborhood park or playground. To enjoy such facilities as campgrounds, beaches, ski slopes, tennis courts, and golf courses requires a certain amount of investment in equipment, in possible travel expenses, and in experience or training needed to use the facility. What little we know about user characteristics indicates that the consumers of such facilities are mainly from middle- and higher-income groups who could afford private alternatives. To the extent that such public facilities are financed out of general tax revenues, the implication is that the resultant redistribution is toward the upper end of the income scale. Furthermore, if the users of specific facilities are reasonably affluent, they may well be willing to pay fees to improve the quality of a facility that cannot be properly maintained because of inadequate financing through general taxes.

Though some surveys have been conducted to obtain information on use of federal park lands and camping grounds, the type of information on user characteristics mentioned above is at present not available on any large scale for local recreation services.[5] The existing surveys, which have identified users by income, residence, travel distance, and use, indicate that most users are reasonably affluent and willing to incur significant cost in traveling and in preparing for use of the facilities; they also feel that a charge is fair and are willing to pay it.[6]

Costs and Data

Information about the cost of providing a public service and the use made of the service by different categories of users is crucial in determining how the service ought to be priced. Unfortunately, however, such information is not readily available. At best, cities provide information concerning level of use and the total cost of recreational facilities clasified by activities. Although these data may prove useful for some purposes, they must be cautiously used for intercity comparisons since they do not flow from standardized accounting procedures. Furthermore, no cities appear to collect information on use of facilities by different income classes—information that is essential to the design of pricing systems consistent with equity as well as other objectives.

Figures on the variation in percent of city operating expenses devoted to parks and recreation, and the variation in per capita levels of expenditure on these two items, have been prepared by the National League of Cities for fifteen selected cities of varying sizes. (See Tables 14.1 and 14.2.) However, because cost accounting practices differ significantly and the functions classified under parks and recreation vary from city to city, these figures are not really a good measure of each city's relative commitment to provision of recreation services.

Current Charging Practices

The variations in charging practices for similar facilities both within a given city government's jurisdiction and from city to city are considerable. Every local government charges in some way for certain of its facilities. The following classification of types of charges indicates a few of the methods employed: entrance fees—to enter a park, garden, or developed recreational area; admission fees—to enter a building or exhibit that may be within a recreational area; rental fees—for exclusive use of property or equipment, such as golf clubs, a boat, etc.; user fees—for use (may not be exclusive) of a facility or participation in such an activity as a ride of some kind, an archery range, boat launch, picnic area, or sightseeing bus; license and permit fees—for a legal privilege such as a camping permit or a fishing and hunting license.

Several of these methods may be used in combination in a single facility. A zoo, for example, which may or may not charge for entrance, may have a fee for parking, for admission to special exhibits, for a ride on a train through the zoo, and for rental of such things as baby strollers. In many cases the use of a facility such as a tennis court, playground, or picnic area involves little or no marginal cost, provided there is no queuing or congestion. Therefore, no charge is made for general use. But a charge will be made for a specific extension of service that does involve a marginal cost—for example, coin-operated lights for

TABLE 14.1

Park-Recreation Spending Compared with Total City Operating Expenditures, 15 Selected Cities, 1967

City	City operating expenditures[a]	Park and Recreation		
		Operating expenditures[b]	Capital expenditures[c]	Percent of city expenditures[d]
New York	$3,741,580,000	$47,300,000	$42,700,000	1.3
Chicago[e]	382,932,000	36,586,748	2,775,898	8.7
Los Angeles	254,427,000	15,022,505	4,189,052	5.9
Baltimore	299,899,000	9,174,036	2,787,696	3.1
San Antonio	28,607,000	1,836,775	492,545	6.1
St. Louis	100,349,000	3,558,294	1,405,000	3.5
Pittsburgh	59,144,000	4,740,357	1,800,000	8.0
Atlanta	51,770,000	3,744,000	530,000	7.2
Minneapolis	43,567,000	3,885,000	663,000	8.9
Nashville	92,415,000	2,084,087	1,635,476	2.3
Oakland	43,198,000	4,660,355	170,000	10.8
Tampa	24,669,000	2,219,854	Not available	9.0
Dayton	24,233,000	2,297,152	661,662	9.5
Peoria[f]	7,375,000	1,607,287	522,869	17.9
Portland	14,234,000	572,540	70,636	4.0

[a] Excludes federal grant funds.

[b] Excludes federal grant funds and expenditures for park and recreation purposes other than park and recreation departments.

[c] Excludes federal grant funds and capital outlay expenditures for heavy equipment and other items.

[d] Derived by dividing operating expenditures for parks and recreation by the city's total operating expenditures. Comparison of expenditures for parks and recreation with expenditures for other municipal services is of limited value because of the wide variation in services provided by the general purpose governments and the performance of services by special districts. In St. Louis, New York, Nashville, and Baltimore, for example, the city performs both city and county functions, and consequently expenditures for parks and recreation constitute a smaller percentage of total municipal expenditures than in cities not providing such functions.

[e] Park and recreation expenditure figures stated are for the Chicago Park District, which is a special district independent of the city government.

[f] Park and recreation expenditure figures stated are for the Peoria Pleasure Driveway and Park District, which is a special district independent of the city government.

night tennis games and fees for reserving a playground or picnic table for exclusive use.

In general, however, municipal parks, playgrounds, and community centers do not charge additional fees. Use of such facilities generates almost no marginal cost, aside from the cost of maintenance,

TABLE 14.2

Per Capita Operating Expenditures for Parks and Recreation in
15 Selected Cities[a]

City	Expenditures 1960	Expenditures 1965	Budget 1968	Estimate 1973
New York	$4.22	$ 6.48	$ 6.19	$10.81
Chicago	7.57	8.97	11.72	14.45
Los Angeles	4.78	5.67	4.77	NA[b]
Baltimore	5.31	8.67	12.32	16.64
San Antonio	1.72	2.56	2.83	NA
St. Louis	4.82	5.57	5.85	6.90
Pittsburgh	5.71	7.73	9.13	NA
Atlanta	3.67	4.76	9.11	NA
Minneapolis	7.14	6.17	9.09	NA
Nashville	5.09	4.50	4.52	7.81
Oakland	8.59	9.87	13.21	15.56
Tampa	2.30	5.82	7.33	NA
Dayton	5.70	7.15	8.90	11.12
Peoria	8.63	10.63	14.69	NA
Portland	4.44	9.12	8.76	9.21

[a] Derived by dividing financial data obtained from recreation personnel by actual or estimated population figures.
[b] Not available.

which can be considered fixed from an individual user's viewpoint. Golf courses, camping areas, boating areas, skating rinks, ski slopes, and swimming pools almost invariably charge fees; these facilities are costly to operate, and often involve queues or congestion or a definite marginal cost for each user. Tennis courts, museums, and zoos vary in their charging practices. For all of these types of services, the cost of providing the service varies from city to city depending, for example, on the city's natural endowment, the way in which its land has been set aside, and the structure of land values, wages, and other resource prices.

Where fees are charged, they are not always uniform over time. Golf, swimming, and camping facilities often sell season passes in addition to fees for single use. Museums, zoos, and cultural exhibits usually have reduced rates for children and for certain categories of users such as school groups and disadvantaged persons; these special considerations may be intended to represent income redistribution to disadvantaged persons and investment in the mental and physical health of children. In addition, price may be varied to ration the resource in peak demand periods, on a daily, weekly, or seasonal basis. Golf and swimming facilities, for example, usually charge more on weekends and holidays. Zoo entrance fees also provide good examples of such practices.[7]

Price and Income Elasticities of Demand

Very little is known about the income and price elasticities of recreation expenditure or consumption. However, a priori consumption of recreation would seem to bear many similarities to consumption of other similar goods. Many forms of recreation—e.g., sailing, skiing, and camping at distant national parks—represent fairly luxurious consumption, and the demand for them is probably quite income elastic. However, when recreation is taken as a single commodity, the little that is known about preferences indicates that many individuals have similar ideas about the amount of time they would like to devote to recreation and the proportion of their income they are willing to spend on it. Variations exist in tastes, which are to some extent conditioned by the exposure a given person has had to recreational experiences (e.g., most inner-city residents have had little experience with water skiing or mountain climbing) and by the type of recreation they can afford.

The total amount a person pays to use a recreation facility should be an important factor in determining his willingness to pay a fee, or to accept an increased fee. That total amount includes the cost of (1) transportation to the facility, (2) the necessary equipment, and (3) recreation experience; it also includes the value of the leisure time the person has set aside to enjoy the facility. If this total is large relative to the fee that must be paid to use the facility once the user is there, the fee itself should have little if any effect on his demand for the facility. This is probably the case for most nonurban types of facilities such as national parks, ski areas, and boating areas, for which large travel and equipment costs are associated with use. The Arthur D. Little study of fees and permits for national park use concluded that fees in the range of $1 to $5 for use of a distant park (and therefore costly to reach) would not reduce demand for use to any significant degree.[8] However, for many urban facilities, especially for playgrounds, parks, or swimming pools in neighborhoods where the users are far from affluent, even a small new charge or an increase in an established fee might reduce demand drastically.

Very few empirical data are available on this question, but the experience of the Oakland, California, Department of Recreation furnishes some clues. In the summer of 1967 two swimming pools were operated on an admission charge basis. One of the pools is located in the de Fremery area, which is a low-income, minority neighborhood in the Model Cities District of Oakland. The other pool is in the Castlemont area, which has a half-and-half residential mix of middle class whites and low-income blacks. In the summer of 1968 use of both pools was made free, and the change in attendance was dramatic. Attendance at the Castlemont pool increased from 14,000 to 18,000, a 29 percent increase, and at the de Fremery pool by two-thirds, from 10,000 to 17,000. Clearly, the demand seems to have been extremely responsive to price. Furthermore, although the effect was larger in the less affluent area (de Fremery), the composition of the users at the mixed Castlemont pool shifted to include more of the low-income group after the fee was removed. This may be attributable to a relatively high price elasticity among low-income users or to a change in low-income tastes induced by contact with a relatively unfamiliar form of recreation.

A further point with regard to elasticities is that one must look at the whole and decide whether recreation should be treated as a collection of differentiated, yet similar, competing products or as a collection of separate commodities. Obviously the demands for different recreational services are interrelated, and such services are thus not completely separate commodities. Some, such as camping, hiking, and visiting national parks, may be complements. In this case, an increase in camping fees may affect the number of people who come to a national park, even if the entrance fee is unchanged. On the other hand, services such as zoos and other exhibit-type facilities (e.g., marinas and museums) may be substitutes. And in certain cases the relationships are not clear: does tennis, for example, substitute for golf, swimming, or horseback riding? If it does, the demand for one is affected by a change of fee in one or more of the others. In addition, there may be various substitution responses to changes in income. People may shift demand to new forms of recreation as their income levels change.

The interrelation of demand for recreation and availability and price of transport services must also be considered. If a significant portion of the cost of using a nonneighborhood recreational facility is the cost of getting to the facility, then a change in the availability—new mass transit lines and (to a lesser degree for low-income urban dwellers) new highways—or price (transit fares and change in the time spent traveling) of transportation to the facility should influence demand. The same is true of changes in the price or availability of equipment and/or experience necessary for the use of more specialized recreation services. We need more understanding about shifts of the demand curve caused by changes in prices of complementary goods and services, compared to a movement along a particular demand curve in response to a change in the actual price of the service itself.

Pricing Strategies

The basic issue in pricing recreation is whether charges are to be set at the marginal cost of use, at average cost, or in some other way.[9] The actual pricing policy chosen depends on the objectives pursued. If full recovery of all costs is desired, prices must be set at average cost, a course of action that violates efficiency criteria but avoids the income redistribution that results from an operating profit or loss. On the other hand, if efficiency is desired, price should be set at marginal cost so that the user is charged only for the incremental resources he ties up in his use of the facility. But this does not solve the problem of financing investment in the project. For facilities such as zoos or national parks, fixed expenditures may be very high while the marginal cost of additional users up to the point of congestion may be close to zero.

Assuming that marginal cost pricing is appropriate, the problem is then to define a user's marginal cost including not only operating and maintenance costs, but also congestion costs (a cost in the sense of reducing the quality of the service provided to other users) and depreciation or depletion. These costs may be very difficult to measure.

Marginal-cost pricing can be fitted into a peak-load scheme. During high-use times, costs (total and marginal) of operation, congestion, and deterioration are higher, and the price can reflect this in a peak-load differential. Moreover, collection costs are smaller relative to marginal cost. Some zoos (and such other facilities as golf courses) do in fact increase prices on weekends or during peak seasons. Differential peak-load pricing also has the effect of shifting demand to offpeak times and reducing overall costs of congestion, maintenance, and deterioration.

Strict marginal-cost pricing conflicts with the employment of preferential charges for such groups as children or the disadvantaged. In theory, the marginal cost of their use is probably no different from that of the general adult user; therefore, if efficiency of pricing is to be achieved, such groups should be charged marginal costs. However, society may wish to redistribute income to these people in this way or invest in their health and welfare through a preferential price. Such a rationale may underlie the pricing policy of the Cleveland Zoo, for example, which manages demand with an offpeak price and practices reverse price discrimination in favor of the group with little or no "ability to pay."

If the goal is to maximize revenue or minimize the cost of collecting fees, rather than equity or efficiency, other pricing schemes are appropriate. In addition to one-day fees for use of park facilities, a recent study recommends the sale of an annual permit which allows limited use of all parks (or parks in designated regions) for an entire season.[10] (Such a permit would be an extension of the "Golden Eagle" passes for national parks.) Permits could be obtained through the mail, from post offices, or from designated retail establishments in the areas of the park. It was felt that a system of this kind would stimulate demand because, as surveys indicate, passholders use facilities much more frequently than other persons (that may have been why they bought the pass), and it would reduce the administrative costs of fee collection. To enforce the permit requirement and obviate the need for an administered admission gate, spot checking of people within the parks could be employed as a means of inducing people to comply with prior purchase of permits. Because of the high costs of travel and equipment required to reach the parks, it is felt that such a system will not reduce attendance and therefore will significantly increase park revenues.

If arrangements can be made for some officials to be on hand periodically to check users for permits, the system seems reasonably adaptable to almost all municipal-type recreation facilities. Certainly such facilities as golf courses, swimming pools, tennis courts, and zoos could adopt this system and thereby reduce costs of collection relative to revenue obtained. There may be objections to the method, however, because of its implications for allocative efficiency.

As a compromise solution one might consider the multipart or two-part tariff which is discussed in the literature on public utility pricing. This system consists of two parts: (1) an initial fee to any potential user set at the difference between average and marginal cost, and (2) a running user charge equal to marginal cost for each usage of the facility. This has the advantage of better meeting revenue requirements (avoiding the redistribution problems of an operating loss), and it also has most of the resource and demand management advantages of price equal to marginal cost. The system probably offers a good practical compromise solution for high fixed cost, high capacity, and low marginal-cost enterprises, such as zoos, museums, and exhibits.

The administrative infeasibility of fee collection at certain facilities creates some problems. A large city park cannot restrict entrance without totally changing its character. Also, where demand is slight and irregular, the costs of fee collection can be high relative to revenue, although mechanical devices and the permit system may reduce such costs. Questions also arise from generalized, "philosophical" concepts, such as the argument that one cannot and should not put a price on an opportunity to view and enjoy the natural beauty resources of the nation. In the same vein it is argued that charging for visits to historical sites such as the Lincoln Memorial would be in poor taste. Those who use these arguments have not come to grips with the question of whether society should in fact discriminate in favor of these uses of output.

Fees and charges have long been imposed on certain recreational facilities (national or state parks, ski runs, and golf courses) that involve fairly heavy public expenditures; since the charges have not deterred use, it would appear that the charges could perhaps be extended and increased. However, we have little comparative evidence so far of the extent of use that might result from no fees. We also have little evidence to help us determine whether ghetto residents and other lower-income groups would be deterred from using urban parks and playgrounds if a nominal fee were charged, and, if they were deterred, whether such charges could eventually be used to so improve the facilities that their attendance might increase despite the charge. We need further experimentation to show whether an urban facilities system that would include both free entrance gate admittance and charges for certain selected services inside the facility could lead to a more efficient allocation of resources and to increased revenues without entailing all of the problems and questions mentioned above.

NOTES

1. Marion Clawson, *Methods of Measuring the Demand for and Value of Outdoor Recreation* (Resources for the Future, Reprint #10, February 1959). Also, Harry P. Hatry and Diana R. Dunn, *Measuring the Effectiveness of Local Government Services: Recreation* (The Urban Institute, 1971).

2. Peter H. Pearse, "A New Approach to the Evaluation of Non-Priced Recreational Resources," *Land Economics*, 44 (February 1968): 87–99. Pearse contends that within each income class, the longest distance traveler represents the marginal user in terms of maximum outlay. Within that income class the difference between the longest distance traveler and each of other individuals' travel represents the maximum toll that could be levied on that individual. This is summed in each class and then over all classes for the total consumer's surplus resulting from free use of this particular service facility. The analysis depends on some restrictive assumptions; however, it does have great advantages over other attempts at this type of measurement. Although Pearse aimed his study at federal park lands, it seems applicable to facilities such as zoos, museums, marinas, etc., which involve travel costs. In addition, the analysis suggests an excellent use for the type of information on income, travel, and occupation of users referred to in this chapter.

3. James W. Kitchen and William S. Herndon, "Land Values Adjacent to an Urban Neighborhood Park," *Land Economics*, 43 (August 1967): 357–361. See also: Jack L. Knetsch, "The Influence of Reservoir Projects on Land Values," *Journal of Farm Economics*, 46 (February 1964): 231–243.

4. Ruth P. Mack and Sumner Myers, "Outdoor Recreation," in Robert Dorfman, ed., *Measuring Benefits of Government Investments* (Brookings Institution, 1965).

5. Arthur D. Little, Inc., "Marketing Study and Recommendations Concerning Federal Recreation Area Permit and Fee Systems" (Report to Bureau of Outdoor Recreation, U.S. Department of the Interior, December 1967).

6. In Canada this type of information is being collected for all levels of recreation facilities, both national and local.

7. Thomas M. Van Dusen and Eugene M. Huhtala, "Entrance Fees," *Revenue Sources Management School* (National Recreation and Park Association, Washington, D.C., 1966). Zoos vary their prices for adults and children, as well as by

day, by time of day, and by season. A detailed elaboration of the fee and charge practices for the various facilities provided by states is presented in *State Park Fees and Charges Survey, 1966,* The National Conference on State Parks (National Recreation and Park Association, Washington, D.C.), in cooperation with Maine State Park and Recreation Commission, Augusta, Maine.

8. See note 5 above.

9. Warren C. Robinson, "The Simple Economics of Public Outdoor Recreation," *Land Economics,* 43 (February 1967): 71–84; also Jack L. Knetsch, "Financing Public Outdoor Recreation," *Proceedings of the National Conference on Policy Issues in Outdoor Recreation, 1966* (Bureau of Outdoor Recreation, U.S. Department of Interior).

10. See note 5 above.

The Pricing of
Hospital Services

*H*OSPITAL care is different from other public services: (1) it is primarily a consumer good, especially in municipal hospitals traditionally responsible for care of aged and indigent patients; (2) it allows for payment by the consumer of the service, for the most part, at a time other than that when care is received, and often allows payment to be made by third parties whether the production of the service is under public or private auspices; (3) it requires a most complex mix of professional skills, both in length of training and number of different medical disciplines, and accordingly requires a high investment in human capital.

Municipal Hospitals

Municipal hospitals are usually for short-term treatment. They are operated as city, county, city-county, or state institutions, but most of them are operated by cities. In the late 1960s municipal hospitals accounted for about 25 percent of short-term beds, 20 percent of admissions, and 22 percent of all short-term hospital expenditures in the United States.[1]

The significance of municipal hospitals in urban medical care may be illustrated by the somewhat extreme case of New York City. In a recent year the public hospitals provided about 40 percent of beds and patient days (or care), 49 percent of ambulatory care (through outpatient departments), 53 percent of emergency room cases, and 59

Sylvester E. Berki is Associate Professor of Medical Care Organization at the School of Public Health, The University of Michigan.

percent of emergency ambulance calls.[2] In fiscal 1967–68, $794 million, or 15.5 percent of the total city executive budget, was for "health care." This was close to $227 per capita, about 60 percent above the national average. Of this amount, 55 percent ($440 million) was for inpatient and 31 percent ($248 million) for ambulatory care. Eleven percent was spent for public support beneficiaries in private institutions known as the charitables or voluntaries.

New York City's health budget was financed as follows: 42 percent ($331 million) from its own tax revenues, 23 percent ($182 million) from state aid, and 31 percent ($245 million) in federal contributions. The remaining $15 million was from other sources.[3] The health budget was distributed by 6 federal, 5 state, and 14 municipal agencies. While New York City is a particularly dramatic case, the situation in other urban centers differs only in degree.

In the early 1960s about a third of personal health care received in New York City was paid for by public funds.[4] By the late 1960s, fully 50 percent of the city's population met the standards of "medical indigency" as established by state and federal regulations.[5]

When half of the population is considered to be medically indigent because of high medical costs, access to public care at public expense is broadened. Moreover, it is further enlarged in communities where alternative private facilities for medical care are largely absent and when the municipal hospital in fact becomes the "family doctor." The outpatient departments and emergency rooms in urban areas have become the major source of primary care for the poor, which includes a majority of the blacks.

There are great regional variations in hospital service, however. In some localities the *function* of the public hospital is no different from that of the private hospital. Throughout the South, for example, the voluntary hospital of the North does not exist. Municipal hospitals in the largest cities provide medical care principally for indigent patients. Both private and municipal hospitals serve as teaching hospitals.

Even the so-called voluntary hospital of the present cannot operate without support from the public sector. Consequently, both municipal and private hospitals are subject to a wide variety of public regulations on accountability and operating controls. One analyst has described the voluntary hospital, with its public controls, as a "special kind of public utility which remains for the most part in private hands, yet provides service to all of the people."[6]

Toward Defining the Product and Its Cost

The major obstacle to economic study of hospital care is that "there are no generally accepted measures of output, input, and productivity in the hospital sector."[7]

The hospital may be conceived as an institution producing a mix of multidimensional services through a flexible set of departments. The services include health care and hotel-type care, inpatient and ambulatory care, personal and community care. While there are some services in the medical care sector of our economy that the hospital alone produces, there are no services in this sector that are not also produced within, or under, the institutional aegis of the hospital. The choices between inhospital and outpatient services are many. Visits to private physician offices *or* to outpatient clinics, diagnoses in independent laboratory facilities *or* in hospital laboratories, or even home care by private practitioners *or* by hospital staff in progressive patient care programs illustrate the many interdependencies or substitutabilities.

The technical substitutability of processes varies with the disease or the condition of the patients. For any given diagnostic category for which treatment substitutability is technically feasible, the interaction of the following six sets of complex factors determines which of the feasible production paths will be chosen: (1) the stocks of service capabilities; (2) the prices of those service capabilities; (3) the preference functions of potential patients; (4) the preference function of the physician; (5) the reward system facing the physician; and (6) the budget constraint faced by the patient. The choice, for instance, between diagnosis in the office, in the hospital's ambulatory program, or in the hospital's inpatient department results from the interaction of these six sets of factors and their relative weights.

The demand for and utilization of hospital services are not determined by any single-valued function such as medical knowledge, physicians' preferences, or number of available beds. In many cases the chosen diagnostic or therapeutic process (what we may call the "production ray") will be determined by the flexibility of the input coefficients, their relative prices, and the nature of the payoffs to both physician and patient. Since the hospital is the most resource-intensive of alternative production facilities, it is also the most expensive. Hence shifts of production rays, or differential utilization of alternative treatment processes, influence costs and prices.

The questions of hospital costs, utilization, efficiency, and pricing thus cannot be meaningfully posed unless the hospital is seen as an important cog in an interrelated system.

In analyzing the hospital as a producing unit, I posit that it produces the following set of services:

1. Personal medical care for patients
   1.1 Ambulatory care
   1.2 Inpatient care
       1.2.1 Direct patient care services (i.e., nursing)
       1.2.2 Indirect patient care, ancillary services (i.e., pathology)
       1.2.3 Direct patient nonmedical services (i.e., "hotel" services)
       1.2.4 General housekeeping and maintenance services
       1.2.5 Administrative services
2. Community medical care—ambulance services, social work services, community health centers
3. Information dissemination services—medical staff affiliation, medical seminars, continuing education
4. Teaching and training services—intern and residency programs, nursing school programs, medical technician and paramedical training
5. Research in medicine and medical technology

In accepted economic theory, final output is that which yields satisfaction to the consumer. The consumer's role in converting products and services purchased in the market into levels of satisfaction is not considered because his preferences are assumed to be expressed directly through his choices of commodities and services per se. A recent argument is that commodities and services are basically bundles of characteristics, and that the consumer transforms the bundles from possibly different commodities into satisfaction-yielding activities.[8]

For medical care, and hospital production specifically, one can argue that the consumer receives satisfaction from expected improvements of his health. (The definition of "health" is complex. For the present purpose it is used to mean the highest attainable level of functional ability, given the state of the medical arts.) In this formulation, the consumer does not purchase, say, two office visits, five days of hospital care, three X-rays, and sixteen tablets of antibiotics, but rather the expectation that his level of health will be improved.

Preferences are formulated in terms of health levels, and not of specific services or commodities. Such satisfactions are not directly measurable. In markets where optimality conditions exist to a sufficient degree, it can be assumed that relative preferences as reflected in marginal rates of substitution correspond to observed relative prices. Without an explicit and direct measure of consumer satisfaction, prices can be used to indicate relative preferences.

In the literature on medical care and hospitals the definition of output is unclear and there is no agreement as to what, in principle, should be measured. V. R. Fuchs argues, for example, that "conventional measures of medical care output such as physician-visit, or a hospital day, are patently unacceptable to economists because they come close to measuring input instead of output."[9]

The literature presents six approaches to the definition of hospital output:[10]

1. Patient days, weighted or unweighted
   Patient days weighted by case mix
   Adult patient days
2. Hospital services
   Weighted classes of services
   Hospital services by type of hospital
3. Episode of illness
4. End results and health levels
   Altered status, symptoms, and functions
5. Intermediate inputs
6. Composites of one or more of the above

The problem of measuring output takes on different meanings in different contexts. If hospitals attempt to maximize their objectives defined in terms of the number of patient days per year, then, for the purpose of evaluating how well they succeed, the appropriate definition of output is in patient days. If physicians are seen as coordinators of medical services or medical entrepreneurs, the hospitals' products are intermediate outputs to be defined in terms of those characteristics the physician considers as his relevant inputs. These may be patient days, or the number of laboratory and other ancillary services, or nursing care. If the purpose of the analysis is the determination of the social efficiency of medical resource allocation, the relevant outputs are those that contribute to increases in health levels, or more specifically, the end results of treatment processes for defined diagnostic categories. But the lack of conceptual clarity, the absence of modeling, and the confusion of patient and physician roles have permitted the development of multiple and inconsistent definitions of output and, as a corollary, the imprecise and sometimes tautological measurement of costs.

Prices and Incentives

Those most closely concerned with hospitals advocate what might be called "compensatory full-cost pricing" of outputs. Prices, they urge, "should be designed to recover full cost of services used and to provide a further margin of return to offset losses in departments which are in the nature of a community service, such as emergency departments and clinics for indigents."[11] Such a pricing system is subject to the usual economists' objections to full-cost pricing and its arbitrary allocation of joint costs; more importantly, it increases the likelihood that consumption would be discouraged unduly.

Price as the basis for an incentive structure in hospital care is affected by the dual system of pricing produced by third-party payments. A set of price ratios designed to induce "efficient" use patterns by consumers may be precisely that set of prices that induces "inefficient" production by suppliers. Over time, of course, the price ratios designed to face suppliers are reflected in prices faced by consumers. If the objective is to reduce the utilization of resource-intensive patterns of care such as hospital use, the price of hospitalization relative to that of ambulatory care facing the consumer should be increased, for example. But to induce providers to produce more ambulatory and less inpatient care, the prices facing suppliers would have to be adjusted in the opposite direction: the price of services to the suppliers on an ambulatory basis would have to be higher than the prices on an inpatient basis. If the dual-pricing were effective over some period of time, changes in the pattern of care in the desired direction could be expected. That means that some excess capacity in the production of inpatient services would be created. If such excess capacities were to exist, utilization on an inpatient basis would be less expensive in real resource terms in the short run. If the excess capacities were not utilized, over time, one would expect a reduction in the capacity to provide services on an inpatient basis. This reduction, in the long run, would drive up the supply price of inpatient services.

Behavior of the adjustment mechanisms, even in well-functioning markets where forward trading is not feasible, is at best difficult to isolate and to analyze. Here, however, the "demand determinants" are also likely to be shifting over time. Incomes, demographic patterns, conceptions of what medical science can and cannot accomplish (and should or should not do), notions of "demand versus right," and environmental factors—in other words, all the structural and behavioral parameters of the system—change over time. In a system of such complexity, "efficient" pricing is not simple.

Productivity Cost Changes

As the Gorham report shows, the cost-production structure, as well as third-party payments, reduces incentives for efficiency.

At present, hospitals have inadequate incentive to be efficient. They are not under strong pressure from patients, because a substantial part of the patients' bills are paid by third parties. Third parties have usually reimbursed hospitals for cost incurred without pressing for greater efficiency. Hospital administrators often lack the training required for effective management. The medical staff of the hospital often presses the hospital administrator and board of trustees for acquisition of the latest medical equipment without regard to the cost implications involved. Trustees are often subject to pressures imposed on them by the community and medical staff. Even where the incentive does exist, initiation and application of cost reducing innovation is often beyond the resources of an individual institution.[12]

The largest single cost component in hospitals is labor costs. It is generally assumed that the single most important source of hospital inefficiency is to be found in the combined lag in productivity in hospitals and competitive wage increases for labor in the hospital; these are attributed to a variety of factors: "archaic licensing regulations and professional mores, . . . unassimilated revolution in hospital labor relations, . . . lack of flexibility in labor use, . . . increased unionization."[13] And productivity must be increased if we are to keep costs of hospital care in check. The issue posed, then, is that of incentives for increasing productivity.

In a classic study, Lytton examined "labor productivity" in federal agencies, among them the hospital system of the Veterans Administration. Output is defined as unweighted patient days and the labor component of input as personnel. He then shows that personnel per patient day has increased over time. This result has since been cited by many.[14] However, it is not even an approximate measure of either productivity or of productivity change over time, since (1) the output is defined in terms of a complex and unspecified aggregate; (2) any change in any of the undefined output dimensions, such as length of stay, quality, case complexity, patient demographic characteristics, and disease distribution over an extended period, will change "output" but will not be reflected in the "measure"; (3) the composition of "personnel" is not known and it may have changed; and (4) service intensity and complexity is not specified, but we know that this has changed.

In a more recent study, Fuchs estimated that labor productivity in hospitals has increased somewhat over time, but by less than in the rest of the economy. For the period 1929–65, his measure of output is deflated national total dollar expenditures. Labor input is again personnel, now appearing as "per man."[15] The increase in "real output per man" is shown to be 0.9 percent per year. The same criticisms apply but in somewhat stronger terms. Changes in patterns and outcomes of hospital care between 1929 and 1965 make shambles of his measures of "real output and input."[16]

However labor productivity is defined, the argument is often advanced that decreasing hours and increasing wages imply higher hospital costs. Klarman has several times suggested that decreases in hours worked necessarily lead to decreases in productivity.[17] Not lags in technical productivity but rapid increases in wages are held to blame by others. The theory that has been offered to explain higher than average wage increases in hospitals may be labeled "the closing of the gap." The basic argument is that wage rates and working conditions in hospitals have been traditionally lower than those in industry in general. Unionization and presumably greater horizontal labor mobility have resulted in the gradual elimination of the hospital-industry differentials. Since hospitals had to "catch up," so to speak, increases in wages paid by hospitals necessarily rose faster than some national averages. The "gap" has not been closed yet: there was still, in 1963, a "depressed state of hospital wages."[18] This has been attributed to the eleemosynary nature of hospitals.[19]

For this argument to hold we must assume either that (1) horizontal labor mobility exists but employees are themselves at least partly motivated by eleemosynary tendencies—that is, they could have moved, within skill categories, to higher paying jobs out of the hospitals, but preferred not to; or (2) little horizontal mobility obtains in that segment of the market from which hospitals draw their labor force. It may also be, at least in the recent past, that both mobility and organization were absent in the pool of Negro and Puerto Rican workers from which urban hospitals tend to recruit an overwhelming proportion of their low-skilled and semiskilled employees. Klarman has argued that while there may have been a gap sometime in the past, it is not present in the post-1948 period.[20]

Price incentives alone may not yield higher productivity. An obstacle to increased productivity is to be found in the hierarchical system of hospitals that inhibits reallocation of tasks and hence limits "efficient" specialization of functions and changes in labor inputs of various skills. Wessen, for example, has identified no less than twenty-three occupational status groups, ranging from the janitor at the bottom to the visiting staff physician at the top.[21]

The literature on labor productivity in the hospital is poor, but the literature on the other factors of production is practically nonexistent. There is some discussion of the sources of capital funds that is informative but in general purely descriptive: it assumes that "the hospital will use whatever capital is available."[22]

Capacity, Size, and Economies of Scale

Many studies have been made of such public policy issues as: Should larger or smaller hospitals be built? Should hospitals have more or fewer beds? A greater scope of services? Should hospital capacity be used at a higher rate—i.e., should there be fewer hospitals in certain areas? Conversely, does excess bed capacity raise costs? Are cost increases, as measured by per diem units, the necessary corollaries of the improved quality of care resulting from the use of the products of medical knowledge and technology? Finally, should we improve training, management, and other aspects of hospitals to provide the present level of care at lower cost? Or should we aim to provide a better level of care at the present cost?

The main conclusion from these studies is that we have to learn more about how hospitals function before these questions can be answered. A number of studies of hospital costs, for example, agree that economies of scale exist.

P. J. Feldstein, for example, concludes that economies of scale do exist,[23] and Carr and Feldstein find a shallow U-shaped curve with a minimum at around 190 average daily census, which implies that beyond that rather small size diseconomies exist.[24] Ingbar and Taylor, on the other hand, find that not only are there no economies of scale, but also that there is an inverted U-shaped cost curve, with a maximum at around 150 beds—or 200, depending on the year of the data.[25] Their "least efficient hospital" is almost exactly Carr and Feldstein's "most efficient" hospital. They reasonably conclude that "whatever its exact shape—the average cost curve does not fall monotonically, at least in the 30–300 bed range of hospital size." Berry, on the other hand, finds economies of scale to exist over the entire range.[26]

Cohen too finds economies of scale to exist, with the minimum of a U-shaped curve at around 160–170 beds in one sample, and a minimum at around 290–295 in another sample, and hence concludes that "hospitals between 150 and 350 beds are most efficient for ordinary patient care."[27] When allowance is made for the "more output" of affiliated hospitals, however, the economies are even more pronounced and now the minimum cost is reached at 540–575 beds with "unweighted" output, and at either 640, 700, or 790 beds, depending on how the affiliated output is weighted. When inpatient days are used as the measure of output, Cohen finds the minimum cost at either 240 or 320 beds, depending on the presence of the quality variable. On the other hand, the Panel on Hospital Care, in its analysis of data from "12 distinguished hospitals" ranging in size from 300 to 1,500 beds, concluded that there are no economies of scale.[28]

Marginal-Cost Pricing Rules

Weisbrod has advocated marginal-cost pricing in the context of instability in demand facing a given hospital. He suggests that prices should reflect occupancy rates.

If patients entered the hospital with the lowest occupancy, aggregate hospital costs would be reduced to some extent in the short run by cutting certain staff requirements, and in the long run by reducing capacity requirements.[29]

By assumption hospitals are considered substitutable homogeneous units, and the distribution of beds between services is the same within all hospitals. However, a low occupancy rate of a hospital that specializes in maternity care is not quite a substitute for the high occupancy in another hospital that specializes in diseases of the heart. Within the set of hospitals with the same or similar service-facility mix, surgical, medical, maternity, pediatric, obstetrical, and intensive care, beds are not by any means perfect substitutes.

Empirically or institutionally, the argument for marginal-cost pricing disregards the referral patterns of physicians and their admitting privileges—factors that are neither independent of each other nor equally distributed over specialists and hospitals. Physicians admit patients to hospitals where they have attending privileges, and also refer patients to those specialists who practice in those hospitals.

Feldstein has suggested that "efficient utilization will exist only when the price is equal to marginal cost."[30] Presumably, "efficient utilization" is that level of utilization observed "when price is equal to marginal cost." His major contribution to the discussion is his clear and explicit recognition of some of the obstacles in the path of the marginalist principles. Among these obstacles are: (1) the interaction between patient and physician preferences, (2) the stochastic nature of demand, (3) the ubiquity of uncertainty, (4) the interdependence between ambulatory and inpatient utilization, (5) the interdependence among physician income, hospital "prestige," and inpatient utilization, (6) option demand, (7) standby capacity, (8) economic vs. technical efficiency, (9) private vs. social efficiency, (10) the oligopolistic nature of the market in just about *any* given community, (11) the incompatibility between price competition and an oligopolistic nonprofit "industry"—i.e., that some hospitals are nonprofit and tax-financed, whereas others operate for profit, (12) the relevance of price competition between organizations, some of which are taxpaying and some tax-exempt, and (13) the fact that private physicians also in some sense compete with outpatient clinics, and pay taxes, while voluntaries do not.

Peak-Load Pricing

One obstacle to utilization of existing capacity is the uneven distribution of demand over time—for example, the peaks associated with the time of day, day of the week, holidays, month of the year, and changes in disease incidence. To smooth off the peaks and fill in the troughs is the objective of peak-load pricing. The theoretical and empirical discussion of this is very extensive.[31]

The most comprehensive analysis of hospital utilization has been made by M. F. Long and Feldstein. They have suggested that, to ration capacity, peak-load pricing should be practiced.[32] They advocate this pricing scheme for all services, but their discussion actually relates uniquely to their specific example—obstetrical care. For example, the implicit assumption is made that the demand for obstetrical beds (if not length of stay, which they don't consider) is perfectly inelastic. If the demand is price inelastic, how can it be shifted by price changes? An additional (and usually unrecognized) problem arises if peak-load pricing is instituted—and then shifts the peak. The argument is made that since maternity ward capacity is only 65 percent used, for example, between Friday noon and Sunday noon, the marginal cost of the service is lower then and ought to be reflected in a lower price. Experimentation could establish the evening-out process by which peaks are reduced.[33]

It is generally recognized that demand peaks are significantly influenced by *supply* conditions. Admission variations with time of day and day of week reflect not only the admitting physician's convenience but also his appreciation that during certain periods the likelihood of using ancillary facilities and personnel is very much reduced. The laboratories, X-ray departments, operating rooms, and the full nursing staff tend to slow down after 5 p.m. from Monday through Friday and on all weekends.[34] To maintain these systems at full steam would involve either a second, and possibly a third, shift, or the payment of overtime. Either case would appear to entail more cost. However, there is in fact no available analysis to judge whether eliminating supply-induced demand peaks for hospital care would be more or less costly than accommodating them.

I do not suggest that current operating levels of hospitals are in any sense optimal. I am simply saying that proposals for changes to attain better, more desirable, more "efficient," or less costly operating procedures need analysis within the framework of an explicit model of medical care. The champions of marginal-cost and/or peak-load pricing have no model, or even a theorem. What they have is a postulate: that marginal-cost and/or peak-load pricing will lead to the efficient use of resources. However, the postulate is taken from the conclusion of a general theory that requires as its conditions precisely those characteristics that do not obtain in the hospital sector.

Recent Proposals on Price Incentives

Feldstein has proposed a number of incentive mechanisms. Correctly, he distinguishes between two kinds of goals and, hence, two kinds of incentives to elicit their attainment: (1) process incentives, designed to encourage desired changes in the process of care, such as the establishment of a committee of experts that establishes that an operation is appropriate, and (2) output incentives, designed to reward the production of specified output dimensions.[35] Four specific incentive plans are then proposed: (1) reimbursement on the basis of the mean of the average costs of all hospitals in a given community, (2) payments based on individual hospital performance, (3) payments based inversely on the length of stay, and (4) schemes based on targeted quality criteria.

Certain difficulties remain. For example, unless plans (3) and (4) were combined, high patient turnover, very short length of stay, and very poor quality would be rewarded. Use of the mean of average costs is meaningful, if at all, only where hospitals of similar facility service mix are compared. A further difficulty lurks in the assumptions underlying the schemes: that both the shortrun and longrun cost curves are U-shaped, that there is some optimal shortrun capacity and operating level, and that economies of scale exist. There is neither strong evidence nor agreement in the literature about costs that these assumptions, in fact, are tenable.

S. Waldman has proposed an "average increase plan" under which each hospital would be reimbursed for cost increases, regardless of their actual magnitude in a given hospital, in the amount corresponding to the average of cost increases for all hospitals in the same classification in the relevant community.[36] Neither output nor quality is specified; the impact of outpatient and training programs is not considered—unless included in the "same classification." In general, it is hard to know what this means other than some incentive to incur cost increases below that of the average. One problem may be posed by the size of the given hospital relative to that of others, even in the same classification, in the relevant community. The larger the size of a hospital, relative to others, measured, say, in beds, the weaker the incentive effect of the plan, unless the standard is the "average of all, excluding the specimen." Many communities with one or two acute hospitals would not fit the scheme at all. A somewhat similar plan, but for physicians, has been proposed by W. J. McNerney.[37]

Both Feldstein and R. M. Sigmond suggest a capitation method.[38] Sigmond's proposal is to reimburse the hospital on a capitation basis. One difficulty would be the establishment of "patient lists." The patients would be expected to (and in fact would be obliged to) associate with a given hospital on a more or less permanent basis. Feldstein, on the other hand, would reimburse on a capitation basis, not hospitals, but *medical groups*. The hospital would in general be expected to be associated with medical groups; in any case the estimated yearly costs for complete services provided by the group, including hospitalization, would be paid to the group on a capitation basis. The group would then become responsible for the medical management of the patient. The underlying assumption is that the organization of prepaid group practice leads to the more efficient practice of medicine. In addition, this would clearly reduce the incentive to hospitalize.[39]

Feldstein's suggestion that medical groups be reimbursed on a capitation basis merits attention even though it presents some difficulties. It is the *only* suggestion that is based on the realization that incentives to attain hospital "efficiency," usually defined simply in terms of reduced costs (or at least costs not greater than the average, or cost increases no greater than average increases), cannot be seriously proposed without considering that hospital utilization, on both ambulatory and inpatient basis, is not independent of the organization of medical care service outside the hospital.

The major premise of this proposal is that unless the system for delivering care *as a whole* is made rational, the hospital cannot be rational. It further assumes, and there is some evidence for this, that the attainment of acceptable or better quality would be enhanced or guaranteed by the internal medical controls characteristics of large group practice. The proposal, however, does not consider how hospitals could or should set prices to the groups.

A method developed by Ro and Auster would make reimbursement a function of the difference between the standard cost of treating a well-defined diagnosis in a relevant area and the realized cost of the hospital.[40] It is actually a weighted average reimbursement formula with variable weights by which both the "incentive" and "penalty" factors could be changed, depending on the degree of deviation from standard cost and its definition. The standard cost is defined in terms of the mean of observed costs and deviations around it. This plan not only considers the hospital as an isolated unit within the medical care system, but also generates other problems: e.g., what is the "relevant area" and which factors of interhospital variation are to be included in standard cost and which not. Nevertheless, it is an imaginative step in the direction of devising efficiency-enhancing alternatives to the full-cost formulas now in use.

The National Advisory Commission on Health Manpower has rung changes on a similar plan by proposing a Variable Incentive Payment (VIP) plan that would be "a percentage figure and its size would depend on the categorization of the hospital on the basis of its standard of care. In the category for the lowest standard of care VIP would be set equal to zero, and in the highest category might be as high as 15 percent."[41] Why this would attain anything other than the maximation of the quality element in the decision-makers' objective function is hard to see.

An additional proposal is to reimburse the hospital on last year's cost, plus a VIP component, plus the average increase in per diem during the current year in an "appropriate" group of hospitals. This appears to mean: "the average of usual and customary, plus something extra for better quality." It can be properly viewed as a quality incentive, but otherwise its incentive effects are minimal, particularly since per diem is the basis. It might even encourage longer stays, since the argument is that the last few days of care are less expensive than the first few. Even if they were not, the impact of the plan, under the present system, might well be to (1) induce a few extra days of stay during which few or no ancillary services are provided, (2) reduce the turnover, and thereby (3) reduce the average per diem for a given hospital.

Since per diem below that on the average for all hospitals is "rewarded," whatever the relevant area and "appropriate" groups for comparative bases may be, the longer stays would be rewarded. Attending physicians might not be averse to this plan either, since the longer their patients were hospitalized, and the more patients, the more the physician's earnings would be increased. An additional problem with this plan (as well as all others, with the possible exception of the group plan of Feldstein) is that the hospitals would still be completely free to allocate costs and to charge fees at will.

There are very few empirical studies of the differential impacts of various reimbursement and pricing schemes.[42] Cost per patient day is a very inaccurate measure at best. Full-cost pricing results in perverse incentives. Substitutes are necessary, and only research in the context of a model of the entire medical care system will yield a range of new options and provide a basis for careful analysis of those options.

NOTES

1. *Hospitals (Journal of the American Hospital Association)*, Guide Issue (August issue, yearly).

2. H. E. Klarman, *Hospital Care in New York City: The Roles of Voluntary and Municipal Hospitals* (Columbia University Press, 1963), p. 34.

3. *Community Health Services for New York City:* Report and Staff Studies of the Commission on the Delivery of Personal Health Services, Gerard Piel, chairman (Praeger, 1969), pp. 76–79, 116–117.

4. N. Piere, "Metropolitan Areas and Public Medical Care," in *The Economics of Health and Medical Care* (University of Michigan Press, 1964), pp. 64 ff.

5. Piel, p. 115. See note 3 above.

6. E. L. Hamilton, "The Voluntary Hospital in America: Its Role, Economics, and Internal Structure," in W. Richard Scott and E. H. Volkart, eds., *Medical Care* (Wiley, 1966), pp. 393–405.

7. *Medical Care Prices: A Report to the President* (Department of Health, Education, and Welfare, February 1967), p. 32 (the "Gorham Report").

8. K. J. Lancaster, "A New Approach to Consumer Theory," *Journal of Political Economy,* 74 (April 1966): 132–57.

9. V. R. Fuchs, *The Service Economy* (National Bureau of Economic Research, 1968), p. 126.

10. For each approach to output definition, the following references are suggested:

Patient days: M. S. Feldstein, see note 14 below: Ch. 2; P. J. Feldstein, see note 23 below; I. B. Kravis, "Discussion," in V. R. Fuchs, ed., *Production and Productivity in the Service Industries* (Columbia University Press, New York, 1969): 84–93; J. R. Lave and L. B. Lave, "Hospital Cost Functions: Estimating Cost Functions for Multiproduct Firms," Graduate School of Industrial Administration, Carnegie-Mellon University, December 1968 (Xeroxed); and C. N. Stevens, "Hospital Market Efficiency: The Anatomy of the Supply Response," paper delivered at the Second Conference on the Economics of Health, Baltimore, Md., December 1968.

Services: American Hospital Association, *Cost Finding for Hospitals* (Chicago, 1957); R. E. Berry, see note 26 below: 123–139; R. E. Berry, "Product Heterogeneity and Hospital Cost Analysis," *Inquiry*, March 1970; 67–75; H. A. Cohen," Variations in Cost Among Hospitals of Different Sizes," *Southern Economic Journal*, January 1967: 355; H. A. Cohen, "Costs and Efficiency: A Study of Short-Term General Hospitals," unpublished Ph.D. dissertation, Cornell University, 1967; H. A. Cohen, see note 27 below; M. S. Feldstein, see note 14 below; M. L. Ingbar and L. D. Taylor, see note 25 below; D. E. Saathoff and R. A. Kurtz, "Cost Per Day Comparisons Don't Do the Job," *The Modern Hospital*, October 1962: 14; J. W. Kovner, L. B. Browne, and A. I. Kisch, "Income and the Use of Outpatient Medical Care by the Insured," *Inquiry*, June 1969: 27–34; and J. K. Mann and D. E. Yett, "The Analysis of Hospital Costs: A Review Article," *Journal of Business*, April 1968: 191–202.

Episode of illness: K–k. Ro and R. Auster, see note 40 below; and A. A. Scitovsky, "Changes in the Cost of Selected Illness," *American Economic Review*, December 1967: 1182–95.

End results: C. L. Chiang, *An Index of Health: Mathematical Models*, National Center for Health Statistics, Series 2, No. 5, U.S. Department of HEW, PHS (Washington, 1965); *Health Planning: A Programmed Instruction Course*, Public Health Service Programmed Instruction, Series No. 2, Bulletin 1846, Department of HEW, PHS (Washington, 1968); *Health Planning, Problems of Concept and Method*, Scientific Publication No. 111, Pan American Health Organization (Washington, 1965); M. Lerner, "Mortality and Morbidity in the United States as Basic Indices of Health Needs," *Annals of the American Academy of Political and Social Sciences*, September 1961: 1–10; J. J. May, "Physician Productivity in the Hospital—An Introduction," *Inquiry*, September 1969: 57–58; P. J. Sanazaro and J. Williamson, "End Results of Patient Care," *Medical Care*, March–April 1968: 128; and H. M. Somers and A. R. Somers, *Medicare and the Hospitals* (Washington, 1967).

Intermediate inputs: P. J. Feldstein, "Research on the Demand for Health Services, *Milbank Memorial Fund Quarterly*, July 1966, Part 2: 128–165; and J. J. May, see paragraph above.

Composite units: *A Decade of Change in U.S. Hospitals, 1953–63*, A Study Comparing Utilization, Staffing and Cost Trends in Civilian and CONUS Army Hospitals, Office of the Surgeon General, DOA (Washington, May 1965); and M. L. Ingbar and L. D. Taylor, see note 25 below.

11. W. F. Foyle, "Accounting and Finance," in W. J. McNerney, *Hospital and Medical Economics*, Vol. II (Hospital Research and Educational Trust, Chicago, 1962), p. 997.

12. *Medical Care Prices*, pp. 7–9. See note 7 above.

13. A. R. Somers, "Hospital Costs and Payment—Suggestions for Stabilizing the Uneasy Balance," *Medical Care* (September–October 1969): 358.

14. H. D. Lytton, "Recent Productivity Trends in the Federal Government: An Exploratory Study," *Review of Economics and Statistics*, 61 (November 1959): 341–359; H. E. Klarman, "The Increased Cost of Hospital Care," in *The Economics of Health and Medical Care* (see note 4 above, pp. 227–254); M. S. Feldstein, *Economic Analysis for Health Service Efficiency* (Markham, 1968).

15. Fuchs, p. 117. See note 9 above.

16. For a discussion of such changes, see American Medical Association, Report of the Commission on the Cost of Medical Care, Vol. 4: *Changing Patterns of Hospital Care* (1964).

17. See notes 2 and 14 above.

18. H. Ginsburg, "Wage Differentials in Hospitals, 1956–1963: A Study Emphasizing the Wages of Nurses and Unskilled Workers in Nongovernmental Hospitals" (unpublished Ph.D. dissertation, New School for Social Research, 1967), p. 293.

19. M. W. Reder, "Some Problems in the Measurement of Productivity in the Medical Care Industry," in V. R. Fuchs, ed., *Production and Productivity in the Service Industries* (National Bureau of Economic Research, 1969), p. 127.

20. See notes 2 and 14 above, specifically pp. 230–232 of the latter.

21. A. F. Wessen, "Hospital Ideology and Communication Between Ward Personnel," in E. G. Jaco, ed., *Patients, Physicians, and Illness* (Free Press, 1958), pp. 448–468; specifically p. 450.

22. M. F. Long, "Efficient Use of Hospitals," in *The Economics of Health and Medical Care* (see note 4 above), pp. 211–226.

23. P. J. Feldstein, *An Empirical Investigation of the Marginal Cost of Hospital Services* (Studies in Hospital Administration, Graduate Program in Hospital Administration, University of Chicago, 1961), p. 51 and p. 64, respectively.

24. W. J. Carr and P. J. Feldstein, "The Relationship of Cost to Hospital Size," *Inquiry*, 4 (June 1967): 45–65.

25. M. L. Ingbar and L. D. Taylor, *Hospital Costs in Massachusetts* (Harvard University Press, 1968).

26. R. E. Berry, "Returns to Scale in the Production of Hospital Services," *Health Services Research*, 2 (Summer 1967): 123–139; also "Product Heterogeneity and Hospital Cost Analysis" (mimeo), no date.

27. H. A. Cohen, "Hospital Cost Curves with Emphasis on Measuring Patient Care Output," paper delivered at the Second Conference on the Economics of Health, Baltimore (December 1968), p. 4.

28. *Report of the National Advisory Commission on Health Manpower,* Vol. 2 (1967), p. 161.

29. B. A. Weisbrod, "Some Problems of Pricing and Resource Allocation in

a Nonprofit Industry—The Hospitals," *Journal of Business*, 38 (January 1965): 18–28, quote from p. 23; see also K-k. Ro, "Incremental Pricing Would Increase Efficiency in Hospitals," *Inquiry*, 6 (March 1969): 28–36.

30. P. J. Feldstein and J. J. Gorman, "Predicting Hospital Utilization: An Evaluation of Three Approaches," *Inquiry*, 2 (June 1965): 13–36.

31. O. E. Williamson, "Peak-Load Pricing and Optimal Capacity Under Indivisibility Constraints," *American Economic Review*, 56 (September 1966): 810–827.

32. M. F. Long and P. J. Feldstein, "Economics of Hospital Systems: Peak Loads and Regional Coordination," *American Economic Review*, 57 (May 1967): 119–129.

33. When peak-load pricing was first introduced in the Bell Telephone System, trunk lines became unavailable between 9 and 10 p.m. The peak shifted. Only after further experimentation was the shifting peak fairly evenly distributed, to everyone's benefit.

34. According to Arnold J. Toynbee, "It is . . . imprudent to fall sick or die between 6:00 p.m. on a Friday evening and 9:00 a.m. on a Monday morning. If you fall sick between those hours, you may get no medical attention; and, if, in consequence, you die, you will certainly not be able to get yourself buried till Monday comes." See Toynbee, *Change and Habit: The Challenge of Our Time* (Oxford University Press, 1966), p. 220.

35. P. J. Feldstein, "An Analysis of Reimbursement Plans," in *Reimbursement Incentives for Hospital and Medical Care*, Research Report No. 26, 1968, U.S. Department of Health, Education, and Welfare, Social Security Administration: 17–38.

36. S. Waldman, "Average Increase in Costs—An Incentive Reimbursement Formula for Hospitals," *ibid.*, pp. 39–48.

37. W. J. McNerney, "M.D.s Need Incentives for Medical Efficiency," in an interview for *Medical Economics*, 46 (November 10, 1969): 25 ff.

38. P. J. Feldstein, "A Proposal for Capitation Reimbursement to Medical Groups for Total Medical Care," and R. M. Sigmond, "Capitation as a Method of Reimbursement to Hospitals in a Multihospital Area," both in *Reimbursement Incentives for Hospital and Medical Care* (see note 35 above), pp. 49–60 and 61–72.

39. For a discussion of the effects of prepaid groups on hospitalization, see A. Donabedian, "An Evaluation of Prepaid Group Practice," *Inquiry*, 6 (September 1969): 3–27.

40. K-k. Ro and R. Auster, "An Output Approach to Incentive Reimbursement for Hospitals," *Health Services Research*, 4 (Fall 1969): 177–187, specifically, 177.

41. *Report of the National Advisory Commission on Health Manpower* (see note 28 above), p. 147.

42. For an exception, see M. V. Pauly and D. F. Drake, "Effect of Third Party Methods of Reimbursement on Hospital Performance," paper delivered at the Second Conference on the Economics of Health, Baltimore (1968).

Pricing Primary and Secondary Education

The confusion between state provision and state financing is so
prevalent in most discussions of the welfare state that we might pause
a moment to establish firmly [the] distinction. For example, to show
that many people cannot afford to educate their children beyond the
statutory leaving age at best established a case for a cash grant by the
state, an income tax rebate, or a personal loan from the public
authorities, but has absolutely nothing to do with the issue of private
versus public ownership of schools. . . . External benefits, parental
incompetence, and equality of opportunity do not stand up as
arguments for state-provided education.

Mark Blaug[1]

THE rebirth of interest in the market as a mechanism for allocating resources[2] stems from an increasing disillusion with
bureaucracies, or nonmarket-oriented organizations, as agencies for doing this.[3] Education is a representative case. Current debate
focuses on the alleged technological inefficiency of education, the lack
of responsiveness to client demands, and the lack of innovativeness.[4]

One provocative remedy to the problem of the administrative
overburden of bureaucracy in education is to subject production, distribution, and possibly the financing of schools to market forces.[5] Competitive markets can be introduced for the services that produce learning either for entire schools (or even entire school systems) or for parts

Martin T. Katzman teaches at the Institute for Economic Research, University of São Paulo, Brazil.

Author's Note: In preparing this paper, I have benefited tremendously from discussions with Christopher Jencks, Marvin Lazerson, Stephen Michelson, Marshall Smith, and Stanley Paul.

of the learning output—for example, reading or foreign language skills. Information about consumer demands for learning products can be obtained through the political process (as it is obtained at present), or through a greater measure of parent or citizen participation in the educational policy decisions, or by a system of pricing. The market test of consumers' willingness to pay a price can be thought of as a package price for services, at a grade level, or as separate prices for learning individual skills.

Intervention of Government

Public intervention in the provision of education may be justified on several grounds: (1) the technological characteristics of education that contribute to failures of consumers and producers to behave in conformity with axioms of perfect competition, (2) externalities, and (3) institutional failures in adjacent markets (especially for human capital and housing).

Technological characteristics

Unlike the output of firms in the market sector, the output or product of schools is difficult to define. Student learning is the intent. But aspects of this performance and their relation to goals of ultimate concern evade reliable measurement. For example, schools are supposed to "educate" children for "adult life." Generally, schools measure proxies for this preparation by cognitive test scores. How these short-run measures relate to longrun achievement continues to be obscure.[6]

Schools have poorly understood production functions. Perhaps the best-known characteristic of the educational production function is that any output is influenced by multiple inputs, the most important of which—the social background of the child—is exogenous to and relatively uncontrollable by the public school system. Schools serving students of different social backgrounds have generally used different inputs; thus, whether the inputs or the students themselves account for any interschool differences in performance is rarely obvious.[7] Parents are generally unable to determine which of several schools serving similar student populations will provide the best education for their children. Producer-educators are similarly hard pressed to evaluate which of several alternative policies will produce the most of a given educational goal.

In spite of this ignorance, both consumers and producers have strong preferences on the proximate goals that should be produced as well as how the goals should be attained. The consumers' preferences appear to be strongly related to social class. For example, as several writers point out, the working class in general stands for the traditional and conservative three R's approach to education.[8] Higher-income groups appear to favor schooling that will teach children not only to gain skill in the three R's but also to get along with each other, to achieve some measure of independence from adult direction, and to be creative. As for means of attaining such goals, this class tends to favor "innovation" (i.e., *new* practices), smaller classes, aggressive building programs, and the recruitment of highly trained teachers.[9] The educators' goals tend to reflect those of their wealthier constituents.[10]

The relevance of these points for a discussion of pricing is the assumption of perfect knowledge in a market system. Although parents may know what goals they want, they do not necessarily have accurate perceptions of (1) the relationship between those proximate goals and matters of ultimate concern, and (2) the relationship between what the school is doing and what their children are learning. Although professionals have clear-cut norms of teaching and administration, again it is unclear how they are related to what children learn. In other words, the "knowledge" both parties possess is of questionable validity.

Externalities in education

There are four major classes of externalities that exist in education. One of them refers to the functioning of the school and the other three refer to the functioning of society.

Externalities in production. The "peer effects," i.e., the reciprocal effects of students on the academic performance of others.

Externalities in quantity of consumption. A minimal level of literacy is necessary for a smooth functioning of the major legal, political, and economic institutions of society. A lack of literacy in one part of the population can increase the costs of communication for others. In a more subtle sense, if a minimal ability to communicate and participate in the society is absent in a certain segment of the population, such a deviant segment may become either dependent on or threatening to the rest of society—or "social dynamite," according to James Conant.[11] Potential underconsumption of schooling to this degree is presumably prevented by compulsory attendance laws.

Externalities in quality of consumption. The kinds of things that are learned are not a matter of indifference. Externalities in quality are internalized by specifying the language of instruction, the religious contents of the curriculum, the courses of study, the textbooks, as well as such "extraneous" characteristics of teachers as foreign accent and political views.

Externalities in distribution of educational attainment. Equality of opportunity is an explicit American value, and education is seen as the most important controllable influence on opportunity. Under the current institution of compulsory schooling without charge, the degree of inequality in educational attainment is considerably less than the inequality in income, wealth, health expenditures, or housing.[12]

In short, the American belief appears to be that it is a good thing for people to consume not only *great quantities* and *similar kinds* of education, but also *equal quantities.*

Failures in capital markets

The market for education fails in an allocative sense because of the absence of financial markets for "human capital."[13] Although an individual child might benefit from attending high-quality schools for a long period of time, he would, in the absence of free public education or a capital market, have to rely upon his parents to pay for tuition and living expenses from current income. Even if parents were willing to exchange their own present consumption for their child's future consumption, they are limited in their ability to do so by their current earnings and stock of savings.

To some extent the availability of free schooling compensates for failures in the capital market. However, direct tuition costs are only one facet of private and social costs of schooling. Leisure and income foregone, especially at the higher grades, are an implicit private cost that again may be greater than social costs because of the inavailability of consumption loans.

On balance, despite the lack of a user charge, there is probably an *under*consumption of schooling by the poor: the internal rate of return for completing eighth grade instead of dropping out at seventh is roughly 30 percent, and for completing twelfth grade instead of dropping out in the eleventh is roughly 14 percent.[14]

Historical considerations

The existing system of free compulsory education evolved historically out of compromises among groups whose private interests usually conflicted and whose visions of the public interest were often incompatible. The copious literature on this evolution is replete with descriptions of the differences in quantity and quality of product sought by different groups in the population; nevertheless, the creed of equality of opportunity and boundless social mobility emerges clearly from the record.[15]

Intervention as to the quantity, quality, and distribution of education is probably agreed to by most people in American society (although the precise range, form, and magnitude of intervention are subject to considerable dispute). The desirability of public intervention in education does not, however, logically imply the production and distribution of education through the current publicly administered institutions. The questions of financing and production can be separately considered.

The Administration and Financing
of Educational Enterprises

Production decisions in the schools are influenced by geographically designated groups of voters rather than by unrelated individuals who bid through a price mechanism. Although the voters are involved to the extent that they presumably all pay taxes (the financial basis of the production decisions), they usually include people who are not parents of school-age children, as well as people who are not interested in public schools as a mode of education. As a corollary of the geographical factor, residents of communities outside a given school system can have little or no direct effect on the production decisions, even if for various reasons they might like to.

In contrast, production decisions in the private sector are not based on the decisions of a geographically delimited collectivity (school districts), but on the decisions of individual consumers. Because of competition for consumer dollars, producers may even be responsive to the demands of individuals who are *potential* consumers.

Under the present production-financing method, the community decides how much of available resources should be allocated to education as opposed to other publicly and privately consumed goods. The amount allocated depends upon the relative costs of education and other goods, the community's preferences, and the community's income.

It is significant for the "school market" that schools can operate efficiently at relatively low levels of enrollment. In a production analysis of big-city school districts, economies of scale were found for four outputs and diseconomies in none, as enrollment varies from 500 to 2,300; in addition, administrative costs were minimized at enrollments of about 1,900.[16] Two studies—one of urban high schools in New York State, the other of unified school systems in California—found economies of scale when enrollments were less than 2,000 and diseconomies when enrollments were greater.[17] Burkhead, in examining Chicago high schools with an average enrollment of 2,000, found no scale effects, which is not surprising if the maximum (minimum) of the production (cost) function is near the average.[18] Finally, in a study of high school expenditures in Wisconsin, Riew found a minimum cost at 1,675 students.[19] In none of these studies did the costs (in terms of either inputs or outputs) of operating at nonoptimal enrollments seem particularly high. These findings suggest that large numbers of school systems are viable, if not technologically efficient. In this respect, elementary schooling resembles many enterprises in the private sector of the economy (such as restaurants and barbershops), more than some enterprises in the public or quasi-public sector (such as atomic power plants).

In the case of the big-city school system, users of a particular school comprise only a small fraction of the electorate in determining their school's policies. The city neighborhood, unlike the suburb, has no mechanism for equating supply of school services and demand. Users of a particular school, to improve quality, must persuade a majority of the rest of the city through a cumbersome political mechanism, or somehow elicit favoritism from the central administration.

Usually school services are free to those living within the school district, and proscribed to those living outside its boundaries. Within big cities, a policy of "open enrollment" is followed generally, which permits students to transfer between schools when there are vacancies. No such free transfers exist among school systems. In effect, each public school system has a local monopoly. If inequalities among systems exist, "arbitrage" by transfer to the better system is often impossible, even were tuition to be paid.

School districts, because of housing markets, segregate families on the basis of income, ethnic identities, occupation, and so on.[20] In the context of present financial sources, residential patterns almost guarantee that school districts will differ in their ability and willingness to pay for education as well as in their styles of operation. (Only to the extent that schools are financed by the state government or the national government is the support for schools divorced from local ability to pay and intrastate inequalities reduced.)[21]

The institutions for producing and distributing education, dubbed by Tiebout the "Municipal Services Market Model," force people to consume housing and educational services jointly.[22] The choice of housing, which is influenced by a large number of considerations, and school taxes and expenditures cannot be separated. "Voting with their feet," the higher income families, by segregating themselves, can obtain public support for higher taxes and expenditures on education, pay a "fair" or roughly equal share of these taxes, obtain a consensus as to how the schools should be run and avoid having to suffer the adverse peer effects of the poorer students.

The current big-city educational system may be compared to two suggested radical alternatives: (1) decentralization, and (2) the voucher system. Both decentralization and some type of voucher or allowance plan are implicit components of a charge system in education. The possible combinations of these alternatives are numerous, but we focus here on these two extreme forms to emphasize their differences.

Suggested organization: decentralization

Decentralizing the administration and control of schooling is urged to better reconcile the goals of equality of educational opportunity and freedom of consumer choice. We start our analysis by assuming that big-city school systems would be split into neighborhood districts with fiscal and administrative autonomy. Each district would raise its own school taxes and hire its own personnel in accordance with the income and preference of the voters.[23]

Drawing on the documented experiences of small towns, we find that educational opportunities may tend to be less equal under decentralization than under a more centralized system. Inequalities among small towns result from the consumer–voter decisions in socially segregated and fiscally autonomous school systems. Towns of different income and/or taste tend to choose to spend different amounts on schooling. The income elasticity of educational expenditures per student among towns is about .26—i.e., per capita income differentials of $100 translate into per student expenditure differentials of roughly $26 at the mean.[24]

Within centralized big cities there are also sources of inequality, but these are more complex. They include teacher preferences to teach white, upper income children; inflexibility in salary; rules that prevent higher pay for unfavorable teaching posts; and the varied political pressures on school administrators.[25]

While inequalities within big-city school systems have been criticized, the facts show they are less than the inequalities among towns of different income. Evidence from Boston and Chicago suggests that the politically and fiscally united big-city districts vary in quality less than do fiscally autonomous suburbs.[26] For example, the three wealthiest Boston districts receive no greater expenditures per student than the three median income and lowest income districts (Table 16.1). The same maximum salary for teachers with bachelors' degrees applies to all city districts; moreover, the percentage of teachers with masters' degrees is somewhat lower in the wealthy districts.

On the other hand, in Massachusetts the towns that are predominantly upper-middle income spend much more per student than the poorest towns. Both the maximum salary and the percentage of teachers with masters' degrees suggest that the better towns have better teaching staffs. The discrepancy between rich and poor towns would be further accentuated if the wealthiest towns in Massachusetts were included in the table. Paradoxically, despite Boston's income inequalities, its big-city school system more effectively narrows the gap in educational opportunities afforded different income groups than do the fiscally autonomous small towns. Low-income districts in Boston receive more expenditures per child and have more highly trained staffs than small towns of equal income.

TABLE 16.1

Comparisons of School Quality Measures
(Boston school districts and Massachusetts towns matched for income
and size of public elementary school enrollment, 1964)

Type of district	Median family income	Percent white collar	Expenditures per student	Maximum B.A. salary	Percent M.A. degrees	Percent public elementary
High income districts						
highest income Boston districts[a]	$7,934	50.4	$337	$7,860	45.0	62.3
upper-middle income towns in Massachusetts[b]	7,926	60.7	470	7,691	25.0	83.9
Medium-income districts						
medium income Boston districts[c]	5,283	30.8	349	7,860	53.0	71.4
Low-income districts						
lowest income towns in Massachusetts[d]	5,157	36.6	405	7,200	17.5	80.6
lowest income Boston district[e]	3,757	16.5	449	7,860	55.0	85.8

[a] Districts #56, 55, 50
[b] Bedford, Belmont, Hingham, Melrose, Reading, Sharon (all are Boston suburbs)
[c] Districts #6, 18, 23, 38, 44, 49
[d] Adams, Ayer, Bourne, Chelsea, Lynn, Revere (latter three are suburbs)
[e] Districts #10, 15, 17.
SOURCE: Adapted from Massachusetts Teacher Association, "Background data for comparing towns in respect to payment of adequate salaries to teachers." (October 30, 1964).

Big city school systems, in general, upgrade the educational opportunities of the poor, but are inadequately organized for permitting the expression of consumer preferences and for spreading the burden of upgrading the poor within an economic region beyond the city. Decentralization (plus external aid) is a way to achieve the efficiency of improved consumer choices.

Suggested organization: private markets and the voucher system

While there were originally good evolutionary reasons for the traditional role of government in education, not all forms of government intervention are necessarily adaptive today. Among the various ideas for change in this regard, the most radical proposal for school reorganization is that the production of educational services be turned over to the private or market sector of the economy. The most carefully detailed form of the proposal comes from Friedman, who suggests that the federal government "require a minimum level of schooling, financed by giving parents vouchers redeemable for a specified maximum sum per child if spent on approved education."[27] Under this system, parents can supplement the vouchers with private expenditures, and the role of government is simplified to financing and insuring minimum standards of quality.

The private market. Such grants to parents would open up a competitive market for education, with all its ramifications. First, private entrepreneurs could enter the education industry on terms equal to the current public "entrepreneurs," and compete for consumer dollars. Like producers in the private sector, public schools would become responsive to consumer demand because they would no longer have a public education monopoly. In turn, the consumer would have greater freedom of choice, without having to "vote by his feet," or try to persuade a community to alter its collective policies.

At present a well-defined constituency has more or less direct control over a single school system. If, however, a competitive market were established, the control would be indirect over a whole set of schools via the market, and those schools that did not respond to consumer demands might very well fold. We do not actually know whether indirect control would in this situation provide greater responsiveness to consumer needs than direct control would. Consumers may be apathetic or as easily manipulatable by a profit-seeking market as they have been by vote-seeking educators.[28]

Friedman argues that the creation of a private market will produce technological efficiency because of the profit motive. Greater efficiency would translate into either lower costs or greater quality for the consumer, while the inefficient schools would succumb. The line of reasoning that underlies the proposal needs to be carefully analyzed with due regard for the inherent difficulty of inventing and innovating in education and the many inefficiencies resulting from institutional restraints. For example, a strong teachers' union may be able to establish a metropolitan single-salary schedule in bargaining with a large number of independent school boards.[29] Such a development would limit the ability of schools catering to lower class children to offer differential pay to teachers in ghetto schools.

Producers of education, whether public or private, may not be able to distinguish frills from essentials any more than can consumers. The value of alternative resource allocations may be difficult to assess. The most likely result is the kind of professional paternalism that exists in medicine and auto repairing, in which the producer makes judgments of value and of fact for a nominally sovereign consumer.[30]

A second kind of efficiency is, however, likely to emerge from privatization. At present, the purchase of a home and of an option to attend public school are indivisible. Residential location decisions are often contingent upon the quality of the latter option. Privatization may tend to weaken the nexus between home location and schooling decision; educational policy would tend to become fiscally neutral with respect to residential land use.

Private schools and minorities. Privatization reverses the traditional public policy of denying subsidy to schooling controlled by "divisive" or separatist minorities. Without involving the constitutional aspects of church-state relations, we can speculate on the impact of such a reversal on segregation in the schools on racial, religious, and economic grounds and, ultimately, on national unity.

Unless there are supplementary controls on private choices, privatization is likely to increase educational segregation because consumer freedom extends to choice of peers as well as to choice of place of learning and tangible inputs.[31] A new breath of life would be infused into the parochial school systems were they to be eligible for the private funds. Ambitious lower class children might leave the ghetto neighborhood public school with its more impoverished peer group. But such progress as has been made toward desegregation in the South would probably be undone. Nondiscriminatory admissions policies may have little effect on these tendencies if segregation is self-imposed on ideological or pedagogical grounds.

If privatization leads to a marginal increase in racial, class, and religious segregation, it is worth asking how divisive this trend might be for the social order. At least in the case of Catholic education, segregation does not seem to produce divisiveness. Comparisons between Catholics who had parochial education and those who had public education show little difference in community involvement, tolerance, and interaction with non-Catholics.[32] A more complete answer on the consequences of segregation for social solidarity cannot be given at this time.

Alternative forms of the suggested market system

The workings of the market system may depend crucially upon the specific institutional arrangements that are established for financing and regulating the educational enterprises. Variations in the magnitude of the voucher can affect segregation, responsiveness, and equality of opportunity.

Zero voucher. Under this formula, the poor will no longer be subsidized by the property and income taxes of the well-to-do. They will tend to go to schools with poorer resources and for fewer years than at present. Consequently, inequality in educational attainment will increase. Schools will become more segregated on the basis of income because heterogeneous families now sharing a common neighborhood school will be willing to spend different amounts on education. While the degree of ethnic segregation may also increase (partly because income is associated with ethnic identity, partly because of the drives for self-segregation), income segregation within ethnic groups now sharing the same neighborhood school may also increase. Schools for the poor will be marginal enterprises, about as responsive as other enterprises affecting the lives of the poor.

Moderate vouchers (national average expenditures) with permission to add parental supplements. In contrast to the zero voucher plan, the degree of inequality of opportunity will be limited by the floor set by the moderate voucher. The poor will not only attend better schools, but will attend them somewhat longer than under the zero voucher variant. The degree of segregation between the low- and middle-income students will diminish unless informal self-segregation mechanisms can be found. The schools catering to the poor will become potentially more profitable, hence more responsive.

Large vouchers (maximum current state expenditures), no parental supplements possible.   The degree of inequality and segregation might diminish further. The rich will still be able to attract better resources than the poor because of teacher supply factors. However, the average quality of teachers may rise, since more money will be spent on education than at present.

Vouchers inversely related to income.   The quality of resources for the poor will be equal to or greater than that of the rich. If the vouchers for the poor were large enough, schools catering to rich students would have an incentive to admit some poor students because the excess would be used to upgrade the quality of instruction for all. Higher numbers of poor children could be admitted with marginally increasing voucher payments high enough to offset the perceived adverse peer effects for the rich students.

Contracting for services.   With or without vouchers, there is another market approach. Instead of buying a whole educational package from a given school, a student might purchase math services from one school, reading from another. While this might produce finer grained choices than the previous proposals, the transportation and transaction costs to a student might be formidable.

Contracting by schools.   The school might contract for services from firms specializing in particular subject matters, utilizing equipment with high fixed costs.

Summary of alternatives

We can now compare three alternative forms of educational organization with respect to the degree of economic efficiency, equality of opportunity, and integration they foster. Although different aspects of these organizations may be combined, the ideal types are characterized as follows:

1. Status quo: multidistrict systems in a big city, under central control, monopoly of neighborhood schools tempered by open enrollment with transportation costs privately borne (no "bussing"); fiscally autonomous suburban systems; no intersystem transfers permitted without tuition payment.

2. Decentralization: big-city districts assume same autonomy as suburban systems; no open enrollment.

3. Privatization: Students given vouchers equal to national average expenditures to attend school of choice; supplementary private funds may be added.

To make the three organizations comparable, we assume that the average level of state-federal support per student is identical under all plans and that there are no programs whose primary purpose is integration (although different degrees of integration are a consequence of various approaches).

In terms of the goals of equality and integration, the current system ranks highest because all big-city public schools would be of nearly equal quality; however, many families would obtain better private and suburban education producing a bimodal distribution of overall quality. On the other hand, privatization produces the greatest inequality and segregation. In terms of freedom of choice, or economic efficiency, privatization ranks highest: the status quo lowest (Table 16.2).

TABLE 16.2

Rankings of Forms of Educational Organization:
Attainment of Goals and Preferences of Interest Groups

| | Policy Goals | | | Interest Groups | | | |
Organization	Equality	Free Choice	Integra- tion	City Rich	Suburb Rich	Minority Poor	Educational Establishment
Status quo	1	3	1	3	1 or 2	3	1
Decentralization	2	2	2	2	3	1 or 2	2
Privatization	3	1	3	1	1 or 2	1 or 2	3

The four interest groups are likely to have widely divergent preference orderings.

a. The high-income groups in the big city would favor privatization because it would permit them to live where they want without compromising their preferences, subsidizing the local poor, or sharing facilities with those whose educational motivations appear to be at variance with the values they hold. Decentralization might be their second-best option because the high-income groups could control their own schools.

b. The suburban rich are probably indifferent between the status quo and private schools, which may not be very different from public schools in exclusive suburbs. Decentralization in the big city leaves them unaffected.

c. The preferences of the poor and minorities are less clear. Decentralization or privatization gives their groups control but no integration. The status quo gives them neither.

d. The educational establishment, like all establishments, would probably resist any change. Privatization would be the most threatening if unionism were abandoned in favor of "free market" forces. On the other hand, if teachers' organizations survived, they might have greater bargaining power vis-à-vis the many independent schools than they have against monopsonistic urban boards.

It seems likely that some combination of decentralization and privatization could be reached that would make all major interest groups better off than under the status quo. For example, all students might be granted vouchers inversely proportional to family income. These students would have a choice of attending a private school or the fiscally autonomous public school, which would be locally controlled. A metropolitan agency might serve as an employment exchange for teachers, disseminate information on the relative quality of different schools, operate an educational television station, or offer cooperative purchasing services. Finally, the state or federal government might offer fiscal incentives for integration.

Experimentation with Educational Markets

Forecasting the consequences of the market system would be facilitated if the validity of the underlying assumptions were tested. While some of the assumptions may be tested crudely by observing existing patterns of behavior, others are testable only by planned experimentation. The four major assumptions stated below need this latter kind of inquiry.

> If present and potential educators were given freedom and financial resources, they would create schools that were significantly different from each other and from those operated by local school boards.

There is little reason to believe that, in the short run, freedom of choice for producers would result in a greater variety in the characteristics of schools. Today there are tens of thousands of local educational authorities, each serving a clientele with unique class and ethnic characteristics, hence differing attitudes toward schooling. These differences in parental characteristics notwithstanding, there is relatively little variety in the way in which schools are run.[33] Variety might be introduced if a new set of entrepreneurs entered the market for schooling, ignorant of the norms of the professional subculture and mentally prepared to consider alternatives to "best professional practice."

> *If parents were given an opportunity to choose among significantly different schools, they would enroll their children in those schools that teach more of the things they wanted the children to learn.*

It has often been stated that the market system works well for those with the means to obtain information, but not for the poorly informed, who generally comprise the poorest classes. There is some evidence that all classes are vulnerable to faulty judgments regarding educational quality, and presumably would be so at the marketplace. A prior condition for intelligent choice is the existence of reliable and valid assessment systems that would force educators to compete on the basis of "value added" to learning.

> *Equality of opportunity would be strengthened by the voucher and not impaired.*

If the income elasticity of education is high, wealthy families would tend to add considerably more to the basic voucher than poor families. Each family can be said to have a demand for a bundle of school inputs that is a function of both its income and the price at which these inputs are available. The observed expenditure bundle is an index of the quantity and price of these inputs.

Before translating expenditure differences into quality differences, we must know the *supply elasticity of teachers and administrators* to the social characteristics of students. Little is known about the price differential that must be paid by lower income and nonwhite children to attract resources equivalent to those attracted by other children. That such a differential exists is suggested by teacher turnover rates and the distribution of experienced teachers in systems that employ a single-salary schedule, with right of transfer depending upon seniority. My calculations in Metropolitan Boston suggest that the supply of teachers with a given level of formal training is highly sensitive to the social class of the community and almost totally unresponsive to salary differentials, within a wide range.[34]

A final step in estimating the effect of inequalities in expenditure on opportunity is identifying the *elasticity of educational output to expenditures*. If we talk about the potential output of schools for a marginal increase of expenditures, when these schools are efficiently run, we then need to: (1) discover the production functions for the several outputs of schools, (2) minimize the cost of obtaining some weighted index of these outputs, where weights reflect marginal utilities, and (3) relate the output to the expenditures. No studies have adequately performed these analyses. On the other hand, if we are concerned with the actual output attained by schools from marginal expenditures, we can say that they are quite low.[35]

The voucher system would broaden choices among socioeconomic and ethnic groups.

The degree to which there is variation in desired private expenditures on education within and between ethnic class subpopulations requires more study. Cross-sectional analysis of small towns suggests that relatively little (roughly 30 percent) variance in school expenditures is explicable by mean community income.[36] Presumably the variations in family income would explain even less variation in desired school expenditures. If schools were chosen only on the basis of tuition —i.e., desired school expenditure—then there would be considerable socioeconomic and ethnic mixing. Housing segregation, and consequently differential access to available schools, would be one limiting factor on school integration. There are several other important factors, including the degree to which parents select schools on the basis of peer characteristics.

We do not know how large a differential in quality would be sufficient to induce parents of majority children to place them in schools with members of the minority. This differential may be surprisingly small. In Boston a brand new, highly touted "balanced" school (at least 50 percent whites) in the middle of a black neighborhood has been notably successful in attracting whites, despite the fact that the public school has been "tipping" for years. One factor in this success may be the guarantee that black enrollment will not exceed 50 percent; another, that the school has developed an image of quality. Research has to be done on the quality-peer tradeoffs that parents are willing to make.

Experimental directions

The voucher debates focus on several propositions about the behavior of parents, educators and, ultimately, the American system of social stratification. The major questions are whether parents can choose among schools on the basis of their merits, whether educators can be innovative in a meaningful way, whether the self-segregation of students by ability, class, and ethnicity will be greater than at present, and whether segregation would be divisive for society.

These questions can be solved only by experimentation with long-term followup. The practical problem is finding areas of education in which experimentation on the voucher plan is feasible without stepping on too many vested toes. Four such areas may be identified.

Preschool education. An advantage of experimenting with a voucher plan for preschool children is that relatively little capital is needed (the school premises can be in a basement, or an old house), so that the risk to the entrepreneur is low—i.e., risk against the program shutting down after five years. If the program were successful, vouchers could be granted to the original cohort as those in a cohort advanced a grade a year. However, if a nursery school is to be educational and not merely custodial, a high ratio of adults to children is required. Consequently, the costs of these schools are high. To perform the experiment properly, we may grant vouchers of $500 per year to children of age 3 or 4, and observe the following: (1) the degree to which parents utilize the vouchers (send their children to school), (2) the degree to which parents supplement the basic voucher as related to parental income, ethnic identity, or other factors, (3) the degree to which parents segregate their children from children of different backgrounds, (4) the degree to which entrepreneurs respond to the vouchers by creating new schools, (5) the variety the schools possess, and (6) the degree to which parents can distinguish schools of varying quality.

Vocational education. In cooperation with private industry, the federal government might give students vouchers for training in various industrial or commercial settings where sophisticated modern equipment is used. The student will take one or two days a week of academic courses in high school (language, mathematics, history, etc.), but he will also have an opportunity to develop skills that will be useful in the marketplace. From contact with workers in the industrial and commercial enterprises, he may learn something about the labor market, the demands for various skills, and the value of further education. Such a program might apply to a wide range of techniques—i.e., skilled stenography, computer programing, auto and other machine repair, medical or other scientific laboratory skills, electronics, and so on.

Cultural courses. Public schools generally provide instruction in a variety of "cultural" courses—e.g., music, art, and foreign languages—that are also provided on the free market. Smaller school systems are sometimes unable to provide a large enough variety of such offerings or to gather enough students to a given skill level in a given course, but larger systems often have specialized music, art, or language high schools. Rather than providing these services directly, a school system might contract a private enterprise to provide specialized instruction where demand is insufficient to warrant a full-time teacher. Or the school might give vouchers for instruction in music, art, and foreign languages at accredited private institutions; this would provide (1) greater variety of courses, (2) access to a wider range of teaching specialists, and (3) opportunity to associate with a more homogeneous peer group.

Community schools. One of the boldest proposals would permit community corporations in the Model Cities areas of the nation to establish community schools that would bid for the vouchers of all children living in designated Model Cities areas.[37] The community school-cum-voucher would allow ideological minorities within the Model City area to obtain the education of their choice either in the community schools, public schools, parochial schools, or even suburban schools.

Simulating the competitive system: open enrollment

The introduction of competition does not necessarily have to await such a radical revolution in financing and control as the voucher system would entail. A first approximation is the "open enrollment" system, which many big-city school systems already use. Under this institution, children from one attendance zone are permitted to transfer to any other school in the city, provided there is no "overcrowding" in the host school. In other words, places in a school are open first to all children in its attendance zone (regardless of the crowding constraint), and then to outsiders if space is available. Often such a system can be thwarted if the definition of crowding is low enough.

Because the desirable host schools cannot expand to meet demand indefinitely, and the undesirable schools consequently cannot lose all their students, the open enrollment system does not generate as great a selection pressure on the survival of schools as the voucher system does. Open enrollment could be given greater flexibility if high-quality mobile class modules could be easily shifted from the undesirable schools to the desirable schools as demands changed.

One factor attenuating the leverage of this approach on efficiency and responsiveness is that various schools in big cities are not so very different from each other, or at least are more similar than the schools in various suburbs. Consequently, the range of choice may be less than the threshold sufficient to trigger search for better schools. Another obstacle to the workings of the open enrollment system (and also of the voucher system) are the effects of transportation costs on freedom of choice. At most, children would have access to the nearest schools.

A further suggested modification of the current system is to permit "open enrollment" across municipal boundaries. This would invite considerable arbitrage from low tax/low quality school districts to high tax/high quality school districts. Taxpayers of the better school districts would presumably not tolerate such flagrant exploitation. To prevent such manipulation, school boards of the undesirable districts may be required to pay the average daily student expenditure to the host district. This would mean that the undesirable district would not profit and might lose financially if students left (spreading fixed costs on fewer students). The state or the "arbitrageur" would make up to the host community the difference between its per student costs and the payment received from each out-of-district student.

NOTES

1. Mark Blaug, "Economic Aspects of Vouchers for Education," in *Education: a Framework for Choice* (Institute for Economic Affairs, London, 1967), p. 33.

2. Charles E. Lindblom, "The Rediscovery of the Market," *The Public Interest*, 4 (Summer 1966) : 89–101.

3. Anthony Downs, *Inside Bureaucracy* (Little, Brown, 1967); and James Q. Wilson, "The Bureaucracy Problem," *The Public Interest*, 4 (Winter 1967): 3–9.

4. See, for example, Charles V. Hamilton, "Race & Education: A Search for Legitimacy," *Harvard Educational Review*, 38 (Fall 1968) : 669–684.

5. Milton Friedman, "The Role of Government in Education," in *Capitalism and Freedom* (University of Chicago Press, 1962), pp. 85–107; also see Blaug (note 1 above).

6. Martin T. Katzman, *The Political Economy of Urban Schools* (Harvard University Press, 1971), Chap. 1.

7. *Ibid.*, Chapter 2.

8. William Dobriner, *Class in Suburbia* (Prentice-Hall, 1963), pp. 113–126; and Herbert Gans, *The Levittowners* (Vintage, 1969), Chap. 5.

9. *Ibid.*

10. Werner Hirsch, "Measuring Factors Affecting Local Government Services," in John C. Bollens, ed., *Exploring the Metropolitan Community* (University of California Press, 1961), pp. 317–352; and also Talcott Parsons, "The Professions and Social Structures," in *Essays in Sociological Theory* (Free Press, 1964), pp. 34–39; Alma S. Wittlin, "The Teacher," in "The Professions," *Daedalus* (Fall 1963) : 745–63; cf. Gans (note 8 above).

11. James B. Conant, *The Slums and the Suburbs* (New American Library, 1961).

12. John K. Folger and Charles B. Nam, *Education of the American Population* (U.S. Bureau of the Census Monograph, 1967).

13. Gary Becker, *Human Capital: A Theoretical and Empirical Analysis, with Special References to Education* (Columbia University Press, 1964). Becker discusses the market failures for education loans due to risk and constitutional constraints.

14. W. Lee Hansen, "Total and Private Rates of Return to Investment in Schooling," *Journal of Political Economy*, 81 (April 1963) : 128–141.

15. We discuss these considerations in only the most general way here, because the literature in the field is very large, and our prime purpose in this chapter is to present the pros and cons of the "voucher system." For a sound historical discussion, see Lawrence Cremin, *The American Common School: An Historical Conception* (Columbia Teachers College, 1951). Some of the more recent work in the field includes Michael B. Katz, *The Irony of Urban School Reform: Ideology and Style in Mid-Nineteenth Century Massachusetts* (Harvard University Press, 1968); Robert Dreeban, *What Is Learned in School?* (Addison-Wesley, 1968), and "Socialization and Schools," *Harvard Educational Review*, Reprint Series, No. 1 (1968); Milton M. Gordon, *Assimilation in American Life* (Oxford University Press, 1964), pp. 132 ff., and references, on the reaction of English-speaking legislatures to German attempts to develop language schools and ultimately German-speaking states in the Midwest; John Higham, *Strangers in the Land: Patterns of American Nativism, 1860–1925* (Atheneum, 1967), on the

cultural threat of foreigners to the ideal of Anglo-conformity; Don Erikson, ed., *Public Controls for Private Schools* (University of Chicago Press, 1969).

16. Katzman, Chapters 3 and 4 (see note 6 above).

17. Herbert J. Keisling, "Measuring a Local Government Service: A Study of School Districts in New York State" (unpublished Ph.D. dissertation, Harvard, 1965); also, Charles S. Benson, *State and Local Fiscal Relationships in Public Education in California* (Senate of California, 1965).

18. Jesse Burkhead, *Input and Output in Large City High Schools* (Syracuse University Press, 1967).

19. John Riew, "Economics of Scale in High School Operation," *Review of Economics and Statistics*, 48 (August 1966): 280–287.

20. Otis Dudley Duncan and Beverly Duncan, "Residential Distribution and Occupational Stratification," *American Journal of Sociology*, 60 (1955): 493–503; Karl Taeuber and Alma Taeuber, "The Negro as an Immigrant Group," *ibid*, 69 (January 1964): 374–382.

21. See H. Thomas James, *School Revenue Systems in Five States* (Stanford University School of Education, 1961); Jerry Miner, *Social and Economic Factors in Spending for Public Education* (Syracuse University Press, 1963).

22. Charles M. Tiebout, "A Pure Theory of Local Public Expenditures," *Journal of Political Economy*, 64 (October 1956): 416–424. Also see Robert Warren, "A Municipal Services Market Model of Metropolitan Organization," *Journal of the American Institute of Planners*, 30 (August 1964): 193–204.

23. Cf. Mayor's Advisory Panel on Decentralization of the New York City Schools, *Reconnection for Learning: A Community School System for New York City, passim*. Commonly known as the Bundy Report, this study does not recommend fiscal autonomy, a function reserved by the central administration, presumably to provide a broader fiscal base for the poor districts. Such support, however, could be granted by state or federal funds as suggested above.

24. Miner (see note 21 above); also see Burton A. Weisbrod, *The External Benefits of Public Education* (Princeton University Press, 1964): pp. 107–11.

25. Katzman, Chap. 5 (see note 6 above).

26. Thomas I. Fox, "A Study of Educational Resource Transformation in a Large Public High School System" (unpublished doctoral dissertation, Syracuse University, 1966), presents evidence that intrasystem differences in school equality in Chicago are minor; also see Katzman, Chap. 4 (note 6 above).

27. Milton Friedman, pp. 85–107 (see note 5 above). Cf. Theodore R. Sizer, "The Case for a Free Market," *Saturday Review* (January 11, 1969): 34 ff; Kenneth Clark, "Alternative Public School Systems," *Harvard Educational Review*, 38 (Winter 1968): 110–113; West and Blaug in *Education: A Framework for Choice* (Institute for Economic Affairs, London, 1967).

28. See Lawrence W. O'Connell, "The Citizen Reform Group in Central City School Politics" (unpublished doctoral dissertation, Syracuse University, 1968), Chap. 5, on the creation and exploitation of the "Negro problem" in Boston's school politics.

29. Joseph Kershaw and Roland N. McKean, *Teacher Shortages and Salary*

Schedules (New York: McGraw-Hill, 1963); Eugene J. Devine and Morton J. Marcus, "Monopsony, Recruitment Costs, and Job Vacancies," *Western Economic Journal* (September 1967), on the inefficiencies due to single-salary schedules, monopoly, and monopsony in local government.

30. See Milton Friedman, "Occupational Licensure," in *Capitalism and Freedom*, pp. 137–160; Henrik Blum, "Introduction to Comprehensive Planning for Health" (Brookings Institution, unpublished manuscript, March 1, 1968).

31. John F. Kain, "Housing Segregation, Negro Employment, and Metropolitan Decentralization," *Quarterly Journal of Economics*, 82 (May 1968): 175–197, on the costs of housing segregation to Negroes in terms of employment.

32. Andrew M. Greeley and Peter H. Rossi, *The Education of Catholic Americans* (Aldine, 1966).

33. James S. Coleman, et al., *Equality of Educational Opportunity*, Report for U.S. Office of Education, National Center for Educational Statistics (1966).

34. Henry M. Levin, "Recruiting Teachers for Large City Schools" (Brookings Institution, unpublished manuscript, 1968).

35. Katzman, Chap. 3 (see note 6 above).

36. Miner (see note 21 above).

37. Sizer (see note 27 above).

Chapter 17

MARJORIE C. WILLCOX
SELMA J. MUSHKIN

Public Pricing and
Family Income: Problems
of Eligibility Standards

ONCE it is decided to impose charges for certain services, it usually becomes apparent that some people simply do not have the financial means to pay the charges, or that some could pay the charges for a particular service only at an opportunity price that is deemed unfair. In many cases the choice that would have to be made by individuals and families could have serious implications for the community at large, because of the public diseconomies that might result from the individual decision. Therefore, if policies on fees and charges are not to run counter to national and local commitments (e.g., for programs designed to assure a generally satisfactory community environment and to overcome poverty and unequal opportunities for economic advancement), they will have to be developed in the context of these program objectives.

Two major questions are encountered when policies and standards for remission of charges for public services are being set. What level of income should be protected for family maintenance? What services are so essential that they should be provided without invading the protected income? Or, put another way, what maintenance costs is the protected income expected to meet?

Each set of particular program policies usually endeavors to build on the community services and assistance programs that are otherwise available—that is, policies are designed in the expectation that any

Marjorie C. Willcox is an attorney resident in Washington, D.C. (See p. 3 for Dr. Mushkin.)

assistance the program provides will be in addition to, and not in re-placement of, other resources already available to the aided families and individuals. For example, the development of welfare budgets and cost standards assumes the general availability of some services free of charge from other public programs in the community that need not, therefore, be included in developing the monthly cost standard for basic maintenance needs. If it is now proposed to charge for some of these basic services, the assumptions that underlie the ability-to-pay policies and income standards developed for remission or adjustment of charges might call for re-examination and adjustment of welfare and other program standards as well as of proposed charge policies.

Definitions of Income

An initial problem is to define family income; there are many definitions to choose from and not all types of income are counted for all purposes. For example, in furtherance of a public policy of providing a work incentive, the states, when applying a means test to determine eligibility under federally aided public assistance programs, are now required to disregard all the earnings of school children and a portion of the earnings of other family members (the first $30 per month of earned income, plus one-third of the remainder). The public assistance programs of some states also exempt a portion of earnings from income as "necessary work expenses."[1]

The various public housing programs also have complex income determination rules (see Appendix B to this chapter).

One difficulty in making annual income the sole test of need is that this does not take into account prior accumulations of income, the existence of insurance coverage, or the ownership of property. Most means-test programs therefore establish policies covering the amounts and kinds of resources that they will consider "available" for expenditure for the kinds of costs the program would otherwise meet, and these are expected to be exhausted before the individual or family is aided under the program at public expense. The federally aided cash public assistance and medical assistance programs have policies of this kind. Home, household goods, and personal effects are usual exemptions, plus also a fixed dollar amount of cash or other liquid assets per family member. Within dollar limits, the cash surrender value of life insurance and an equity in a car may sometimes be exempted also. Here again the central policy issue will be the level of living that is considered socially desirable in order to protect against erosion by charges for service.

Identification of the Basic Public Service Package

What services in what amounts should be supplied charge-free to families that are within the established income and resources ceiling? The living standard that the community decides to protect against charges has two parts: (1) the private goods and services that the individual purchases with whatever income he has, and (2) the goods and services that public authority has undertaken to provide, with or without charge, e.g., fire and police protection, sanitation, water, sewer systems, public health services, transportation services (including streets and highways), car inspections, schools, libraries, etc.

There may be many reasons, aside from the issue of charges, why a particular function is a public activity rather than a private activity. One reason may be that the function is so important to the community at large that its performance cannot safely be left to private market incentives, nor can the use of the service provided safely be left to individual consumer choice. An example is the community's interest in a clean city and the provision of adequate sanitation services, coupled with the antilitter laws. At the opposite extreme, while there is a public interest in every family's having an adequate food budget, the choice of foods and the source of supply have for the most part been left to the individual consumer choice and to the initative of private production and marketing.

Federally aided vocational rehabilitation and student aid for higher education are examples of government programs in which considerations of economic need or ability-to-pay are outweighed by other objectives—at least in the sense in which those benefit or eligibility conditions are usually understood. Until 1965 the Vocational Rehabilitation Act prohibited the imposition of a means test for certain specified rehabilitation services, left the imposition of such a test to the option of the various states in the case of training services, and required a finding of an individual's economic need as a condition of federal participation in expenditures for other classes of rehabilitation services. In addition, this class of services was to be provided to an individual only "after full consideration of his eligibility for any similar benefit by way of pension, compensation, and insurance." The 1965 amendments to the Vocational Rehabilitation Act deleted the federal requirement of a finding of economic need for any class of rehabilitation services, leaving the states a much broader option.[2] However, the act's original provision requiring consideration of other sources for some classes of rehabilitation goods and services was not changed.

Several kinds of questions must thus be considered in developing the package of charge-free essential services that should accompany the protected level of income and resources. For example:

1. Which public services are essential components of the standard of living that the community regards as a desirable minimum?

2. Is the same standard appropriate for all types of public service programs?

3. Are there some types which should have no means test at all?

4. In each case, what level or volume of use should be supported by the community?

5. Is individual consumer choice a reliable way of obtaining the desired level of use, or of controlling excessive use?

6. If not, what controls and incentives should be devised?

7. For services the consumer wants to use, should limits be placed on the volume of use permitted without cost? Or should charges be instituted, with the income standard adjusted to allow for payment of the volume of service considered desirable?

8. For services the community wants the consumer to use, should there be penalties for failure to use some facilities and services? Or, should there be incentive payments (or other types of rewards) to encourage the level of use that is deemed to be in the public interest?

From even this brief discussion, it is apparent that identifying essential public services, working out reasonable standards for selecting the population group to whom the services should be provided without charge, and establishing yardsticks for the scope and volume of charge-free services will require great care if charge policies are not to undercut many of the social objectives of a number of existing programs.

There is thus a clear need for analysis of the interactions of the presently wide-ranging rules and dollar standards concerning income level determination for public services and payments. Only subsequent to such an analysis can a rational charge policy be developed for individual services or groups of services, where the charge policy and its required eligibility standards are to be income related. A preliminary analysis along these lines with respect to public housing is included as Appendix B of this chapter.

Partial Payment Consideration

Charges for public services may be adjusted in accordance with the income levels of their users in two basic ways: (1) by identifying in some manner those persons who may use the services without charge or at reduced charges, and (2) by identifying the services, or the amount of service, that will be provided to all persons without charge or at reduced charges. For example, Title IV of the Social Security Act (Grants to States for Aid and Services to Needy Families with Children and for Child-Welfare Services) authorizes financial assistance to the states for the costs of child welfare services provided on a community-wide basis, for costs of certain other services when provided to former, current, or potential recipients of cash payments, and for costs of day care provided free to the needy and to others on the basis of ability to pay. For some public services, one or the other of these two methods may be wholly impractical or inappropriate; for others a combination of the two may be desirable.

The income of some families is so low that public policy would tend to excuse them from paying any charges, at least for "basic" services. Certain other families might reasonably be expected to pay some part of the charges for even the basic services, but their circumstances are such that their progress toward economic self-sufficiency and social stability might be undesirably impeded if they were asked to pay in full. And there is danger that families just above the no-charge income level might be reduced below that level if they automatically became liable for some portion of all the charges for all the basic services. Other considerations seem to argue for the development of partial-charge policies on a service-by-service basis, taking into account the nature of the service, the way in which the charge is measured, and the method of collection. However, such service-by-service charges may have adverse effects on the near-poor family and such effects would be compounded by problems of fixing partial charges and administering multiple or even unrelated eligibility tests.

To discuss such problems except in relation to a specific charge for a particular service is difficult. Nevertheless, there are some general possibilities for fixing different levels of payment.

1. Graduated charges fixed in relation to income levels. If the overall charge pattern is intended to make the service self-sustaining, a system of graduated charges would have to be designed, with the rate of charge based on classification of users by ability to pay (income bracket). (A "Robin Hood" theory has sometimes been used in practice, for example, to justify variable charges in hospital and medical practice.) Even when less than the total cost is to be returned through charges so that only those with "full ability" would be charged actual cost, or something next to it, differential billing procedures would be needed. Methods of this kind, "charges by pay-ability," are in use in public hospitals, private universities, and private social service agencies.

2. Uniform charges with side subsidies. The reverse of the preceding approach is to charge uniform rates for a given service to all comers, then to return some percentage of expenses to the individual, depending upon his level of income. Rent supplement programs are a good example of this approach, while the GI education benefits are an indirect form. The two kinds of programs reflect the complex variations this approach may entail.

3. Self-administered consumer choices. Another possibility would be to provide a minimum level of some, or all, basic services free to all, with charges for use in excess of that minimum. For example, each family might be allowed a once-a-week trash collection for a prescribed number of trash containers of prescribed size; those with greater trash collection requirements would pay a fee based on number of containers and frequency of collection. The advantage of a charge system of this type is that it could produce a kind of self-administered graduated charge roughly in proportion to the consumer's standard of living. The request for the additional service would provide the basis for the billing. A number of European countries run their national health services on this basis. Or, "no-charges" could be restricted to poor families; all other families would elect the level of service they wished, knowing the charge and deciding whether they were willing to pay it.

Some Criteria for Administrative Arrangements

Any administrative arrangements for systems that seek to provide services at no charge to some, at reduced charges to others, and at full charge to still others will have to satisfy a number of criteria, among which the following may be suggested:

1. The administrative cost should be small. How much "small" is will depend on the purposes of the system. For example, an administrative system developed to prevent eligibility errors in admissions to some restricted service should cost no more than the cost of the errors that would exist without it. In general, administrative costs for services provided should be small relative to the cost of the services or to the revenue yield from the service.

2. The administrative system should be convenient and not impair the quality or the use of the service. Many services are impaired by methods of administering no-charge or part-charge policies. Examples include discriminatory tests such as complex eligibility criteria (common in most public welfare service systems); servicing centers that are inconveniently located for a great many potential consumers (common in U.S. public medical systems); lunchroom work requirements for children qualifying for free school lunches; inconvenient "approved" methods of collection or payment (e.g., the location of food stamp centers in banks not easily accessible to those using food stamps, or the demand for payment in some form other than checks by mail, as was common in many government agencies a few years ago); cumbersome manual methods of adjusting payments while the consumer waits (common in many sliding scale pricing systems in social agencies); ineffective or nonexistent distribution or transportation systems (as has been sometimes the case in governmental food and commodity distribution systems, and in service systems for the handicapped).

Collection arrangements should be consistent with both the objectives of the public service program and the purposes of the charge. Thus, if the purpose of the charge is merely partial reimbursement for costs of providing a service for which it is hoped to encourage wide and frequent use, payment mechanisms should be simple, convenient, unobtrusive, and, usually, without requirements for prior reservation or advance payment. If, however, one of the purposes is to control overuse, payment arrangements should be designed for maximum prominence of the charge, and might be coupled with prior reservation requirements and perhaps an incremental charge for the most burdensome types of use.

3. Administrative arrangements should include a convenient method by which the administering agency can evaluate and adjust the

arrangements for discriminatory pricing. Most public administrative systems are extremely difficult to change after a certain period of program initiation is past; very few systems have a mechanism for change built into the administrative design. In providing variable-priced services conditioned on income, a built-in method should exist for changing the pricing arrangements and eligibility standards when new data on the effects of the initial policies become available. If, for example, the pricing mechanism is intended to be redistributive for the available services—and the reduced prices charged to persons on the lower end of the income scale are still somewhat too high (as was, for example, the case in the food stamp program)—some method should exist to provide this information routinely, rather than requiring unusual and extraordinary efforts to make such a determination.

4. The administrative arrangements should avoid placing a stigma on those persons receiving special benefits from the program. Some services for the poor have foundered, in part, on the stigma problem. For example, checkout clerks in supermarkets often receive a customer's presentation of food stamps with not-quite-concealed scorn. And medicaid recipients might sometimes wait in line at prescription counters until the "cash customers" have been served. Administrative arrangements that confer anonymity upon the consumer tend to be superior, unless the program's objective includes making an equal-product good less desired than another by differential packaging, or by adding waiting time as an automatic eligibility test.

5. The methods for determining eligibility or payment level should be simple to administer. This criterion has most often been honored in the breach. Two distinct aspects need consideration: (1) determination of income status of each family applying for remission of charges; and (2) mechanisms for evidencing such entitlement.

In regard to income status, any family on one of the cash assistance programs would presumably be included in the no-charge consumer group for all basic services. These families could be certified by the agencies administering the welfare program; thus no supplementary procedures would be needed for determining their income status. Any additional individuals and families above the cash assistance income levels (but below a higher no-charge income standard) would require some sort of procedure for establishing their income status. It might be possible to delegate this function to the agency that in the first place established entitlement for cash assistance, using the same procedures and substantiating the claim of entitlement in the same way, but simply using a different dollar yardstick. (This has been the pattern used for establishing medicaid eligibility under Title XIX programs.) More consideration is increasingly being given to the practice of reliance on the affidavit of the applicant, then checking for fraud and error on a sample basis. On the surface, there appears to be no good reason why entitlement to selected basic services (or some quantum thereof) without charge should require more elaborate substantiation than entitlement to the payment of cash benefits.

Ideally, the information-gathering process should be as nondiscretionary as possible for purposes of both consumer convenience and easy administration. With such a requirement, the influence of individual tastes and prejudices of those gathering the information can be reduced to a minimum. The burden of proof for showing that an applicant does not need the program should be on the program, and administrative procedures should reflect this. The only behavior required of the applicant for entry into the program should be that of information exchange directly related to the purposes of the program. All administrative arrangements for checking on information offered should be "symmetrical," i.e., at least as much should be spent on preventing, identifying, and rectifying possible negative errors as on preventing ineligible persons from gaining access to a public service.

In regard to mechanisms to assure entitlement, the frequency of verification would seem to vary with the kind of service in question. For recurring services—such as those for water, sewage, heat, light, trash—and billing procedures, the beneficiary might be certified periodically by the determining agency directly to the billing agency. For intermittent use of certain services, such as recreation facilities (tennis courts, swimming pools, summer concerts in parks), the no-charge consumer might be given a card that he could present at the time of using the facility or service, or at the time of making a reservation for future use. Appendix A outlines in more detail a possible credit card system for identification and billing, as applied to the school lunch program.

Identification or credit cards might be good for a certain period of time (e.g., until the next affidavit was required) or for a certain number of occasions of use (e.g., X number of concerts, X hours of use of a tennis court, golf course, swimming pool). The period for which an identification card would continue valid might vary for different population groups. For example, cards for persons receiving old age assistance and whose incomes do not usually change much from year to year, might be good for as long as a two-year period, whereas younger families with a wage earner member might be expected to renew their cards more frequently, perhaps as often as quarterly.

Distribution of coupon books, stamps, and tokens are other methods that should be explored in relation to specific services. For example, school children are sold low-priced books of coupons for use on busses going to and from school. When there are no quantitative considerations, the multipurpose identification or credit card might be most appropriate (e.g., if there were a charge for a required annual car inspection). But if the volume of use to be permitted is an important consideration (either to prevent overuse by the legitimate holder of the card, or to prevent lending for use by unauthorized persons), the indicia of entitlement to free use should carry some quantitative limitation, as a coupon book or a card that is good until punched a specified number of times. Most such evidences of entitlement could probably be mailed out by the certifying agency at the time of making cash payments.

NOTES

1. See 1967 Amendments to the Public Assistance titles of the Social Security Act.

2. Public Law 89–333. House Report No. 432 of the House Committee on Education and Labor gives the following explanation of the economic need amendment: "The committee wishes to emphasize its feeling that rehabilitation services should be made available on the basis of the person's handicap and not on the basis of economic need. With this in mind, the reported bill proposes a deletion of the economic need requirement in the Federal law with the result that the states may, if they wish, offer rehabilitation services without regard to economic need. In permitting greater flexibility in the selection of persons for rehabilitation service programs in the states, it is the committee's hope that appropriate, yet reasonable, revision will occur in state procedures."

APPENDICES

TO CHAPTER 17

A SELMA J. MUSHKIN

Designing a Credit Card
Experiment

A CREDIT card approach could easily be designed initially as an experimental demonstration, particularly in the school meal program. Such a demonstration would seek to gather information on the pertinent effects upon (1) demand, (2) children's nutritional needs, (3) parental responses, (4) child tardiness, (5) absenteeism, and (6) learning. The proposed approach depends heavily upon a central computer with inexpensive remote readers. Since a number of school systems are now using computers at this level, and since the economics of remote computing is fast becoming more and more favorable to such approaches, the incremental costs for such a demonstration may not be very large. On the other hand, learning about the effects of differing approaches to school feeding programs, about the costs and benefits of such programs, and about the problems of instituting credit card systems for social services to the poor is extremely important to future policy in education and in social services.

The experiment might be designed more or less as follows. Each child in a school would be issued a numbered plastic card that could be read by a machine. On inserting the card in a computer card reader, the child is admitted to the lunch room. The machine would scan each number presented to ensure (if repeated use is considered a problem) that the number had not been presented before during that particular meal period.

If there are problems regarding card exchanges or card thefts, a random number generator can provide the basis for a quality control check on the match between card user and card ownership. The information is stored to be used to prepare monthly billing to all parents.

The bill would be adjusted for the income of the parents on a sliding scale. Thus, for example, lunches might be "free" to all children in families with an income equal to less than one and one-half times the current welfare maximum allowance for that size of family (the current rule in public assistance administration for eligibility, for those starting out below the public welfare maximum), plus an extra allowance of $30 per month. Then, for income intervals beyond this level, a sliding scale of payments might be used, up to the point where the family would be obligated to pay full cost. For those parents with incomes below the minimum payment line, the "billing" might simply present the information on the number of meals taken during the month and the number of meals missed. Further, if an incentive feature is to be used to encourage more adequate nutrition, there might be a "negative billing," in which a small payment is provided to the parents for each lunch consumed. Such an incentive payment might reinforce *against* school absenteeism and *for* adequate nutrition.

The method of collection—monthly billings to the family—avoids problems that might arise from a cash requirement, which entails that each child carry money to school. It also avoids the stigma problem that results when some children are identified by their peers as "charity cases" with the reported result that this discourages participation by some poor children and deprives them of adequate nutrition.

A computer-based program also allows for keeping statistics on daily and seasonal variations in school lunch purchases, variations by income class, and variations by type of menu offered. With sufficient experience in the program, these statistics can provide the basis for the most economical order algorithms for the school's purchasing agents and allow for prediction of menu choices over time. Further, data would be provided for the estimation of price elasticity of demand.

More importantly, the information on school meals generated by a price system would serve analytical needs as a guide to other school meal programs, including breakfast programs now being implemented in some places. Data provided for these programs would help to resolve some controversies on school meal utilization under different times and costs of serving, and by children of different family income groups.

B GEOFFREY CARLINER

Fees and Charges in Federally Subsidized Housing

SINCE the 1930s, the federal government has accepted the view that regular market forces are unable to provide certain segments of the population with levels of housing that the nation deems adequate. For some twenty years the primary means of correcting this deficiency was "public housing"—i.e., housing projects built and operated by local housing authorities (LHA's), and occupied by low-income renters. Since 1959, however, several new programs have been started to correct perceived failures and shortcomings in the existing system. These have incorporated a variety of pricing schemes and have been designed to serve income groups ignored by traditional public housing but considered deserving of subsidized housing. The relevant aspects of seven federally subsidized low-income housing programs may be summarized briefly.

Public Housing

Traditional public housing is developed, owned, and operated by local housing authorities. These LHA's are independent agencies of the states, under the supervision of the Housing Assistance Administration (HAA). Since the start of the program in 1937, over 780,000 units have been built, making it by far the oldest and most important of the low-income housing programs.

Geoffrey Carliner was a summer student intern at The Urban Institute when he wrote this chapter. He is now a Lecturer in the Department of Economics and Research Associate with the Institute for Research on Poverty at the University of Wisconsin.

409

After the LHA has obtained HAA approval and finished construction of a housing project, it issues a bond, generally lasting 40 years. The federal government assumes payment of all interest and amortization of the bond. The local community grants the project exemption from local property taxes, though the LHA makes payments in lieu of taxes at a lower level. Federal law further specifies that maximum rents for newly admitted families must be no more than 80 percent of rents for the cheapest decent private housing in the community. Beyond this and the loose supervision of the HAA, the LHA is granted broad freedom in setting income limits for admission and continued occupancy, and for determining rents.

In general, all unusual and nonrecurring income such as overtime, inheritance, gifts, and job connected expenses, e.g., for uniforms, transportation, or day care centers, is excluded from calculations of income for both eligibility and rental purposes. Some income excluded from eligibility definitions, such as that from secondary wage earners about to leave the family, is included in rental income. Exemptions are granted for dependents.

The most common rental scheme, and that sanctioned by law until 1959, provides for minimum rents for each apartment, and maximum rents equal to market value. Between these limits, tenants pay 20 percent of their rental incomes each month. Very poor tenants pay the minimum, and tenants with incomes more than five times the maximum must leave. Rents for tenants on welfare are set through direct negotiations with the local welfare department, for "the highest rents which the welfare agency would agree to."[1] Recently, LHA's have been experimenting with other schedules. To promote economic integration through retention of higher income tenants, some LHA's have decreased rent/income ratios for families close to the upper income limits. Others have tried to reduce management costs of certifying incomes by establishing fixed rents for most tenants, with special hardship rents for tenants who can prove their extra need.

Section 23 Leased Housing

Under this program that started in the mid-sixties, LHA's can rent standard housing from private landlords, sublet to low-income families eligible for regular public housing, and receive a subsidy from the federal government to cover the difference between payments to landlords and receipts from tenants. Landlords are paid market rents. Tenants pay the rents they would in project housing, with allowance made for the extra cost of maintaining a home. The government ends up paying what it would for equivalent project housing.

These rented properties must be decent, but need not be new and are not exempt from local property taxes. To prevent the LHA from pushing up rents in private housing, the program is only permitted in communities with vacancy rates above 3 percent.

Section 202

The oldest of the new programs, section 202 was authorized in 1959. Project sponsors, who must be nonprofit organizations, can obtain mortgages from the federal government of up to 50 years covering 100 percent of construction costs, at a subsidized 3 percent interest rate. Only elderly individuals or families are eligible. Income limits are $4,500 for single persons, $5,400 for couples, or 80 percent of the approximate 221(d)(3) BMIR limit (see below). Rents are fixed at levels to cover project costs and are not a function of income. Local community approval is not needed for 202 projects. By the end of fiscal 1969, the number of units built had reached 46,000.

221(d)(3) Below Market Interest Rate Program

This is very similar to the 202 program. The federal government buys 3 percent mortgages from sponsors, and rents are fixed to cover costs. Admissions limits are set by the FHA at median income levels or at some slightly lower figure. In practice, the limits are about 60 to 100 percent higher than comparable public housing limits. Local approval is required, and profit-oriented sponsors are eligible, though they can only obtain 90 percent mortgages instead of 100 percent for nonprofit sponsors. Approximately 150,000 dwelling units have been built under this program.

These two programs, along with the others described below, are administered by the Federal Housing Administration. They receive considerably less subsidy than public housing and can be afforded only by families that are considerably better off than other low-income families. Therefore, to achieve some measure of economic integration, 202 and 221(d)(3) BMIR projects are allowed to rent up to 20 percent of their units to low-income families further subsidized under the rent supplement program discussed below.

Section 236

To fill the gap between the two preceding programs and public housing, Congress in 1968 authorized section 236 rental housing. Income limits are 135 percent of admissions limits for public housing, or in special circumstances 90 percent of 221(d)(3) BMIR limits. Private parties hold the mortgages, but the federal government pays an interest subsidy that can reduce each family's share of interest payments to a minimum of 1 percent. Families pay rent to cover operating amortization, and at least 1 percent of interest, or 25 percent of income, whichever is higher. Maximum rents are equal to market rents for similar units, and families with incomes more than four times these rents are encouraged to stay. The FHA estimates that the 1 percent interest limit will result in minimum rents of about two-thirds of market rents. Local approval is not required, and rent supplement families may rent 20 percent of the units in a project.

Rent supplement

Income limits for rent supplement are set by the FHA equal to or slightly below admissions limits in public housing. However, income for eligibility and for rents is defined more inclusively than in public housing. Tenants must pay 25 percent of their incomes or 30 percent of the market value of their apartments, whichever is more. When income exceeds four times rent, the subsidy ceases, but the tenant need not move as under traditional public housing. Commercial builders are eligible sponsors. They must obtain FHA approval and local approval for their projects, which must not cost more per unit than legally specified limits. Sponsors are encouraged to have unsubsidized as well as subsidized tenants, but the cost limits for rent supplement projects generally have led to building features that make them unattractive to families with enough income to afford new housing without subsidy.

Section 235

This program subsidizes home ownership for low-income families. Eligibility limits and technique and limits on subsidies are the same as under 236. Limits are also placed on the value of the home. The homeowner must make a down payment, which can be in the form of labor, and then must pay the minimum amount corresponding to the maximum subsidy, or 20 percent of his adjusted income, whichever is larger. He must pay for utilities, maintenance, and repairs. Local approval is not required. Generally, only new or substantially rehabilitated housing is allowed.

Pricing Problems in Subsidized Housing

Most goods in a market economy are allocated to buyers with the money and the desire to purchase them. The richer the individual, the more the market gives him. Subsidized housing programs, however, have just the opposite intent: to provide the poor with more housing than they could normally obtain with their incomes. To allocate these subsidized goods by a price mechanism, i.e., to those most able to pay, would defeat the main purpose of the programs. Therefore, tenants have been admitted in order of application, with priorities for the elderly, the handicapped, those displaced by government action, persons whose homes were destroyed by natural disaster, and individuals who are currently living in substandard housing.

Once admitted, families pay widely varying percentages of their incomes for rent. In the private market, this is always the case, of course; similar units have similar prices, and families with similar incomes do not necessarily pay similar amounts. Most housing programs, however, are designed so that each family gets what it "needs," and pays what it can. It seems equitable that families with similar incomes and needs should receive similar subsidies.

However, rent supplement families must pay at least 25 percent of their incomes, broadly defined, while public housing families usually pay about 20 percent of narrowly defined income. Rents of families in 221(d)(3) BMIR projects do not vary with income at all. Maximum subsidies in government programs range from complete interest, amortization, and up to one-third of operating costs, to 30 percent of cost, to all but 1 percent of interest costs, to all but 3 percent of interest costs. Even within the same project of the same program tenants with similar incomes but different sources or expenses often pay quite different rents. In all programs and projects the poorest families pay the highest percentage of their income to the landlord, because of fixed or minimum rents or exclusions from income that increase with income.

There are some reasons—though possibly more rationalizations— for the seeming inequities among families in subsidized housing. First, local situations may actually differ, as the HAA claims in justifying the diversity of rules among the LHA's under its supervision. Second, some experimentation is certainly a good thing, and differences in rules may imply that housing officials do learn from their mistakes. This is true for programs as well as individual projects. Third, treating all income identically might be more inequitable than making distinctions with exclusions.

However, the main explanation for the most glaring inequity— the high rates for the very poor—lies in efforts to restrict the size of subsidies. Because of housing's special characteristics—its important externalities, the imperfections in the capital market, rigidities in the construction industry, its effects on other aspects of life—the federal government has supplied housing at especially low prices for poor families. However, in trying to keep down the costs of each program, limits on the amount of subsidy per family have been set. The subsidized housing programs have not been designed to take care of the poorest of the poor, and perhaps should not be expected to. But in the absence of a broader income maintenance program, the housing programs could, and probably should, do more for the very poor than they are doing, even within current total financial constraints.

In another attempt to keep subsidies small, HUD set limits on construction costs in most programs. At some times in some areas, this has had the effect of stopping new construction completely, since standard housing just could not be built within the limits. Even without such drastic results, the cost limits have tended to defeat the goal of social and economic integration within specific projects. One of the main criticisms of public housing has been that it concentrates the poorest families in the community. Such great concentrations, housed in inexpensive and unattractive buildings, have not been popular neighbors. Moreover, families receiving subsidies have not benefited from contact with families with higher incomes and fewer problems. In public housing, the more stable and upwardly mobile families, those most able to be leaders, are forced to move out when their incomes exceed occupancy limits.

All the new FHA programs allow tenants who become ineligible for subsidy to remain in their apartments if they pay market rents. However, cost limits and the prohibition of amenities, especially in rent supplement projects, have made the new apartments too unattractive for families not eligible for subsidy. Section 23 Leased Housing has probably been more successful in dispersing poor families throughout the community because, in some cities at least, no more than 10 percent of a building's units can be leased by the LHA. Combination projects, where most of the families are middle income and subsidized under 221(d)(3) BMIR or 236 programs, but where up to 20 percent of the families are poorer and subsidized under rent supplement, have also avoided the concentrations of traditional public housing. These efforts are the exception, however. The conflict between cost limits and the goal of economic integration continues to plague low-income housing programs.

A similar problem has been the difficulty of building subsidized housing outside the poorest sections of the city. Public housing projects, by and large, have been restricted to the central cities of metropolitan areas, because of a ruling that an LHA only operate within its city and can only get federal money if it has a "Workable Program." Theoretically, the Workable Program merely demands some sort of local planning and code enforcement but, in practice, communities have used the absence of a Workable Program as a way to exclude public housing.

Thus the central city LHA cannot build on relatively cheap suburban land, cannot build in middle class sections of the city because of zoning and financial or political structures, and is usually forced to build on high-cost land in the slums. Between 1937 and 1954, 89 percent of public housing was built on occupied sites, and only 11 percent on vacant land.[2] Even with greater attempts at dispersal since then, the increasing scarcity of vacant land in central cities has made site selection a real problem for many LHA's—increasing cost per unit and often forcing construction of high-rise projects when low-rise would have been preferable.[3]

To facilitate increased dispersal, attempts have been made to reduce the external diseconomies that subsidized housing imposes on its neighbors. Smaller projects with fewer high rises, scattered-site housing outside of projects altogether, more expensive and less institutional-looking projects for higher income groups, and more imaginative design for low-cost housing have all increased acceptability. However, the greatest hope for a decrease in land costs and dispersal of subsidized housing throughout the metropolitan area lies in eliminating the requirement for a Workable Program. Under the new sections 235 and 236, builders do not need the approval of local governments, whereas they do under all older programs except section 202, which is restricted to the elderly.

As an alternative to building relatively high-cost, high-subsidy housing for the very poor, it is sometimes suggested that we build slightly higher cost housing with a much lower subsidy for middle-income groups. The newly vacated housing would then (presumably) filter down to low-income families.[4] The success of such a filtering scheme depends on the supply elasticities of used housing. The units left empty by middle-income families may be too expensive for low-income families, and when rents decrease maintenance by landlords may also decrease. If the government provided subsidies to poor families for existing housing, the result might merely be higher rents and windfalls for landlords, not better housing for the poor.

Very little is known about these supply elasticities, and the Congress has been reluctant to start a program that enriches landlords without helping the poor. Traditional public housing has been entirely in new buildings: Section 23 Leased Housing is an exception. Rent supplement, 236 projects and 235 projects that are not cooperatives must be new or substantially rehabilitated. Sections 202 and 221(d)(3) BMIR must be new. The acceptance of substantial rehabilitation sometimes means that sound dwellings can be provided at far less expense than new ones, but rehabilitation is often scarcely cheaper than starting from scratch. Little has been done to connect subsidized housing programs with efforts to prevent further decay of old but sound housing by combining the elements of code enforcement, payments to landlords adequate to cover maintenance, and rental subsidies. Indeed, a preliminary study of Section 23 Leased Housing in Washington, D.C., found inadequate landlord maintenance to be its biggest problem.[5]

Efforts to reduce the stated cost (not necessarily the real economic cost) of low-income housing in the federal budget have resulted in several forms of subsidy. Public housing receives annual grants that appear in the budget, but also receives tax exemptions for the interest on bonds and on property that do not appear in the budget. Sections 202 and 221(d)(3) BMIR seem very expensive, since their mortgages are bought by the government, and the entire cost of a 40-year project is included in one year's budget. The new programs—sections 235 and 236—remedy this by having private parties hold the mortgages, while the government pays annual interest subsidies.

The innovation of home ownership for poor families under the new section 235 may also result in decreased costs for the government. Although the family pays only 20 percent of its income for shelter, it must maintain and repair its home, and provide utilities normally supplied by a project. Extra payments in the form of "sweat equity" (labor) are encouraged. This program should enable poor families to participate in the American dream of being property owners, and hopefully avoid the alienation and hostility felt by many tenants in traditional public housing. The program is not feasible for the old or for broken and unstable families, but the primary obstacle to its success could be the combination of cost and subsidy limits, which might make it too expensive for those who want it and unwanted by those who can afford it.[6]

Tenant-landlord relations in the best of circumstances are often subject to some strain, and in subsidized housing projects, where rent is a function of income and families are poor and often troubled, the strain is greater. The management of a project may find it desirable to provide services not usually associated with housing, and it may relax income/rent rules to avoid distrust and suspicion. For the first twenty years of public housing, however, most LHA's required tenants to report increases in their incomes, so that their rents could be increased. Tenants who failed to do this were fined or evicted from the project. Currently, under public housing and the newer programs, tenants' incomes are checked only every one or two years, but they need not report increases between recertification dates. If their incomes should fall, they can often have their rents decreased.

Extra services are more often provided by public housing than by privately managed projects. The simplest of the services is merely explaining the unusual rules of the project to new tenants. Others include organizing a tenants' association, helping troubled families to find the aid they need from an appropriate agency, establishing day care centers for working mothers, providing recreation for children and old people, and policing the project with special guards.[7] The simplest way (yet sometimes the least pursued) for the management staff to establish a feeling of community in the project is to be responsive to tenants' complaints (even when at times unreasonable) and consistently to make clear that the staff and the tenants are fellow human beings.

Conclusion

Since 1960, serious attempts have been made to correct some of the mistakes of the first twenty years of subsidized housing. There has been a great deal of flexibility and experimentation, although certain programs, such as rent supplement, seem to be repeating some of the mistakes of earlier public housing. It is still too early to see what will happen in the most promising programs, sections 235 and 236. Public housing itself has become considerably less rigid and institutionalized, but the problems of rising operating costs and of poorer, less upwardly mobile families may be more serious than ever.

Changes in pricing policy alone, however, can do relatively little to meet the housing needs of the poor. Much more can perhaps be done through a program that combines subsidized low- and middle-income housing with code enforcement, community organization, and all the dynamics of the private market. Without considerably larger appropriations for subsidized housing, no pricing policies can provide decent housing for every family.

NOTES

1. HUD, HAA, *Local Housing Authority Management Handbook*, Part VII, Sec. 4, "Special Rents" (May 1964).

2. Charles Adams, quoted in Martin Meyerson and Edward C. Banfield, *Politics, Planning, and the Public Interest: the Case of Public Housing in Chicago* (Free Press, 1955), p. 20.

3. Jack I. Berkman, "Behind the Shortage of Sites for Public Housing," summary of a study for the National Capital Housing Authority (November 1957).

4. Irving H. Welfeld, "A New Framework for Federal Housing Aids" (July 1969, mimeo); also, Eugene Smolensky, "Public Housing or Income Supplements —The Economics of Housing for the Poor," *Journal of the American Institute of Planners*, 34 (March 1968): 94–102.

5. Eunice S. Grier, "Large Family Rent Subsidy Demonstration Project" (National Capital Housing Authority, May 1966).

6. George von Furstenberg, "Improving the Feasibility of Homeownership for Lower Income Families Through Subsidized Mortgage Financing," cited in President's Committee on Urban Housing, *Technical Studies*, Vol. 1, 1968.

7. National Association of Housing and Redevelopment Officials, "Change for the Better" (publication N468, May 1962); also, Jack L. Wank, "Final Report, Grace Abbott Homes Pilot Study" (Chicago Housing Authority, 1958); and *Procedures for the Hartford Housing Authority Tenant Relations Advisors Program.*

An Agenda
for Research

T
HE previous chapters in this book demonstrate that the present state of knowledge about both concepts and institutional processes falls far short of that required to decide finally about the relative efficiency response of either the market or the administrative economy. The agenda for research thus laid out is sizeable. In addition to the necessary initial determination of what urban services lend themselves, at least potentially, to the use of prices or charges, the agenda may be viewed in the perspective of the six key policy questions outlined here.

(1) *Is the market test really the preferred allocation device?*

Prescriptions for pricing start from the notion that if individual households choose from among all goods those they deem appropriate to their tastes and budgets, and if productive resources fully respond to demand as registered by the market price, efficiency is achieved. Accordingly, if commodities and services now produced by local government lend themselves to the market's function because the beneficiaries and the units of benefits are identifiable, then the purposes of efficiency will be best served by permitting demand to signal production responses within the market's sphere.

Market failure in its several dimensions has not dampened the search for ways to extend the price system to public products. Yet, in terms of a research agenda, further study is needed of transaction costs, including private costs, in rationing or exclusion, costs of becoming informed about the product (its supply condition and prices), costs to individuals and firms in computing optimum choices of goods or factor use, and costs of contracting in the private market.[1] These costs have to be weighed, for example, against the costs of administrative planning and of benefit evaluation to determine relative rates of return of public investment valued at shadow prices,[2] the use of some lesser criteria of measurement of effectiveness, or the optional administrative resource allocation.[3]

Correcting price signals.   On a different plane the market tests of earlier years have failed to gain efficient use of air, water, and landscape resources. What are the responsibilities, and what the solutions, to improve incentives? What role can the urban community play in correction of air and water "cost" so the supply response to market price can take account of those costs?

The general notion is that the market in the past has not had the correct signals to which to respond. With the assimilative capacity of our resources becoming overloaded, use of scarce resources of air and water needs to be rationed through the price system. A research agenda on effluent and emission charges as a way of pricing air and water is long, but given the currency of many proposals to adopt such charges, there is special urgency to this research. Some of the problems for which additional research is needed have been suggested in this volume; other important issues have not.

Recent action taken to implement an 1899 statute by requiring the recording of industrial discharges into the nation's rivers and harbors will provide essential information nationwide for determining amounts of damage to rivers so that levies can be assessed for damage done. What account should be taken of the differences in volume and speed of water flow, of chemical interactions among different wastes, of time of year, and water temperature, to mention only a few factors on which damage depends? Are effluent charges to be varied or not in relation to technological possibilities of averting or reducing damages? Research is clearly needed on the specifics of pricing policies in the framework of our intergovernmental system. Localities are better able to reflect local conditions affecting damages done. They are far less likely than the national government to be able to impose charges that could adversely affect industry and employment in their own region.

Should prices be based on costs of abatement rather than of damages done? Should the charge based on costs of cleanup be a uniform amount per volume of water or air discharge, or should it be varied by pollutant material? In local practices on sewerage charges examples can be found of both uniform charges and charges varied by type of discharge. Effluent charges based on costs of cleanup undertaken by a governmental agency are far easier to compute than are charges based on damages that require detailed knowledge not only of the pollution-causing activities but of the net pollution impact on the water or air.

Is it, in any case, politically feasible to consider an effluent charge policy that calls for variable charges? When the amount of the damage done by a pollutant such as lead or sulphur oxide is about the same for each unit of the material, and its pollutant qualities are about the same, an emission charge on that pollutant provides the appropriate incentive for the market to function and to reduce the use, within efficient margins, of the damaging product. In localities levies of this kind are limited by the possible market response. For example, as an environmental control measure a few localities tax throw-away bottles; they are less likely to be able to tax lead in gasoline, or the internal combustion engine. Their control over the market, except in the case of a few states and major cities, is small. Yet response in competitive markets to pricing of the use of the waste discharge potential of air and water depends on costing the discharge in amounts equivalent as nearly as possible to the damage. Only in that way would competition set in motion forces yielding the optimum industrial output relative to resource inputs, including in such inputs the waste assimilative powers of air and water. The effluent charge mechanism would cause different plants in an industry to reexamine the damage potential of raw materials and production processes so that, on balance, lower net costs would result. In this assessment, various optional abatement control processes would be considered as well. If the charge is set too low, it becomes cheaper for a plant to pollute than to abate, thus yielding the argument that effluent charges may be a license to pollute. If it is set too high, it could reduce production below an efficient level. What is the politically feasible strategy for local or state governments concerned about out-migration and competitive disadvantage?

Study of the potential role of state and locality in environmental protection by emission and effluent charges is especially of interest when inter-governmental competition is a limiting factor. What are the relative responsibilities of each of the levels of government; and as a preliminary consideration, what criteria are applicable to determine the respective roles?

Economic modeling to determine the impact of environmental control measures among industries and among jurisdictions—state and local—is just getting started, yet a vital component of policy depends upon such information. A quantum increase in research is indicated to yield the required policy backup.

Common Property. Now under way is a reassessment of property rights. That reassessment may provide a very different set of concepts from which to evaluate the market economy and administrative decision making as well. New avenues of research are using as a starting point the concept that improvement in the environment requires more than marginal changes in institutions, particularly in property rights, to recognize *common property.* In this research, common property is being defined in two somewhat different ways. One set of research studies uses common property much in the same sense as Henry George in *Progress and Poverty,* as property belonging to all the people. (This volume of the 1870s might well be revived as the cornerstone of the policies of the 1970s.) Air and water as property rights of all the people call for payment of a price for use, or more accurately, for a set of rules within which the property is used to assure efficiency. Pricing of air- and water-use to count social costs is discussed by Kneese and by Gerhardt earlier in this volume.

A second concept is basic to another set of research studies. This views common property as rights acquired by long-term practice. Recognition of such common property rights in air, water, and landscape could alter the effluent or emission tax remedies proposed by Kneese and Gerhardt. In place of a tax equivalent to water or air damage to alter incentives, the common property use of a waterway by a utility, for example, would require explicit purchase or other recognition of rights through compensatory payment. To illustrate, one recent proposal calls for purchase of such common property assets when value is substantially destroyed by public policy, but only when there is no duplicity on the part of the owners. Present property law which permits losses and gains to fall where they may in the course of market response, regardless of the cause, is viewed as a deterrent to change. Public policy now, for example, creates assets or destroys their value by regulations or licensing. A minor example is the regulation against the billboard; a major illustration is zoning. These illustrations are intended to give some idea of the issues involved—issues that are large and compelling in our mixed economy and that raise a multitude of separate research questions.

Who benefits now from restricted supplies brought about by governmental licensing and exclusion? Are there ways, through taxation or otherwise, of capturing the rents for the common purpose? In such cases as licensing of liquor stores, taxis, and even nursing homes, some persons are benefited as a consequence of the action taken by the city. Should those receiving the benefits pay? Should the general public share in the surplus values created by the restrictions? If benefits generated by public action are claimed for the public, what transition is needed from the present methods, recognizing that property assets such as taxi license rights have been transferred among persons in the past? Is a start to be made only on rents created by new actions taken by the government? What are the optional processes for recapture if such recapture is indicated?

(2) *How are prices to be determined?*

To formulate a pricing policy and to implement it with some assurance of "success"—assurance, that is, that expectations with respect to allocation and funding will be met—require a considerable range of data on characteristics of demand and of supply of each of the public products. Even assuming that the product itself has been identified and can be quantified in some measurable unit (perhaps somewhat less precisely than existing counts of tons of coal or bushels of apples), data on which to analyze the demand characteristics of product and the conditions determining supply are most deficient.

A public price policy does not start from scratch; there are now many public prices in each community. Cities make much use of prices even when priced services are somewhat narrowly defined. Many units of service are now priced, but the machinery for collection of information about price has not been developed to the point where there is a substantial body of data to share among the cities. In preparing many of the chapters included here, the authors searched the available literature to determine what is known about the characteristics of demand and supply and about types of pricing arrangements. As the results suggest, little is known except perhaps in the area of water, transportation, and to some extent recreation.

This is so partly because most economists have not turned the spotlight of investigation on the detail of city finances; they have been dissuaded from that venture by the lack of a data base, and the need to start by collecting the required information from one public marketplace or city after another. But progress in policy guidance can only be made if detailed investigations are undertaken. This means fewer reviews of general concepts and far more concentration on the specifics of public products and pricing policies, centering on the appropriateness of present charge practices in terms of efficiency and equity, and the optional pricing methods that could be applied to improve the incentives generated by those pricing practices.

Demand for public products. An initial question in deciding on price and resource allocation is: What is the demand for the product? How many persons will purchase home health services in accord with what price schedule? How many, in a city market, will demand after-school extension services for play, further education, or child care, at different price levels?

The available information on the demand response to price of public products, most of which has been presented in previous chapters, is summarized in Table 18.1. Although the table notes whether demand is price elastic or inelastic for the product type listed, in fact the product type is far too broad for a consideration of demand and its characteristics. In the case of water supplies, perhaps the simplest of public products, for example, Steve Hanke and, earlier, Charles Howe differentiated demand between industrial and household users.[4] Even when concentration is on domestic or household water use (omitting the intermediate use through the production, for example, of electricity or fire services) a distinction is required between outdoor or sprinkling use and use for food, washing, waste disposal, and so forth. The characteristic inelasticity of demand for water that is generally assumed relates principally to indoor household uses, and Hanke in Chapter 12 questions even that. In concept, at least, water applied to different uses need not be of the same grade and, accordingly, while water is the general class of the product in the same sense that an apple is the general class of a product, there are different types and grades of apples and different types and grades of water. Demand for each of the defined types and

TABLE 18.1

Data Availability and Approximate Demand Elasticities

Product	Data Availability	Information Available on Illustrative Prices	Information Available on Demographic, Economic, and Social Characteristics of Users	Approximate Price Elasticity of Demand
Water	National data collection on water use by type (household or industrial): Federal Power Commission and Census Bureau	Metered water rates and schedules by class of user, and volume of demand not routinely collected	Few data on domestic purposes classified by income, family size, etc.	Demand generally regarded as price inelastic for domestic in-house use, elastic for sprinkling and other similar purposes
Mass rail transport	No national data collection	Comparative intercity data not routinely collected	Few data on users classified by income, family size, etc.	Inelastic price over small price changes but elastic over large price movements
Private motor vehicles	Passenger-vehicle mileage and gasoline consumption data available: Department of Transportation	Comparative intercity data not routinely collected	Expenditure data by income groups collected nationally	Price inelastic for small price changes but elastic over large price movements
Airports	National data collection on number of passengers vs. freight: Federal Aviation Administration	Comparative intercity data not collected routinely	Special studies	Generally regarded as price elastic

TABLE 18.1 (Continued)

Product	Data Availability	Information Available on Illustrative Prices	Information Available on Demographic, Economic, and Social Characteristics of Users	Approximate Price Elasticity of Demand
Waterways, harbors, and terminals	National data collection on value and volume of shipments: Department of Army, Corps of Engineers	Not collected routinely for statistical comparisons; intercity data available from N.Y. Port Authority	Not available	Generally regarded as price elastic
Elementary and secondary education	National collection of much relevant data on demand: Dept. of HEW	Data on private education offerings by price, not collected routinely	National data: private school users by age, sex, income, etc. (census CPS Series P–20)	Price elastic
Hospital care	National data collection, also American Hospital Association	National data on cost reimbursement formulae exist but are not generally available; municipal hospital pricing data not routinely collected	Data on hospital use by social, economic and demographic characteristics available but not identified for municipal hospitals; special studies available	Demand is price inelastic over a range of prices—third party payments make price elasticity and price rationing major issues
Recreation	No national data collection	Sparse and sporadic	Sparse and sporadic	Price elastic
Fire	National data collection: National Fire Protection Association	Now zero priced	Data on fire service use, by industrial and domestic users, not routinely published	Now zero priced—price inelastic over a range of price movements

TABLE 18.1 (Continued)

Product	Data Availability	Information Available on Illustrative Prices	Information Available on Demographic, Economic, and Social Characteristics of Users	Approximate Price Elasticity of Demand
Public housing	National data collection: Department of Housing and Urban Development	Cost and rent data collected nationally but not compiled for intercity comparisons	Use subject to eligibility tests	Price inelastic over a range of small price changes
Solid waste collection	No national data collection	Comparative intercity data not routinely collected	Sparse and incomplete	Generally regarded as price inelastic for small price movements
Solid waste disposal	No national data collection	Comparative intercity data not routinely collected	Sparse and incomplete	Generally regarded as price inelastic for small price movements

grades can have different demand responses to price variations. Other public products encompass much more diverse subproduct classifications.

It is difficult enough to characterize price elasticity of demand for a single product without taking account of substitutes. But the research agenda necessarily includes not only extension and correction of the tentative findings set forth in Table 18.1 but also analyses of cross-elasticities. While substantial public funds have been spent in determining, for example, the effect of beef price changes on consumption not only of beef, but also on consumption of pork, lamb, veal, etc., hardly any resources have been devoted to the exploration of the effect of a change in the price of one outdoor recreational service on the demand for other forms of outdoor recreation, or the effect of changes in price of parking on the use of alternative forms of commuter transportation or on the choice to risk a fine for a standing auto violation.

In some instances where private services are closely related to a public service, it would appear possible to use private market data as indicative of demand functions of the product. Private tennis court charges may suggest the effect of price on demand (assuming other things are the same). Or commercial vocational educational offerings may provide data on demand response that could be usefully applied to the public sector. Police services similarly have a private analog of public policing services. Yet it cannot be assumed that the similar inputs yield precisely the same product and therefore that private price data will necessarily serve the cities. For example, detective services purchased privately by large department stores are intended to reduce shoplifting and thus to keep the margin of inventory losses down. They are also intended, as I understand it, to keep the department store out of the stream of legal apprehension and prosecution and thus reduce the costs to the store in such legal processes. Thus public and private policing services, while similar, are far from identical.

A city government faced with price determinations often does not have sufficient data to make the necessary decisions. The government, however, is in a situation not unlike that confronting many new business ventures. Demand has to be estimated by new data collection that could take the form of tests by market surveys and limited trials of the market, and measured demand response to price. In general, the way to find out about demand and its price elasticity is to begin to price and to record the response of users.

Experimentation with prices and different price schedules is an important agenda for future research. In cooperation with various levels of governments, experimental demonstrations might, for example, be undertaken on pricing of particular public products so that more can be learned about the demand for identified public services and the response to assorted pricing methods and optional pricing policies.

Costs and their functions. Application of pricing rules requires knowledge not only of demand but also of supply and its cost characteristics. Table 18.2, based primarily on the work of Carl Shoup, depicts in summary form total cost, average cost, and marginal cost of different public services for (1) an increase in level of service, (2) population growth, and (3) enlarged areas served.[5] Once again, the "facts" shown in this table are not facts but estimates for further empirical study to reject, support, or modify. In its multiple dimensions Table 18.2 thus provides a mapping of questions for research. The separation of cost functions by level of service, population size, and area (or volume, density and distance, as Vickrey classified them) needs to be reassessed. And those cost functions must be redefined on a dynamic basis to take account of cost response to unemployment, to growth in city gross product, to changes in value of time.

Furthermore, Table 18.2 includes primarily those services that are commonly supplied by governments with zero direct charges. Shoup divides the services in the case of education, housing, and medical care into two parts—marketable services and externalities—dealing with the cost characteristics of each part separately. The marketable service and its externality are viewed as joint products so that neither total cost nor marginal cost can be allocated between them. As a collectively enjoyed benefit, externalities have characteristics of decreasing per capita cost, falling per person as the number of users or consumers increases. Indivisibilities and collective enjoyment suggest zero prices for the externalities but positive prices for the marketable component, Shoup concludes. He derives a supply price computed by subtracting from total cost for a given level of joint product output the demand at that level of one of the joint products.

The multiplicity of products considered as a single item in Table

TABLE 18.2

Presumed Cost Functions of Government Services

	Increase in Level of Service Quality Scale			Increase in Population Density Factor			Increase in Area Distance		
	Total Cost	Average Cost	Marginal Cost	Total Cost	Cost Per Capita	Marginal Cost	Total Cost	Cost Per Capita (also Avg. Cost Per Unit)	Marginal Cost Per Unit of Area
Public Health	Up	Down, then up	Down, then up	Up	Down	Slightly positive and unchanged	Down (?)	Down (?)	Negative and unchanged (?)
Fire Protection	Up	Up	Up	Up	Down, then up	Down, then up	Down, then up	Down, then up	Negative, then positive
Police Protection	Up	Up	Up	Up	Up	Up	Up	Up	Up
Highways	Up	Up	Up	Up	Up	Up	Down	Down	Negative
Streets	Up	Up	Up	Up	Up	Up	Up	Up	Up
Flood Control, Drainage	Unchanged, then up	Down, then up	Zero, then up	Unchanged	Down	Zero	Up	Up	Up
Education	Up	Up	Up	Unchanged, then up	Down, then up	Zero, then up	Up	Up	Up
Sewerage, and Garbage Refuse Disposal,	Up	Up	Up	Up	Up	Up	Down, then up	Down, then up	Negative, then positive
Medical Care	Up	?	?	Up	Down	Positive, then unchanged	Down, then up	Down, then up	Negative, then positive
Recreation, Cultural Facilities	Up	Up	Up	Up	Up	Up	Down, then up	Down, then up	Negative, then positive

a Marginal cost also rises as cumulative service over time rises

TABLE 18.2 (Continued)

	Increase in Level of Service Quality Scale			Increase in Population Density Factor			Increase in Area Distance		
	Total Cost	Average Cost	Marginal Cost	Total Cost	Cost Per Capita	Marginal Cost	Total Cost	Cost Per Capita (also Avg. Cost Per Unit)	Marginal Cost Per Unit of Area
Water Supply	Up	Up	Up	Up	Down	Down	Up	Up	Up
Mass Transport	Up	Up	Up	Up	Down	Down	Up	Down	Down
Airports	Up	Up	Up	Up	Down, then up	Down, then up	Unchanged	Unchanged	Unchanged
Waterways	Up	Up	Up	Up	Down	Down	Unchanged	Unchanged	Unchanged
School Meals	Up	Down, then up	Down, then up	Up	Unchanged	Unchanged	Up	Unchanged	Unchanged
Public Housing	Up	Up	Up	Up	?	?	Down	Down	Down
Externalities from:									
Education	Up	Not defined	Not defined	Unchanged	Down	Zero	Unchanged	Unchanged	Zero
Housing	Up	Not defined	Not defined	Unchanged	Down	Zero	Unchanged	Unchanged	Zero
Medical Care	Up	Down, then up	Down, then up	Unchanged (but see text)	Down	Zero	Down	Down	Negative (and unchanged?)

SOURCE: The rows 1–10 (reading down), and Externality rows 1–3 from: Carl Shoup, *Public Finance* (Chicago: Aldine Publishing Company, 1969), I, p. 143. Entries in rows 11 through 16 are rough guesses for the purposes of this volume and may not be consistent with Shoup's analysis.

18.2 immediately points to qualification. That public services in a particular functional area such as public health are not simply a differentiated product must be empasized. They are distinctly different types of services, often with different immediate types of clients. The customers for VD and TB control are not the same as the customers for school public health nursing services, eating place inspections, or vital records collection. Cost functions for each separate item are required if decisions on price or on administrative resource allocation are to be based on adequate information.

(3) *How is the stickiness of public prices to be overcome?*

Whatever the findings for yesterday, they are not necessarily applicable to tomorrow. The city is a living entity composed of neighborhoods that change shape and face, that grow and decay. In the course of the city's pulsations, industrial-commercial patterns are altered, population moves, income flows are enlarged or reduced, tastes for different goods change. New technology transforms methods of working, playing and indeed the essential interpersonal contacts of living. These transformations occur when congestion becomes characteristic and speed of communication and transportation is swift. Static pricing policies in this dynamic environment are inappropriate, yet the methods of quick response are not ready at hand, nor is the result of current sticky pricing practices fully understood.

Some localities report, for instance, that charges once set are continued unchanged for substantial periods of time despite higher maintenance costs or sharp increases in product demand. One remedy for this lag in administrative price setting, when revenue bond issue obligations permit, is periodic evaluation and formulation of routine proposals for change. It is also reported that changes in fees are often made with the objective of stability in amount of revenue, but with the hypothesis of stability in demand. Thus, if the revenue from charges is less than expected, price increases are sought to continue to cover average costs, as if demand were totally inelastic. Further, little account is reportedly taken of trends in employment or income in the city that would affect the purchases of the priced service and the resulting revenue yield at a specified price.

Among the research questions is the study of methodology for analyzing the revenue and efficiency results of alternative pricing policies under specified demographic and economic developments in the city. A small beginning toward the development of a model for analyzing shifts in costs and in demand was made in the 1967 State-Local-Finances Project study on long range revenue estimation.[6] Improved analysis along these lines would facilitate the implementation of continuing reviews. Moreover, it would provide the pattern for empirical study of charge revenues for specific public services under conditions of employment and of income growth at various rates.

Income elasticities of fee revenues may be considered as a composite of (1) price elasticities, (2) income elasticities of demand for the specific public product for which fees are imposed, and (3) cost changes (or price-cost ratio) as income levels grow or shrink. Income elasticities are summarized in Table 18.3 for selected items of consumer demand

TABLE 18.3

Income Elasticities of Selected Items of Demand

Item of demand	Elasticity
Electric utilities	3.00
Water utilities	.58
Local bus transportation	1.41
Intercity bus transportation	1.89
Airline travel	5.66
Educational offerings	2.00
Doctors' services	1.08
Dentists' services	1.00
Participant amusements (e.g., bowling)	1.88
Legitimate theater	1.98
Other recreation (e.g., camping fees)	2.19

SOURCE: *Long-Range Revenue Estimation*, The State-Local Finances Project (The George Washington University Bookstore, October, 1967), p. 104.

for products on which governments levy charges. These figures are subject to many qualifications. They represent expenditure elasticities as reported by consumers on surveys of consumption, rather than income elasticities; they are for the national economy only and do not necessarily indicate the variations in elasticities among localities. Research is needed to determine income elasticities on the basis of time series data, and for individual cities in place of the cross-sectional data by family income now available for the nation. Far more information on demand characteristics of each of the public products and ways in which the demand is affected by the dynamics of the city is needed for guidance on even this one aspect of a continuing policy of reassessment and price modification.

In an initial small effort to gain insight into the kinds of problems raised publicly, one part of this study was a preliminary inquiry of mayors' offices in a number of cities to determine whether in the immediate past proposals had been advanced for a change in user charges.[7] This inquiry was carried out as a screening process to facilitate the selection of a subset of those cities for purposes of a study of newspaper coverage of reactions in selected cities to user charge proposals. For varying periods of time the newspapers in nine selected cities were read and digests prepared of the issues discussed.[8]

One purpose of the news coverage study was to throw light on the issues identified in the public debate with respect to two conflicting hypotheses frequently advanced: (1) that additions to user charges are easier to implement than additions to general taxation because of the tie of benefits to charges, and (2) that additions to charges are as difficult to achieve as the upping of general taxes, if not more so.

The preliminary findings suggested that consideration be given not only to service-by-service pricing, but also to an across-the-board pricing policy in a city. Would it be feasible, for example, to formulate a general set of price guidelines that specify for classes of public products (classified as appropriate in the light of efficiency and equity considerations) conditions under which prices are raised (1) for the general class of products, (2) after a specified length of time, and (3) in a prescribed manner? Or, stated differently, is it possible to formulate guidelines and seek city council adoption of general rules about price changes? If the guidelines laid down are specific and workable, they would help to achieve a more flexible system of public product pricing with established processes for change that do not in each instance require additional debate and public discussion. For example, if it should be decided that water rates and all such similar charges be adjusted annually to reflect growing marginal costs, then without further debate at the time of user charge review the price would be raised in accord with the adopted guidelines.

(4) *Would prices reduce city-suburban disparities?*

The spatial distribution of population and business firms within any urban economic area is responsive to relative costs, including those of transportation, of housing, and of doing business. Taxes are a component part of each cost item. It is frequently hypothesized that the city that depends on its own local taxes for much of its revenue is constrained in its fund raising and provision of public services by area-wide tax competition—that is, by the levies determined separately by nearby local governments, each of which is assumed to act individually and competitively rather than in concert. Each government is thus strategically obliged to view the potential effect of its tax levies on its own citizens and business firms in the light of the tax rates of its neighboring governments.

The possible substitution of prices for general revenues, at least for some broadened categories of products, raises several important questions on city–suburban competition and its consequences.

Is there a difference between taxation and pricing in impact on interjurisdictional revenue competition? Would not the same forces that constrain tax rates among local governments within an economic area also constrain to competitive levels such charges as water rates, bus fares, garbage collection charges, hospital rates, and so forth? The essential difference between taxation that is compulsory and general and user charges that are voluntary and specific suggests that the constraints of interjurisdictional revenue competition may not be the same. For most public services—and this seems to be true even of the necessary water supplies—the tax makes the payment compulsory as long as the individual chooses to remain in the area, whereas households can re-align their activities, and thus their spending, in the light of their own preferences if the user charge is involved.

The question may also be raised whether incentives for population outmovements would be reduced by pricing services that are especially sought by industry and by the more affluent taxpayer. Pricing may work to reduce incentives for outmigration of persons and industry in two separate ways: (1) by encouraging the production of those kinds of public services that are considered desirable by the more affluent members of the city community, or by industry, and (2) by lowering taxes. If all persons were required to pay the specified price without city subsidy, then the general own city revenues would be relieved of the burden of such services. (Prices substituted for local taxes, however, reduce the offset against local taxes provided by federal income tax deductibility.)

On balance, public prices may provide less of an incentive to continuing outmigration from the city than the present property tax does. Charges would be paid only by those who choose to benefit from the services provided; hence important costs for those services would be removed from the general tax base with its perverse economic effects. Moreover, additional or incremental costs that are incurred because city services are made available directly to the suburbs (or to the suburban dweller), e.g., the added investments in water supplies, can sometimes be recovered through the use of public prices appropriately designed to reflect marginal costs.

Does pricing city products relieve city financing by facilitating interjurisdictional purchases? If prices are set on the services provided within the city boundary, it would follow that persons who entered the city to buy would pay the market price. How large a share of city expenditures goes to service the out-of-city resident is not fully known. It takes a detailed study of uses of library, zoo, museum, park, roadway to determine the distribution of users between city residents and those from outside who find in the city the characteristic urban amenities.[9] Some argue that a large share of city expenditures is made on behalf of the suburban commuters; but even if the share is as little as 10 percent, city development could be adversely affected by the greater pressure exerted on a relatively low tax base.

Many governments now purchase from their neighbors some of the products that are already priced. Presumably, intergovernmental purchases are intended to take advantage of economies of scale in the actual production of public services while at the same time retaining small units for purposes of voting resource allocation.

A major facet of the issue of intergovernmental purchases is thus the cost characteristic of the service. For some classes of services, production units are necessarily large, with sharply decreasing costs at the margin. Services that have a heavy capital component, or are capital intensive, tend to be of this type. For example, electricity generation and water desalinization require large capital plant. Within capacity limits costs per unit drop as output is increased. Mass screening of individuals as a disease-control service requires large initial investment in equipment and personnel training; unless the volume of demand is sufficient to use that fixed investment to near capacity, short-term costs per unit of service are high. Similarly, computerized instruction requires a heavy equipment investment; costs are high per unit of output at low levels of demand, and drop sharply with increased use. The larger the market area for mass screening or computerized instruction, the greater the prospects of high use and low costs per unit.

The scale requirements of the market are determined in other cases by the specialized characteristics of the market itself. Small numbers (at risk) need to be brought together over a wide geographic area to have sufficient market size to permit accommodation of that market at public expense. Rehabilitation services for emotionally disturbed children, for children with congenital heart diseases, or for paraplegics can only be provided economically where there are substantial numbers of persons who require the services. The scale of production is set in these cases, not by production technology, but by the characteristics of demand.

Study of economies of scale offers some guidance to the appropriate geographic units for the production of different services. Studies on water wastes point to regional river basin-wide planning and provision for use of the streams as discharge agents both for municipal government and industrial wastes. The geographic area for production at least cost differs for each product. For example, it is not the same area in the production of specialized diagnostic services for heart disease and cancer as it is in the case of hospital care for the mentally ill or for maternity beds, or cobalt radiation, or kidney transplants.

It would be useful to study current pricing experience as it relates to interjurisdictional purchases, to gather data on those current practices so that we understand to what extent, if at all, the center city has been subsidizing the suburban use of such services as trash disposal, public hospital care, water supplies, parks, libraries, museums, and so forth. Indeed, would the services to those in the metropolitan areas be improved in quality and lowered in cost by incentives for more intergovernmental purchases?

(5) *Are taxes fairer than charges?*

Questions about distributional aspects of public prices are repeatedly raised in any public discussion of user fees. Milton Z. Kafoglis, who has given perhaps more thought to this question than other researchers, could reach few definitive conclusions:

Although much research remains to be done before the distributional implications of service charge finance can be assessed fully, it has been suggested that in some communities increased reliance on cost-of-service finance might ameliorate the condition of the low-income classes. Promotional utility rates and flat rates per house are especially suspect since they encourage inefficiency and lead to service rate structures that are more regressive in their effects than the property tax. The distributional problem created by service charges may be due to faulty pricing practices rather than to faulty principle.[10]

But he continues with the caution that uneconomic and inequitable service charges can hamper the attainment of the objectives of programs directed to relieve poverty in the core of the city.

Payment of prices for educational services, along with charges for hospital care, water supplies, electricity, parking meters, and so on, would plainly reveal the cost to the poor of public services. Taking the formula under the existing public welfare programs as an example, additional public assistance payments would become necessary, financed largely, if not exclusively, out of federal and state monies. The basic urban services would simply become part of the measured "needs" in the budget of poor families that require additional resources under a public assistance standard. At present, such costs are not disclosed; an accounting for local services is not given; and cities are called upon to finance them even for the poor public assistance recipient. Thus, through the use of prices for public services, if assistance standards are maintained, upward of 50 percent of the cost of public services to the poor would be shifted through the public assistance payment to the national government and the major part of the remaining share to the state governments. Federal income taxes and state sales taxes would take the place of property taxes as the source of redistributive funding. With this shift in mind, what is the net result of prices vs. taxes? The question for research is complex and not readily answered.

Historically, in the interest of greater equity, general taxation took the place of fees as the method of financing many public services. Children, it was held, should have equal opportunity for an education without regard to their parents' ability to pay school fees; the poor should not be excluded from needed hospital and other health care because they could not afford to pay. The dominant doctrine came to be that citizens should pay for public services through compulsory tax levies based on capacity to pay, and that public services should be uniformly available, with special charitable provision for those who did not have the means to care for themselves.

"Fairness" must be viewed in terms of relative burdens of user charges, on the one hand, and general tax levies, on the other. A fee or public price could very well be a more progressive source of revenue than the property tax. That is, the burden on low-income groups would be less if a charge were imposed, since poor families may now pay more in rent as a consequence of general property taxation than they would under some alternative pricing arrangement. The formulas or optional price schedules or methods of applying user charges affect their distributional outcome. Charges for solid waste collection, for example, may be uniform, or they may be varied in accord with property values or with the amount or the type of waste. A recent study by Johnson of sewer charges examines the burden of those charges by type of charge formula and type of user and illustrates the very wide divergence in their distributional effects.[11]

The equity of alternative revenue sources cannot be viewed in isolation from the benefits provided. Who pays the taxes, who gets the benefits, and the value of those benefits—all must be considered. Benefits flowing from air pollution control measures may increase real estate values, and thus property tax receipts would be enlarged by reduced air pollution. A study in St. Louis, for example, found that property values were related linearly to mean annual sulfation rates. When sulfation levels were divided into eight equal zones of rising intensity, values appeared to decline about $250 per lot per zone when other factors remained constant.[12]

To take another case, analysis of outdoor recreation activities in a city may disclose that "use" is heavily concentrated. Middle-income groups may be found to be the chief users, rather than the low-income families. Similarly, findings may suggest that libraries and other amenities in a city are not used by the low-income groups, or not used proportionate to their representation in the population.

It could turn out on analysis that the distribution of both benefits and taxes would work disadvantageously for the lower income groups and to the comparative advantage of people with middle-sized incomes. An opposite finding also would be possible in other cities; that is, the principal users might turn out to be the lowest income groups and the tax burdens may not rest on them in proportion to the benefits they receive. Or the findings might be intermediate with respect to income for both taxpayers and benefit recipients. In other words, any generality about the distributional impact of taxes as opposed to fees is likely to be misleading; the facts of specific cases are more to the point. Furthermore, the incidence of any particular charge formula (or tax) is less significant from the point of view of public policy than the distributional effect of the tax-transfer system as a whole.

Prices can be used to discourage certain classes of users and to encourage others, for example, by negative prices. They can be used as well to stimulate more effective provision of public services. The types of service, the classes of customary users, the methods of pricing, all affect the distributional outcome. Price payments by some (high-income) users can be supplemented by general revenues to meet costs for other (low-income) users. The pattern of priced services and eligibility tests to determine "payability" is used typically in financing health care services, in public housing, in certain welfare services such as family counseling, and in school meal programs. Payments from those who can afford to pay, and financing from general tax revenues for those in low-income groups can, if desired, operate to enhance the progressivity of a fee-charge system even when charges would otherwise be more regressive than other optional forms of revenue.

Many public services that are offered at no charge are nevertheless rationed. The rationing device that is most used is "waiting time," with a cost to the beneficiary in the time spent queuing up for public products. Waiting-time costs to the user raise the cost of the public product to that user but without adding to the city's revenue. Thus, hospital services are controlled or rationed by restrictions on the number of hospital beds. Swimming pools and tennis courts are similarly rationed by the size and number of the facilities made available. The check or control demand is directly exercised by increasing the waiting time for use of the service. The length of the queues instead of a higher price becomes a partial signal for demand pressures on the existing supplies of services. As Smolensky and his coauthors point out in Chapter 5, prices in effect may be quoted in time or money. Long queues may provide an automatic rationing device just as price does.

Time, however, has a very different cost for different groups in the population. Clearly the value of time is related to the opportunity cost of that time or, more specifically, the value of the earnings that would have been gained during the time of the wait. Thus for the young and the retired, queuing time frequently has a low cost; in fact, for older persons, the wait may be a positive gain in the relief from loneliness and in the "no value" of time itself.

Thus, queues may make benefits from public services more nearly equal among income groups. This suggests, however, that the quality of services could be brought more nearly in line with public demand by the differentiation of quality (or quantity) of services, with prices set in proportion to higher quality of service as measured by reductions in waiting time. If persons with a high value on time demanded the service, they would have it available, and without the cost of queuing. Those who place a lower value on time could choose the more crowded services that have no charge, or a lower charge.

(6) *Are budget resources enlarged by use of prices instead of taxation?*

Numerous studies have recommended a greater use of fees and charges for public services and more realistic charge or fee schedules than those already in force in order to increase city revenues. The extent to which revenues can be expanded through user charges will depend on the outcome of a political bargaining process involving groups whose interests are differently affected by the particular fee expansion being considered. These include the groups who (1) formerly paid for the service through general taxes but did not use it, (2) those who formerly paid for the service through general taxes and did use it, and finally (3) those who do not pay general taxes because of the location of their residence but have used the services on which a fee is to be levied.

It is impossible to predict the general feasibility of expanding net revenues by implementing new fees, but it will clearly depend on the relative size and political strength of these groups with respect to the particular fee being considered. Thus, for example, it should be relatively easy to implement a fee on a service used predominantly by nonresidents, since they are likely to have relatively little political influence outside their own jurisdiction. Similarly, fees would seem more easily implemented on narrowly used services than on broadly used ones, since the latter would result in broader opposition. Yet all the effort required to tap narrowly used services, especially from the view of those on the political front who have to push for pricing, does not promise much total revenue increment. In the extreme case of a fee on an essential service used by virtually all residents, the fee, if used to expand net revenues (rather than substitute for other sources), will appear similar to a general tax increase and is likely to face similar opposition.

A wide variety of services has in fact been provided by cities through user charges. The bulk of the revenue from these has come from charges on utilities (water, gas, electricity, and transit), although some revenues have come from fees on goods with a strong externality component (e.g., fire inspection fees). The forms of public-charge levies have ranged from flat fees to fees varying in proportion to use. It is quite possible that cities could raise these charges in a number of instances, but the *degree* of the rise is vital. Stockfisch estimated that the Los Angeles city government in the late 1950s could have in fact increased its revenues approximately 40 percent by rationalizing and increasing the levels of user fees and charges levied for a number of service categories. [13]

Estimates such as these seem to imply that such revenue increases are possible, whether or not the existing level and structure of public prices is reasonable, and regardless of potential community opposition. This view appears to be contrary to experience reported in some cities. It is probably more feasible to expand city revenue by increasing the prices of already priced services than by imposing prices on services that the public has traditionally received free of charge. Yet there is also the important question of consumer reaction to increased prices: Is there any guarantee that price increases, even when possible, will yield net additions, and not net losses, to the volume of total municipal revenues? Revenue can either fall or rise depending on the elasticity of demand for the particular service. This suggests that prices can only be raised in those service areas where demand is relatively inelastic, if the purpose is net revenue expansion.

As noted earlier, the argument is rather different when our concern is with pricing services that are not currently provided. There may, for example, be a need expressed for day care centers, homemaker services, homes for the aged, and so forth. Effective demand may exist among some potential users, but the community may fail to provide the service because of inadequate funds. Provision by the public sector may, nevertheless, be justified on a number of grounds, including the failure of the private sector to enter the field, the need for quality controls, and the ability of the public sector to take account of equity considerations in pricing. External benefits that accrue to nonusers of the service may also justify placing the service in the public sector and charging less than full costs for use of the service.

In instances where desired public services cannot be provided due to a lack of funds, user-charge financing may provide at least a partial bypass around the revenue obstacles. This tactic, however, requires that the public's perception of and reaction to a new fee on a new service must differ from its perception of and reaction to, for example, a property tax increase.

Public prices may be differentiated from tax increases for new services in several ways. First, payment of the user charge is optional and not compulsory, as a tax payment is. Those individuals who decide to pay for the service will simultaneously garner a new benefit with their new burden. Also, a fee, when it falls on a relatively small proportion of consumer-voters, regardless of their place of residence, may generate a smaller and less effective amount of community opposition than the burden of a tax increase that must be shouldered by all.

This reasoning suggests, therefore, that when fee revenues are increased by charging for a newly established service, the revenue increment can be regarded as a net addition to total city revenue, since it is unlikely to require any offsetting decline in taxes, grants, borrowing, or other kinds of user charges. The use of public prices may thus permit expansion into new services the city could not otherwise provide.

The revenue-increasing potential from much more intensive use of beneficiary charges, however valuable such charges may be in pursuit of other governmental objectives, may be limited. Increased use of pricing for urban services is not likely to provide a solution of the cities' revenue problems by itself, though it can be a useful component of a balanced program of revenue expansion. Such a judgment must be tempered by the fact that the entire area of user charges in the public sector is still greatly under-researched as compared to other revenue instruments. There is, therefore, an urgent need for comparative studies that would catalog the pricing policies of various cities, examine consumer response to price alterations, and identify external markets for municipal public goods and services.

Conclusion: Next Experimental Steps

We are entering an area of experimental economics in which measurements will be carried out for control and test groups. While inter-city comparisons can help provide information somewhat akin to experimental material, experimental designs in the analysis of city experience are also increasingly necessary.

Such study would encourage experimentation with prescribed price schedules for particular functional areas. The notion would be to design, in cooperation with governments, experimental demonstrations on pricing of particular public products so that, without impairing local government revenues, more can be learned about the demand for identified public services and the response to alternative pricing policies. Ideally, this research would identify the economic characteristics of the commodities and services produced by cities on behalf of their residents, along with the cost and demand characteristics of those products and the special groups of persons, industries, and governments who receive appropriable benefits from public sector activity.

Without more experimentation and research on pricing urban services, the many questions raised in this volume cannot be answered with much more certainty than is done here. Yet, if public pricing policies are to be extended and expanded in a rational fashion, as both economic analysts and hard-pressed urban finance officials are now urging, they must be answered.

NOTES

1. Harold Demsetz, "The Cost of Transacting," *Quarterly Journal of Economics*, 82 (February 1968): 33–53.

2. Julius Margolis, "Shadow Prices for Incorrect or Nonexistent Market Val-

ues," in *The Analysis and Evaluation of Public Expenditures: The PPB System*, Joint Economic Committee (91st Cong., 1st Sess., 1969), Vol I, pp. 533–546.

3. Selma J. Mushkin, Harry P. Hatry, John F. Cotton, et al., *Implementing PPB in State, City, and County* (The George Washington University Book Store, 1969).

4. Steve H. Hanke, "Demand for Water Under Dynamic Conditions," *Water Resources Research*, 6 (October 1970): 1253–1261, and Charles W. Howe, "Municipal Water Demands," in W. R. Derrick Sewell and Blair T. Bowen, eds., *Forecasting the Demand for Water* (Ottawa, Canada: Department of Energy Mines and Resources, 1968), pp. 43–79.

5. Carl S. Shoup, *Public Finance* (Aldine, 1969).

6. Eugene P. McLoone, Gabrielle C. Lupo, and Selma J. Mushkin, *Long-Range Revenue Estimation*, The State-Local Finances Project (The George Washington University Bookstore, October, 1967).

7. I am greatly indebted to Hugh Mields for his help in writing to the mayors and paving the way for city selection.

8. Remi Boelart, "Project on User Charges: Public Discussion in Newspapers" (August 21, 1969, rough draft; processed).

9. William B. Neenan, "Suburban-Central City Exploitation Thesis: One City's Tale," *National Tax Journal*, 23 (June 1970): 117–139.

10. Milton Z. Kafoglis, "Local Service Charges: Theory and Practice," in Harry L. Johnson, ed., *State and Local Tax Problems* (University of Tennessee Press, 1969).

11. James A. Johnson, "The Distribution of the Burden of Sewer User Charges Under Various Formulas," *National Tax Journal*, 22 (December 1969): 472–485.

12. R. G. Ridker and J. A. Henning, "The Determinants of Residential Property Values with Special Reference to Air Pollution," *Review of Economics and Statistics*, 49 (May 1967): 246–257. See also Kenneth F. Wieand, "Property Values and the Demand for Clean Air: Cross-Section Study for St. Louis," paper prepared for the Committee on Urban Economics Research Conference, September 11–12, 1970 (processed).

13. J. A. Stockfisch, "The Outlook for Fees and Service Charges as a Source of Revenue for State and Local Governments," in *Proceedings of the Sixtieth National Tax Conference* (National Tax Association, October 1967).

Subject Index

449

Persons Index

Adams, Charles, 419
Anderson, R. J., Jr., 170
Auster, R., 365, 367, 369
Ayres, Robert U., 206, 208, 212

Bateman, Worth, xvi
Baumol, William J., 49, 50, 92, 240
Becker, Gary, 391
Benson, Charles S., 392
Berki, Sylvester E., 351–369
Berkman, Jack D., 419
Berry, R. E., 360, 367, 368
Bird, Richard, M., xvi, 3–25
Black, R. J., 207
Blair, George S., 215
Blaug, Mark, 371, 390, 392
Blum, Henrik, 393
Boelart, Remi, 447
Boiteux, M., 263, 266
Boland, John J., 283n
Bonbright, James C., 49
Bowen, Blair T., 133n, 151
Bowen, Howard R., 123
Boyle, Gerald J., 25
Bradford, David F., 49, 92
Brazer, Harvey E., 48
Browne, L. B., 367
Buchanan, James M., 25, 49, 51, 206, 207, 212
Bugg, Paul, 283n
Burkhead, Jesse, 376, 392

Cafiero, A. S., 211
Carliner, Geoffrey, 409–419
Carll, R., 264

Carr, W. J., 360, 368
Carter, R. L., 332
Cassell, Eric J., 213
Chernick, Howard, 307n
Chiang, C. L., 367
Clark, Kenneth, 392
Clarke, Edward H., 24, 125–130
Clawson, Marion, 349
Clemens, Eli W., 49
Cohen, H. A., 360, 367, 368
Coleman, James S., 393
Conant, James B., 391
Cotton, John F., 447
Cremin, Lawrence, 391
Crocker, Thomas D., 170

Darnay, Arsen, 206, 209, 211–213
Davies, J. Clarence, III, 171
Davis, Robert K., 283n, 306
DeAlessi, Louis, 283n
de la Vallee Pousin, D., 111n
deTorres, Juan, 25
Demsetz, Harold, 446
Devine, Eugene J., 393
Dobriner, William, 391
Dolbear, F. Treney, Jr., 212
Donabedian, A., 369
Downing, Paul B., 305
Downs, Anthony, 391
Drake, D. F., 369
Dreeban, Robert, 391
Dreze, J. H., 111n
Duba, John G., 267–271, 278–282
Duncan, Beverly, 392
Duncan, Otis Dudley, 392

457